EDITORIAL TEAM

Managing editor
and senior analyst
Jeff Crisp

Production and
translations editor
Marina Ronday-Cao

Editor and analyst
Rachael Reilly

Consultant
Nicholas Van Hear

Produced by UNHCR's Centre
for Documentation and
Research, under the direction
of Eric Morris.

Designed by Studio PAGE
De Pol-Tazza, Rome.

Acknowledgements

The editorial team wishes to thank all those who have assisted in the preparation of this book. For contributions to the main text: Kenneth Bush, Dylan Hendrickson, Maria Stavropoulou. For contributions to boxes: Nazare Albuquerque Abell, Julie Bisland, Christina Boswell, Philippa Candler, Anne Encontre, Kemlin Furley, Kris Janowski, Karen McClure, Asmita Naik, Francesca Naylor, Frances Nicholson, Elizabeth Tan, UNHCR offices in Kampala, Mexico City, Moscow and New Delhi. For assistance with maps, graphics, statistics and photos: Jean-Yves Bouchardy, Anneliese Hollmann, Bela Hovy, Yvon Orand and Simon Raiser. For comments on draft chapters: Jean-François Durieux, Wilbert Van Hovell, Karin Landgren, Bohdan Nahajlo, Karola Paul, Sharon Stanton Russell and Volker Turk. For other assistance and support: Claire Bessette, Denise Carroll, Johan Cels, Catrin Crisp, Marika Fahlen, Stefano Guerra, Cathy Mohtashemi, Carla Di Napoli and Astri Suhrke. Thanks to Carol Batchelor, Roberta Cohen, Elizabeth Ferris, Pierre-Michel Fontaine, Guy Goodwin-Gill, John Horekens, Andrew Shacknove and Patricia Weiss-Fagen for their contributions to 'People of Concern', a *State of the World's Refugees* conference held in Geneva in November 1996, kindly supported by the Ford Foundation.

Contents

Figures

Preface
by the United Nations Secretary-General

When the United Nations was established in 1945, the international community was intent on averting a third world war. Today, just over 50 years later, that objective appears to have been attained. With the end of the period of superpower rivalry, reductions in nuclear weapons arsenals and the process of economic globalization, there is a real prospect of lasting peace between the world's most powerful states. More generally, it has become clear, governments are increasingly reluctant to resolve their differences by resorting to the use of military force. Wars between sovereign states appear to be a phenomenon in distinct decline.

Tragically, however, the lives of millions of people around the globe continue to be blighted by violence. In some parts of the world, states have collapsed as a result of internal and communal conflicts, depriving their citizens of any effective protection. Elsewhere, human security has been jeopardized by governments which refuse to act in the common interest, which persecute their opponents and punish innocent members of minority groups. As *The State of the World's Refugees* explains, such conditions have made it impossible for those millions of people to exercise a basic human right: to live safely, peacefully and without fear in their own homes.

The problem of forced displacement is one of the most pressing challenges now confronting the United Nations. This timely and important publication describes in detail the many dangers experienced by the world's uprooted and displaced people. It also presents a wide-ranging set of policy proposals concerning the protection of such populations and the resolution of their plight. Such efforts, it must be stressed, are inextricably linked to our work to prevent and resolve armed conflicts, to defend human rights and to promote sustainable development in every part of the world.

No-one should be obliged to flee from their own country in order to stay alive. No-one should be displaced because others want to seize their land, occupy their homes or control their territory. I am sure that *The State of the World's Refugees* will assist the international community to reach a better understanding of these issues and to respond to them more effectively.

Kofi Annan

Foreword
by the United Nations High Commissioner for Refugees

The word 'refugee' tends to evoke images of a sprawling camp, housing large numbers of distressed and impoverished people who have had to escape from their own country at short notice and with nothing but the clothes on their back.

This perception is not an entirely false one; a majority of the 22 million people who are cared for by UNHCR come from the world's poorer countries. And many of them are obliged to live in large camps and settlements, waiting for the day when it is safe enough for them to go back to their homes and resume a more normal way of life.

As this book explains, however, the problem of forced displacement has become a much broader and more complex phenomenon than is suggested by the conventional image of a refugee camp. Indeed, refugees in the legal sense of the word now constitute little more than half of the people who are protected and assisted by UNHCR. The organization's other beneficiaries include a variety of different groups: internally displaced and war-affected populations; asylum seekers; stateless people and others whose nationality is disputed; as well as 'returnees' - refugees and displaced people who have been able to go back to their homes, but who still require some support from the international community.

While such groups of people may differ considerably with regard to their specific circumstances and legal status, they have one thing in common: a high level of human insecurity, arising in most instances from the inability or unwillingness of a state to protect its citizens. The primary function of UNHCR is to compensate for this absence of national protection by safeguarding the life, liberty and other rights of people who have been uprooted or threatened with displacement.

That task has become increasingly difficult in the past few years. On one hand, much higher expectations have been placed upon humanitarian action, often because states and regional organizations are reluctant to commit themselves to more decisive forms of intervention when confronted with armed conflicts and crimes against humanity. On the other hand, the circumstances in which humanitarian organizations are required to function have become increasingly difficult and dangerous. Whether in Afghanistan, Bosnia, Liberia, Rwanda or the former Zaire, aid agencies have found themselves working in zones of active conflict, and in many instances have been deliberately singled out for attack by one or more of the warring parties.

The tools available to UNHCR and other humanitarian organizations are thus limited in their nature and impact. However proficiently such agencies are managed and coordinated, they cannot bring civil wars to an end, oblige states to respect the human rights of their citizens or bring a halt to the deliberate displacement of civilian populations.

Even so, in situations where armed conflict has erupted and where people have been uprooted or threatened with displacement, humanitarian action has an essential role to play. It can feed the hungry and shelter the homeless. It can reunite divided families and help displaced people return and reintegrate in their own community. Humanitarian organizations have the capacity to alert the world to impending emergencies and to mobilize public opinion on behalf of people who are in need of international protection. In some circumstances, such organizations can also help to foster the growth of attitudes and institutions which reduce the risk of violence and forced population displacements.

The pages which follow provide a wealth of policy proposals and practical recommendations concerning the problem of forced displacement. Refugee and humanitarian problems, the book suggests, are inherently transnational in nature, not only because they involve the movement of people across state borders, but also because as human beings we have a responsibility to safeguard the security of all people. At the threshold of the 21st century, we are faced with the challenge to assure the universal protection of people by reinforcing even more than before the bonds of human compassion and solidarity. We yearn for the day when people in every part of the world can live safely within their own country and community.

Sadako Ogata

Displaced people in Monrovia, Liberia ©A. Herzau/Signum

People in need of protection

'Fresh wave of displaced people arrives in Afghan capital'. 'Rwandan refugees dying in Kisangani'. 'Hong Kong forces more boat people home'. 'UNHCR says right to asylum in Europe under threat'. 'Georgian refugees insist on the right to return'. 'Thousands displaced by violence in Colombia'. 'Military intervenes to stem Albanian exodus'.

Those are some of the headlines which appeared in the newspapers during a single week in April 1997. As they suggest, the problem of forced displacement now affects every part of the world and has become a major subject of public and political concern. This introduction identifies a number of the new and most important dimensions of the problem and outlines some of the themes and issues examined in the following chapters of the book.

Forced displacement: new dimensions and dilemmas

Throughout the centuries, people have been obliged to flee from their own country or community as a result of persecution, armed conflict and violence. And in every part of the world, governments, armies and rebel movements have resorted to moving people by force in order to attain their political and military objectives.

The people most seriously affected by the problem of forced displacement are often the most marginalized members of society: minority groups, stateless people, indigenous populations and others who are excluded from the structures of political power. Persecuted by their governments or by other members of their society, many find themselves living in a state of constant insecurity and uncertainty. Even if they have managed to find a safe refuge, they may never know if or when it will be possible for them to go back to their homes.

It would be unduly alarmist to suggest that the problem of forced displacement is more serious now than it has ever been in the past. The period since the late 1980s has certainly been an unusually turbulent one, but this is not the first time that the international state system has undergone a fundamental change. In the post-cold war years, as in the period after the first and second world wars, forced population displacements have proven to be a prominent consequence of the demise of old ideologies, the collapse of existing empires and the formation of new states.

While it may be an age-old problem, the issue of forced displacement has assumed some particularly important - and in several senses new -

dimensions in the final years of the 20th century. First and foremost, the numbers have been staggering. UNHCR - the Office of the United Nations High Commissioner for Refugees - is now responsible for the welfare of some 22 million people around the world, around 13 million of whom are refugees in the conventional sense of the word: people who have left their own country to escape from persecution, armed conflict or violence (see Figures 0.1 and 0.2). To this figure can be added a very large number of uprooted people who do not receive any form of international protection or assistance, the majority of whom remain within the borders of their own country.

In total, some 50 million people around the world might legitimately be described as victims of forced displacement.(1) Many of this number are to be found in areas which were not significantly affected by refugee problems during the cold war years: the Balkans, the Caucasus, Central Asia and other parts of the former Soviet Union.

Second, it has become increasingly clear that forced displacement is a complex phenomenon which assumes many different forms. This development has given rise to a somewhat bewildering variety of terms. As well as the familiar notion of a refugee movement or mass exodus, academic analysts and humanitarian organizations now also make frequent use of concepts such as asylum flow, mass expulsion, ethnic cleansing, disaster-induced displacement, development-induced displacement, forced migration, internal dis-

Fig. 0.1

**People of concern
to UNHCR
by category**

Millions (rounded)

Refugees: 13.20
IDPs: 4.85
Returnees: 3.31
Others of concern: 1.36
Total: 22.72

Statistics at January 1997

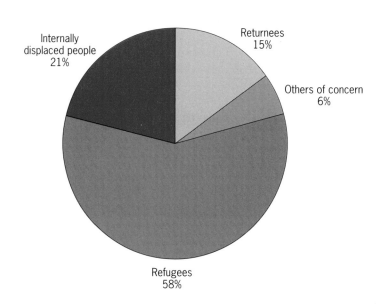

Internally
displaced people
21%

Returnees
15%

Others of concern
6%

Refugees
58%

placement, population transfer, population exchange, involuntary repatriation and imposed return.

The circumstances and characteristics of the people affected by these different forms of displacement vary substantially. There are clearly some important differences between the peasant farmer who has been displaced by the fighting in southern Sudan, the middle-class Bosnian from Sarajevo who has taken refuge in Germany, and the second-generation Palestinian refugee who has never set foot on the territory which she considers to be her home. Nevertheless, such people have a similar need for protection and a common right to be treated in a way that is consistent with humanitarian principles and human rights standards.

Third, while refugee movements have always been intimately linked to political and military conflicts, forced population displacements have in recent years been perceived as an increasingly important element of national and regional security. In Bosnia, for example, the successful implementation of the Dayton peace accord is widely considered to hinge upon the return of the many refugees and displaced people created by the conflict. In the Great Lakes region of Africa, it is impossible to understand the dynamics and dimensions of the current crisis without reference to the long history of forced displacement in the region.

Large-scale displacements of people may also prompt other states and regional organizations to deploy their armed forces, as witnessed in countries

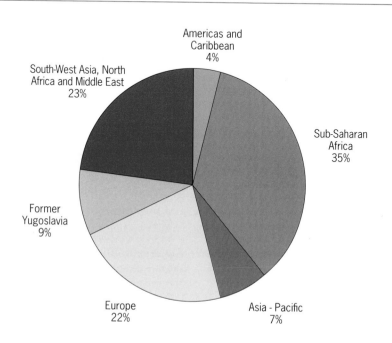

Americas and
Caribbean
4%

South-West Asia, North
Africa and Middle East
23%

Sub-Saharan
Africa
35%

Former
Yugoslavia
9%

Europe
22%

Asia - Pacific
7%

Fig. 0.2

**People of concern
to UNHCR by region**

Millions (rounded)

Sub-Saharan Africa 7.84
South-West Asia, North Africa
and Middle East: 5.26
Europe: 5.01
Former Yugoslavia: 2.16
Asia - Pacific: 1.57
Americas and Caribbean: 0.88
Total: 22.72

Statistics at January 1997

such as Albania, Iraq, Liberia, Somalia and former Yugoslavia. Whether such action is taken with or without the consent of the country concerned, and whether it is prompted by humanitarian or strategic considerations, it inevitably has an important impact on the local balance of political and military power.

Fourth, and in many cases precisely because of the link between forced displacement and the security concerns of states, forcibly displaced people are faced with mounting rejection when they attempt to seek safety elsewhere. As a result of the physical and administrative barriers erected by states, it is becoming increasingly difficult for the victims of persecution and violence to gain access to the territory of potential asylum countries.

Safety during asylum is also threatened, whether as a result of armed attacks on refugee camps, the forced recruitment of young men into military forces or sexual violence inflicted upon displaced women and girls. And the principle that refugees should only return to their homes on a voluntary basis has been undermined by the frequency with which states and other actors have forced displaced people to repatriate, often to conditions that are far from safe. According to some commentators, the international regime of refugee protection, painstakingly developed since the beginning of the 20th century, is now under unprecedented pressure.(2)

As a result of these developments, UNHCR and other humanitarian organizations have in recent years been confronted with a wide range of difficulties and dilemmas, many of which are examined in subsequent chapters of this book. For example:

• to what extent have the world's more powerful states used humanitarian action as a substitute for the decisive political and military action that is sometimes required to bring armed conflicts to an end?

• how can the integrity and impartiality of humanitarian action be preserved in the increasingly political context in which it is undertaken?

• what action can be taken to protect and assist displaced and other war-affected populations, and what role can multinational military forces play in this task?

• why are many traditionally generous asylum countries now closing their borders to displaced populations, and how can they be encouraged and assisted to provide refugees with a satisfactory degree of security?

• how can the civilian character of refugee camps be maintained, and what can be done to demilitarize those which have come under the control of armed groups?

• under what - if any - conditions is it legitimate for humanitarian organizations to encourage or even insist upon the repatriation of refugee populations to their country of origin?

- how does the return and reintegration of displaced populations affect the broader process of peacebuilding in countries which have experienced civil wars and communal conflicts?

- to what extent can refugees be distinguished from other migrants, and what kind of procedures can states establish to assess large numbers of individual asylum applications in a fair, thorough and sufficiently speedy manner?

- how is the question of citizenship related to the problem of forced displacement, and how can governments be encouraged to desist from actions which leave large numbers of people stateless and vulnerable to expulsion?

The changing parameters of international interest

In order to examine these and other elements of the international humanitarian agenda in a coherent manner, this book focuses on those forms of forced displacement and groups of displaced people which are of direct concern to UNHCR: refugees, internally displaced people, returnees, asylum seekers and stateless people. The opening chapter of the book places these issues in their contemporary context, examining recent changes in the notion of international security, the nature of armed conflict and the role of humanitarian action.

As the second chapter of the book explains, more than 45 years after its establishment in 1951, the main focus of UNHCR's work continues to be on refugees in the conventional sense of the word. Totalling some 13.2 million, the majority are to be found in low and middle-income regions of the world, particularly Africa, Asia and parts of the former Soviet Union.

Unfortunately, as already indicated, those people who attempt to take refuge in a neighbouring or nearby state increasingly find that they have simply swapped one situation of insecurity for another. Chapter Two examines the declining standard of protection experienced by refugees in many parts of the world and suggests some ways in which this disturbing trend might be halted.

In recent years, UNHCR and other humanitarian organizations have become increasingly involved with other forms of forced displacement. Perhaps the most important, at least in numerical terms, is that of internal displacement. According to United Nations figures, there are up to 30 million people around the world who have been forcibly displaced and who remain, whether by necessity or choice, within their country of origin. Around five million of this number now come under UNHCR's responsibility.

Given these alarming figures, it is not surprising that the problem of internal displacement, and the closely related issue of war-affected populations, now occupies a prominent position on the international humanitarian agenda.

Nevertheless, as Chapter Three explains, recent multilateral efforts to protect such populations have raised a wide range of conceptual, legal, operational and organizational questions, many of which remain to be resolved.

Despite the turbulent nature of the post-cold war world and the general increase in the number of forcibly displaced people, there are also some positive trends. Since the beginning of the 1990s, many longstanding conflicts have come to an end or have significantly reduced in intensity, enabling millions of refugees and internally displaced people to go back to their homes. The countries to which they return, however, are frequently characterized by continued instability and insecurity. Chapter Four assesses the international community's changing approach to the reintegration of displaced populations, and examines the close relationship between that task and the broader challenge of peacebuilding in war-torn societies.

While the problem of forced displacement is concentrated in the poorer countries of the world, it is certainly not confined to them. Since the beginning of the decade, more than five million claims for refugee status have been submitted in the industrialized states. Up to a million asylum seekers in those states are currently waiting for their status to be determined.

Asserting that many of these asylum seekers are economic migrants rather than refugees, the governments of the more affluent countries have in recent years made a concerted effort to limit the number of new arrivals on their territory. Chapter Five examines the consequences of these restrictive practices and identifies some of the steps that might be taken to ensure that people who need some form of protection are able to receive it.

The sixth and final chapter of the book focuses on a relatively neglected humanitarian issue and on another group of people who may lack the protection of the state in which they live: those who are legally stateless or whose nationality is disputed. The dissolution of several states and the creation of new political entities in Eastern and Central Europe and the former Soviet Union has certainly been instrumental in bringing these issues to the attention of the international community. But as this chapter argues, statelessness is a global and growing problem and stateless people are at particular risk of displacement. If new refugee movements are to be averted, this issue must be addressed more vigorously.

Human security and state responsibility

In terms of their legal status, some clear distinctions can be drawn between refugees, the internally displaced, returnees, asylum seekers and stateless people. In terms of their human needs and the humanitarian issues associated with their plight, however, they share a number of important characteristics.

All of the manifestations of forced displacement examined in the subsequent chapters of this book entail varying forms and degrees of human insecurity. In the most dramatic and tragic cases, that insecurity may be such as to threaten the very existence of the people concerned. Bosnians living in an area that is about to be 'ethnically cleansed', for example, or internally displaced people caught up in the fighting in Liberia, or refugees who have been forcibly returned to a conflict zone in Burundi, are all likely to be confronted with very immediate threats to their life and liberty.

In other instances, the insecurity experienced by forcibly displaced people is more subtle and insidious in nature. The asylum seeker waiting for a decision on his or her claim to refugee status, for example, may spend months or even years in a situation of hardship and uncertainty. Even in the world's most prosperous states, he or she may be denied the right to seek employment, disqualified from claiming social welfare benefits and kept in detention while waiting for the authorities to make their asylum decision.

Similarly, while stateless people may not in most instances be threatened with death or serious injury, individuals who lack an effective nationality may live in constant fear of expulsion from the country which they consider to be their home. Even if they are allowed to stay, they may be subjected to systematic discrimination and be deprived of the sense of belonging and identity that citizenship normally provides.

What can be done to safeguard the security of forcibly displaced people, to provide them with the protection to which they are entitled and to find a lasting solution to their plight? As each of the following chapters suggests, humanitarian action has a valuable role to play in the effort to achieve these objectives.

Humanitarian action is a very broad concept, covering a variety of different activities undertaken by many different institutions. This book focuses primarily on international and multilateral humanitarian action, particularly the activities of UNHCR and the organizations with which it works on a daily basis: other UN agencies, non-governmental or voluntary agencies and governmental bodies.

In the popular consciousness, humanitarian action is most commonly associated with the provision of relief assistance such as food, water, shelter materials and medical care. During a complex emergency or refugee crisis, the rapid and equitable distribution of such scarce resources can evidently help to save lives and prevent unnecessary human suffering. Even if it does little to restore people's livelihoods or enable them to return to a more settled way of life, emergency assistance can safeguard the most fundamental components of human security.

Humanitarian action can also assume many other and no less important forms. It can mean removing the land-mines which make it impossible for refugees and displaced people to go back to their homes. It can mean trying to ensure that the parties to a conflict respect the laws of war and the rights of civilian populations. It can take the form of advocacy activities, intended to persuade a government that it is wrong to act in a manner that is contrary to international refugee or human rights law. And the concept of humanitarian action can also be understood in terms of military intervention, if armed forces are deployed to safeguard the security of a displaced or war-affected population.

The importance of such activities cannot be overstated, especially in a period of turbulence in the international system and at a time when the world's most powerful states are demonstrating a reduced willingness to take action other than to support humanitarian relief operations. As one eminent analyst reminds us, "humanitarian efforts have achieved some important results since 1991... It enabled Iraqi Kurds, stranded in the mountains, to return home to relative albeit temporary safety. It averted the worse consequences of famine in Somalia in 1992-93. It subsequently prevented or mitigated at least two widely predicted disasters - mass starvation in Sarajevo and the uncontrolled spread of cholera and dysentery in the camps on the border of Rwanda in 1994."(3)

At the same time, however, there is a need to acknowledge that humanitarian action has some important limitations. It cannot avert armed conflicts or bring them to an end. It cannot act as a substitute for political will. It may have a variety of unintended and even negative consequences, and be exploited by the parties to an armed conflict. And it can never act as a satisfactory substitute for national protection.

National protection can be said to exist as long as the state is able and willing to ensure the security of its citizens, as long as those citizens recognize the legitimacy of the state, and as long as different groups within society acknowledge the need to reconcile their differences by peaceful means. National protection is manifested most clearly in the maintenance of the rule of law and an absence of social or political violence; in effective law enforcement mechanisms and impartial judicial systems; in constitutional, participatory and non-discriminatory forms of governance; and in the equitable distribution of resources and access to public services. There is abundant evidence to demonstrate that the states and societies which lack these attributes are precisely those whose citizens are most likely to suffer the trauma and hardship of displacement.

If such displacements are to be averted and the growing number of displaced people around the world are to return safely to their homes, then states must individually and collectively pursue a political and economic agenda as well as a humanitarian one. While these agenda can accommodate a diversity of ideological, religious and cultural traditions, they must nevertheless be founded on the principle that everyone has a right to security and freedom: security from persecution, discrimination, armed conflict and poverty; and the freedom to fulfil their personal potential, to participate in the decisions which affect their lives and future; and to express their individual and collective identity. If such rights and freedoms could be realized, then millions of people around the world could be spared the physical and emotional pain of being uprooted.

Angola: a war-torn society © *S. Salgado*

1   **Safeguarding human security**

Refugee movements and other forms of forced displacement provide a useful (if imprecise) barometer of human security and insecurity. As a rule, people do not abandon their homes and flee from their own country or community unless they are confronted with serious threats to their life or liberty. Flight is the ultimate survival strategy, the one employed when all other coping mechanisms have been exhausted.

For the citizens of many states, life has become more difficult and dangerous over the past decade. As a result, the problem of forced displacement has become larger, more complex and geographically more widespread. Refugee movements and other forms of population displacement have also assumed a new degree of political importance, largely because of their impact upon national and regional stability. The security of people and the security of states are in that sense intimately linked.

The international community's primary response to the problem of forced displacement has been to develop new forms of humanitarian action and to devote additional resources to emergency relief. This response has undoubtedly helped to reduce human suffering and has substituted in some measure for the inability or unwillingness of the states concerned to protect their own citizens. As this chapter explains, however, it has become increasingly clear that in situations of internal armed conflict, humanitarian action is limited in its impact and can have a number of unintended and even negative consequences.

CHANGING CONCEPTS OF SECURITY

During the past decade, the notions of international and state security have undergone a fundamental reassessment by scholars, politicians and other decision-makers. Prompted in large part by the end of the cold war, this new approach to the security question provides some valuable insights into the themes which run throughout this book: the growing scale and complexity of forced displacement; the responsibility of the state to protect its citizens; and the role of humanitarian action in situations where states are unable or unwilling to provide such protection.

The changing concept of security has been examined in some detail by a number of academic analysts, as well as organizations such as the Commission on Global Governance, the International Institute for Strategic Studies and the UN Development Programme (UNDP).(1) Three broad conclusions can be drawn from this discussion.

First, the notion of security has in recent years assumed a broader and more holistic meaning. Traditionally, security analysts were preoccupied with a relatively narrow range of issues, most notably the military balance of power between different states and alliances, as well as the ability of such entities to defend their sovereignty. With the end of the era of superpower rivalry, however, and the growing number of armed conflicts taking place within states, the international community has become increasingly concerned with other sources of instability, including issues such as communal conflict and social violence, poverty and unemployment, organized crime and terrorism, as well as migratory movements and mass population displacements.(2)

Many commentators have also drawn attention to the close connections that exist between these new security concerns and the way in which they interact and reinforce each other. As the president of a leading US refugee organization has suggested, "terrorism, drug smuggling, illegal migration and environmental destruction are mightily stimulated when people are tossed about by civil war or ethnic violence and left without hope or legitimate occupation."(3)

Epitomizing this new and more integrated approach to the question of international security, in January 1992, the UN Security Council issued a declaration, formally recognizing that "the non-military sources of instability in the economic, social, humanitarian and ecological fields have become threats to peace and security."(4) While the subsequent action taken by the permanent members of that body has in many situations been disappointingly limited, international priorities have clearly been reordered. Humanitarian issues and ethical questions, which previously played a very limited role in the global security discourse, now enjoy a central place in that discussion.(5)

Second, recent years have witnessed a growing recognition of the intimate relationship that exists between the security of states and the welfare of the citizens who populate such political and territorial entities. On one hand, it has become clear that states which are militarily and strategically powerful are not necessarily strong or stable. The armed forces of the Soviet Union and its allies in Eastern Europe, for example, were enormously powerful by international standards. But those states or their governments collapsed very rapidly at the end of the 1980s, due in large part to their lack of socio-political cohesion and their failure to meet the needs and aspirations of their citizens.

On the other hand, as the World Bank has suggested, effective, responsive and inclusive states are required if people are to be properly protected, to lead healthier and happier lives, and, one might add, to avoid the trauma of displacement.(6) Historical experience has demonstrated that authoritarian and exploitative states are prone to treat their citizens as political and economic pawns, relocating them by force, imposing stringent controls upon their freedom of movement and expelling them from the territory if they are perceived to be disloyal.

Nevertheless, when state structures disintegrate and disappear, forced population displacements are also very likely to ensue. As one scholar has commented, "states constitute the primary nexus when it comes to security for individuals and groups."(7) As the recent cases of countries such as Afghanistan, Liberia and Somalia suggest, forced displacements of people are a clear indication that the web of rights and obligations which links the citizen to the state has broken down.

A third recent evolution in the notion of security is to be found in the growing focus on international cooperation, in contrast to the more traditional emphasis on competition and conflict. The principal threats to international, state and human security, it has been recognized, are transnational in nature, and cannot be effectively addressed by means of unilateral action. At the same time, the demise of communism in its established forms has removed one of the most important impediments to cooperation between states.

Of course, continuing ideological differences and competing national or regional interests continue to obstruct such cooperation, as witnessed in relation to a number of recent or contemporary crises involving refugees: the deployment of a multinational force in the Great Lakes region of Africa; the use of force by external powers and alliances during the war in former Yugoslavia; and the continuing differences of opinion expressed in relation to the Palestinian question, to give just three examples.

Nevertheless, there is substantial evidence to confirm the general trend towards multilateralism and international cooperation: the growing size and influence of regional organizations such as the Organization for Security and Cooperation in Europe, the Southern African Development Community, and the Association of South-East Asian Nations; the participation of states and other actors in a series of international conferences on global issues such as human rights, women, the environment, population and social development; and the new degree of consensus which has emerged in the UN Security Council, reflected in the declining use of the veto by that body's permanent members.

The growth of international cooperation can also be seen in the activities of non-state actors. Increasingly, non-governmental organizations, advocacy groups and the institutions of civil society are pooling their resources at the regional and international levels. Greatly facilitated by the introduction of new information and communications technologies, this development has also contributed to the weakening of principles such as national sovereignty and the inviolability of borders. In the era of the fax machine, satellite dish and internet, even the world's most authoritarian governments are finding it difficult to impose controls over the circulation of images, information and ideas.

THE SOURCES OF HUMAN INSECURITY

As suggested in the preceding section, the notion of security has in recent years been given a broader meaning and has assumed a more human and 'people-centred' aspect. UNDP's *Human Development Report* has played a particularly important role in the development of this new paradigm. As the 1994 edition of that publication explained, human security has two principal aspects: safety from chronic threats such as hunger, disease and repression, and protection from sudden and hurtful disruptions in the pattern of daily life. "The loss of human security," the report explains, "can be a slow, silent process or an abrupt, loud emergency. It can be human-made - due to wrong policy choices. It can stem from the forces of nature. Or it can be a combination of both."(8)

The balance sheet of human security suggests that many gains have been made in recent years. The global economy continues to expand, bringing tangible benefits to millions of people around the world. More people than ever before are living in democratic states, and therefore have an opportunity to participate in the governance of their country. And the longstanding threat of superpower confrontation and nuclear war has effectively been removed from the international environment. Unfortunately, however, a substantial proportion of the world's population has gained little or no benefit from these advances. Indeed, for the citizens of many states, life has become progressively more difficult and dangerous.

Polarization and poverty

Although aggregate global incomes have now reached unprecedented levels due to the forces of technological innovation and international trade, recent years have also witnessed a further widening in economic disparities, both within and between states.(9) During the past three decades, the income differential between the richest and poorest fifth of the world's population has more than doubled, from 30:1 to 78:1. In the less-developed regions, no fewer than 89 countries now have lower *per capita* incomes than they had ten years ago. Nineteen of these states, including Haiti, Liberia, Rwanda, Sudan and Venezuela, are poorer today than they were in 1960.

About a quarter of the world's 5.7 billion people now live below the World Bank's official poverty line, including more than 100 million people in the industrialized states. As this statistic indicates, the disparities are not simply restricted to the less-developed regions. In both Britain and Australia, for example, the richest 20 per cent of the population earn 10 times more than the poorest 20 per cent.

The growth of such striking inequities within the industrialized states has stimulated a greater awareness of the fact that economic growth alone does not automatically lead to an across-the-board improvement in living standards. Moreover, while international trade is clearly a powerful instrument of economic development, serving in many cases to strengthen the less dynamic economies, it may also marginalize those which are least able to adapt in the face of growing, and often unregulated, competition. To illustrate the disparities which have emerged, the poorest 20 per cent of the world's people enjoy only one per cent of global trade. The whole continent of Africa currently accounts for less than five per cent of global trading activity.

According to many analysts, the restructuring of the global economy and the penetration of market forces is leading to the emergence of a two-tier system of states quite different from the one suggested by the notion of a rich 'North' and a poor 'South'. Thus in recent years, the traditionally prosperous regions of North America and Western Europe have been joined by the dynamic economies of East and South-East Asia. In sharp contrast, many countries in Africa, the former Soviet Union, the Caribbean and South Asia have recorded much lower rates of growth and income (see Figure 1.1).

Many of the world's poorer nations are now locked into a vicious circle of economic stagnation, environmental degradation and impoverishment, reinforced in some cases by rapid rates of population growth. In order to meet their debt repayment obligations while maintaining standards of living at a minimum survival level, some countries have felt obliged to cannibalize their capital base and to exploit their natural resources in a completely unsustain-

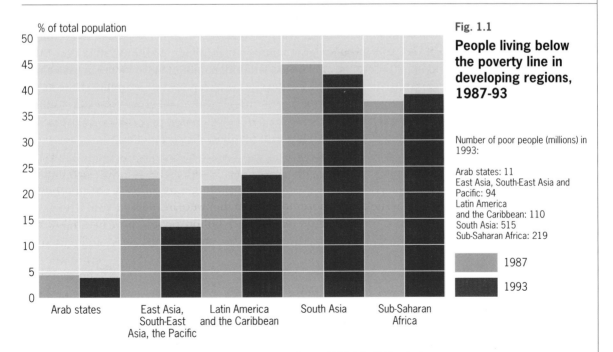

Fig. 1.1

People living below the poverty line in developing regions, 1987-93

Number of poor people (millions) in 1993:

Arab states: 11
East Asia, South-East Asia and Pacific: 94
Latin America and the Caribbean: 110
South Asia: 515
Sub-Saharan Africa: 219

1987
1993

Source: United Nations Development Programme, *Human Development Report 1997*, Oxford University Press, New York, 1997; Figure defines poverty line as an income of less than $1 a day, $2 a day in the case of Latin America and Caribbean, based on 1985 purchasing power parity in $ (PPP$); East Asia excludes China.

able manner. It is particularly disturbing to note that a major share of the bilateral and multilateral aid provided to low-income countries is being used to service debts, instead of being used for its original purpose: human development and the alleviation of poverty.

Those countries which exhibit the greatest potential for growth often receive the highest level of external investment and aid, while the least dynamic and strategically unimportant countries have become increasingly dispensable. Since 1990, aid to the least developed countries has fallen by seven per cent while assistance to the states of Eastern Europe and Central Asia has more than doubled. This comes at a time when the richer countries are giving less in official development assistance: the $59 billion provided in 1995 represents the lowest ratio of aid to gross national product - just 0.27 percent - since the United Nations adopted a target of 0.7 percent in 1970. (10)

In this context, the primary response to crisis in the poorest economies has often been a tough prescription of economic reform or structural adjustment. While reform is certainly needed, experience has demonstrated that the type of economic policies demanded by the world's most affluent states and most influential financial institutions can carry a high human and social price: unemployment, declining wages, reduced public services and growing income differentials.

Poverty and economic polarization alone do not produce forced population displacements. In fact, there are a number of countries which, although very poor, have in recent years been largely unaffected by the persecution, conflict and human rights abuses which oblige people to abandon their homes: Lesotho, Namibia, Tanzania and Zambia, to give four examples from Southern Africa. But such cases are the exceptions which prove the rule. In general, there is ample evidence to demonstrate that countries with low and declining standards of living are particularly prone to complex emergencies, refugee outflows and other forms of forced displacement. (11)

The process of economic polarization also has an obvious relevance to migratory movements of a more voluntary nature. Some of those people who are unable to satisfy their needs and aspirations at home will inevitably try to move to a country where their prospects appear to be better. And if they cannot achieve that goal by regular and legal means, they may be tempted to seek admission by submitting a claim for refugee status.

Social and political instability

As we move towards the end of the 20th century, more people than ever before are living in countries with relatively pluralistic political systems. According to one estimate, the number of states with civilian governments, appointed by means of competitive elections, has doubled since 1984. (12) Whole regions that were once under authoritarian rule - the former Soviet Union, Eastern Europe and South America, for example - have now made at least a partial transition to democracy. Nevertheless, the citizens of many countries continue to suffer from human rights abuses, social turmoil and political instability.

A good number of states, primarily but not exclusively in Africa, Asia and the Middle East, remain under authoritarian forms of government. In many instances, moreover, such states have come under relatively little pressure to reform, usually because the world's more prosperous countries have allowed their quest for trade and investment opportunities to override any commitment which they have to democracy and human rights. In the light of events in countries such as Haiti, Iraq, Myanmar and Zaire, it hardly needs to be said that states which lack a pluralistic political system and which disregard human and minority rights are particularly prone to refugee movements, mass expulsions and other forms of forced displacement.

Many of the countries which have in recent years established the formal structures of democracy are now affected by varying degrees of social and political instability. In the second half of the 1980s, a number of related phenomena prompted authoritarian governments in many parts of the world to introduce political reforms: the growth of pro-democracy movements and other forms of popular protest; the declining legitimacy of Soviet communism and the eventual demise of the USSR; and the mounting pressure for political and economic liberalization exercised by the more prosperous states and the international financial institutions.

It would be profoundly foolish to mourn the passing of regimes which were responsible for terrible violations of human rights. Nevertheless, it is now quite clear that a proportion of the states that introduced more pluralistic political structures and more liberal economic systems in the late 1980s and early 1990s lacked the socio-political cohesion and civic culture required to underpin such rapid and far-reaching reforms.

The resultant instability has been manifested in a particularly vivid manner in parts of the former Soviet Union. Sadly, for many people living in the Commonwealth of Independent States (CIS), the economic and political freedoms of the post-communist era have actually been associated with declining levels of physical, material and legal security, a situation which has given some legitimacy to calls by anti-reformists for a halt, or even a reversal, to the process of change (see Figure 1.2). Three manifestations of that insecurity are of particular relevance to this book: the spate of ethnically-based conflicts which have erupted in many of the newly-established CIS states; the displacement or involuntary migration of some nine million former Soviet citizens during the past six years; and the many problems related to statelessness and citizenship which have emerged with the dissolution of the USSR and its replacement by 15 different states.

While such problems have structural origins, they have undoubtedly been exacerbated (and in some cases even created) by people who have an interest in disrupting the democratization process: politicians, government officials, diaspora communities, arms dealers, mercenaries and criminal syndicates. As one expert from the region explains, "violent conflicts have now become a routine reality because a highly militarized society, with low civic morality amongst its members, was confronted with the sudden collapse of state control in many areas... permitting a large number of ambitious and corrupt persons and groups to exercise their activities in a social space which had lost many of its identity parameters and legal constraints."(13)

While the process of state formation is proving to be a turbulent one in many parts of the post-communist world, other parts of the globe are also witnessing the progressive weakening of established state structures and the emergence of new political entities (see Figure 1.3). In many parts of Africa, for example, governments have made a substantial retreat from their role in the provision of basic services such as health, education and social welfare, and have lost their ability to undertake the basic functions of the state: collecting taxes, paying its officals, maintaining law and order and defending the territorial integrity of the country.(14) As a result, the state has been stripped of its legitimacy and has lost its ability to act as a social and political mediator in the face of growing civil unrest.

In situations of declining prosperity and opportunity, people have tended to seek security in communal allegiances, a process which has reinforced the potential for social and political conflict. In order to maintain a semblance of stability and to protect their privileged position, ruling elites have in many instances become dependent on the repressive machinery of the state (and increasingly on private security companies) thereby reducing its legitimacy still further. In this context, calls for political liberalization have often been met by an authoritarian backlash, manifested in the repression - and sometimes the mass expulsion - of people who pose a threat to ruling regimes.

Fig. 1.2

Poverty in former communist countries 1987-94

People living below the income poverty line ($4 a day)

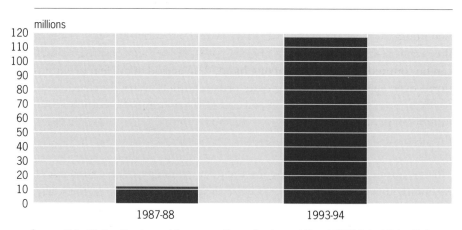

Source: United Nations Development Programme, *Human Development Report 1997*, Oxford University Press, New York, 1997

Armenia	Lithuania	**Fig. 1.3**
Azerbaijan	Macedonia (FYR)	**New states, 1990-97**
Belarus	Moldova	
Bosnia and Herzegovina	Russian Federation	
Croatia	Slovak Republic	
Czech Republic	Slovenia	
Eritrea	Tajikistan	
Estonia	Turkmenistan	
Georgia	Ukraine	
Kazakstan	Uzbekistan	
Kyrgyzstan	Yugoslavia (FR)	
Latvia		

In the most extreme cases, exemplified by countries such as Afghanistan, Burundi, Liberia, Rwanda, Sierra Leone and Somalia, the political nexus between state and citizens - which was never very strong - has been definitively ruptured. The general pattern in such countries has been for the state to lose control over increasing amounts of territory as armed challenges to its power have mounted. With the progressive destruction of the public infra-structure, informal and illicit economic activity has become the main gener-ator of wealth, further undermining the reach of the state and its ability to protect its citizens.

These extreme cases of state dissolution are both a cause and consequence of armed conflict, and have provided the background for many of the largest flows of displaced people during the past few years. Elsewhere, as in the Great Lakes region of Africa, the social nexus between different groups of citizens has broken down, leading to terrible forms of violence and massive population movements (see Box 1.1).

VIOLENCE AND WAR-BASED ECONOMIES

According to some criteria, the world is now a much safer place than it was in the recent past. The number of ongoing conflicts between sovereign states can be counted on the fingers of one hand. The period of nuclear prolifera-tion is over, and many of the regional 'proxy conflicts' that were characteris-tic of the cold war era have also been brought to an end. Nevertheless, for millions of people around the globe, violent conflict remains the most direct threat to their life and liberty and their ability to remain peacefully in their own homes.

During the 1970s and 1980s, in countries ranging from Angola and Mozambique in Southern Africa to El Salvador and Nicaragua in Central America and to Cambodia in South-East Asia, the pattern of armed conflict was broadly similar. If the government of a third world state was backed by one of the superpowers, then the other superpower would attempt to unseat

1.1

Population displacements in the Great Lakes region of Africa

Forced population displacements have been a central characteristic of the political crisis which has gripped the Great Lakes region of Africa during the past three years. In many instances, moreover, such displacements have been deliberately provoked by the warring parties, employed as a means of securing or reinforcing their control of territory, resources and people.

While the crisis in the Great Lakes has a long and complex history, international attention began to focus on Rwanda in the second quarter of 1994, when at least 500,000 people, usually described as Tutsis and moderate Hutus, were killed in the space of six weeks. In fact, the question of ethnic and national identity in the region is far more subtle than these categorizations might suggest.

The genocide stopped only when the government was ousted by the Rwandese Patriotic Front (RPF), a rebel movement composed primarily of exiled Tutsis, whose repatriation from Uganda had for many years

been blocked by the regime in Kigali. As the RPF drove south, the organizers of the genocide recognized their imminent defeat and organized a mass evacuation of the Hutu population. Around 1.75 million moved to the neighbouring countries of Zaire, Tanzania and Burundi, where they were accommodated in camps and provided with international assistance. As the Hutus were leaving, approximately 700,000 Tutsi refugees - including children who had been born in exile - returned to Rwanda, the largest number of them from Uganda.

Soon after the primarily Hutu camps were established in 1994, approximately 160,000 of the refugees returned voluntarily to Rwanda. But as members of the former Rwandese government, army and militia forces tightened their grip on the refugee population, the repatriation came to a halt. UNHCR's efforts to promote return had only a limited impact. In fact, the number of people repatriating was almost exactly matched by the number of babies born in the refugee camps. As a result, the total refugee population remained stable.

The size of the refugee camps in Zaire and Tanzania, their proximity to the border, as well as their political and military character, posed a serious security threat to the

new Rwandese government. UNHCR soon recognized the extent of the problem and repeatedly called upon the international community to separate the armed elements and intimidators from the civilian refugee population. The political will required for such action to be taken, however, was simply not in evidence.

Conflict in Burundi

Burundi, whose ethnic composition is almost identical to that of Rwanda, has been ravaged by internal armed conflict since 1993, when the democratically elected president Melchior Ndadaye was assassinated. His murder was followed by ethnically motivated killings of both Tutsis and Hutus, and a more general descent into chaos. As a result of the violence, some 160,000 Burundian refugees (mostly Hutu) fled to Tanzania and Zaire. Many thousands more were internally displaced. The camps for Burundian refugees, like those of their Rwandese counterparts, were also used as bases for Hutu rebels engaged in cross-border attacks on their country of origin.

The influx of 270,000 Rwandese (primarily Hutu) refugees into Burundi in 1994, came at a time when the situation in that country was already spinning out of control. As the crisis in Burundi deepened and the violence around the camps

increased, the exiled Hutus came under growing pressure to repatriate from the country's Tutsi-dominated government. Eventually, in July 1996, up to 90,000 refugees were forced back into Rwanda while some 30,000 others fled to Tanzania.

Throughout the period described above, tension and violence were mounting in eastern Zaire. Hutu refugees who wished to return to Rwanda were intimidated or eliminated by armed elements in the camps. North Kivu became the scene of a three-way war between Hutu, Tutsi and local peoples such as the Hunde, entailing the killing and mass expulsion of many Tutsi. In South Kivu, people of Rwandese origin, primarily Tutsis known as the Banyamulenge, also started to be harassed and displaced by local Zaireans, supported from Kinshasa.

Having witnessed with great concern the fate of the Tutsis in North Kivu, the Banyamulenge, some of whom had assisted in the RPF victory in July 1994, began to resist. Well armed and highly motivated, they became a central component of the Alliance of Democratic Forces for the Liberation of Congo-Zaire (AFDL). Led by Laurent Kabila, a lifelong opponent of President Mobutu, the AFDL was supported in various ways by other states in the region who wished to see a change of government in Kinshasa: Angola, Eritrea, Rwanda and Uganda.

As the AFDL advanced, Rwandese refugees were scattered in all directions from the camps in eastern Zaire. Some 70,000 Burundian refugees, who were mostly living in camps

around Uvira and Bukavu, returned to their country of origin. Half a million Rwandese refugees regrouped at Mugunga, near Goma, and were finally encircled by AFDL soldiers, who obliged them to repatriate. Most of these refugees crossed the border into Rwanda between 15 and 19 November 1996, with tens of thousands of

Map A

Displacement of Rwandese and Burundian refugees, 1996-97

☐ Capital
● Town or village
━ State boundary
── District boundary
➤ Principal movements of displaced refugees

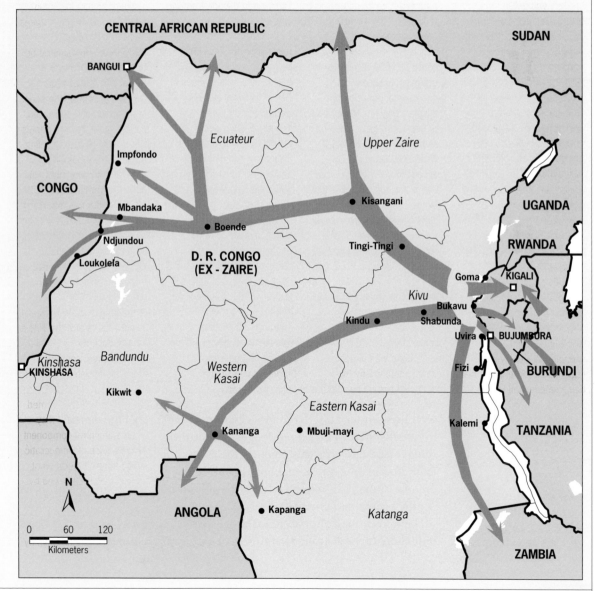

stragglers returning in the following days.

By the end of the year, around 685,000 Rwandese refugees had returned from Zaire. At the same time, large numbers of Rwandese and Burundian refugees (more than 400,000 according to UNHCR estimates) fled into the Zairean interior, some of them under the influence of military and militia forces associated with the former regime. Large numbers of local Zaireans were also displaced by these events.

The unpaid and ill-disciplined Zairean army offered practically no resistance to the AFDL. In March 1997, the rebels took control of the second city of Kisangani as well as the important mining town of Lubumbashi. As the march on the capital began in earnest, President Mobutu fled the country. On 20 May 1997, the AFDL entered Kinshasa. Zaire was renamed the Democratic Republic of Congo and Laurent Kabila declared himself to be president.

Peace and prosperity?

The demise of the Mobutu regime, some commentators initially suggested, might usher in a new era of peace and prosperity right across Central Africa, from Eritrea in the east to Angola in the west. But such hopes were overshadowed - if not dashed - by growing evidence that the AFDL forces had committed atrocities against the Hutu refugees in eastern Zaire, in revenge for the 1994 genocide of Rwanda's Tutsi population. By June 1997, some 215,000 displaced refugees remained unaccounted for, either because they had been killed or because they were hiding in the dense Zairean forest. While UNHCR did not have access to many of the areas where the Rwandese had fled, by that date, the organization had been able to organize the return of more than 54,000 refugees by air and 180,000 by land.

By this time, the crisis in the region had spread well beyond the Great Lakes. While thousands of Rwandese and Burundian refugees had disappeared in eastern Zaire, others had walked hundreds of kilometres and crossed the border into Angola, Congo Brazzaville, the Central African Republic and Zambia, with smaller numbers arriving in Cameroon, Kenya and other nearby states. Refugees from Burundi were also continuing to move into Tanzania to escape from the conflict in their own country.

Return from Tanzania

By this time, the vast majority of Rwandese Hutus who had fled to Tanzania in 1994 had also returned to their homeland. Two weeks after the massive return of Rwandese refugees from eastern Zaire, on 5 December 1996, the Tanzanian government and UNHCR had issued a joint declaration, setting a deadline of 31 December 1996 for the return of all Rwandese refugees living on Tanzanian territory. The statement said that the government of Tanzania had decided "that all Rwandese refugees can now

return to their country in safety."

On 12 December 1996, camp leaders in the Ngara area began to move the refugees away from the border and further into Tanzania, so as to maintain their control over the exiled population. In response, the Tanzanian army forced the refugees to turn round and redirected them towards Rwanda. Hundreds of thousands of refugees were taken to the Rwandese border during the next few days. Those who had managed to flee into the surrounding countryside, and those who had stayed in the camps, were rounded up over the next few weeks and trucked back to Rwanda under military escort. In total, an estimated 483,000 Rwandese refugees were returned from Tanzania.

Regardless of the nature of the Rwandese repatriation from Zaire (where the refugees returned as a result of violence and the AFDL advance), Tanzania (where the refugees were returned

or at least undermine that regime by supporting a rebel movement, not infrequently, it must be acknowledged, under the guise of humanitarian and refugee assistance programmes. This rivalry fuelled the militarization of many low-income states, enabling regimes and ruling elites which lacked any popular support to remain in power, while underlying political and social conflicts remained unresolved.

The end of the cold war, it was widely expected, would lead to a general reduction of such armed conflicts. First, it was assumed that with the

by the national army) and Burundi (where refoulement, murders and general insecurity prompted a mass return), few observers doubted the need for these refugees to go back to Rwanda. Without the return of the refugees, it seems clear, the Hutu militia and former Rwandese army would have continued to mount attacks on Rwanda from their bases outside the country, indefinitely obstructing any process of stabilization.

Even so, the months that followed the mass repatriation of refugees from Tanzania and Zaire witnessed a sharp increase in the level of violence within Rwanda, especially in the north-west of the country. There is little doubt that much of this violence was committed by Hutu militia who had been obliged to repatriate with the refugees. By prompting the authorities in Kigali to respond to this threat with the use of military force, supporters of the former and genocidal regime achieved their primary objective: to perpetuate the instability of Rwanda, and of the Great Lakes region as a whole.

Fig. 1.4

Displacement of Rwandese and Burundian refugees, 1996-97

Number of Rwandese refugees	
Present in eastern Zaire (before Oct. 1996 conflict)	1,100,000

Repatriations from eastern Zaire	
Spontaneous returns (Nov.1996)	600,000
Organized returns by land (Dec. 1996-June 1997)	180,000
Organized returns by air (April-June 1997)	54,000
Total returns	**834,000**

Refugees who have moved from Zaire (July 1997)	
Congo (Brazzaville)	20,000
Central African Republic	3,800
Angola	2,500
Total	26,300

Refugees remaining in Zaire (July 1997)	26,300
Total refugees location known	**52,600**
Total refugees location unknown	**213,400**

Number of Burundian refugees	
Present in eastern Zaire (before Oct. 1996 conflict)	150,000

Repatriations from eastern Zaire	
Spontaneous returns	77,000
Registered returns, (Nov. 1996 - June 1997)	23,000
Total returns	**100,000**

Refugees who have moved from Zaire (July 1997)	
Tanzania	10,000
Total	**10,000**

Refugees remaining in Zaire (July 1997)	4,500
Total refugees located and repatriated	**14,500**
Total refugees location unknown	**35,500**

Estimated statistics at 2 July 1997

disappearance of the east-west ideological dispute, the underlying rationale for these wars would also vanish. Second, there was good reason to believe that the dramatic reduction of superpower support for states and rebel groups in developing countries would lead many conflicts to burn out, or at least to diminish in intensity.

Third, it had been expected by some commentators - somewhat naively perhaps - that a generous 'peace dividend' stemming from global disarmament might lead to higher flows of development assistance to the

Fig. 1.5

Internal armed conflicts, 1990-95

Country	War began	Site of war	Combat status at 31 December 1995
Algeria	1992	general	continuing 1995
Bosnia and Herzegovina	1992	general	suspended 1995
Croatia	1991	Slavonia/Krajina	suspended 1992
Croatia	1995	Western Slavonia/Krajina	suspended 1995
Djibouti	1991	Afar	continuing 1995
Egypt	1992	general	continuing 1995
Georgia	1991	western region	suspended 1993
Georgia	1991	South Ossetia	suspended 1992
Georgia	1992	Abkhazia	suspended 1993
Ghana	1994	northern regions	suspended 1995
Haiti	1991	general	suspended 1991
India	1990	Kashmir	continuing 1995
Iraq	1991	southern Shia regions	continuing 1995
Libya	1995	general	continuing 1995
Mali	1990	northern Tuareg regions	suspended 1995
Mexico	1994	Chiapas	suspended 1995
Moldova	1991	Dniestr Republic	suspended 1992
Myanmar	1991	general	suspended 1992
Myanmar	1992	Arakan	suspended 1994
Myanmar	1992	Kaya	continuing 1995
Niger	1991	northern Tuareg regions	continuing 1995
Niger	1994	eastern region	continuing 1995
Pakistan	1992	Karachi/Sind	continuing 1995
Russian Federation	1992	North Ossetia/ Ingushetia	suspended 1992
Russian Federation	1993	Moscow	suspended 1993
Russian Federation	1994	Chechnya	continuing 1995
Rwanda	1990	general	suspended 1995
Senegal	1990	Casamance region	continuing 1995
Sierra Leone	1991	general	continuing 1995
Somalia	1991	general	suspended 1995
Sudan	1994	Beja	suspended 1995
Tajikistan	1992	general	continuing 1995
Togo	1991	general	suspended 1991
Trinidad and Tobago	1990	general	suspended 1990
Turkey	1991	western region	suspended 1992
Uganda	1994	central region	suspended 1995
Uganda	1994	south-eastern region	suspended 1995
Venezuela	1992	general	suspended 1992
Yemen	1994	general	suspended 1994

Source: Dan Smith (et al.) *The State of War and Peace Atlas*, Penguin, London, 1997
Figure shows only internal armed conflicts beginning in or after 1990. Not an official UN record.

poorer countries, enabling them to address their social and economic problems.

These assumptions, it is now realized, greatly underestimated the strength of the internal forces driving some of these wars, as witnessed in the continuation and transformation of the conflicts in countries such as Afghanistan and Angola. At the same time, the optimistic outlook which characterized the end of the 1980s neglected the extent to which new conflicts would emerge in different parts of the world, many of them the manifestation of deep-rooted processes and problems that were ignored by the international community during the cold war.

This is not to suggest that the armed conflicts which have erupted during the past few years can simply be regarded as the product of 'tribal hatreds' or 'ancient animosities', phrases which are employed far too freely by journalists and believed far too readily by politicians and policymakers. Recent experience has demonstrated that hatred and animosity are political resources which can, if the circumstances are right, be mobilized (and even manufactured) by groups who are struggling for political power. Unable to gain external support for their cause by exploiting the rivalry of the superpowers, governments and other actors alike have resorted to 'playing the communal card', a process which has often culminated in social violence and armed conflict.(15)

The privatization of violence

Up to 35 civil wars and a much larger number of lower-intensity conflicts are currently being fought around the world (see Figure 1.5). The parties to these conflicts have in many cases flagrantly violated international humanitarian law by adopting tactics which rely upon the brutalization of civilian populations. As one commentator has written, these include "conspicuous atrocity, systematic rape, hostage-taking, forced starvation and siege, the destruction of religious and historic monuments, the use of shells and rockets against civilian targets (especially homes, hospitals and crowded places like markets or water sources) and the use of land-mines to make large areas uninhabitable."(16)

In many war-affected countries, the absence of adequate resources to pay or feed the combatants has forced soldiers and other fighters to fend for themselves, whether through the informal taxing of civilians at roadblocks, for example, or by the outright looting and pillaging of the population. While this crude process of 'privatising violence' has helped to address the problem of payment, it has also led to the growing fragmentation of armed groups and a loss of control over the combatants.

With formal military authority breaking down, combatants have tended to mobilize around loyalties and allegiances which have as much to do with personal survival and enrichment as with any political or ideological agenda.

Such predatory tactics have undoubtedly been facilitated by the widening availability (and declining price) of light weapons, land-mines and other instruments of war.

Recent experience has also demonstrated that internal wars do not necessarily come to an end when foreign support has been withdrawn or reduced, nor do they necessarily finish when a large proportion of the civilian population has been displaced or impoverished. In fact, in countries such as Angola, Afghanistan and Sudan, where war has raged for many years, the intensity of violence has taken a number of periodic upturns since the beginning of the 1990s.

One of the reasons for this development is that in the absence of external support, governments, armed opposition movements and local warlords have all been able to establish sophisticated 'war-based economies' to sustain and even expand their activities. In Afghanistan, for example, poppy cultivation has more than doubled during the past decade and has become a vital resource in the country's armed conflict. Similarly, in countries such as Angola, Cambodia, Liberia, Myanmar and Sierra Leone, armed groups and state officials have supported and even enriched themselves through the systematic extraction of natural resources such as timber, rubber and precious stones.

In such situations, the function of violence has also changed. While the parties to these conflicts may continue to evoke a social, political or ideological rationale for their struggle, their activities are actually aimed at the illicit accumulation of wealth. The line between political action, social banditry and organized crime has become very difficult to draw in many parts of the world, not least in relatively developed conflict areas such as former Yugoslavia and the Caucasus.

The resource flows which sustain many of these war economies have in many senses been facilitated by the process of globalization. For example, a number of multinational companies have shown little reluctance to establish deals with the armed factions in Liberia, so that they can gain access to the valuable natural resources which that country has to offer. In return, the hard currency provided by those companies allows the armed factions to purchase additional weapons on the international arms market - a market which has been eager to find new customers.

At the same time, the impact of the globalization process can be seen in the activities of certain diaspora or transnational communities, channelling financial and human resources to conflicts in places such as Armenia, Azerbaijan, Sri Lanka, Turkey and former Yugoslavia. While information on this issue is not easy to collect, there is considerable evidence to suggest that the wars in these and other countries have been sustained in part by emigrant and exiled populations in Europe, North America and other parts of the world. (17)

War-based economies are thus both a cause and a consequence of the failed state syndrome. On one hand, they are symptomatic of a state's inability (or unwillingness) to protect its citizens, to regulate the economic activities which take place on its territory and to prevent the use of public resources for private gain. On the other hand, by systematically exploiting these conditions, armed groups, warlords and corrupt government officials deprive the state of revenue and legitimacy, thereby reinforcing its disintegration.

Such conditions, of course, provide very fertile ground for political instability, social violence and forced population displacements. They also provide a major obstacle to the repatriation and reintegration of displaced populations as well as the broader task of post-conflict reconstruction.

War-based economies will not disappear with the signing of formal peace agreements and the introduction of large-scale aid and development programmes. Nor will the process of demobilization necessarily bring an end to social violence, rooted as it usually is in poverty, inequality and the absence of opportunity. The recruitment of child and adolescent soldiers, for example, which in many cases is voluntary, represents a crude form of social advancement for young people, providing them with an identity and status which has been denied to them in civilian society. Enabling such youngsters to survive without resorting to the use of violence constitutes a vital component of the peacebuilding process.

PATTERNS OF FORCED DISPLACEMENT

As the preceding sections of this chapter have shown, the security of many people is currently being threatened by a complex mixture of factors: by unbalanced development, economic decline and environmental degradation (see Box 1.2); by state collapse, state formation and the authoritarian exercise of state power; and by new forms of violence and warfare, which, although based in many instances on communal allegiances, also serve as a camouflage for personal or factional gain.

Given the difficulties involved in quantifying human security and insecurity, it is not easy to say whether such threats are more widespread and intense today than they were in the past. On one hand, there are many analysts who point to 'the new world disorder' and 'the coming anarchy'. Taking it as almost self-evident that life in the contemporary world is nastier and more brutish than it was in previous years, the representatives of such schools of thought tend to envisage a future which in certain parts of the world is characterized by mounting lawlessness, an irreversible process of social and political fragmentation, as well as growing conflict over scarce natural resources. (18)

On the other hand, there are scholars who believe that such pessimism is unwarranted and based upon a faulty reading of both historical and contem-

1.2

Environment and migration: the case of Central Asia

Ecological and environmental change are a common cause of migration and human displacement. The forms which such changes take, however, are extremely varied. They can be sudden and unexpected, as is usually the case with disasters such as earthquakes or cyclones. Or they can be more gradual in nature, as is the case with long-term processes of desertification and land degradation.

People who have been displaced as a result of environmental change are not normally considered to be refugees, even if they have been obliged to cross an international border and move into another country. Refugees are distinguished by the fact that they lack the protection of their state and therefore look to the international community to provide them with security. Environmentally displaced people, on the other hand, can usually count upon the protection of their state, even if it is limited in its capacity to provide them with emergency relief or longer-term reconstruction assistance.

The exception to this rule is to be found in situations where acts of environmental destruction, such as the poisoning of water wells, the burning of crops or draining of marshlands are deliberately used to persecute, intimidate or displace a particular population. In such cases, the affected populations might legitimately be considered to be refugees if they leave their homeland and seek safety in another state.

Environmental degradation and the ensuing competition for scarce natural resources is often at the root of refugee-producing conflicts. The Zapatista rebellion in the Chiapas state of Mexico, for example, which led at one point to the displacement of up to 35,000 people, has been attributed in part to the growing grievances of peasants affected by the problems of deforestation, soil erosion and land scarcity. According to many commentators, the coming years may also witness a growing number of refugee-producing 'resource wars', in which states fight for control of rivers and other valuable environmental assets.

The Soviet legacy

Some of the clearest examples of environmentally induced migration and displacement are to be found in the former Soviet states of Central Asia. According to a recent UNHCR report, in the first half of the 1990s, around 270,000 people in the region were displaced for such reasons.

Much of Central Asia is affected by problems such as soil degradation and desertification, a situation created by decades of agricultural exploitation, industrial pollution and overgrazing. During the Soviet years, irrigation schemes were introduced throughout the region, so that cotton could be cultivated on an intensive and continuous basis. Poorly designed and badly managed, these irrigation schemes led to the large-scale wastage of scarce water resources and the degradation of the land as a result of salinization.

Under the monocultural agricultural system practised by the Soviet authorities, massive amounts of chemicals were used to control the growth of weeds and to replace lost nutrients in the soil. The residues of those additives are now poisoning the region's land and water and contaminating the food chain, making it increasingly difficult for some populations to remain in their usual place of residence.

Although many parts of Central Asia suffer from such problems, degradation of the environment has reached its worst proportions in and around the Aral Sea, a large lake situated between Kazakstan and Uzbekistan. As a result of Soviet efforts to maximize the area's cotton crop, most of the water flowing into the Aral Sea was siphoned off and used for irrigation; the annual flow was reduced from an average of 50 cubic kilometeres a year between 1930 and 1960 to less than five cubic kilometeres by the early 1980s. Since 1960, the surface area of the sea has been reduced by half, while its volume has dropped by around 65 per cent.

Dust from the dried-up bed of the Aral Sea, containing large quantities of agricultural and industrial chemicals, is now carried long distances by the wind, contributing further to the pollution, salinization and desertification of the land. The economic and social consequences of this phenomenon have been substantial. They include a sharp decline in agricultural production, an increase in the price of foodstuffs, the demise of a once significant fishing industry and declining health standards amongst the local population. Not surprisingly, a considerable number of people have chosen to move.

Since 1992, some 100,000 people are believed to have left the Aral Sea area as a result of these environmental problems. Ethnic Russians,

Kazaks and Uzbeks have tended to be the first to move, leaving behind the members of poorer and less mobile groups who lack the social networks required to establish new homes elsewhere.

Disaster zones

Semipalatinsk in Kazakstan is another environmental disaster zone. Almost 500 nuclear bombs were exploded in the region between 1949 and 1989, 150 of them above ground. With the consequences of nuclear radiation becoming more widely known amongst the local population, around 160,000 people have decided to leave the area. Around half of this number have moved to other parts of Kazakstan, with the remainder migrating to Russia, Ukraine and other former Soviet states.

Several other forms of environmental disaster and population displacement have also been witnessed in Central Asia. The mountainous states of Kyrgyzstan and Tajikistan, for example, have both been affected by serious earthquakes, as well as landslides, mudslides and avalanches. According to the Kyrgyz government, in 1994 alone, landslides caused the displacement of some 27,000 people. In the area of Lake Balkash in Kazakstan and in parts of the Ferghana Valley of Kyrgyzstan and

Uzbekistan, many of the better educated and more affluent members of the population have moved away to escape from high levels of air, land and water pollution - a result of the poorly regulated agricultural, industrial and mining activities undertaken in those areas.

Tackling the issue of environmental degradation and displacement in Central Asia will not be an easy task. The problem is so deep-rooted and was kept hidden for so long under the Soviet authorities that it may in some instances be too late for effective remedial action to be taken. Moreover, the political sensitivity of the issue is such that accurate information on the true dimensions of the problem is difficult to compile. Governments in the region are confronted with a host of other pressing issues and generally lack the capacity and resources to address the problem in a systematic manner.

At the international level, obstacles to effective action also exist. No single UN agency is responsible for the issues of environmental degradation and displacement. Without effective coordination, these problems are likely to be addressed in a fragmented manner. And while the international community has an evident interest in

promoting stability and sustainable development in the region, the states of Central Asia, especially those which continue to be affected by political conflict and human rights violations, are not currently a high priority for many donor states.

Despite these constraints, some positive steps have been taken. The problem of environmental displacement was, for example, discussed at the recent conference on population movements in the Commonwealth of Independent States (see Box 1.3), an initiative which has helped to place the issue on the international agenda. As part of the follow-up process to the conference, in February 1997, organizations such as UNHCR and the International Organization for Migration issued an appeal for funds, which will be used for the resettlement and integration of environmental migrants in the Central Asian states. Donor states and international organizations have also taken a particular interest in the Aral Sea basin, although the environmental problems in that area are so extreme that remedial and preventive activities will be required for many years to come.

While environmental problems can easily become a source of disagreement between states, there are some hopeful indications that the effort to resolve such

difficulties in Central Asia could actually promote regional cooperation. There has, for example, been extensive coordination between the five countries of Central Asia in relation to the Aral Sea question, including the establishment of a number of international agreements on this matter. In a region which has a high potential for conflict and population displacement, such initiatives are clearly to be welcomed.

porary evidence. According to the editor of the journal *Foreign Policy,* "the cold war period was much more violent than is the current period. Of course, any unnecessary deaths are an outrage... But we have not seen the kind of sustained carnage in recent years that our grandparents and parents did..." "Today," he concludes, "despite increased surface turbulence, the international system is structurally sound because none of the great powers seeks a hegemonic role in the international system."(19)

While such comments are a useful corrective to some of the more apocalyptic descriptions of the contemporary world, they can appear more than a little sanguine when viewed in relation to recent events in different parts of the globe: the genocide in Rwanda; the use of rape as a weapon of war and ethnic cleansing in former Yugoslavia; the deliberate expulsion of minority groups throughout much of the Caucasus region; the deployment of child soldiers in countries such as Sierra Leone and Sudan; the brutal reign of the warlords in Liberia and Somalia; and the bombing of fleeing civilians in Chechnya, to give just a few examples. Nor is this more optimistic interpretation of the post-cold war era supported by the rising number of people affected by forced displacement and the growing level of humanitarian assistance needed to sustain such populations - the subjects which are addressed in the following sections of this chapter.

The scale and complexity of the problem

During the past few years, the global refugee problem has changed in a number of ways. First, the overall scale of forced displacement has increased. In 1987, for example, UNHCR was providing protection and assistance to some 12 million people around the world. Ten years later, that figure has increased to 22 million.

These figures do not tell the whole story, however, as UNHCR's statistics do not include many victims of forced displacement: a large proportion of the world's internally displaced people, Palestinian refugees, and people who have been uprooted by development projects, for example. Significantly, and for reasons that will be explored later in the chapter, a declining proportion of the world's displaced people are refugees in the conventional sense of the word, namely people who are living outside of their own country as a result of persecution or violence.

There is also some evidence to suggest that mass population movements are now assuming a larger scale and occurring within a shorter timeframe than in previous years. This trend has been witnessed most graphically in the flight of more than a million Iraqi Kurds after the war in the Persian Gulf, the internal and external displacement of up to four million people by the conflict in former Yugoslavia, the exodus of over a million Rwandese citizens after the 1994 genocide, as well as the movement of more than two million displaced people within and from Liberia. According to some estimates, almost the whole of Liberia's rural population has been displaced at one time or another since the beginning of the conflict in December 1989.(20)

A number of trends appear to have contributed to the growing scale and speed of forced displacement in these and other parts of the world: the emergence of new forms of warfare, entailing the destruction of whole social, economic and political systems; the spread of light weapons and land-mines, available at prices which enable whole populations - including their youngest members - to be armed; and, perhaps most significantly, the use of mass evictions and expulsions as a weapon of war and as a means of establishing culturally or ethnically homogenous societies.

A number of commentators have also suggested that the large scale of some population displacements and migratory movements can be attributed to a form of mass desperation, provoked by very rapid processes of social, political and economic change. The willingness of many Albanians to pay hundreds of dollars to leave their own country, despite the dangers of the journey across the Adriatic Sea and their limited chances for admission to Italy, provides a possible case in point.

While most commonly associated with Bosnia and other parts of former Yugoslavia, the horror of ethnic cleansing has also been witnessed in other parts of the world, not least in the former Soviet Union. As one analyst has written, "the Caucasus - which has always had a multiplicity of nationalities... is now more ethnically 'pure' than it has ever been. Many refugees, driven out of their homes by people of a different ethnicity, are unlikely ever to return."(21)

Commenting upon such developments, the UN High Commissioner for Refugees has observed that "the forced displacement of minorities, including depopulation and repopulation tactics in support of territorial claims and self-determination, has become an abominable characteristic of the contemporary world."(22) One of the most difficult issues now confronting UNHCR is to find fair, appropriate and durable solutions for people in areas such as former Yugoslavia and the Caucasus who have been deliberately displaced ('ethnically cleansed') from their usual place of residence and who are unable to return safely to their homes .

Forced displacement in general, and rural depopulation in particular, have also become increasingly common weapons of war, even in armed conflicts where ethnic cleansing is not a specific objective of the parties involved. In some countries, such as Liberia or Somalia, the tactic of rural depopulation has been used to permit the theft of cattle, property and other assets, whereas in other situations, such as Afghanistan, Sri Lanka, southern Sudan and eastern Myanmar, civilian populations have been forcibly dispersed or relocated for primarily political reasons, so as to deprive rebel movements of their natural supporters. While it was initially described in conventional terms, as a refugee movement, the massive exodus from

Rwanda in 1994 can also be conceptualized as a strategic population withdrawal by the defeated regime, which wished to retain its control over large numbers of people and to establish a hostile military force on the country's borders.

The geography of displacement

As well as increasing in scale, the geographical scope of forced displacement can also be said to have widened in recent years. But this trend is not a simple one. During the past decade, a number of conflicts and associated problems of forced displacement have been resolved, most notably in areas such as Central America (El Salvador, Guatemala and Nicaragua), Southern Africa (Mozambique, Namibia and South Africa) and South-East Asia (Cambodia, Laos and Viet Nam).

At the same time, however, new crises have exploded in regions which were previously unaffected by the problem of forced displacement or where involuntary population movements did not come to the attention of the international community. The crisis in former Yugoslavia, for example, created some four million refugees and displaced people, the largest population movement in Europe since the end of the second world war. And as indicat-

Map B

Refugee populations in South Asia

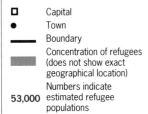

- ◻ Capital
- ● Town
- — Boundary
- Concentration of refugees (does not show exact geographical location)
- 53,000 Numbers indicate estimated refugee populations

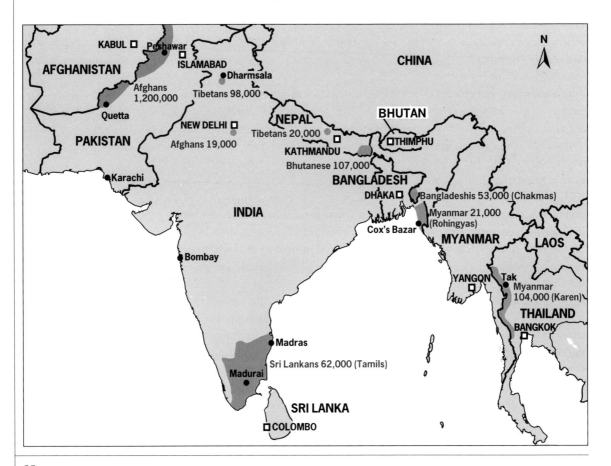

ed earlier, in the CIS region, some nine million people are thought to have been displaced from their homes in recent years.

Other regions with large numbers of forcibly displaced people have featured less prominently in the headlines. South Asia, for example, which is rarely recognized as a 'refugee-affected' region, has in recent years witnessed a succession of cross-border movements: from Bhutan and Tibet to Nepal; from Myanmar to Bangladesh and Thailand; and from Bhutan, Sri Lanka and Tibet to India (see Map B). According to one recent estimate, moreover, the 750,000 people in South Asia who are currently protected and assisted by UNHCR constitute less than half of all the displaced people in the sub-continent.(23)

In a number of locations around the world, whole 'neighbourhoods' of states have become affected by interlocking and mutually reinforcing patterns of armed conflict and forced displacement.(24) This phenomenon can be observed in the Caucasus, for example, a region which includes no fewer than six entities which have produced refugees and displaced people: Abkhazia, Armenia, Azerbaijan, Chechnya, North and South Ossetia. It can also be seen in Central Africa, where forced population displacements have recently taken place within and between nine contiguous states: Angola, Burundi, Central African Republic, Congo, Rwanda, Tanzania, Uganda, Zaire and Zambia. In Central and Eastern Africa, forced displacement is not simply a consequence of conflict and violence; it is also a primary cause of strife and instability.

As these examples suggest, forced population displacements are becoming increasingly complex. Movements of refugees and internally displaced people now often criss-cross each other, collecting and discarding people on the way. At the same time, there would appear to be a growing number of situations in which people are repeatedly uprooted, expelled or relocated within and across state borders, forcing them to live a desperately insecure and nomadic existence.

One of the better-known examples of this trend concerns the plight of 20,000 boys from southern Sudan, who, having initially been displaced within their own country, were subsequently forced into Ethiopia, then back to Sudan and eventually into Kenya.(25) Displaced people in the border areas between Myanmar and Thailand, between Liberia, Sierra Leone and Guinea, and between Burundi, Rwanda and Tanzania have experienced similarly repeated displacements.

During the past few years, a growing proportion of the people who have succeeded in escaping from their own country have found that their new situation is just as - if not more - insecure than the one they left behind. In the Great Lakes region of Africa, for example, refugees have been forcibly expelled from three different countries of asylum. Rwandese refugees in Zaire have effectively been held as hostages by the political leaders and former soldiers responsible for the 1994 genocide, and their camps turned into military support bases. As a result, those settlements have in turn come under attack from forces opposed to the former regime.

Paradoxically, in an era when so many people have become the victims of ethnic cleansing and other forms of mass expulsion, many others have found it impossible to escape from their own country and to find refuge elsewhere. In some cases, as in Bosnia or Sri Lanka, for example, their departure has been blocked by government or opposition forces who wish to maintain control over the civilian population. Elsewhere, such as the case of the Iraqi Kurds who fled towards Turkey, or the Haitian boat people heading for the United States, their flight has been obstructed by potential countries of asylum.

As the Haitian refugee problem (and the US response to it) also suggests, the problem of forced displacement has become increasingly enmeshed with the broader pattern of international migration. Rightly or wrongly, people wishing to move to the world's more affluent countries have increasingly sought entry to such states by submitting claims to refugee status. This trend is a result not only of the material insecurity of life in many parts of the world, but also the progressive closure of official immigration channels in the industrialized states and the penetration of the international media, communications and transportation networks into the remotest corners of the earth.

Diaspora communities, many of which are themselves the product of forced population displacements, have played an important part in maintaining the volume and determining the direction of such migratory movements. The Tamil who decides to leave Sri Lanka, for example, will almost invariably make use of information, resources and contacts provided by compatriots in Europe or North America in the bid to leave his or her homeland. And when that person arrives in a country such as Switzerland, the United Kingdom or the United States, he or she will depend upon the social network established by a previous generation of migrants and asylum seekers in order to find accommodation, work and, perhaps, to make a claim for refugee status.

The public profile of displacement

Finally, while the problem of forced displacement has certainly grown in scale and complexity during the past few years, it has also assumed a new degree of public and political importance. Not so long ago, the refugee question was primarily the preserve of relief agencies, development organizations and human rights bodies. Of course, this issue played an important part in both the ideology and the practice of the cold war; the western states were particularly adept at using exiled populations to discredit and in some cases to undermine those governments allied to the Soviet Union. But in recent years the problem of forced displacement - and humanitarian issues more generally - have been the subject of increasing discussion in political and military fora such as the UN Security Council and the North Atlantic Treaty Organization (NATO).

This development derives in part from the changing nature of the international security agenda, the central role of forced displacement in so many of the world's recent crises, and the fear that growing numbers of uprooted people might try to make their way to richer and more stable parts of the globe. But there is little doubt that the intensive media coverage given to the plight of displaced people has also forced governments and other actors to address the situation of uprooted people, even when they might have preferred to do nothing.

The role of the media is, however, highly selective in nature. When the first US marines landed on the shores of Somalia during the crisis of 1992, they were greeted by the lights and cameras of many television crews. But on the other side of the African continent, in Liberia and Sierra Leone, the massive displacement of the civilian population and the activities of ECOMOG - the West African peacekeeping force - have attracted minimal international attention.

Concepts and categories

While the notion of 'forced displacement' is now an established feature of the humanitarian vocabulary, the distinction between voluntary and involuntary migration is not always an easy one to sustain. It is generally accepted that almost all migration involves some kind of compulsion; labour migration for example, while usually regarded as 'voluntary', is often prompted by poverty.

Equally, almost all migratory movements involve an element of choice. However terrible the circumstances, people frequently have some latitude to decide where to go and, indeed, whether to flee at all. It is a notable but neglected fact that even in the largest population displacements, some people will for one reason or the other decide to stay where they are, rather than to flee.

Looking at the issue in this way has some important implications for humanitarian organizations. Because flight often requires resources and social connections (especially if it involves long-distance, cross-border or intercontinental travel) those people who manage to escape from a situation of danger normally represent just a small minority of those whose lives and liberty are at risk. It is for this reason that the protection and assistance provided to refugees and asylum seekers must be combined with similar if not greater efforts on behalf of those people who are unable or unwilling to leave their own country.

The problem of distinguishing between movement by force and migration by choice is in many situations coupled with a related conceptual difficulty;

that of differentiating between 'planned' and 'spontaneous' population movements. This is not simply an academic question, as it raises the whole question of individual and institutional responsibility for forced displacements - an increasingly important issue given the international community's current interest in the punishment of people who have committed war crimes. Interestingly, the International Law Commission has recently de-

1.3

The CIS conference: objectives and achievements

Like other international organizations, UNHCR was new to the problem of population displacement in the former Soviet Union when it began to assist with emergency operations in the Caucasus and Tajikistan in the early 1990s. It rapidly became evident that the problems emerging in the newly independent states were both complex and interrelated. The various tensions, conflicts and population displacements in the Caucasus and Transcaucasus regions, for example, were so intertwined that none of them could be dealt with in isolation. Similarly, it was impossible to ignore the fact that these states had for many years been part of the same political entity, and that issues such as citizenship and the return of peoples to their ancestral or ethnic

homeland could only be tackled by means of an integrated regional approach.

While the predicted outflow of former Soviet citizens to the western states has not taken place on the scale once feared, the international community has continued to be concerned about the social and political impact of mass population movements in the Commonwealth of Independent States (CIS): first, because the citizens of those states have already suffered substantially as a result of the socio-economic and political dislocation created by the demise of the Soviet state; second, because large-scale movements of people might place excessive strain on the region's fragile economies and democratic institutions; and third, because large population outflows would have obvious ramifications for states outside the CIS, many of which are also poorly equipped to cope with refugee problems. Thus a combination of humanitarian and security concerns led

the CIS countries themselves, other states and international organizations such as UNHCR to recognize the need for a concerted effort to resolve the problem of forced displacement in the former Soviet Union.

The scale of that problem is enormous. Around nine million people are believed to have been displaced in the region since the collapse of the Soviet Union, a phenomenon which has resulted from many different factors: armed conflicts, human rights violations, environmental problems and economic stagnation or decline, as well as the desire of certain populations to return to countries which they consider to be their natural home.

In 1994, at the request of some CIS countries, UNHCR began to organize a regional conference on the problem of forced displacement, together with the International Organization for Migration (IOM) and Organization for Security and Cooperation in Europe

(OSCE). The objectives of this initiative were threefold: to provide a neutral and non-political forum for the CIS and neighbouring countries to discuss refugee and migration issues; to establish a better knowledge of the scale and scope of population displacements in the region; and to devise a comprehensive strategy at the national, regional and international levels to cope with this problem.

As the planning process for the conference revealed, these were not simple objectives to achieve, given the political sensitivities surrounding these issues, the difficulty of coordinating the actions of so many states and uncertainty over the commitment of governments to address the problem of forced displacement in a practical manner. The last of these factors has been a particular concern, as the non-binding programme of action eventually adopted by conference participants in Geneva in May 1996 proved to be a very general statement of principles and objectives. Only now are the

fined the practice of 'arbitrary deportation or forcible transfer of population' as a 'crime against the peace and security of mankind' in a draft code on this matter.

According to one expert on international migration, "most of the world's population flows since World War II did not merely happen; they were made to happen."(26) But the way in which they were made to happen, and the de-

governments and organizations concerned trying to translate those principles into practical activities.

As a result of the conference, UNHCR has extended its activities in the CIS region to a broader range of displaced populations, including peoples such as the Crimean Tatars and Meskhetian Turks, who were deported *en masse* in the Stalinist era and who now wish to return to their previous place of residence. The organization is also helping to strengthen the capacity of CIS governments to deal with migratory problems, to establish independent judicial systems and to address the issues of citizenship and statelessness.

The programme of action adopted at the conference emphasized the need to strengthen civil society throughout the CIS. To fulfill this objective, UNHCR has been helping a number of non-governmental organizations to become involved in legal, assistance and research activities, to

establish programmes that will be of assistance to the various groups of displaced people of concern to the conference, and encouraging them to establish better linkages with governments, international organizations and with each other.

UNHCR has also paid increasing attention to the issue of public awareness, providing information to Crimean Tatars who wish to go back to their place of origin and to prospective emigrants from Armenia. At the same time, educational projects have been established to inform the population about refugee issues and to promote ethnic tolerance, activities which will hopefully contribute to the prevention of social tension, political violence and population displacements. UNHCR and the IOM issued a joint appeal for funds in November 1996, which will be used for the implementation of national plans of action in 1997, drawn up by the two organizations in association with the respective governments of the region.

The New York-based Open Society Institute (OSI), which has closely monitored the CIS conference process, has expressed some disappointment about the progress which has been made in the region since the Geneva meeting was held. Describing the international community's response to the programme of action as "sluggish," the OSI states that most of the ideals expressed by the conference "remain unfulfilled in practice." More specifically, the Institute points to the failure of states to accept specific legal obligations in the programme of action, the poor response of donor countries to the UNHCR/IOM fund-raising appeal, the limited role which non-governmental organizations have been able to play in the conference follow-up process and the dearth of concrete implementation activities undertaken by mid-1997.

While these comments may not give due recognition to the wide range of initiatives that are being undertaken to

address the problems of forced displacement and migration in the CIS, they provide a useful indication of the many difficulties encountered in the region. Internally, the states and societies of the former Soviet Union are still struggling to deal with the legacies of communism: distorted economies, ethnic cleavages, authoritarian political structures and the absence of a civil society. Externally, the response to the problem of forced displacement in the region has undoubtedly been weakened by the fact that so few people have sought safety outside of the CIS. As international migration expert Aristide Zolberg has written, "although the population displacements generated by the conflicts that accompanied the disintegration of the Soviet Union are of the same order of magnitude as those triggered by the destruction of Yugoslavia, the latter have occasioned much greater concern because they have spilled over into the world of affluent democracies."

gree of intent and organization involved, clearly varies from case to case. Flight may be the unintended or incidental outcome of armed conflict or persecution. And yet, as recent events in former Yugoslavia and the Caucasus have demonstrated, refugee movements and internal population displacements may be the very purpose of the violence inflicted by one group of people on another.

The growing complexity of forced displacement, and the growing recognition that refugees represent just one category of uprooted and vulnerable people, has had some important implications for UNHCR and other humanitarian organizations. In the words of the High Commissioner for Refugees, "although my office is a refugee protection agency, it is increasingly having to deal with a wider range of civilian victims in refugee-like situations and whose flight must be addressed if we are to seek solutions to humanitarian crises... "(27)

In few places is this comment more clearly illustrated than in the former Soviet Union, a region which in recent years has experienced a bewildering variety of forced population displacements. According to the plan of action drawn up at a recent international conference on this problem, no fewer than eight different categories of displaced person or migrant can be found in the CIS region: 'refugees', 'persons in refugee-like situations', 'internally displaced people', 'involuntarily relocating persons', 'repatriants', 'formerly deported peoples', 'illegal migrants' and 'ecological migrants' (see Box 1.3).

Such typologies are always imperfect. A forcibly displaced person or population may straddle several categories simultaneously or over time; someone may initially be displaced within their own country, then become a refugee in a neighbouring state, then be displaced again within their country of asylum, before finally repatriating to their homeland.

Such categorizations are also of little relevance (and may even be the source of inequity and conflict) when different types of displaced person - not to mention the local population - are living alongside each other in equally difficult circumstances. It is for this reason that UNHCR and other humanitarian organizations often provide relief and rehabilitation assistance on a community-wide basis and to all needy people in a given geographical area, irrespective of whether they are refugees, returnees, internally displaced people or local residents.

At the same time, there has been a growing recognition of the need to respond to the problem of forced displacement on a regional basis, rather than establishing separate humanitarian programmes for individual countries. In the Great Lakes region of Africa, for example, the displacements which have taken place within and across national borders are so complex and interrelated as to make a regional approach the only viable means of resolving the problem.

Despite the definitional difficulties and operational dilemmas identified above, it would be misleading to suggest that the distinction between forced and involuntary migrants, and between different types of displaced person, no longer have any relevance. Indeed, some of the most pressing and problematic issues on the international humanitarian agenda derive from such distinctions.

As later chapters of this book will ask, what can be done to safeguard the security of internally displaced people, who, unlike refugees, remain in their own country? To what extent is it useful to distinguish the internally displaced from other populations who are affected by war and violence, but who remain in their own homes? What responsibility do UNHCR and other international organizations have towards returnees - people who were once in need of asylum and international protection, but who have now gone back to their homeland? And what methods can be used to determine whether an asylum seeker should be granted refugee status, or considered as an irregular migrant who can be returned to his or her own country?

HUMANITARIAN ACTION: ACHIEVEMENTS AND LIMITATIONS

The world's response to the problem of forced displacement - and UNHCR's role in relation to that problem - has changed significantly during the past decade. Until the mid to late 1980s, the international community was primarily concerned with cross-border refugee movements, and devoted most of its efforts to providing refugee populations with protection and assistance in the countries of asylum to which they had fled.

During this period, there was a broad international consensus that UNHCR could only respect its humanitarian and non-political status by confining its activities to those countries of asylum and by responding to refugee movements once they had taken place. Any effort to address the problems of human insecurity and displacement within countries of origin, it was agreed, would have involved the organization in activities which fell beyond the scope of its mandate.

In recent years, a number of different factors have combined to bring about a fundamental reassessment of this traditional approach to the refugee problem.(28) These include, for example:

- the mounting concern of host and donor countries about the financial and other costs incurred in providing refugees with indefinite protection and assistance, and their growing unwillingness to admit large numbers of displaced people;

- a growing awareness that refugee movements can constitute a serious threat to national, regional and even international security;

- the changing military and strategic value of refugee populations in the post-cold war period;

- an initial willingness amongst some of the world's more powerful states to intervene in countries affected by acute political and humanitarian crisis, particularly when those states are weak or have some strategic significance;

- a recognition of the need to protect, assist and find solutions for groups of uprooted and vulnerable people other than refugees, especially those who are displaced within their own countries; and,

- a desire to consolidate peace and prevent the recurrence of violence in war-torn societies through measures designed to ensure the return and effective reintegration of displaced populations.

As a result of these and other developments, a new international consensus has emerged, recognizing the need to address humanitarian problems within countries of origin and to avert those situations in which people are obliged to abandon their homes in order to survive. Thus it has been proposed that the traditional right to asylum, as enshrined in the Universal Declaration of Human Rights and other international instruments, should be joined by another: the right to stay in one's own country and community, in conditions of physical, material, legal and psychological security.

While this right has not been formalized in international law, the UN Human Rights Commission has affirmed "the right of persons to remain at peace in their own homes, on their own lands and in their own countries." Similarly, the former UN High Commissioner for Human Rights has asserted that "the right to live in one's native land is a very precious and fundamental right." Displacement and expulsion, he observes, "by its very nature deprives victims of the exercise of many other rights and is frequently accompanied by physical abuse and even by the ultimate violation of the right to life."(29)

The growth of humanitarian assistance

There was a widespread belief at the beginning of the 1990s that the international community would be able to uphold its commitment to maintain peace and security in the world's less stable regions, thereby addressing the problem of forced displacement in a more proactive manner and realizing the right of people to live safely in their own homes. The UN Secretary-General's 1992 *Agenda for Peace,* for example, evoked the establishment of a collective security system which would be capable of bringing stability to troubled regions by, if necessary, imposing peace upon the parties to armed conflicts.

Since that time, however, the mixed results of UN-mandated military operations in countries such as Somalia and former Yugoslavia have led to a very evident retreat from the more ambitious and interventionist approach of the early 1990s. This trend has been unambiguously demonstrated in the Great Lakes region: first, in the Security Council's decision to reduce the UN's military presence in Rwanda, even after the genocide had taken place in 1994; second, in the Secretary-General's subsequent inability to gain support for a UNHCR proposal later in the year, urging the deployment of a force to separate Rwandese refugees and military elements in eastern Zaire; and again in the latter half of 1996, when states failed to deploy a multinational force in that area, despite the magnitude of the humanitarian crisis which had erupted there.

As these and other examples suggest, the world's more powerful states are becoming increasingly reluctant to take the decisive action that is sometimes required to avert political crises and bring an end to massive human rights abuses. As the International Institute for Strategic Studies has observed, such countries "are in no mood to sacrifice their well-being for supposed international advantage... Even the brief post-cold war sense of humanitarian obligation has begun to give way to colder realpolitik calculations of what can be done."(30)

The exceptions to this statement tend to prove the rule. It is now widely acknowledged, for example, that the eventual decision of the NATO states to intervene more actively in former Yugoslavia was prompted as much by the need to sustain the North Atlantic alliance as any humanitarian consideration. Similarly, there is little doubt that in the more recent case of Albania, the eagerness of certain states to lend military support to the delivery of humanitarian relief has derived primarily from a desire to stem an unwanted exodus of asylum seekers.(31) Significantly, at a Security Council debate on the protection of emergency assistance held in May 1997, the permanent members of that body effectively buried the concept of 'humanitarian intervention' which had achieved such prominence in the early 1990s. As the US government stressed, "the UN cannot send peacekeepers into each and every emergency."(32)

Nevertheless, and as the case of former Yugoslavia demonstrates again, it has proved impossible for the industrialized states simply to turn their back on complex emergencies taking place in other parts of the world. Prompted in many instances by public opinion and the international media, states have often responded to situations of armed conflict and forced displacement with humanitarian action, often on a massive scale.(33)

During the past decade, the resources devoted to humanitarian assistance have soared (see Figures 1.6 and 1.7). Among official aid agencies, spending on emergencies has increased five-fold over the last decade. The rise in the share of emergency assistance in the total bilateral aid spending of the industrialized countries is even more dramatic, increasing from 1.5 per cent in 1991 to 8.4 percent in 1994. Although the two trends may not be directly linked, it is significant that this increased spending on emergency aid has been matched by a steady decline in the level of official development assis-

Fig. 1.6

**People in need
of humanitarian
assistance, 1983-95**

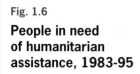

Total

Internally displaced
people

Refugees

Other

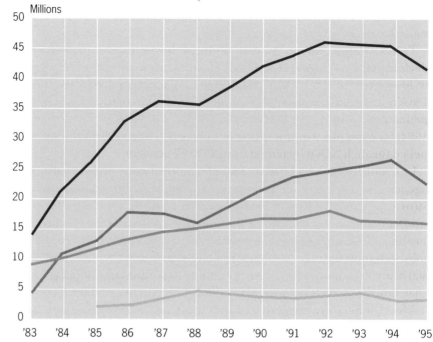

Source: United States Mission to the United Nations, *Global Humanitarian Emergencies*, 1996
Figure shows only displaced populations in need of humanitarian assistance.
'Other' refers to people in refugee-like situations who have not been recognized as refugees.

Fig. 1.7

**Bilateral emergency
assistance, 1990-95**

Other emergency aid

Refugee relief

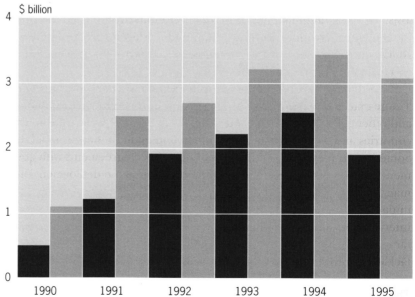

Source: Organization for Economic Cooperation and Development, *Development Cooperation Report 1996*,
OECD, Paris, 1997
Figure shows bilateral non-food emergency aid of Development Assistance Committee members.

tance. Only in the last two years has the amount spent on emergency relief started to decline.

The expansion of the humanitarian sector has gone hand-in-hand with a decline in the role of state structures in the provision of basic public services in low-income states. Today, some 1,500 non-governmental organizations (NGOs) are registered with the United Nations, many of whom act as competing subcontractors for UN agencies and donor states. Between 1990 and 1994, for example, the proportion of European Union relief funding channelled through NGOs increased from 45 to 67 per cent.

In countries such as Liberia, Rwanda, Sierra Leone and Somalia, such agencies have tried to plug the gap created by the disintegration of state structures, ensuring the provision of a whole range of services that would normally be considered the responsibility of government: food, shelter, health care, water supply, education, transport, commercial contracts and jobs. It is therefore not wholly accurate to suggest that the world's wealthier states are reluctant to intervene in complex emergencies. In many senses, that function has been devolved to humanitarian organizations.

The growth of the humanitarian sector has clearly been facilitated by the growing ability of humanitarian organizations to work in situations of ongoing violence. Because of the importance attached to the principles of sovereignty and non-interference during the cold war years, the governments of war-torn countries often denied relief agencies access to areas controlled by rebel groups. Relief assistance therefore tended to be channelled through state structures, or simply dealt with the symptoms of war by means of refugee assistance programmes. The principal exceptions to this pattern were to be found in the cross-border relief operations established by international NGOs and indigenous agencies, such as those from eastern Sudan to Eritrea and from Pakistan to Afghanistan.

This situation has changed quite dramatically in recent years, facilitated to a large extent by a succession of Security Council resolutions, enabling UN and other agencies to mount emergency operations inside conflict-affected countries and to gain direct access to uprooted and besieged populations. Sometimes undertaken on the basis of negotiated agreements with governments and rebel groups, and sometimes backed by the deployment of UN-mandated forces, either in a logistical or more assertive capacity, these initiatives have established a new paradigm of humanitarian action and intervention.(34) And the emergence of this new paradigm has had some far-reaching implications for the way in which the international community tackles the problem of forced displacement.

The limitations of humanitarian action
Responding to the changing nature of the international environment, humanitarian organizations have in recent years been able to expand their op-

erations geographically and extend their activities functionally. In the process, they have saved an unknown number of lives, reunited many families, educated large numbers of children and assisted massive numbers of people to return to their homes. In situations where the relationship between state and citizen has broken down, humanitarian action can help to compensate for the absence of national protection and provide affected populations with a degree of security which they would otherwise lack.

While few commentators would query such achievements, it has become increasingly clear that humanitarian action has some important constraints and limitations, and that it can also have a number of unintended and negative consequences. Although a full exploration of these complex issues goes beyond the scope of this chapter, a number of related points deserve to be underlined.

First, humanitarian action alone cannot resolve complex political emergencies and situations of forced displacement. As the UN High Commissioner for Refugees has stated, "while stressing the importance of humanitarian action we must also recognize its limitations. Agencies such as UNHCR can do a lot. Through their presence and interventions they can sometimes help to stabilize a tense situation and mitigate human rights abuses. But humanitarian action cannot be a substitute for political action or decisions."(35)

Unfortunately, states have tended to use humanitarian action as a substitute for political action rather than as a complement to it. Security Council members and other governments have generally found it easier to reach agreement on humanitarian issues than on more controversial and risky strategies, especially those entailing the deployment of troops and the use of force. And by donating large amounts of money to highly-publicized relief operations, governments have to some extent been able to satisfy the demands of public opinion and the international media.

By placing primary emphasis on the role of humanitarian action, governments have been able to minimize their own responsibility for mistakes and failures. Thus when the safe areas in Bosnia are attacked, when thousands of refugees go missing in eastern Zaire, or when an international peacekeeping force is obliged to withdraw from Somalia, the fault lies with 'the United Nations' rather than the states which comprise and control that body. As one eminent scholar has observed, "a failure to develop serious policies regarding the security of humanitarian action, and of affected peoples and areas, has been the principal cause of the setbacks of humanitarian action in the 1990s." While recognizing the inherent difficulties of developing such policies, he suggests that such issues "have been handled repeatedly in a short-term and half-hearted manner, often with elements of dishonesty and buck-passing."(36)

Second, as the preceding quotation suggests, it has become all too clear that humanitarian action can play only a very limited role in protecting human rights and safeguarding human security in situations of ongoing conflict. As the tragic events in Srebrenica and Zepa demonstrated in 1995, when the 'safe areas' established by the UN Security Council were overrun by Serb forces, more assertive forms of action are required to safeguard the physical security of vulnerable populations, especially when they are confronted by forces which flagrantly flout international opinion and humanitarian law.

Recognizing the limitations of conventional humanitarian action in such situations, many commentators have looked to the military - usually in the form of multinational forces - to provide the necessary protection to affected populations. But the many difficulties associated with such proposals will not easily be resolved. Does a right of international intervention exist, and if so, under what circumstances can it be invoked? Can humanitarian organizations and the military work together in the same location, especially if those troops are obliged to work in a non-consensual manner and to make use of their coercive capabilities? Should the military be used to apprehend and bring to justice those individuals who are responsible for crimes against humanity? And in view of the events in Srebrenica, where some 8,000 people are believed to have been killed, does the 'safe area' notion still have any potential as a means of protecting vulnerable populations within their own country? At the moment, it should be noted, there is very little consensus on any of these issues.

Third, there is a need both to acknowledge and address some of the unintended consequences of humanitarian action. Contrary to popular and journalistic opinion, most displaced people and other victims of violence do not rely upon external assistance in order to survive, but make use of their own coping mechanisms.

If it is carefully planned and targeted, and based upon an intimate knowledge of the beneficiary population, humanitarian assistance can play an important part in supporting those coping mechanisms. But when food and other aid is indiscriminately pumped and dumped into a crisis area, local markets and social security networks are liable to be undermined. At the same time, large-scale relief operations can easily create a harmful dependence - both physical and psychological - amongst the beneficiaries of external assistance.

International aid and the logic of war

There is perhaps an even more important need to recognize that humanitarian action can easily be drawn into the logic of an armed conflict, thereby prolonging or even intensifying it. Because of the need to negotiate with armed groups for access to displaced people and other conflict-affected populations, aid agencies often implicitly accept that a proportion of their relief will go to the very groups which are waging the war.

The precise ways in which armed groups exploit international assistance are complex, varying in accordance with their political objectives, their level of popular support and the social environment within which the conflict is taking place. Food aid can be used to feed soldiers or can be sold on local markets to finance the purchase of weapons. International assistance serves as an important source of political legitimacy for both governments and rebel groups, particularly where they can control and channel its distribution among the local population. Most cynically of all, international assistance can be used as a means of attracting displaced people into areas where they can be attacked and killed.

The parties to recent conflicts have shown themselves to be particularly adept at exploiting international concern for forcibly displaced populations. As the Liberian warlords have discovered, by deliberately creating conditions of acute impoverishment and displacement, and by using the victims of such tactics to attract relief assistance, armed groups can gain access to additional

1.4

Humanitarian codes of conduct

The international community has placed increasing emphasis in recent years on its right to intervene in war-torn states to alleviate the suffering of people affected by conflict. But the rights of war-affected populations to receive effective and appropriate assistance remain largely unclarified and unformalized. Until quite recently, moreover, little had been done to establish a code of conduct or set of standards to guide the work of organizations providing relief to the victims of war.

That situation has now changed for a number of

related reasons: the recent expansion of humanitarian activities around the world and the associated proliferation of aid agencies; the growing involvement of such organizations in areas where armed conflicts are taking place; the eagerness of donor states and UN agencies to channel their funds through non-governmental organizations (NGOs); and the mounting competition amongst NGOs for media exposure, public recognition and contracts.

Slipping standards?

As a result of these factors, there has been growing concern that relief organizations have in some situations lost sight of their true objectives, allowed standards to slip and have paid insufficient attention to

the impact of their work. In the words of the Red Cross and Red Crescent movement, "the increasing scale, complexity, speed and cost of emergencies mean that humanitarian agencies must confront questions of the quality of their work and issues of success and failure, even whether what they are doing is right or wrong."

Such considerations have stimulated a new interest amongst NGOs in the question of standards and self-regulation. An initial step in this direction was taken in 1994, when more than 70 agencies from around the world established an NGO Code of Conduct. Since that time, an additional 30 agencies have adopted the code, which has also been welcomed by almost 150

states which are signatories to the Geneva Conventions, which set out the laws of war. UNHCR and other UN agencies are also considering how the code can be incorporated into the criteria which they use when selecting operational partners.

Under the terms of the NGO Code of Conduct, signatory organizations agree to abide by the ten principal points summarized below:

- the humanitarian imperative comes first;

- aid is given regardless of the race, creed or nationality of the recipients and on the basis of need alone;

- aid will not be used to further a particular

resources. As events in Bosnia demonstrated, when a civilian population is placed in grave danger, humanitarian organizations may have little alternative but to arrange an evacuation programme, thereby hastening (and even paying for) the process of ethnic cleansing. And as the Rwanda emergency demonstrated in 1994, by effectively manufacturing a highly-publicized refugee crisis, it is possible for a genocidal regime to protect itself against any retribution, to retain control over large numbers of civilians, and to maintain a large, threatening and destabilizing military force in exile.

Until quite recently it may have seemed irrelevant or even morally objectionable to examine the negative implications of humanitarian assistance, especially since its driving values are so evidently different from those responsible for the suffering which it seeks to address. However, as wars have become more intense and prolonged, and as relief organizations have become more centrally involved in such conflicts, the humanitarian space avail-

political or religious standpoint;

- aid organizations will endeavour not to act as instruments of government foreign policy;

- aid organizations will respect culture and custom;

- aid organizations will attempt to build disaster response on local capacities;

- ways will be found of involving programme beneficiaries in the management of relief aid;

- relief aid must strive to reduce future vulnerabilities to disaster as well as meeting basic needs;

- aid organizations hold themselves accountable to those they assist and to those from whom they accept resources;

- aid organizations will recognize disaster victims as dignified humans, not as hopeless objects, in their information, publicity and advertising activities.

Physical protection
In addition to the NGO Code of Conduct, other efforts are under way to guide the work of organizations involved in emergency relief. A group of UK-based agencies known as People in Aid, for example, has established a 'code of best practice' for relief workers, focusing on issues such as employment and training policy as well as staff security. A 'beneficiaries charter' is also being

developed, covering topics such as the minimum and relative entitlements of disaster victims, the delivery of assistance and the accountability of aid agencies.

While these initiatives represent an important attempt to regulate the work of aid organizations and to hold them accountable for their activities, they are not without their critics. According to a study by Oxford professor Adam Roberts, the new codes of conduct address humanitarian problems "in an abstract manner, far removed from the harsh realities resulting from war." In recent armed conflicts, the author notes, the key issue has not been the delivery of humanitarian assistance, but the physical

protection of displaced and threatened populations, not to mention aid workers themselves.

Roberts also notes that there is currently little consensus on how to combine impartial relief work with the coercive measures which are sometimes required to bring wars to an end, to halt human rights violations and gain access to people in need. In the absence of such action, the effectiveness or ineffectiveness of humanitarian agencies remains of secondary importance. As an international evaluation of the Rwanda emergency concluded, "humanitarian action cannot serve as a substitute for political, diplomatic and, where necessary, military action."

able to them has been progressively degraded, making it more difficult and dangerous for aid agency personnel to carry out their responsibilities.

In recent years, employees of relief organizations have been exposed to much greater psychological stress and physical danger, a trend epitomized by the recent murder of UN, NGO and Red Cross personnel in places such as Burundi, Chechnya and Rwanda. At the same time, aid agencies have been confronted with a range of dilemmas arising from the way in which humanitarian assistance can be abused and exploited by the parties to a conflict. As a result of these developments, humanitarian organizations have in recent years begun to examine the principles underlying their work more systematically and to articulate those principles in formal codes of conduct (see Box 1.4).

Containment or asylum?

Finally, there is little doubt that the international community's recent emphasis on notions such as 'humanitarian access' and 'in-country protection' has to a considerable extent been driven by the growing reluctance of states to admit large numbers of refugees. As suggested earlier, the political incentive to grant asylum has diminished. Refugee flows are increasingly seen as a political, economic and social threat to potential host countries. People fleeing from violence and human rights abuses at home are consequently confronted with rejection when they arrive in another country. According to some critics, the willingness of UNHCR and other humanitarian organizations to operationalize these new approaches by working in countries of origin and assisting other groups of displaced people has legitimized the increasingly restrictive attitude of states towards refugees and asylum seekers.(37)

On a number of recent occasions, states have closed or attempted to close their borders to refugees from war-torn countries such as Afghanistan, Bosnia, Burundi, Liberia and Rwanda. In almost all of the industrialized states, there has been a flurry of official activity over the past decade to obstruct or deter the arrival of asylum seekers from other parts of the world. And on numerous occasions, refugees have been forced or induced to return to their countries of origin, even if conditions there continue to be insecure. The recent decline in the world's refugee population, and the simultaneous increase in the number of internally displaced people, is one obvious manifestation of these disturbing trends.

The international community's declining commitment to asylum and growing interest in policies of confinement and containment is a retrograde development which flies in the face of international refugee law, human rights principles and humanitarian norms. It is certainly true to say that the internal problems of unstable states cannot be resolved by means of refugee assistance programmes. Of course it is better for people to remain safely in their homes, and, if they move, to do so out of choice rather than necessity. And there is an evident need to recognize the immense strains that refugee flows can place upon countries of asylum, especially when those countries are themselves economically weak, politically unstable and socially divided. But the problem of forced displacement cannot be resolved - and may even be exacerbated - by efforts to obstruct the departure or compel the premature repatriation of people from countries where the state is unable or unwilling to protect its citizens.

A Sri Lankan refugee child in Tiruchi, India © *J. Vink/Magnum Photos Inc.*

2   Defending refugee rights

For many people who are confronted with threats to their life and liberty, fleeing to another country is the only way in which they can find safety. At the beginning of 1997, just over 13 million people found themselves in this situation. The vast majority of this number come from and live in the world's poorer countries, and it is their plight which forms the focus of the following pages.

Sadly, it is becoming increasingly difficult for refugees to find a place of safety beyond the borders of their homeland. Confronted with pressing domestic problems and declining international support, a growing number of countries have closed their borders to impending large-scale refugee influxes. In many parts of the world, moreover, people who have taken refuge in another country have been harassed, attacked and even forced to go home against their will.

This chapter explains why refugee protection standards are under such threat in the developing regions and discusses some of the difficulties and dilemmas which this trend has created for UNHCR and other humanitarian organizations. The chapter also sets out an agenda for action, which, if effectively implemented, would help to reinforce the institution of asylum, safeguard the security of refugees and help them to find lasting solutions to their plight.

THE REFUGEE DEFINITION AND REFUGEE REGIME

The word 'refugee' is frequently used by the media, politicians and the general public to describe anyone who has been obliged to abandon his or her usual place of residence. Normally, when the word is used in this general manner, little effort is made to distinguish between people who have had to leave their own country and those who have been displaced within their homeland. Nor is much attention paid to the causes of flight. Whether people are escaping from persecution, political violence, communal conflict, ecological disaster or poverty, they are all assumed to qualify for the title of refugee.

Under international law, however, the refugee concept has a much more specific meaning. As established in the 1951 UN Convention relating to the Status of Refugees, the word refugee refers to a person who, "owing to a well-founded fear of being persecuted for reasons of race, religion, nationality, or membership of a particular social group or political opinion, is outside the country of his nationality and is unable or, owing to such fear, is unwilling to avail himself of the protection of that country."(1)

In the years since the 1951 Convention was established, legal experts have examined this somewhat complex definition in great depth, focusing particularly on the meaning of phrases such as 'well-founded fear', 'persecution' and 'membership of a particular social group'. Such details are not a direct concern of this chapter, which uses the refugee concept to denote those people who have had to leave or remain outside of their homeland because of serious threats to their life and liberty.

This inclusive approach to the refugee definition has been formalized in the Organization of African Unity's 1969 Refugee Convention, which was established in response to the growing scale of the African refugee problem during the period of decolonization and national liberation. "The term refugee," it states, "shall apply to every person who, owing to external aggression, occupation, foreign domination or events seriously disturbing public order in either part or the whole of his country of origin or nationality, is compelled to leave his place of habitual residence in order to seek refuge in another place outside his country of origin or nationality."(2)

Regional refugee instruments in other parts of the world, most notably in Central and South America, have adopted a similar approach, placing less emphasis on a fear of persecution and more on objective conditions of violence and disorder in the country of origin. This is also the definition favoured by UNHCR.

Experience in the less-developed regions of the world has demonstrated that when large numbers of people move across an international border, it is not usually possible to ascertain whether every person involved in the influx actually meets the criteria for refugee status. Low-income countries simply do not have the logistical, administrative and financial capacity to undertake such a demanding and time-consuming task. When conditions are objectively dangerous in a country of origin, individual screening of new arrivals may also not be necessary. It is for this reason that refugees in Africa, Asia, Latin America and the Middle East are frequently recognized on a group or *prima facie* basis.

The international protection system

As the preceding discussion suggests, refugees leave their homeland and seek admission to another country not from choice or for reasons of personal convenience, but out of absolute necessity. As nationals of states which are either unable or unwilling to perform their primary function - ensuring the well-being of their citizens - refugees are obliged to rely on international rather than national protection.

Throughout the 20th century, and more specifically since the end of the second world war, states have devoted a considerable amount of effort and resources to the task of providing refugees with international protection. Their purpose has been twofold: first, to safeguard the lives and liberty of people whose basic rights have been threatened in their country of origin;

and second, to safeguard their own interests by ensuring that large-scale population movements are managed in a predictable manner and in accordance with agreed principles. Demonstrating the importance which governments attach to this issue, no fewer than 134 states have now ratified either the 1951 Convention or its 1967 Protocol, making it one of the most widely endorsed of all international legal instruments. (3)

The laws, agreements and institutions which have been established to regulate and resolve the refugee problem are often collectively referred to as the 'international refugee regime' or 'international protection system'. At the centre of this system is UNHCR. The broad-based nature of the international protection system is also to be seen in the composition of UNHCR's Executive Committee, which oversees the organization's budget and provides general guidance to its activities. Consisting of some 53 states, the Executive Committee includes representatives from all parts of the world and from almost every political, religious and cultural tradition.

As its name suggests, the international refugee regime was established in relation to one particular category of people. Over the years, UNHCR has become increasingly involved with groups of displaced and threatened people who do not conform to the refugee definition. In many parts of the world, the organization has also implemented area or community-based programmes, designed to safeguard the security of all those in need, irrespective of their nationality or legal status. Despite the importance of these innovations, refugees remain a specific group of people under international law, with a particular set of rights and obligations.

With regard to their rights, refugees benefit from the principle of 'non-refoulement', which forbids states from returning them in any manner to countries where their safety would be at risk. In addition, countries of asylum have an obligation under international law to ensure that refugees enjoy a range of economic, social and political rights, as well as freedom of movement. Moreover, as stated very clearly in the Preamble to the 1951 Convention, people who have been obliged to leave their homeland and seek safety elsewhere are assured "the widest possible exercise" of all the other fundamental rights affirmed in the UN Charter and 1948 Universal Declaration of Human Rights. (4)

As well as enjoying such rights, refugees are required to respect a number of obligations. Most notably, they must abide by the laws and regulations of the country which has granted them asylum and conform to any measures taken for the maintenance of public order. Under the terms of the 1951 Convention, people who have committed serious criminal offences, crimes against humanity and war crimes can be denied refugee status. As these provisions of the 1951 Convention suggest, the founders of the international refugee regime were particularly eager to prevent the refugee problem from becoming a cause of tension between states. This principle was made more specific in the OAU Refugee Convention, which affirms that the granting of asylum to refugees "is a peaceful and humanitarian act, and should not be regarded as an unfriendly act by any member state."(5)

REFUGEE NUMBERS, LOCATIONS AND CHARACTERISTICS

While there is a popular perception that the international refugee problem is growing inexorably in size and geographical scope, the statistics collected by UNHCR tell quite a different story. Certainly, the problem of forced displacement has by most measurements become considerably larger and more complex over the last decade. But the number of refugees in the strict sense of the word has actually declined in recent times: from 18.2 million in 1993 to 13.2 million at the beginning of 1997 (see Figure 2.1).

Fig. 2.1

Global refugee population, 1978-97

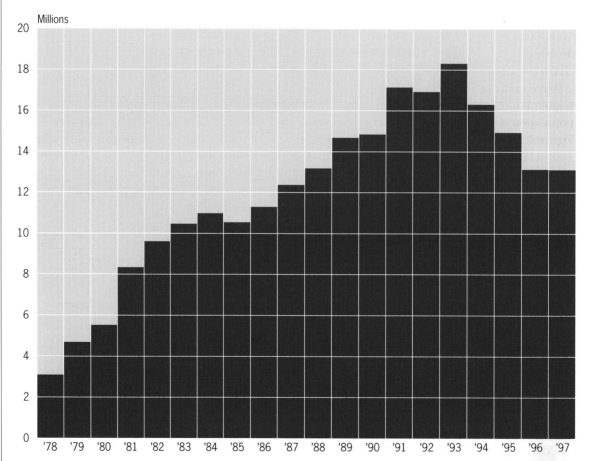

Statistics at January each year. Totals do not include other groups of concern to UNHCR and Palestinians assisted by the UN Relief and Works Agency for Palestine Refugees in the Near East.

This trend appears to be the result of two principal factors. First, the re-duction in refugee numbers can be attributed to the succession of large-scale repatriation movements which have taken place since the beginning of the 1990s, involving countries such as Afghanistan, Cambodia, Mozambique, and Rwanda. Altogether, more than 10 million refugees are thought to have gone back to their homes since the beginning of the decade, either voluntar-ily or because they had little or no other option. Second, recent years have witnessed a dramatic increase in the number of people who have been up-rooted by persecution and violence but who have not crossed the border into another country. While the problem of external displacement has dimin-ished in scale, therefore, so the problem of internal displacement (discussed in the following chapter) has augmented.

Despite the recent reduction in numbers, by the middle of 1997, large-scale refugee populations were still to be found in most parts of the world, most notably in Central and West Africa, the Horn of Africa, South and South-West Asia (see Map C). In addition, some three million Palestinian refugees, assisted by the UN Relief and Works Agency, are to be found on the West Bank, in Gaza and other parts of the Middle East. As these Palestinians do not fall under the mandate of UNHCR, they have not normally been in-cluded in the organization's refugee statistics.(6)

While many of the world's largest refugee populations are the result of population movements that took place a decade or more ago, cross-border population displacements continue to take place on a regular basis (see Figure 2.2). The second half of 1996 and the first half of 1997, for example,

Fig. 2.2

Major refugee movements in 1996

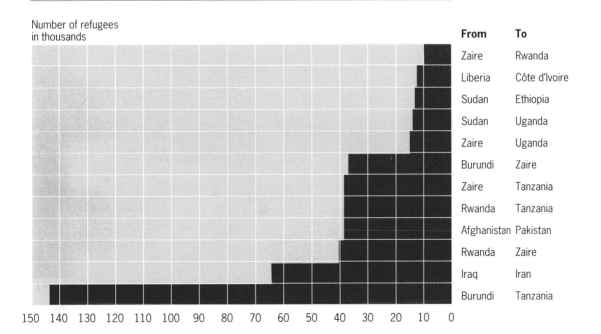

Number of refugees
in thousands

From	To
Zaire	Rwanda
Liberia	Côte d'Ivoire
Sudan	Ethiopia
Sudan	Uganda
Zaire	Uganda
Burundi	Zaire
Zaire	Tanzania
Rwanda	Tanzania
Afghanistan	Pakistan
Rwanda	Zaire
Iraq	Iran
Burundi	Tanzania

150 140 130 120 110 100 90 80 70 60 50 40 30 20 10 0

Map C
Major refugee populations worldwide

Palestinians

The Palestinian diaspora has spread to practically every corner of the globe, but the largest number - over three million - are still be to found in Jordan, Syria, Lebanon, the West Bank and Gaza. It is one of the oldest refugee problems in the world. The fourth generation of refugees is now growing up in camps initially constructed by their great-grandparents.

Algeria

There are around 165,000 refugees from Western Sahara in the Tindouf region of south-western Algeria, of whom half are assisted by UNHCR. In addition, Algeria has granted asylum to nearly 30,000 other refugees, most of them Tuaregs from Mali and Niger, as well as Palestinians.

Mexico

The 32,000 Guatemalans recognized as refugees in Mexico at the end of 1996 constituted the largest refugee population in Latin America. Almost half of this number were born in exile and will eventually be able to apply for Mexican citizenship. Many other unregistered Guatemalans - between 50,000 and 100,000 according to many estimates - have also taken up residence in Mexico.

Côte d'Ivoire and Guinea

The civil war in Liberia, which began at the end of the 1980s, has prompted large numbers of people to take refuge in neighbouring states: around 420,000 in Guinea and up to 300,000 in Côte d'Ivoire by early 1997. Guinea, one of the poorest countries in the world, has also offered asylum to as many as 250,000 refugees from Sierra Leone.

Zaire

Some of the largest and most complex population displacements of 1996 and 1997 took place in Zaire. Despite the armed conflict affecting parts of the country, by mid-1997, Zaire continued to host a large number of refugees: 160,000 from Angola, 40,000 from Burundi, around 20,000 Ugandans and 110,000 Sudanese. At this date, UNHCR and other humanitarian agencies were continuing to trace the whereabouts of almost quarter of a million missing Rwandese refugees.

Uganda

Uganda has pursued a notably liberal asylum policy in recent years and now has a refugee population of around 265,000, predominantly from southern Sudan. By mid-1997, armed attacks by Ugandan rebels had displaced 30,000 of the refugees and disrupted a UNHCR-financed local settlement programme.

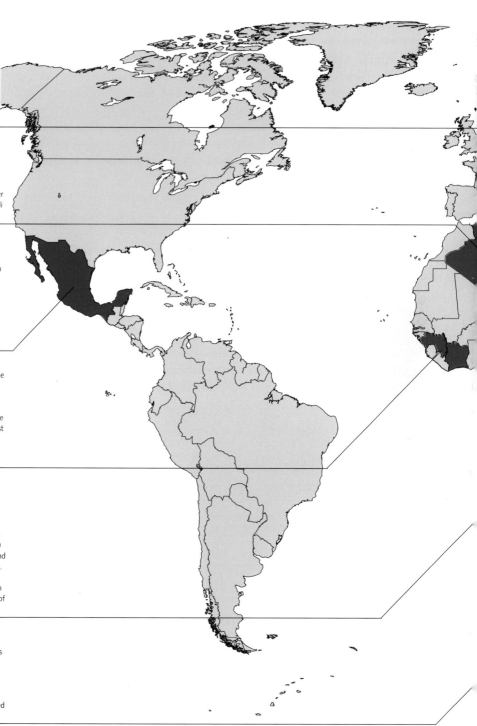

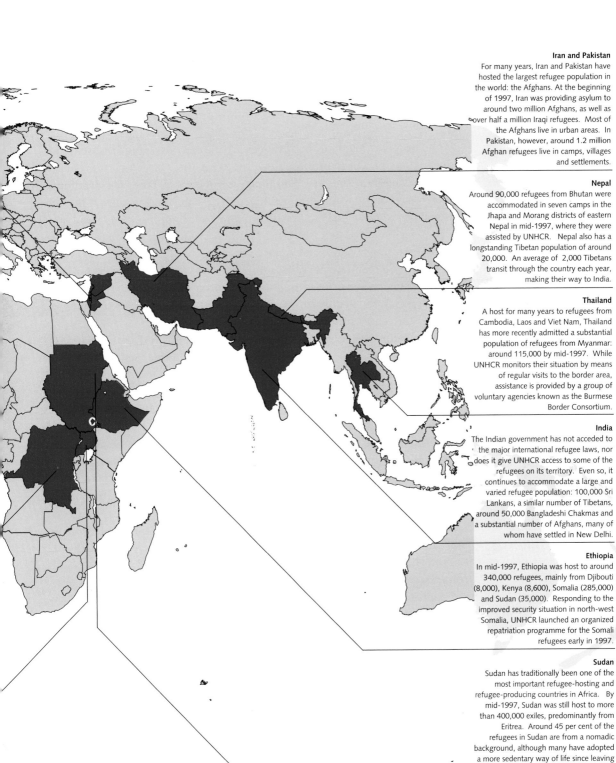

Iran and Pakistan
For many years, Iran and Pakistan have hosted the largest refugee population in the world: the Afghans. At the beginning of 1997, Iran was providing asylum to around two million Afghans, as well as over half a million Iraqi refugees. Most of the Afghans live in urban areas. In Pakistan, however, around 1.2 million Afghan refugees live in camps, villages and settlements.

Nepal
Around 90,000 refugees from Bhutan were accommodated in seven camps in the Jhapa and Morang districts of eastern Nepal in mid-1997, where they were assisted by UNHCR. Nepal also has a longstanding Tibetan population of around 20,000. An average of 2,000 Tibetans transit through the country each year, making their way to India.

Thailand
A host for many years to refugees from Cambodia, Laos and Viet Nam, Thailand has more recently admitted a substantial population of refugees from Myanmar: around 115,000 by mid-1997. While UNHCR monitors their situation by means of regular visits to the border area, assistance is provided by a group of voluntary agencies known as the Burmese Border Consortium.

India
The Indian government has not acceded to the major international refugee laws, nor does it give UNHCR access to some of the refugees on its territory. Even so, it continues to accommodate a large and varied refugee population: 100,000 Sri Lankans, a similar number of Tibetans, around 50,000 Bangladeshi Chakmas and a substantial number of Afghans, many of whom have settled in New Delhi.

Ethiopia
In mid-1997, Ethiopia was host to around 340,000 refugees, mainly from Djibouti (8,000), Kenya (8,600), Somalia (285,000) and Sudan (35,000). Responding to the improved security situation in north-west Somalia, UNHCR launched an organized repatriation programme for the Somali refugees early in 1997.

Sudan
Sudan has traditionally been one of the most important refugee-hosting and refugee-producing countries in Africa. By mid-1997, Sudan was still host to more than 400,000 exiles, predominantly from Eritrea. Around 45 per cent of the refugees in Sudan are from a nomadic background, although many have adopted a more sedentary way of life since leaving their country of origin.

witnessed refugee movements from Myanmar into Thailand, from southern Sudan into Uganda, from Colombia into Panama, from Afghanistan into Pakistan, and from Zaire into a number of neighbouring states. In the latter case, many of the refugees were Rwandese citizens who had been uprooted twice: initially in their country of origin and subsequently in their country of asylum.(7)

In the popular imagination, refugees are perceived as people who live in sprawling camps where they are dependent for their basic needs on international relief organizations. This image is not entirely false. Governments in many parts of the world prefer refugees to live in camps for two different reasons: because they feel that such an approach minimizes the social and political risks involved in hosting large numbers of foreign nationals; and because it encourages donor states and humanitarian organizations to assume a greater degree of financial responsibility for the refugees. Relief agencies have also tended to favour the establishment of camps, given the relative ease of providing food, health care, education and other services to refugees when they are concentrated in large settlements.

Even so, many refugees live outside organized camps and settlements and receive little or no international assistance. Indeed, some analysts have suggested that in Africa, well over half of all exiles fall into this category.(8) Most frequently, such 'spontaneously settled' refugees are to be found living in the border areas of their asylum country, as close as possible to their homeland. Such is the situation in Guinea and Côte d'Ivoire, for example, which have hosted more than 700,000 Liberian refugees since the early 1990s, almost all of whom are spontaneously settled and many of whom are now partly self-sufficient.

Given the general pattern of rural-to-urban migration in low-income regions of the world, it is not surprising to find that more and more refugees appear unwilling to live in rural camps and settlement areas, preferring to move into a town. This trend can again be witnessed very clearly in Guinea, where urban centres such as Nzerekore, Gueckedou and Macenta have become crowded with young Liberian men, looking for work, income-generating opportunities and a more interesting lifestyle than is available in a village environment. In general, the movement of rural refugees into urban areas is not a trend that has been welcomed by host governments and humanitarian organizations (see Box 2.1).

In terms of their demographic and socio-economic composition, it is not easy to make generalizations about the world's refugee populations. It is frequently stated, for example, that the vast majority of refugees are women and children - an assertion which simply reflects the fact that the vast majority of people in any population are also women and children! Broadly speaking, however, adult males tend to be under-represented in refugee populations, often because they are engaged in other activities, whether farming, working

2.1

Urban refugees

As a result of the images projected to the public by humanitarian organizations and the international media, the popular notion of a refugee is someone of a poor, rural background living alongside thousands of other destitute people in a densely packed camp. While such images certainly reflect the reality of exile in certain parts of the world, they fail to take account of the many refugees who live in other circumstances, most notably those who are commonly referred to as 'urban refugees'.

The urban refugee concept is commonly used to describe at least three different groups of people:

- refugees with an urban, non-agricultural and usually educated background, who take up residence in a town or city so that they can live in a familiar environment, maximize their social and economic opportunities or apply for resettlement in another, more developed country;

- refugees of a rural, agricultural and uneducated background who initially take up residence in a camp, but who subsequently move to a town or city in search of work, trading or income-generating opportunities; and,

- individual and small groups of asylum seekers who arrive independently in the capital cities of low-income countries and who submit a claim for refugee status to UNHCR and the national authorities.

According to a recent UNHCR study, up to 200,000 people around the world can be considered as urban refugees - less than two per cent of the global refugee population. While urban refugees are to be found in almost every capital city in the world, the largest groups registered with UNHCR are to be found in locations such as Cairo, Islamabad, New Delhi and Rio de Janeiro.

Socio-economic profile
In view of the various meanings given to the concept, it is difficult to generalize about the socio-economic profile of urban refugees. Accurate statistics on urban refugees are also difficult to collect, as relatively few receive assistance from or are registered with UNHCR and other humanitarian organizations. Moreover, in the many countries where refugees are officially confined to rural settlement areas and where they are not welcomed in the main towns, urban exiles have a strong incentive to maintain as low a profile as possible.

Most typically, however, those refugees who are to be found in the towns and cities of low-income states are young, unaccompanied males with a secondary or university education, who have held positions as civil servants, teachers, traders or shopkeepers in their country of origin. Fewer refugee women and children live in the urban environment, in contrast to the situation in camps, where they tend to predominate. There is a link between these two phenomena, as in many refugee situations, able-bodied men will head for the towns to look for work, leaving their dependants to benefit from the support systems which are usually to be found in a camp.

In many cases, it would appear, urban refugees originate from groups who have a long history of trade-related migration and who therefore possess the skills required to cope with the difficulties of life in an unfamiliar city. The presence of Somalis throughout east and southern Africa, for example, and the presence of Afghans in much of South-West Asia and the Middle East provide two examples of this phenomenon. Inevitably, the mobility and adaptability of such refugees has led to frequent suggestions that they are actually economic migrants. Similarly, some commentators have suggested that educated men and women in certain low-income countries become refugees with the primary purpose of seeking resettlement in one of the industrialized states.

Refugees in New Delhi
One of the largest groups of urban refugees is to be found in India. New Delhi is home to some 20,000, primarily Afghans, many of whom arrived directly from Kabul when the Soviet-backed government fell. India has no laws on asylum and the Afghans are not officially recognized as refugees. Their presence is tolerated, however, as 'foreigners temporarily residing in India'.

Each asylum seeker who approaches UNHCR in New Delhi is interviewed individually to assess his or her claim to refugee status. Those who are recognized as refugees are issued with a UNHCR refugee certificate, which normally enables them to obtain an official residence permit. For those without any other documents, the refugee certificate is sometimes the only measure of protection against arrest and deportation.

While urban refugees of other nationalities experience certain protection problems in India, the main challenge for the Afghans is to build a new life. What, for example, can a former senior government official from Kabul do to earn a living in New Delhi? Nor is it much easier for the doctor who suddenly finds his Afghan qualifications worth very little in India, or the university student who can no longer continue his studies. For them, the dream is usually either to go home or to move to an industrialized country.

Afghan traders and shopkeepers are generally better able to utilize their entrepreneurial skills in India, but even they are often hindered by a lack of capital or contacts in a strange city. Dispersed throughout the capital, living in cramped and rented accommodation, urban refugees are unable to develop the kind of community support structures which are often available in camps.

When the first Afghan refugees contacted UNHCR in 1981, the organization's New Delhi office responded by paying them a monthly cash allowance. In theory, such assistance was to be for a limited period. In practice, however, because they were not authorized to work, the refugees failed to become self-sufficient. As a result of this problem and the growing number of Afghan refugees in the city, UNHCR's budget

rose: from $2.3 million in 1983 to $4.8 million in 1995. By that time, some of the refugees had been living on UNHCR assistance for more than a decade. There was little hope for their resettlement in a western country, and with the continuing violence in Afghanistan, the prospects for repatriation appeared bleak.

Change of policy

As a result of these considerations, UNHCR was forced to review its policy. A survey undertaken in 1994 found that many of the Afghans actually had substantial resources of their own and had found some kind of gainful employment. UNHCR's assistance was therefore supplementing a lifestyle that was quite prosperous by local standards. In addition, the study showed, many of those Afghans who were living in poverty were able-bodied and had the potential to earn a reasonable income if they were given appropriate training and advice.

Since 1995, UNHCR has shifted the focus of its urban refugee programme in New Delhi, providing a subsistence allowance only to those with a particular need for it, such as some female heads of household, the disabled, elderly and newly arrived exiles. Other refugees have been encouraged to take a lump

sum payment, to set up small-scale businesses and to gain new skills such as motor mechanics, airline ticketing, TV repair, tailoring, embroidery and baking. Since 1996, new arrivals have been provided with assistance for up to a year, during which time they receive intensive counselling and vocational training. Small grants have also been made available to groups of refugees who wish to set up cooperatives.

Refugee women have found it much more difficult to establish an independent livelihood, partly because they have few marketable skills and partly because they are prevented or discouraged from working outside the home. Moreover, some are heads of their household and many have young children which they are expected to care for. Nevertheless, some progress has been made in this area. When one refugee woman found a job, a delegation of Afghan leaders called on UNHCR to protest. The woman replied, "if on the first day of each month, the leaders can pay me the 3000 rupees (about $90) that I am now earning, I will stop working." The leaders then backed down.

UNHCR's local implementing partner, the YMCA, has found great interest and enthusiasm for skills training among Afghan women,

particularly the younger ones, who appreciate the greater freedom which they enjoy in India. Beauty culture is the most popular training course, and New Delhi's thriving beauty parlours provide plenty of employment. Parents and husbands are also happy to see their daughters and wives working in a women-only environment.

The reorientation from subsistence to self-reliance has not been easy. Urban refugees, angry at losing what they had come to regard as their salary, threatened UNHCR staff and smashed its office windows. In several cases, Afghan business ventures have failed and the refugees have come back to UNHCR, asking for a reinstatement of their monthly allowances.

In general, however, the new policy has had some positive effects. By mid-1997, only 2,500 people out of a total caseload of some 20,000 urban refugees were still dependent on a monthly subsistence allowance, many of them because they had medical problems. UNHCR has now established a medical assessment and referral project with the Voluntary Health Association of Delhi, so that their condition can be assessed and treated. If and when their medical problems are resolved, they will be referred to the YMCA for employment counselling, vocational training and placement in a job.

Assistance dilemmas

Given the growing difficulties of life in the rural areas of developing countries, coupled with the declining level of services available in many refugee camps, it seems likely that a growing number of refugees will in future make their way into the towns and cities of their asylum country. At the same time, UNHCR has increasingly been confronted with the problem of 'irregular movers' - urban refugees who have been granted asylum in one country but who have subsequently moved on to another state, and who have approached the organization for material assistance.

A Somali refugee living in a camp in northern Kenya, for example, might initially go to Nairobi, and later move on to Lusaka in Zambia, Harare in Zimbabwe or Johannesburg in South Africa. Iraqi refugees and asylum seekers have proved to be particularly mobile, arriving in capital cites such as Ankara, Islamabad, Bangkok, Beijing and Moscow, as well as the more traditional countries of asylum in Europe and North America.

Both of these trends have created some difficulties and dilemmas for UNHCR. Host governments are generally not very keen to see significant numbers of refugees in their major towns and cities, particularly when they have established refugee camps in rural areas. As in India, UNHCR has found that urban refugees are relatively expensive to assist and may not take the opportunity to become self-sufficient if they are provided with material support. Moreover, as UNHCR's study of this issue concluded, "urban refugees and asylum seekers tend to share a culture of expectation which, if not satisfied, often leads to frustration and violence."

Scarce resources

Responding to these difficulties, in early 1997, UNHCR established a comprehensive policy on urban refugees, the purpose of which is "to ensure protection and to maximize access to solutions, both for individual refugees and for groups, and to make the best use of scarce resources." In brief, the policy document states that irregular movers should not normally receive assistance from UNHCR, but should benefit from the organization's protection. In some circumstances, they might also be helped to go back to the country where they were first granted asylum.

Similarly, refugees who have moved of their own accord from a rural camp to an urban centre in the same country will not normally receive assistance from UNHCR. If they are to settle in a town or city, they must find their own way to make ends meet, as many urban refugees already do. In Sudan, for example, despite strong official discouragement, thousands of Ethiopians and Eritreans have made their way to Khartoum and have found a niche in the local labour market. More recently, many thousands of people from other parts of the continent have made their way to Johannesburg and other cities in South Africa, where they have entered the informal economy.

With regard to urban refugees of the type found in New Delhi - skilled and educated people who do not have the option of going to a camp - the primary objective must be to find a long-term solution. If neither repatriation nor resettlement in another country are feasible, then efforts must be made to integrate the refugees locally, preferably by assisting them to participate in existing activities for nationals, such as job-creation, income-generating and skills-training programmes. As well as benefiting refugees themselves, an integrated approach of this kind will help to demonstrate that exiled populations can make a positive contribution to the country which has granted them asylum. Given the likelihood that the number of urban refugees will increase in the years to come, a more positive and imaginative approach to this issue is now required.

61

or trading in another location, fighting in an army or rebel group, or visiting their country of origin in order to prepare for the repatriation of their family members (see Figure 2.3).

REFUGEE RIGHTS AT RISK

Many of the world's poorer countries have a remarkable record of hospitality towards refugees. Malawi, for example, a country which has few natural resources, a serious shortage of land and a population of under eight million, hosted more than a million Mozambican refugees from the mid-1980s until the early 1990s. During that period, UNHCR recorded very few incidents in which displaced Mozambicans were refused admission to the country or were forced to leave Malawi against their will. Similar acts of generosity have been recorded throughout most of Africa, which continues to accommodate more refugees than any other region of the world.

South and South-West Asia provide several examples of countries which have pursued generous refugee policies. Pakistan and Iran, which jointly hosted more than five million Afghans throughout most of the 1980s, are perhaps the best-known cases. Somewhat less attention has been paid to India, which now provides asylum to some 250,000 refugees, including Tibetans from China, Chakmas from Bangladesh and Tamils from Sri Lanka, as well as a significant number of urban refugees from Afghanistan, Bhutan and Myanmar.

In South-East Asia, Thailand has in recent years constituted the most important refugee-hosting country, having granted temporary refuge to people from four neighbouring and nearby states: Cambodia, Laos, Myanmar and Vietnam. While the country's refugee population had diminished to some 100,000 by mid-1997, in the mid-1980s, it had stood at close to half a million.

Although refugee numbers in the Americas have generally been on a much smaller scale than those recorded in Africa, Asia and the Middle East, the region has witnessed some generous attitudes on the part of host governments and communities. Mexico, for example, provided asylum to over 100,000 Guatemalans during the 1980s and early 1990s. While many have been able to go home during the past few years, Mexico recently announced that up to 30,000 of the remaining refugees could stay in the country indefinitely and benefit from an accelerated naturalization procedure.

Despite these and many other positive examples (see Figure 2.4), the global picture of refugee protection is not a very happy one. Indeed, protection standards appear to have declined quite significantly over the past decade, even in countries which have traditionally pursued the most generous refugee policies. Sadly, some of the fundamental principles of the 1951 Convention and other refugee instruments are now being challenged - and in some cases even flouted - by industrialized and less-developed states alike.

Fig. 2.3

Refugee demographics in selected countries

Somalis in Ethiopia

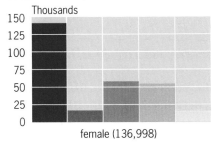
female (136,998)

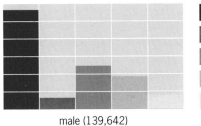
male (139,642)

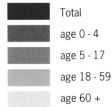
Total
age 0 - 4
age 5 - 17
age 18 - 59
age 60 +

Guatemalans in Mexico

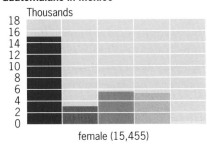
female (15,455)

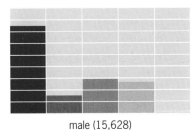
male (15,628)

Breakdown considers
only refugees
in camps or centres
and urban refugees

Afghans in Pakistan

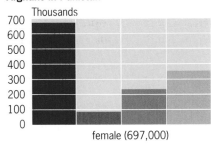
female (697,000)

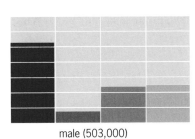
male (503,000)

Refugees 60 +
are included in the
category 18-59

Liberians in Guinea

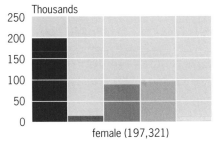
female (197,321)

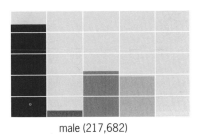
male (217,682)

Statistics at January 1997

The Director of the US Committee for Refugees speaks for most humanitarian organizations when he observes "a continuing deterioration in the quality of protection and assistance which countries are prepared to offer to those fleeing persecution and violence."(9)

In a recent speech to UNHCR's Executive Committee, the UN High Commissioner for Refugees identified the three principal ways in which refugee protection standards are currently being undermined: by the denial of asylum by potential countries of refuge; by threats to the physical safety and human security of exiled populations; and by a weakening commitment to the principle of voluntary repatriation.(10) These comments provide a useful framework for the following analysis.

Denial of asylum

According to the High Commissioner, the declining willingness of states to grant asylum to refugees is now one of the most important issues on the international humanitarian agenda. Many countries, she has pointed out, are "blatantly closing their borders," while others are "more insidiously introducing laws and procedures which effectively deny admission to their territory." "The threat to asylum," she observes, "has taken on a global character." (11)

Some countries, fearing large and potentially destabilizing influxes from neighbouring states, have prevented displaced populations from en-

Fig. 2.4

Major refugee hosting countries in developing regions

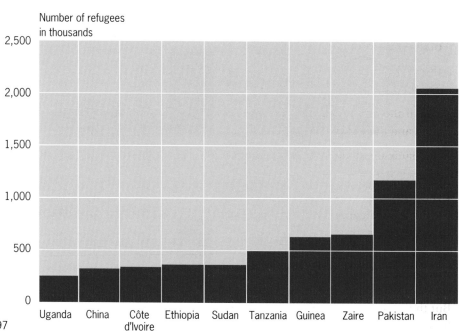

Number of refugees in thousands

tering their territory. Such was the case, for example, with Tajikistan, Uzbekistan and Pakistan, who denied entry to displaced Afghans during the Taliban offensive in the second half of 1996. In the same year, having already admitted very large numbers of refugees from Rwanda, both Tanzania and Zaire closed their borders to uprooted Hutus arriving from Burundi.(12)

Similar events have taken place elsewhere in the world. In early 1997, UNHCR expressed strong concern at the decision of the Thai government to deny asylum to fleeing adult and adolescent males from eastern Myanmar. During the same period, some 900 Myanmar women and children were returned from Thailand to a particularly dangerous part of their homeland, obliging UNHCR to express its alarm again.(13) By mid-1997, however, Thailand had admitted about 100,000 refugees from Myanmar onto its territory.

Physical safety

Regrettably, admission to a country of asylum no longer brings with it a guarantee of safety. Increasingly, the right of refugees to live in peace and security is being threatened, whether by the government of the host country, members of the local population or by other people who belong to the community in exile. More specifically, the safety of refugees has been threatened by a number of different developments. In brief, these include:

- the militarization and politicization of refugee camps by armed groups and rebel factions;

- armed attacks on refugee camps by rebel groups and by the military forces of the country of origin;

- the forced conscription of boys as well as adult and adolescent male refugees into armies, rebel groups and militia forces;

- sexual and other forms of violence committed against refugee women and girls, and their exploitation for sexual purposes;

- the harassment and arbitrary detention of refugees, particularly those living in urban areas; and,

- the obstruction of UNHCR and other humanitarian organizations in their efforts to gain access to, protect and assist refugee populations, as well as the deliberate diversion of aid intended for them.

It should be stressed that none of these security problems is entirely new. Abuses have always taken place in the essentially artificial and often highly volatile environment characteristic of refugee camps and settlement areas. But the growing prevalence and severity of such incidents is a major cause for concern.

Nowhere has this issue been more apparent than in the Great Lakes region of Africa, where the Rwandese refugee camps in Zaire and Tanzania, established in 1994, quickly came under the control of the political leaders, soldiers and militia forces who had been responsible for organizing the genocide in their homeland. In November 1994, UNHCR field staff reported that as many as 30 refugees a day were being killed in the Goma area of eastern Zaire, whether because of their ethnic origin, their political background and affiliation, or because they had expressed the desire or intention to repatriate.

Despite repeated attempts by UNHCR to address the security situation - including a request to the UN Secretary-General and Security Council for the creation of a multinational force which could attempt to separate civilian refugees from those bearing arms - the international community failed to take decisive action. In effect, as a senior UNHCR staff member has pointed out, the organization was left alone to find a way of maintaining law and order in a cluster of refugee camps which housed more than a million people.(14) The only way it could seek to achieve this objective was by engaging a contingent of Zaire's best trained soldiers and by appointing expatriate liaison officers to supervise their activities.

In December 1996, concerns about the militarization of a refugee settlement and intimidation of its population prompted UNHCR to announce the closure of the Atrush camp in northern Iraq, which at the time was home to some 14,000 Turkish Kurds. In a statement on this situation, UNHCR explained that the camp had come under the control of a Kurdish rebel movement, and pointed out that it could "no longer assist a camp where people are deprived of their basic freedoms and which has become politicized to an unacceptable extent."(15)

It has long been recognized that refugee camps are particularly vulnerable to insecurity when they are sited close to an international frontier - because they may be seen as a threat by the authorities in the country of origin, and because they are more easily attacked in a cross-border incursion. Incidents of this type have taken place in the Somali refugee camps of northern Kenya, the Karen refugee camps of western Thailand and the Sudanese refugee settlements of northern Uganda.

Regrettably, insecurity in and around refugee camps presents a growing threat to the welfare of refugees and a mounting obstacle to UNHCR's protection and assistance activities. Some of the most serious incidents of this type occurred in eastern Zaire during 1996 and 1997, where some 250,000 Rwandese refugees went missing as a result of the armed conflict in that area and the advance of the Zairean rebel forces. Addressing the UN Security Council on this matter, the UN High Commissioner for Refugees described the "desperate efforts" that UNHCR was making to reach the refugees, "carrying out impossible negotiations with the rebel forces and overcoming nightmarish logistical hurdles." "We do not yet know," she continued, "how many lives have been lost through exhaustion, war or outright killing."(16)

Human security

While physical safety constitutes the most evident component of human security, people also have essential material, social and psychological needs which must be met if their well-being is to be assured. Refugees cannot be properly protected if such needs are ignored or neglected.

Unfortunately, while the resources devoted to humanitarian relief have increased enormously since the end of the 1980s, there has been a growing tendency in recent years for refugee assistance programmes to concentrate almost exclusively on the most basic and visible forms of relief, particularly food, shelter and medical care. Other activities, such as education, skills training, income-generation, recreational activities, counselling and other community services, have generally been amongst the last programmes to be established in refugee emergencies and the first to be cut when financial savings are required.

In parallel with these developments, the long-established notion that refugees should be active participants in the management of their camps and assistance programmes is quietly being set aside. Increasingly, donor states assess humanitarian organizations in terms of their capacity to deliver emergency relief, rather than their ability to empower marginalized populations and to bring a degree of dignity to their lives.

This trend is the result of several different factors. Donor states now want refugee problems to be resolved with the minimum of delay, and are no longer prepared to finance community and social services programmes which, they erroneously believe, might discourage refugees from going home. Host governments have also come to associate such programmes with the long-term presence of refugees, and have in some instances expressed their concern that refugees have access to better services than the local population. Similarly, a number of governments have discouraged refugees from becoming self-sufficient and have barred them from seeking paid employment, believing that it is easier to induce the repatriation of exiled populations which are dependent on international assistance for their basic needs.

Voluntary repatriation and the right to return

The notion of voluntary repatriation is one of the fundamental principles of refugee protection. Although no explicit reference is made to it in the 1951 Convention, the concept is endorsed in UNHCR's Statute, in a number of resolutions approved by the organization's Executive Committee, and in regional refugee instruments such as the 1969 OAU Refugee Convention. In brief, the principle of voluntary repatriation affirms the right of all refugees to return to their own countries, stipulates that repatriation must be the result of a free and well-informed choice, and forbids any action which is taken with the intention of obliging refugees to go back to a country where their life and liberty would be at risk.

As Chapter Four explains, a significant proportion of the refugees who have repatriated in recent years have done so not because conditions have become safe in their country of origin, but because conditions have become too dangerous or difficult in their country of asylum.(17) When refugees are caught up in armed conflicts, the principle of voluntariness may prove difficult or impossible to uphold. But as UNHCR's Division of International Protection has pointed out, returns which take place under duress do not conform to the principles of international refugee law: "refugee repatriation is *not* voluntary when host country authorities deprive refugees of any real freedom of choice through outright coercion or measures such as reducing essential services."(18)

One of the most disturbing recent examples of such 'outright coercion' was witnessed in July 1996, when the armed forces of Burundi organized the expulsion of up to 90,000 Rwandese refugees. As the UN High Commissioner for Refugees observed in a letter to the country's President, this incident was "a serious violation of a cardinal principle of human rights."(19) It was by no means, however, an isolated example. In its 1997 *World Refugee Survey*, the US Committee for Refugees lists no fewer than 20 states which expelled refugees from their territory during the preceding year.(20)

While the problem of refoulement and involuntary repatriation has attracted a great deal of attention in recent years, much less interest has been shown in those situations where the refugees want to go home but are unable to exercise their right to return - a right that is recognized in several international legal instruments, including Article 13 of the 1948 Universal Declaration of Human Rights, and Article 12 of the International Covenant on Civil and Political Rights.

In some cases, such as that of the Rwandese refugees in Zaire and Tanzania and the Tajik refugees in Afghanistan, large numbers of refugees have effectively been held hostage by militant groups within the exiled population, who believe that repatriation would be to their political and military disadvantage. The 90,000 refugees from Bhutan who have lived in Nepal since the early 1990s have been unable to repatriate for a very different reason: because their nationality - and therefore their right to return - is disputed by the Bhutanese authorities.(21)

PROTECTION AND THE CHANGING WORLD ORDER

The preceding chapter of this book explained how the international community's response to the problem of forced displacement has changed during the past decade. Rather than waiting for refugees to cross a border and seek safety in a country of asylum, there has been a growing recognition of the need to take action within countries of origin, providing humanitarian assistance (and if possible, protection) to displaced and vulnerable populations.

The recent emphasis on multilateral action in countries of origin is potentially positive, in the sense that it could, if undertaken effectively, both resolve existing refugee problems and avert new situations of forced displacement. Unfortunately, however, this approach towards the protection of threatened populations has also in some instances been used as a pretext to obstruct the flight of people whose lives are in danger, to limit their right to asylum and to return them prematurely to conditions of danger.

Sadly, the world's richest and most powerful states have taken a lead in eroding the right of asylum and undermining the principles of refugee protection. As Chapter Five will explain, since the beginning of the 1980s, the industrialized states of Europe, North America and Australasia have introduced a vast array of measures specifically designed to restrict the arrival of asylum seekers on their territory.

When the very countries responsible for establishing the international refugee regime begin to challenge its legal and ethical foundations, then it is hardly surprising that other states, especially those with far more pressing economic problems and much larger refugee populations, have decided to follow suit.

Increasingly, when low-income countries close their borders to refugees, they tend to justify their actions by referring to the precedents which have already been set by the more affluent states. "In the current situation, what country would keep its border open?" asked a government minister in an African country when confronted with an impending refugee influx. "If this was a western country," he continued, "it would have been well accepted."(22)

As the preceding statement indicates, the world's poorer countries feel that they are expected to bear too great a responsibility for the world's refugees and that they are required to observe standards which the industrialized states themselves no longer attempt to respect. Such attitudes have been reinforced by a number of other developments.

First, many of the low-income countries which have admitted large numbers of refugees in the past now feel that the problems created by their generosity have been too quickly forgotten. The regions of Malawi which accommodated large numbers of Mozambicans, for example, have experienced serious environmental difficulties such as deforestation and soil erosion. But now that the refugees have returned to their homeland, the world's attention has moved away from Malawi and the country has been left to cope with the problems which the refugees left behind. Confronted with examples such as this, the world's poorer states have understandably become more wary of opening their borders to large refugee influxes.

Second, donor states can be said to have exacerbated the decline in protection standards by making it increasingly clear that they are no longer prepared to support long-term refugee assistance programmes in other parts of the world. Programmes which have already been in existence for a number of years, they argue, should be brought to an end as rapidly as possible. And when new refugee movements take place, immediate efforts should be made to facilitate the repatriation of the people concerned, thereby averting the need for long-term 'care and maintenance' programmes.

An illustration of this linkage was seen in October 1996, when donor states attending a meeting of UNHCR's Executive Committee said in very certain terms that they wished to see a speedy end to the assistance programme for the Rwandese refugees in Tanzania and Zaire. According to one of the principal donors, resources were "limited and diminishing," and there was a need to break the "intolerable and unsustainable status quo" through a process of "prompt, voluntary and orderly repatriation."(23)

There is evidently a need to avoid the kind of protracted refugee situations associated with groups such as the Afghans, Angolans, Eritreans and Palestinians. But it is equally clear that the recent emphasis on speedy solu-

Fig. 2.5

Official development assistance, 1987-96

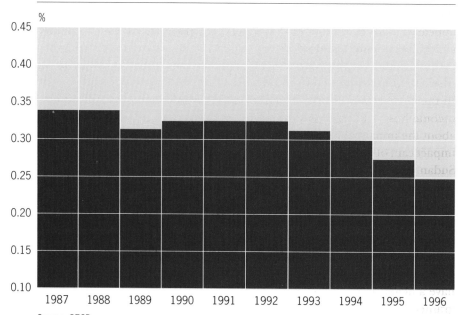

Source: OECD
Figure shows average ODA as % of Gross National Product (GNP) for members of the OECD Development Assistance Committee.

tions has not been conducive to the maintenance of high refugee protection standards. Indeed, it has diminished the willingness of host countries to admit large numbers of refugees, obliged humanitarian organizations to limit the services which they provide to exiled communities, and in some cases has led to the organization of premature and non-voluntary repatriation programmes.

Third, in order to understand the declining commitment to asylum in the low-income states, it is necessary to situate the refugee problem in the broader context of the international economy. When such states began to receive large numbers of refugees in the 1960s and 1970s, they were relatively well placed to cope with this responsibility. The global economy was booming, agricultural commodity prices were high and new employment opportunities were being created in the world's poorer countries.

Over the past 20 years, that situation has changed significantly. During this period, many of the world's less affluent states, particularly in Africa, have experienced low and in some cases negative rates of economic growth. At the insistence of the industrialized states and the international financial institutions, such countries have been obliged to introduce free-market economic reforms and to make substantial cuts to public spending. Since the beginning of the 1990s, however, the level of official development assistance provided by the richer nations has not only been in decline (see Figure 2.5), but has also been increasingly targeted at a relatively small number of states with good development prospects and investment potential. In such difficult circumstances, a growing number of the world's poorest states appear to have concluded that large refugee populations are one luxury which they can no longer afford.

The refugee impact

In the circumstances described above, it is also understandable that low-income host countries should begin to express a new degree of concern about the impact of refugees upon their economy and environment. That impact can, of course, be a positive one. As with the Ugandans in southern Sudan, refugees may introduce new crops and expand agricultural production in the areas where they settle. As with the Afghans in Pakistan, they may open up new trucking and trading opportunities, making cheaper goods available to the local population. And as with the Mozambican refugees in Zambia, they may attract international assistance to an area which has traditionally been neglected in national development efforts.(24) It would, however, be naive to ignore the fact that large-scale refugee populations can have a negative impact on the countries and communities where they are granted asylum.

One of the most obvious consequences of a refugee influx is to increase the level of competition for scarce resources such as employment, income-generating opportunities, education and health care, as well as basic commodities such as food, fuelwood, drinking water and construction materials. A less evident impact of the refugee presence can be seen in the 'brain drain' which takes place when humanitarian agencies move onto the scene of a mass influx and sign up the most skilled and best educated members of the local population, thereby depriving indigenous institutions of their expertise. Moreover, even when generous amounts of international assistance are available, refugee influxes can make heavy demands on the authorities of their host country. Rather than attending to the needs of the local population, government officials may find their time and resources occupied by the management of refugee camps and other emergency-related tasks.

The environmental impact of refugees has attracted a great deal of attention from academic analysts and aid organizations during the past few years. It has also been cited by many low-income states as one of the predominant reasons for their declining willingness to host large-scale refugee populations.

In reality, the environmental damage caused by exiled communities may not always be as great as is sometimes assumed. Recent research has raised some doubts about the hypothesis that refugees tend to deplete natural resources in a reckless manner because they lack a long-term commitment to the area where they have settled. In some cases, moreover, environmental problems caused by other factors have been wrongly (and even maliciously) attributed to the presence of refugees. (25)

Nevertheless, the evidence from many refugee-hosting countries supports the general view that the long-term presence of a refugee population in an area of resource scarcity can have a very detrimental impact upon the physical environment.(26) This is clearly the case in situations where refugees move in very large numbers into an area which has previously supported a much smaller population.

In the Ngara district of Tanzania, for example, Rwandese refugees outnumbered the local population by four to one when they arrived in 1994. As an environmental expert pointed out, in the early days of the emergency, the only provision made for the refugees' shelter needs by the international community came in the form of plastic sheeting. "This leaves the procurement of all other shelter materials and fuelwood completely up to the refugees, who (are forced to) exploit whatever the surrounding natural vegetation offers them. A free-for-all attitude is created within the refugee communities with regard to firewood, poles, timber, grass, animal fodder and any other plant material available within walking distance."(27)

The negative impact of such problems on the local population is frequently reinforced by the perception that refugees receive preferential treatment from the international community. Despite attempts by UNHCR and other humanitarian organizations to promote integrated and area-based assistance programmes in situations of mass influx, most notably in the Horn of Africa, it remains the case that relief efforts are normally focused on refugees, rather than needy members of the local population (see Box 2.2).

Inevitably, such situations can easily lead to resentment, tension and conflict between the two groups. Thus according to the aid agency Médecins sans Frontières (MSF), one of the principal causes of the crisis which erupted in eastern Zaire in 1996 was "the indifference of the international community to the fate of the local population." The growing resentment of Zairean citizens towards the Rwandese refugees, MSF suggested in November of that year, "lies in the living daily parody that the refugees in the camps have a far better quality of life." (28)

The growing reluctance of low-income states and societies to accommodate large numbers of refugees is based in part on a perception that exiled populations constitute a serious threat to social stability and political security. At the local level, refugees are frequently associated with problems such as crime, domestic violence, prostitution, alcoholism and drugs. Sadly, there is often some truth in this perception, although refugees can easily become scapegoats for problems which are not wholly of their own making. Violence and other forms of anti-social behaviour are an almost inevitable characteristic of refugee settlements which accommodate large numbers of young males who are deprived of education, recreation and the opportunity to engage in productive activities, and who are unable to plan for their future.

In many instances, moreover, host countries simply do not have the capacity to maintain law and order in the remote and underdeveloped areas where the largest number of refugees are often to be found. The current decline in protection standards is thus not simply the result of a declining willingness to treat refugees in accordance with humanitarian standards; it also derives from the inability of weak states to guarantee the security of all the people who are living on their territory, whether they be citizens or foreigners.

The increasingly hostile reception received by refugees in many low-income states is also related to political developments at the national level. According to some commentators, there is growing evidence of a linkage between the process of democratization and the decline in refugee protection standards.(29)

Prior to the 1990s, it has been argued, authoritarian governments in Africa and other parts of the developing world were relatively free to offer asylum to large refugee populations when they considered such a policy to be in their own interests. But with the end of the cold war and the introduction of pluralistic systems of government in many low-income countries, the refugee question has assumed a new degree of political importance. As in the industrialized states, in the attempt to maximize their electoral support, both gov-

Map D

The Horn of Africa: principal refugee locations

☐   Capital

●   Town

—   Boundary

⋏   Refugee camp or area

2.2

Refugees from the Horn of Africa

The political crisis in the Great Lakes region of Africa and the continuing violence in the West African states of

Liberia and Sierra Leone have tended to divert international attention from the issue of forced displacement in the Horn of Africa. And yet Djibouti, Eritrea, Ethiopia, Somalia and Sudan - five of the world's poorest countries - continue to be affected by some very large and

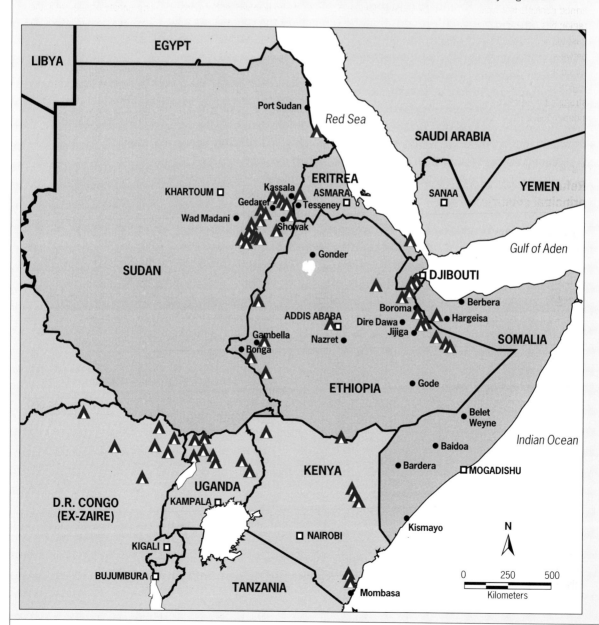

longstanding refugee problems. In total, some 1.3 million refugees from the Horn of Africa are to be found within the region and in nearby states.

Armed conflicts

The refugee problem in the Horn of Africa is rooted primarily in the succession of armed conflicts which the region has witnessed over the past 20 years: the war between Ethiopia and Somalia for control of the Ogaden region in 1977-78; the struggle for Eritrean independence from Ethiopia, which began in the 1950s and was finally achieved in 1993; the battle for territorial control between the clans and warlords of Somalia, prompted by the disintegration of the Siad Barre regime at the beginning of the 1990s; and the ongoing conflict between government and rebel forces in the south of Sudan.

The scale and complexity of the refugee problem in the Horn of Africa has been reinforced by two other factors. First, while armed conflict and human rights violations have been the primary cause of the mass displacements witnessed in the region, environmental and economic factors have also contributed to the refugee problem. In many cases, of course, these different causes of displacement have been inextricably linked. When large numbers of Eritreans and Ethiopians fled to Sudan in the mid-1980s, for example, and when thousands of Somalis fled to Kenya in the early 1990s, they did so not only to escape from violence, but also because the armed conflicts in their respective countries had destroyed their livelihoods and undermined their traditional survival strategies.

Second, the conventional categorizations employed by UNHCR and other aid agencies are not always appropriate or relevant in the socio-economic context of the Horn of Africa. A large proportion of the region's displaced people come from a nomadic or pastoralist background, where movement is the norm and where

Fig. 2.6

Refugees from the Horn of Africa: principal countries of asylum

Countries of asylum and refugee population	Number of refugees	Countries of asylum and refugee population	Number of refugees
Djibouti		**Sudan**	
Somalis	23,000	Eritreans	328,000
Ethiopians	2,000	Ethiopians	51,000
Egypt		**Uganda**	
Somalis	3,500	Sudanese	224,000
Sudanese	1,500		
		Yemen	
Eritrea		Somalis	44,000
Somalis	2,000	Eritreans	2,500
		Ethiopians	1,000
Ethiopia			
Somalis	288,000	**Zaire**	
Sudanese	76,000	Sudanese	97,000
Djiboutians	18,000		
		Total	**1,372,500**
Kenya			
Somalis	171,000		
Sudanese	33,000		
Ethiopians	7,000	Rounded statistics, dated January 1997	

international boundaries have little or no meaning. In such circumstances, it is not always possible to say whether a person is a refugee, a returnee, an internally displaced person or a member of the local population. As a result, the registration and enumeration of refugees in the Horn of Africa has proven to be especially problematic and a constant source of controversy. Responding to these problems, in the early 1990s, UNHCR pioneered a new approach to humanitarian assistance in the region, designed to support all those people in need in a given geographical area, irrespective of their nationality or their legal status.

The search for solutions

As a result of the political, economic and environmental problems experienced by the region, populations in the Horn of Africa have quite literally been scattered in all directions. Citizens of all five countries are living in exile, not only in the region itself but also in nearby countries such as Egypt, Kenya, Uganda and Yemen (see Figure 2.6). Large numbers of Eritreans, Ethiopians, Somalis and Sudanese have also moved to other parts of the world, either as migrant workers or as asylum seekers.

Now that the Horn of Africa is experiencing a period of relative peace, UNHCR's primary concern is to find lasting solutions for people who have lived in exile for many years. In this respect, the organization's efforts are focused on the two largest refugee populations in the region: the Somalis in Ethiopia and, as discussed below, the Eritreans in Sudan.

An estimated 900,000 Eritreans fled from their homeland between 1967 and 1990, the largest number of whom moved westwards to Sudan. When the 30-year conflict with Ethiopia came to an end and a peace settlement was signed in June 1991, there was an evident expectation within the international community that those refugees would soon be able to go back to their homes. In practice, however, progress on this front has been slower than anticipated.

Initially, large-scale repatriation was delayed by the devastation that had taken place in Eritrea, the refugees' caution in returning to such conditions, and the need for discussions with the new government concerning the repatriation and reintegration effort. In 1993, after some intense negotiations, the Eritrean authorities and the United Nations agreed upon a $260 million repatriation and reintegration programme for refugees in Sudan, and in November 1994, UNHCR launched a six-month pilot project involving the return of 25,000 Eritreans.

While the pilot project is generally considered to have been a significant success, the organized movement of refugees from Sudan to Eritrea quickly became stalled, largely as a result of two factors: the deteriorating relationship between the Sudanese and Eritrean governments, which eventually led to a rupture of diplomatic relations; and growing insecurity in the border area, resulting from clashes between the Sudanese armed forces and a rebel group.

Despite the difficulties which have affected the organized repatriation programme, the Eritrean government estimates that around 130,000 refugees had returned independently from Sudan by mid-1997. While the exact number of Eritreans remaining in that country is a matter of some dispute, UNHCR put the figure at around 330,000 at the beginning of 1997, of whom 135,000 were receiving international assistance.

According to a study by Eritrean scholar Gaim Kibreab, over 90 per cent of the refugees are positively disposed towards repatriation, but the risks they have to take in returning without assistance are so great that many prefer to wait until the organized repatriation and reintegration programme resumes. "There is nothing more frustrating than waiting," he observes, "especially when those who are waiting are not in a position to influence either the tempo of the process or its outcome."

ernments and opposition parties are now more prone to encourage nationalistic and xenophobic sentiments, and to blame their country's ills on the presence of refugees and other foreigners. In countries where large numbers of people are living below the poverty line and where income differentials are increasing, such messages can have a potent appeal, irrespective of their veracity.

Finally, recent years have witnessed some important developments in relation to the impact of exiled populations on bilateral state relations and the quest for regional security. During the cold war years, the generous refugee policies pursued by many developing countries were underpinned by the geopolitical interests of the superpowers. With the support of the western alliance, countries such as Honduras, Pakistan, Somalia and Thailand gave refuge to large numbers of refugees from Nicaragua, Afghanistan, Ethiopia and Cambodia respectively, states which were all allied to the Soviet bloc. In a bipolar world, low-income states were often more interested in maintaining a close alliance with one or other of the superpowers than with neighbouring and nearby states.

Now that the cold war has come to an end and there are no longer two superpowers, vying for the support of other states, developing countries have a much greater interest in establishing a good working and trading relationship with countries in the same region. In this new political context, moreover, refugees tend to have a negative rather than a positive value. Even if the granting of asylum is supposed to be a humanitarian act, there is no doubt that it can act as an irritant between countries of origin and countries of asylum.

Evidence for the latter assertion can be found, for example, in the reluctance of Thailand to admit large numbers of displaced people from Myanmar, and in the eagerness of Tanzania to repatriate its Rwandese refugee population. In both cases, the presence of refugees has been contrary to the foreign policy objectives of the countries concerned and a potential impediment to their relationship. With the current strengthening of regional groupings such as the Southern African Development Community (SADC), the Association of South-East Asian Nations (ASEAN) and the South Asian Association for Regional Cooperation (SAARC), the incentive for states to admit refugees from neighbouring and nearby states may diminish further. This tendency is not confined to the developing regions. The European Union (EU), for example, has established an agreement making it very difficult for a citizen of one EU state to seek asylum in another. Such an arrangement, UNHCR has stated, is inconsistent with the provisions of the 1951 Refugee Convention.(30)

UNHCR and the protection dilemma
UNHCR, it must be acknowledged, has been limited in the extent to which it has been able to prevent the decline in standards of refugee protection.

According to its critics, this is because the organization has become involved with a broad range of humanitarian activities, and as a result has neglected its primary task of defending refugee rights. At the same time, it has been argued, the organization has been too ready to become involved in operations which are inconsistent with the principles of refugee protection and too hesitant in taking states to task when they violate those principles. Human Rights Watch, for example, has suggested that UNHCR "has worked in conjunction with states to fashion questionable protection measures that come dangerously close to accommodating rather than challenging [the] global deterioration of refugee protection."(31)

Other commentators have interpreted UNHCR's recent efforts differently, emphasizing the extent to which the agency has adapted to the new world order and thereby helped to safeguard the security of displaced popula-

Viewpoint I

Refugees and human rights: a South Asian perspective
by Kamal Hossain

An intensive review of past experience is currently underway in South Asia, as the region reaches its 50th year of independence from colonial rule. Unfortunately, those five decades have witnessed considerable human suffering and displacement. Indeed, it has been estimated that since 1947, between 35 and 40 million people have moved across the national boundaries of Afghanistan, Bangladesh, Bhutan, India, Myanmar, Nepal, Pakistan and Sri Lanka.

The advent of independence in 1947 was itself accompanied by some massive population movements. The flow of refugees between India and Pakistan at that time is one of the largest ever recorded, anywhere in the world. Another massive exodus took place in 1971, when nearly 10 million people fled from East Pakistan (which emerged as the new state of Bangladesh) to India.

A current survey of the refugee situation in the region records the presence of some 250,000 refugees in India and 1.2 million Afghan refugees in Pakistan. In recent years, Bangladesh has received over a quarter of a million refugees from Myanmar, while Nepal is currently hosting some 90,000 refugees from Bhutan. To this may be added the exodus of Sri Lankan Tamils and Bangladeshi Chakmas to India.

What has been the cause of such movements, and how can displacements of this kind be anticipated and averted in the future? In the exoduses of 1947-48 and 1971, the cause can clearly be identified as violent communal conflict, associated in both cases with the process of state formation. The other involuntary movements mentioned above can broadly be ascribed to human rights violations, resulting from the existence of elite-dominated political systems and a pervasive climate of religious and ethnic intolerance, reinforced by high levels of poverty, landlessness and unemployment. Sadly, those conditions seem likely to persist. A 1997 report on human development in South Asia, for example, states that the area is emerging as the poorest, the most illiterate, the most malnourished and the least gender-sensitive region in the world.

Unless there are determined efforts to address the causes of mass displacement, South Asia could well be the scene of further refugee exoduses in the years to come. Meaningful political reforms are needed to ensure that violence both by the state and by non-state actors is uncompromisingly subordinated to the rule of law. Impartial and effective law enforcement must be ensured. National police and internal security forces must be debrutalized so that they can function as the protectors and not as the violators of human rights.

As in other developing regions, the people of South Asia need to be truly empowered. And such empowerment requires the

tions. According to one academic analysis, "today's UNHCR is regarded by most observers as being at the top of the UN scale of performance - competent, well managed, purposeful, disciplined." Looking at the organization's recent activities in Bosnia, the authors conclude that "reinventing UNHCR to confront the tragedy of the former Yugoslavia was a useful and necessary adaptation to the emerging humanitarian needs of post-cold war disorder."(32)

Whatever the validity of these contrasting viewpoints, it is evident that the emerging world order and the changing attitude of states towards refugee problems and humanitarian action has presented UNHCR with some acute dilemmas.(33) As an organization which is mandated to defend refugee rights, UNHCR has an obligation to uphold the principles of international protection, to ensure that states respect their obligations under internation-

---

nurturing and strengthening of civil society through active popular participation in both governmental and non-governmental bodies. Conscious citizens must be able to articulate their priorities, monitor the activities of those who exercise governmental powers and ensure that the checks and balances written into their constitutions function as more than paper safeguards.

Human rights activism and popular mobilization in support of the values of democracy, tolerance and respect for the rights of others need to be supported. States must be radically restructured to ensure that they do not become the instrument of special interests. Decentralization and the strengthening of local government institutions must therefore be an integral part of any preventive strategy.

The human development report on South Asia underlines the meagre investment which is being made in the region's rapidly multiplying human resources. Less than five per cent of South Asia's combined Gross National Product is spent on health and education. The report recommends that every country of the region should strive to devote 20 per cent of its public spending to the social sector, mainly by means of cuts in military spending.

The needs of South Asian women require special attention. As a recent report on this issue argued, present-day notions of power - evolved in a hierarchical, male-dominated society - are based on divisive, destructive and oppressive values which encourage aggression, competition and corruption, regardless of whether it is

men or women who are wielding power. The need is for a new understanding of power itself; not one of control and exploitation for personal gain, but the power of sharing, giving, creating and developing the potential of every human being.

Regional co-operation is also needed to promote democracy and sustainable human development. Unresolved tensions as well as ethnic and sectarian conflicts must be resolved, given their role in nurturing a climate of intolerance and contributing to the growth of unacceptable military expenditures. The revival of religious fundamentalism in different parts of the region also represents a threat to political stability, both within and between states, and must therefore be addressed.

If undertaken effectively and in a coordinated manner,

such efforts would contribute to the creation of a peaceful and stable environment in South Asia, enabling a culture of tolerance and human rights to be nurtured in that part of the world. This, in turn, would help to reduce (if not to prevent) the kind of refugee movements and population displacements which the region has witnessed on too many occasions during the past half-century.

Dr Kamal Hossain is a Bangladeshi lawyer and former minister of law and foreign affairs. He is also chairperson of the Commonwealth Human Rights Advisory Commission.

al law, and to make the necessary public and private representations when governments and other actors put refugees at risk.

At the same time, however, as an organization which is part of the broader United Nations system, which is guided (and largely financed) by states; which normally relies on the authorization of host governments to establish operations in the field; and which is ultimately incapable of obliging other actors to respect international refugee law, UNHCR does not enjoy complete freedom of action.

Such constraints have been exacerbated by several other characteristics of the post-cold war world: the growing tendency for the parties to a conflict to exploit the activities of humanitarian organizations for their own political and military purposes; the mounting - and in many cases unrealistic - expectations which the international community has placed upon UNHCR and other humanitarian organizations; and the declining willingness of the world's more powerful states to participate in multilateral military operations and to take the decisive action required to bring armed conflicts to an end.

As a result of these interrelated trends, UNHCR has increasingly found itself in 'no-win situations', where it is obliged to choose between a limited number of options, none of which is fully consistent with the principles which the organization is mandated to uphold. Withdrawal is rarely a realistic option. Unless its activities actually begin to endanger the safety of refugees, and unless the lives of its staff members are at serious risk, UNHCR cannot simply pull out of an operation and abandon the people under its care. And while the organization can and should attempt to influence the behaviour of states and other political actors, it cannot make them act in a manner which they consider to be against their interests. As the UN High Commissioner for Refugees explained to the Security Council in April 1997, in some situations, UNHCR has no option but to pursue the "least worse" course of action. (34)

During the past few years, UNHCR has been confronted with such 'dilemma situations' on an almost daily basis. In 1991, for example, the organization was confronted with Turkey's unwillingness to admit the refugees who were fleeing from northern Iraq, and had to decide whether to participate in the US-led effort to protect and assist the Kurdish population within their country of origin. In 1992, UNHCR had to resolve an equally if not more difficult dilemma in former Yugoslavia: should the organization help to evacuate people from situations of danger, and thereby indirectly facilitate the process of ethnic cleansing?

In 1993, UNHCR had to determine whether it could be involved in the repatriation of the Rohingyas from Bangladesh to Myanmar, given the pressures which had been exerted on the refugee population by the former state and the serious human rights problems which still existed in the latter. And from 1994 to 1996, UNHCR had to decide if it could continue to assist the Rwandese refugees in eastern Zaire, when they were known to include people who had been involved in the 1994 genocide and who, despite the organization's strenuous efforts to reinforce security in the camps, were using violence to prevent the repatriation of their compatriots.

In responding to each of these questions, UNHCR ultimately decided to answer in the affirmative and to proceed with a course of action which, while far from optimal in terms of protection standards, nevertheless appeared to be in the best interests of the refugees concerned. Even so, the difficult decisions which UNHCR has felt obliged to take have not met with universal endorsement. (35)

REALIZING THE RIGHTS OF REFUGEES

As suggested already in this chapter, the trends which have led to the decline in protection standards are in many senses deep-rooted, intimately linked to broader changes in the international balance of power and distribution of resources. This should not lead to defeatism, however, as there are a variety of different initiatives that might be taken to reinforce the security and welfare of refugees.

Enhancing protection capacities

Despite the many changes which the world has witnessed since 1951, the UN Refugee Convention remains of vital relevance to the protection of exiled populations. It is also in the interests of states themselves to respect the Convention and other refugee instruments, which were established with the specific intention of ensuring that the refugee problem was dealt with in a consistent and predictable manner.

The right of people to seek asylum in another country and not to be returned to a place where their life and liberty are at risk are fundamental principles which must be upheld by all states, whether or not they have ratified the Convention. All states should, of course, accede to the Convention and Protocol, as well as those regional instruments which stipulate the rights and obligations of refugees.

Considerable progress has already been made in this area, as indicated by the very large number of states which are now parties to the 1951 Convention and its 1967 Protocol. It is, however, particularly disappointing to note that so few Asian countries have signed the international refugee instruments, and that five of the states which sit on UNHCR's Executive Committee have themselves not adhered to these agreements.

By defining the principles and standards which states are expected to observe, international and regional refugee law (not to mention broader human rights instruments such as the 1989 Convention on the Rights of the Child) provide an essential foundation for the protection of exiled populations. But legislation alone does not provide protection, particularly at a time when there is a growing hostility towards refugees. Unfortunately, some of the states which have adhered to the principal legal instruments have nevertheless been responsible for serious breaches of international refugee law.

If this negative tendency is to be countered, active training, education and awareness-raising efforts will be required, and need to be targeted at those people who influence the way in which refugees are treated: politicians, national and local government officials, the security services, community leaders, religious organizations and the media, not to mention the general public. At the same time, greater efforts are required to inform refugee populations of their responsibilities under international and national law, so as to ensure that they do not become involved in activities which threaten or alienate their local hosts.

In some parts of the world, the problems encountered by refugees derive less from the unwillingness of the host government to provide effective protection and more from its limited capacity to maintain the rule of law. In such situations, it is imperative that donor states, UNHCR and other humanitarian organizations provide the necessary support to the authorities by providing financial contributions, equipment and training.

An interesting example of this approach is to be found in the Women Victims of Violence Project, a UNHCR initiative undertaken in north-east Kenya, intended to combat the high incidence of rape and sexual violence occurring in the Somali refugee camps. Adopting an integrated approach to the problem, the project has improved security by providing refugees and the local police with special training, by encouraging women to bring offenders to justice and by making physical changes to the layout of the camps, including the establishment of perimeter fences.(36) Initiatives of this type should evidently be replicated in other situations where female refugees are at risk of assault.

Last but by no means least, if the rights of refugees are to be effectively defended, then UNHCR must have direct contact with them. As the organization recently informed its Executive Committee, "a key element of the institution of asylum is UNHCR's unimpeded, rapid and secure access to persons of concern."(37) An obvious reason for such access is to monitor the physical safety of refugees and to ensure that they are not being subjected to any form of ill-treatment, whether by the host government, the local population or by elements within the exiled community itself. But UNHCR access is also required as a means of ensuring that the different members of a refugee population, particularly those groups with special needs, are treated in an equitable manner.

As demonstrated by events in eastern Zaire during 1996 and 1997, there are situations in which the denial of access is so complete and serious that additional measures may have to be taken to reach refugees who are at risk. As the UN High Commissioner for Refugees told the *International Herald Tribune* in relation to this situation, "international action - not just humanitarian, but political and military action - is long overdue."(38) Regrettably, as indicated earlier in the chapter, such warnings were not heeded, and the proposal to establish a multinational military force in eastern Zaire, endorsed by two Security Council resolutions, never went beyond the preliminary planning stages.

Assistance and protection

There has been a tendency amongst some refugee specialists to talk about 'protection' and 'assistance' as if they were completely different functions.(39) Yet the provision of assistance can legitimately be described as a form of human rights protection, in the sense that everyone, under the terms of the international human rights instruments, has a right to be free from hunger, to be educated and to have adequate shelter. As a result of its assistance programmes, UNHCR also normally enjoys good access to refugee populations and is able to maintain a substantial presence in the areas where they have settled.

Assistance programmes can also make a direct contribution to the protection of refugee populations. Education, training, income-generating and recreational activities sponsored by UNHCR and other humanitarian organizations can play an important part in strengthening social structures in refugee communities, and thereby reduce the risk of conflict and violence.

Meaningful forms of refugee participation in the management of camps and in the design and implementation of assistance programmes also have an important role to play in defending the rights of refugees. It is well known that the principle of refugee participation can be difficult to put into practice and can be manipulated by the most powerful and articulate members of a community to serve their own interests. But when promoted in an effective manner, refugee participation can help to limit the social and economic exclusion of the most marginalized members of a refugee population.

Preserving the humanitarian character of asylum

Another way in which refugee protection can be strengthened is by reasserting the strictly humanitarian and civilian character of asylum. When refugee camps become militarized and overtly politicized, and when they are used as a base for activities intended to destabilize the government in the country of origin, then they inevitably become more vulnerable to retaliatory cross-border raids. Militarized camps are also particularly prone to factional conflict and violence, phenomena which inevitably reinforce the already widespread perception that refugees are a threat to local, national and regional security.

One of the problems associated with the granting of *prima facie* refugee status in situations of mass influx is the likelihood that some of the people who receive international protection may not actually deserve it. As indicated at the beginning of the chapter, the UNHCR Statute, the 1951 UN Refugee Convention and the 1969 OAU Refugee Convention all include provisions which make it possible to deny refugee status to certain categories of people on the basis of their previous activities: war criminals, persons guilty of acts contrary to the purposes and principles of the United Nations, and individuals who have committed serious non-political crimes.

It is now clear that the international community's inability to apply these 'exclusion clauses' to relevant members of the Rwandese population in Tanzania and Zaire was one of the principal reasons for the insecurity which existed in and around the refugee camps in those countries between 1994 and 1996. Even so, a degree of caution is required in invoking this somewhat neglected element of international refugee law. As people who are excluded from refugee status no longer benefit from the principle of non-refoulement and can in most instances be returned to their country of origin, care must be taken to ensure that the exclusion clauses are applied in a fair manner and by means of an examination of each individual case. Moreover, as UNHCR has observed elsewhere, "in a climate of numerous challenges to asylum, exclusion clauses must not become another avenue by which deserving cases are denied access to international protection."(40)

Recent experience in Zaire has also demonstrated that if the exclusion clauses are to be applied effectively and if the civilian character of refugee camps is to be maintained, then combatants must be disarmed and physically separated from their compatriots at a very early stage of a refugee influx. If the authorities of the host country are unable to undertake this task, then multilateral military involvement, endorsed by the UN Security Council, may well be required. Humanitarian organizations evidently do not have the mandate or the operational capacity to carry out this vital but potentially dangerous function.

Even camps which are strictly civilian in character should, as recommended by the OAU Refugee Convention, be situated in locations well away from international borders, thereby reducing the possibility that they will become a source of friction between the country of origin and country of asylum. Ethnic, cultural, economic and environmental considerations should also be taken into account when choosing refugee settlement sites, so as to minimize the potential for conflict between the new arrivals and the resident population.

Sharing responsibility for refugees

The decline in protection standards might also be halted and reversed through a reaffirmation of the principle of responsibility sharing - a principle, it should be emphasized, on which the whole international refugee regime was premised when it was established. In this respect, the primary onus is on the industrialized states to demonstrate a much greater degree of solidarity with those poorer countries where the vast majority of the world's refugees are to be found.

More specifically, the industrialized states might legitimately be expected to share the global responsibility for refugees in three ways: by pursuing less restrictive policies towards those people who wish to seek asylum on their territory; by establishing resettlement programmes for refugees who cannot remain in their country of first asylum (see Box 2.3); and by pursuing humanitarian assistance and development policies which assist and encourage low-income states to cope with the presence of large refugee populations.

With regard to the issues of refugee relief and development assistance, particular emphasis must be placed on efforts that will mitigate the environmental, economic and infrastructural impact of refugee populations on host countries and communities. Without such efforts, both during the refugees' presence and once they have returned to their homeland, the least affluent countries can hardly be expected to pursue generous asylum policies.

If the institution of asylum is to be reinforced, the needs of host communities, particularly their poorer members, should always be taken into account in the design of refugee assistance programmes. There is, of course, nothing very new about this suggestion. Indeed, the first initiatives of this type date back to the 1960s, when countries in Africa and other developing regions began to experience large-scale refugee influxes for the first time.

In recent years, however, interest in this issue has tended to wane, largely because of the international community's preoccupation with the delivery of emergency relief and its belief in the need to resolve refugee problems by means of speedy repatriation movements. Even so, UNHCR and its partners have enjoyed some success with the implementation of community-based environmental rehabilitation projects in countries such as Malawi, Nepal, Pakistan and Zimbabwe, states which have coincidentally been able to maintain generous asylum policies.

Donor states must recognize that an investment in refugee assistance programmes is also an investment in protection and solutions. When funds are available to build roads, bridges, schools and health centres in refugee-populated areas, and when national and local authorities are properly compensated for their work on behalf of exiled populations, then it is far more likely that refugees will be treated in a reasonable manner.

Voluntary and involuntary repatriation

The challenge of protecting refugees is inseparable from that of seeking permanent solutions to their plight. Indeed, the two tasks stand side-by-side in the very first article of UNHCR's Statute.

2.3

Refugee protection and resettlement

Since the end of the first world war, the resettlement of refugees from their first country of asylum to another state has proved to be an effective method of protection as well as an important solution to refugee problems. Indeed, refugees from a very wide range of situations have benefited from resettlement during the 20th century: Russians who fled to China after the revolution of 1917; Jews fleeing from Nazi persecution in the 1930s; European refugees in the aftermath of the second world war, Hungarian refugees who had fled from the Soviet invasion of their country in the 1950s; Chileans and Argentineans in the 1970s; Eritreans and Ethiopians in Sudan during the 1980s; and Iraqis in Saudi Arabia during the 1990s, to give just a few examples.

The largest resettlement programme in recent history was that established for the Vietnamese boat people following the collapse of the Saigon regime in 1975. By 1979, a major protection crisis had developed in South-East Asia. Certain asylum countries in the region refused to accept any new arrivals and pushed them

back to sea. Thousands more languished in camps without a solution to their situation in sight. Confronted with this political and humanitarian crisis, it was agreed at a major international conference that the boat people would be granted temporary refuge by states in the region and then be resettled in other countries. In the years that followed, nearly 700,000 Vietnamese boat people were resettled, most of them going to Australia, Canada, France and, in the largest numbers, to the USA.

The decision to adopt an across-the-board approach to resettlement in South-East Asia undoubtedly helped to save lives and to safeguard the principle of asylum. But it also created new problems. By the late 1980s, resettlement - designed as an important solution and protection tool for individual refugees meeting specific criteria - had also become a factor in inducing large numbers of people to leave Viet Nam, many of whom were subsequently found not to qualify for refugee status. Unfortunately, the notion that resettlement can act as a 'pull-factor' for economic migrants continues to obscure the vital role which resettlement can play in the protection of refugees who, for one reason or another, cannot remain safely in their country of first asylum.

Contemporary resettlement

Ten of the industrialized states have well-established resettlement programmes involving an annual allocation of places and organized reception arrangements. UNHCR plays a central role in identifying refugees needing resettlement and presenting their cases to the governments concerned: Australia, Canada, Denmark, Finland, Netherlands, New Zealand, Norway, Switzerland, Sweden and the USA (see Figures 2.7 and 2.8). While funding for these resettlement programmes comes largely from central and local government sources, other partners such as specialized resettlement agencies, individual sponsors and community associations play a critical role in making resettlement work.

A number of countries also have overseas refugee admissions programmes which function without the involvement of UNHCR. These programmes benefit refugees with family links or sponsors abroad. The USA, Canada and Australia also make allocations for a certain number of persons to be admitted directly from their countries of origin without first seeking asylum in another state.

The number of refugees benefiting from resettlement under UNHCR auspices has dropped considerably in the

recent years, largely as a result of the conclusion of the Comprehensive Plan of Action for Vietnamese refugees. At the peak of the Indo-Chinese programme, resettlement provided a durable solution for one in twenty of the world's refugees. By 1993, this ratio had dropped to just one in four hundred. And while UNHCR helped to resettle over 200,000 people a year in the late 1970s, the number of refugees resettled by the organisation in 1996 was 27,000 (see Figure 2.9).

Why resettlement?

There are four reasons why some refugees need to be resettled. First and foremost, resettlement represents a vital method of protection for those whose safety and security can not be guaranteed in their country of first asylum. Refugees who are threatened with refoulement, refugee women who are at risk of sexual violence, refugees who are threatened with violence or arbitrary detention because of their ethnic, religious or social background all come into this category.

Second, resettlement can be an effective measure to assist refugees with special humanitarian needs which cannot be met in their country of first asylum. Such refugees include, for example, those who are suffering from life-threatening medical problems and who

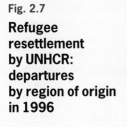

Fig. 2.7

Refugee resettlement by UNHCR: departures by region of origin in 1996

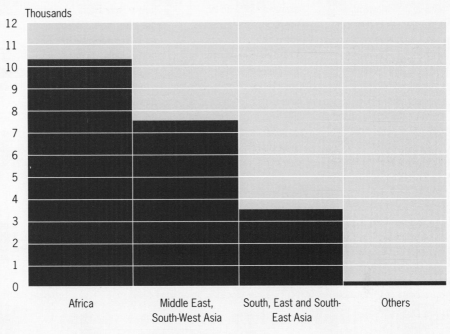

Thousands

Figure shows only departures facilitated by UNHCR

Fig. 2.8

Refugee resettlement by UNHCR: arrivals by country in 1996

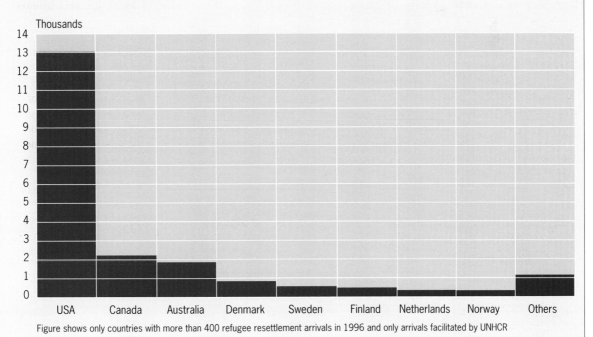

Thousands

Figure shows only countries with more than 400 refugee resettlement arrivals in 1996 and only arrivals facilitated by UNHCR

require urgent evacuation; those with serious injuries, mental problems or physical disabilities; victims of torture and rape and severely traumatized refugees; and refugees who wish to be reunited with family members living elsewhere. In each of these cases, UNHCR tries to ensure that resettlement is arranged only if no local alternatives are available.

A third main reason for resettlement is to be found in the situation of refugees who have already been living in their country of first asylum for some time, who are unlikely to be able to return to their homeland in the foreseeable future, and who are nevertheless unable to remain or integrate in their host society. Such refugees may be considered for resettlement if it is felt that they would have better prospects in another country, or if they have no other way of finding a lasting solution to their plight. Such has been the case for more than 35,000 Iraqi refugees who fled to Saudi Arabia after the Gulf war, and who were offered only temporary refuge in the latter country. By early 1997, around two-thirds of these refugees had been resettled, primarily in the USA, Iran, Sweden, Australia and the Netherlands. This

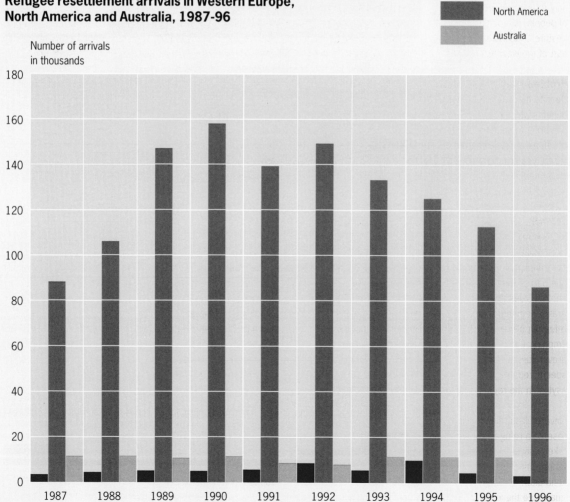

Fig. 2.9

Refugee resettlement arrivals in Western Europe, North America and Australia, 1987-96

Western Europe
North America
Australia

Number of arrivals in thousands

international effort is now drawing to a close as most of the refugees have been resettled.

Fourth and finally, there is a growing consensus that resettlement represents an important means of sharing responsibility for the global refugee problem. While the vast majority of refugees continue to be hosted in some of the world's poorest countries, the offer of resettlement opportunities, if only to a very limited number of people, is a positive gesture of solidarity on the part of the wealthier nations.

Problems and challenges
Despite the very obvious benefits which resettlement can bring to selected groups of refugees, it has tended in recent years to be viewed by governments, UNHCR and some other humanitarian organizations as the least desirable solution to a refugee problem. As has been pointed out elsewhere, the transfer of refugees from one part of the world to another goes against the grain of contemporary refugee policies, which emphasize concepts such as prevention, containment, speedy repatriation, and asylum in the region of origin.

Nevertheless, the decision to resettle a refugee is normally taken only in the absence of other options and when there is no alternative way to guarantee the legal or

physical security of the person concerned. In the light of this observation, the common description of resettlement as a 'last resort' should not be interpreted to mean that there is a hierarchy of solutions and that resettlement is the least valuable or needed among them. For many refugees, resettlement is, in fact, the best (or perhaps only) alternative.

It is certainly the case that some people seek refugee status, and that some refugees move from one country to another, in order to seek a resettlement opportunity. But this unwanted side-effect should not obscure the important role which resettlement has played, and continues to play, in protecting refugees whose human rights are at risk in their country of asylum.

Given the traumatic nature of the refugee experience, resettled refugees in particular can be expected to require extra assistance as they face the challenges of life in a new country. Government bodies and voluntary agencies in countries of final destination often go to great lengths to provide counselling and practical support to those refugees who are granted a resettlement opportunity.

The future
While UNHCR is sensitive to domestic considerations

linked especially to budgetary constraints, unemployment and the politics of immigration policy, it is becoming more difficult for the organization to find resettlement places for some of the most vulnerable refugees. This is largely because resettlement countries are placing more emphasis on the potential of a refugee or a group of refugees to adapt and become economically self-sufficient upon resettlement.

As a consequence, there is a risk that the few countries which are still willing to accept the most difficult and urgent resettlement cases will grow more reluctant to do so. Iranian refugees in northern Iraq, for example, have compelling protection problems, but the number of resettlement places available to them falls considerably short of those needed. Some attempts have also been made to resettle refugees within their region of origin, rather than moving them from one part of the world to another. While few low and middle-income states consider themselves in a position to participate in such arrangements, the possibility of broadening the base for resettlement is now being seriously explored.

Finally, as highlighted by the situation of refugees and displaced people in former Yugoslavia, there is now a growing awareness of the

need to adopt a comprehensive approach to refugee problems, providing different solutions to different groups of people, according to their specific needs and circumstances. In this context, resettlement is a vital tool of protection and a valuable solution for those who are unable to go home and who cannot settle in their country of first asylum.

Refugees can resolve their plight in three basic ways: they can return voluntarily to their homeland, settle permanently in the state which has granted them asylum, or they can move on and establish a new life in a third country. In each case, a refugee can be said to have found a lasting solution when he or she is no longer in need of international protection and when he or she has assumed all of the rights and responsibilities of other citizens living in the same state.

During the past decade, the international community's efforts to find solutions to large-scale refugee populations have focused almost entirely on voluntary repatriation - in contrast to earlier periods of history, when large numbers of refugees found a solution to their problems through local integration and resettlement in a third country. This situation seems unlikely to change, given the general reluctance of both affluent and poorer states to consider the permanent settlement of exiled populations, particularly when they involve many thousands of refugees.

The international community's desire to promote the return of refugees has been so strong that both states and humanitarian organizations have started to re-examine the concept of voluntary repatriation. Most crucially, they are asking, should repatriation always take place on a voluntary basis and at a time of the refugee's own choosing? If conditions have improved in their country of origin and if safety in their country of asylum cannot be guaranteed, could refugees not be expected or required to go home?

A number of comments are required in relation to this important but problematic debate on the principles of voluntary repatriation. First, the suggestion that refugees - people with a need for international protection - should be returned to their country of origin against their will is clearly inconsistent with international refugee and human rights law. As UNHCR has affirmed, the principle of voluntariness, "implying an absence of any physical, psychological or material pressure to repatriate... is the cornerstone of international protection with respect to the return of refugees." A refugee, the organization has stated, "cannot be compelled to repatriate."(41)

Second, in the vast majority of situations, the principle of voluntariness presents no obstacle whatsoever to the repatriation of refugee populations. As Chapter Four of this book explains in more detail, refugees are normally very keen to go back to their own country, and often do so well before the time when peace and stability has been completely restored in their homeland. To give just one example, some 2.5 million refugees have returned from Pakistan to Afghanistan since the late 1980s, despite the continuing violence in their homeland and in the absence of significant pressures to leave their country of asylum.

Third, there is a well established mechanism, incorporated in the 1951 UN Refugee Convention, which can be applied to facilitate the repatriation of people who were recognized as refugees but who no longer need international protection. Commonly known as the 'cessation clause', this mechanism is based on the principle that people should enjoy refugee status only for as long as it is absolutely necessary, and that such status can be withdrawn when fundamental and durable changes have taken place in their country of origin. During the past 20 years, UNHCR and states have applied this principle to refugees from 15 different countries where peace has been restored and where democratic systems of government have been established (see Figure 2.10).(42)

Finally, and most controversially, while established principles governing the repatriation of refugees are unambiguous, there is a need to acknowledge the fact that it is sometimes impossible to ensure that those principles are observed in practice. As the UN High Commissioner for Refugees has explained, "UNHCR faces increasing pressures to support repatriation which is neither strictly voluntary nor strictly safe. Either safety in the country of asylum cannot be guaranteed, because of armed conflict or insecurity, or because asylum is being withdrawn by the host government." In these circumstances, the High Commissioner concludes, "although there may be problems at home, returning in such situations may be better than staying."(43) Such has been the case with regard to the repatriation of Rwandese refugees from Zaire, the return of Rohingya refugees from Bangladesh, and the return of Iraqis who fled to the Turkish border in 1991.(44)

Such situations provide an important example of the protection dilemmas which have confronted UNHCR in recent years. When refugees are under inexorable pressure to repatriate, and when the situation in the country of

Nationality of refugees	Date of application
Mozambicans	November 1975
Guinea-Bissau	December 1975
Sao Tomeans	August 1976
Angolans	June 1979
Zimbabweans	January 1981
Argentinians	November 1984
Uruguayans	November 1985
Polish	November 1991
Czechoslovaks	November 1991
Hungarians	November 1991
Chileans	March 1994
Namibians	April 1995
South Africans	April 1995
Malawians	December 1996
Mozambicans	December 1996

Fig. 2.10

Application of the cessation clause, 1975-96

origin has not improved to the extent that the cessation clause can be invoked, what position should the organization adopt?

In the cases mentioned above, UNHCR decided to become involved in the repatriation of the refugees concerned, primarily by transporting them home, by providing them with material assistance and by monitoring their welfare once back in their country of origin. Examining the dilemma which such situations create for UNHCR, the organization's Division of International Protection concludes that if UNHCR declines all involvement, "refugees who have no alternative but to return may suffer even greater hardship. Their protection will not be monitored and their assistance needs will not be attended to." (45)

As the preceding statement suggests, there is a humanitarian rationale for UNHCR's involvement in repatriation programmes which do not fully meet the standards prescribed by international refugee law. When confronted with such situations, however, the organization has a particular obligation to act in a transparent manner. In practice, this means being honest and open about the fact that refugees are returning under duress, making it clear that the organization's exceptional involvement does not signify any weakening of its commitment to established protection principles.

At the same time, there are a number of practical criteria which UNHCR should strive to meet before becoming involved in situations where refugees are under pressure to repatriate. The organization must examine the case of any refugee whose life and liberty might be at risk if they are obliged to return, and ensure that such individuals are provided with continued protection, either in their country of first asylum or in another state. UNHCR must be satisfied that the repatriation will take place in a safe and dignified manner and that adequate arrangements have been put in place for the reception and reintegration of the returnees. The organization must have free and unhindered access to the refugees once they have returned to their country of origin. Finally, UNHCR must try to ensure that refugees who have been repatriated under some kind of duress are subsequently able to leave their own country and seek asylum elsewhere if they find it impossible to remain safely at home.

An alternative solution: local integration

Although voluntary repatriation is clearly the preferred outcome for most refugees, donor states and countries of asylum, other solutions should not be neglected. Indeed, there is now a growing recognition of the need for a more sophisticated approach to refugee problems, helping different groups of refugees to find different solutions to their plight, according to their varying circumstances, needs, opportunities and aspirations.

Local integration was a popular response to large-scale refugee problems from the 1960s to the early 1980s. This was particularly the case in Africa, where millions of dollars were spent in the effort to encourage self-sufficiency amongst refugee populations, in the hope of allowing UNHCR and donor states to withdraw their support from the continent's many refugee camps.

Reviews of these local integration programmes have demonstrated that they were generally not very successful. (46) Refugees often found it difficult to support themselves on the land which had been allocated to them, and rarely benefited from full social, economic and legal integration in the country of asylum. Host governments, according to one African scholar, had little real interest in the integration of refugees, preferring UNHCR and other international actors to provide indefinite support to displaced populations which had settled on their territory. (47)

As a result of the economic, environmental and demographic problems confronting many low-income states, it seems unlikely that there will be a major revival of interest in the solution of local integration. Speaking at the 1996 meeting of the UNHCR Executive Committee, for example, the representative of the Tanzanian government reflected the views of many countries. "One thing should be clear," he said. "The government of the United Republic of Tanzania is not considering granting permanent residence or offering resettlement to refugees. While we will continue to accept genuine asylum seekers, we expect them to return home as soon as conditions in their countries of origin normalize."(48)

Despite the evident constraints, there may nevertheless be situations where it is possible to pursue the solution of local integration. In Mexico, for example, the government has recently agreed to the permanent settlement of up to 30,000 Guatemalan refugees (see Box 2.4). And in Uganda, around 180,000 refugees, primarily from Sudan, have been given land and agricultural inputs, with the aim of facilitating their long-term integration.

Drawing from these different experiences, it is possible to identify the conditions which must be met for local integration to be pursued successfully. First and most evidently, host governments must be in full agreement with and actively supportive of any effort to facilitate the local integration of refugee populations. This condition is, of course, unlikely to be met in the case of large refugee populations which present any kind of political, social or economic threat to the country of asylum.

Second, the population of the refugees' settlement area must also be supportive of the exiles' long-term presence. If there is already a degree of animosity between the two communities, this is unlikely to be possible. Local integration is more likely to prove successful, however, if there are some ethnic, cultural or linguistic affinities between refugees and the resident population.

Third, local integration must be economically viable if it is to be a lasting solution. Sufficient agricultural land must be made available to the refugee

2.4

Local integration in Mexico

Unlike many other regions of the world, where local integration has largely fallen out of favour with host governments, this approach to the resolution of refugee problems has remained a viable option for limited numbers of exiles in Mexico and Central America. This box focuses on recent developments with regard to the local integration of Guatemalans in Mexico.

By the mid-1990s, the majority of Guatemalans, Nicaraguans and Salvadorans who had been forced to flee abroad during the political violence of the 1980s had been able to go back to their home areas. But smaller numbers of Central American refugees living in Belize, Costa Rica and Mexico have been given the opportunity to settle permanently in their respective countries of asylum, thus acquiring full rights to employment, social, educational and legal services, and to eventual citizenship.

The process of local integration in these countries has been aided by two principal factors. First, in each of these cases the refugees have been living in exile for long periods of

time, many of them for over a decade. Most are at least partially self-sufficient and are already well integrated into the society and economy of their host countries.

Second, according to the nationality laws of the region, children have an automatic right to the nationality of their place of birth. Large numbers of refugee children who were born in exile therefore already enjoy full rights to citizenship and residence in their country of asylum. For parents with such children, local integration represents much less of a rupture in family life than a return to their country of origin.

Guatemalans in Mexico

One of the most recent and largest local integration programmes in the region can be found in Mexico, where the government has agreed to grant permanent residence to those Guatemalan refugees who wish to stay and settle in the country. Over 200,000 Guatemalans, the majority of them from indigenous groups, left their own country in the early 1980s, fleeing from a civil war and a counter-insurgency campaign which made it impossible for them to remain on their land. Many fled to Mexico, where some 46,000 were officially registered by the Mexican government.

The refugees initially settled in camps in the state of Chiapas, on the border with Guatemala. Already an area of extreme poverty and political unrest, the refugees in Chiapas had very poor access to land and few employment opportunities. Between 1984 and 1986, therefore, the government refugee agency and UNHCR relocated nearly half of the refugees away from the border, taking them to the states of Quintana Roo and Campeche.

The Mexican government was keen to pursue a policy of self-sufficiency and local integration for these relocated refugees. With support from UNHCR and donor governments, in particular the European Union and Germany, the refugees were provided with land, seeds and tools. Although in some cases the land provided was insufficient and of poor quality, the refugees were able to attain a degree of self-sufficiency with the help of crop diversification and specialized training.

By 1987, UNHCR and the governments of Mexico and Guatemala had signed a tripartite agreement for the official repatriation of the refugees, although by this time some people had already decided to return of their own accord. Large-scale repatriation did not occur, however, until the

refugees formed the Permanent Commissions of the Representatives of Guatemalan Refugees in Mexico and had themselves entered into negotiations with the Guatemalan government. By 1992, the government and the refugees had reached an agreement on the terms and conditions of repatriation, and by the end of 1996 over 22,000 refugees had gone back to Guatemala.

The signing of a peace agreement between the Guatemalan government and the country's rebel movement at the end of 1996 encouraged smaller numbers of refugees to return in early 1997. Nevertheless, by June 1997 some 27,000 Guatemalan refugees remained in Mexico, of whom only 7,000 had indicated a wish to return. In general, those refugees who have returned to Guatemala are the more politicized element of the refugee population: those who were involved in negotiations with the government concerning the conditions of their return, who have maintained strong links with their homeland and who intend to play an active role in the continuing peace process.

The CIREFCA process

The Mexican government first announced its intention to make local integration an option for the Guatemalan refugees in 1984 and reiterated this option throughout the CIREFCA process, a regional initiative to find solutions to the problem of forced displacement, which ran from 1989 until 1994. Intervening events, however, such as the peasant uprising in Chiapas, meant that the government was unable to pursue this policy in a systematic manner until 1996. Initially, the emphasis of the government's local integration programme was on providing the refugees with land and encouraging self-sufficiency. Most recently, however, the authorities have agreed to provide the refugees with the documents they need to remain in the country indefinitely and to provide them with a secure legal status.

Of the Guatemalan refugees remaining in Mexico, some 20,000 are expected to apply for permanent residency, of whom over half are children who were born in Mexico. By the end of 1996 the government had already provided immigrant visas to up to 4,000 refugees in Quintana Roo and Campeche. Apart from the right to vote, these visas give the Guatemalans the

Map E

Guatemalan refugees in Mexico

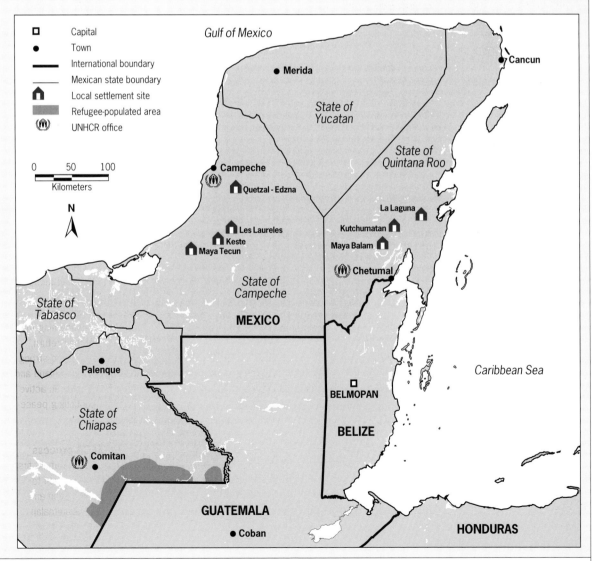

same rights as Mexican citizens and entitle them to apply for permanent residence after five years. Those refugees with Mexican descent or spouses have also been given the opportunity to apply for accelerated naturalization. Some 600 refugees are expected to be naturalized in this way by the end of 1997, and a further 1,800 adults are expected to receive immigrant visas.

So far, the local integration programme has been extended only to refugees in Quintana Roo and Campeche, who are well-established in Mexico and who enjoy a relatively high standard of living. The challenge for 1997, according to the UNHCR office in Mexico city, is to facilitate the integration of refugees in Chiapas, most of whom are still dependent on food assistance. Access to land is a contentious issue in this area, and yet without land it is unlikely that the refugees will ever become fully self-sufficient.

Local integration has been a popular option for the refugees, especially those who were born and brought up in exile, and who acknowledge that life might be more difficult if they were to go back to their nominal homeland. As one Guatemalan youth observed as he watched a group of refugees set off on their journey back home, "I would have to be crazy to go back to Guatemala now: I will wait and see how it goes for the ones who are leaving today. Then I will make up my mind." "We have got to study", he continued, "not like my parents, who have never learned to read and write."

Local integration has also been a desirable option for the Mexican authorities. The remaining Guatemalan refugees are already well integrated and productive, and are generally less politically demanding than those who have returned. They could also make a positive contribution to the local economy. In Campeche and Quintana Roo, for example, refugees constitute only nine per cent of the population, but are responsible for twelve per cent of agricultural production. The Mexican government's support for local integration also represents an important gesture of support for the Guatemalan peace process and the CIREFCA Plan of Action. It is to be hoped that donor states will respond to this gesture by providing the local integration programme with continued financial support.

community, as well as access to markets, employment and income-generating opportunities. Local integration programmes must also assume an appropriate form for each refugee population. Sedentarized agricultural schemes, for example, are unlikely to be suitable for nomadic and pastoralist groups.

Fourth, there must be a guarantee of sufficient external funding if local integration programmes are to succeed, particularly in their initial stages. While donors may not currently be inclined to support local integration programmes, such efforts may actually represent a more cost-effective use of funds than long-term emergency relief or care and maintenance programmes. At the same time, care must be taken to ensure that local integration efforts make use of and develop local skills, expertise and technology, rather than relying on unsustainable external inputs.

Fifth, like repatriation, local integration must be voluntary if it is to be durable. It is unlikely to be suitable for refugees who view their stay in the asylum country as temporary and who are eager to go home.

Finally, for local integration to be a durable solution, refugees must be fully incorporated into their new society, not least by having the opportunity to acquire national citizenship and to exercise all of the rights associated with that status. Once refugees have become fully fledged citizens of their asylum country, then they can genuinely be said to enjoy national protection again.

The opportunity for local integration should not, however, be used as a pretext to limit the right of refugees to return to their homeland - a particular danger in situations where people have become refugees as a result of expulsions on ethnic or communal grounds, and where there is opposition to their return from the authorities in their country of origin. As the UN High Commissioner for Refugees has asked in relation to former Yugoslavia, if there is organized obstruction to the return of refugees to their place of origin, should UNHCR simply give up and settle the people elsewhere? "My answer is no," she has replied, "as that would be tantamount to ratifying ethnic cleansing."(49)

The responsibility of states

The task of protecting refugees is ultimately the responsibility of states and other political actors. Of course, UNHCR and other humanitarian organizations have an important role to play in this area, whether by acting as advocates for the refugee cause, monitoring the situation of exiled populations, providing them with material assistance or ensuring that they are able to repatriate on a voluntary basis. But there is a severe limit to what such organizations can do in situations where refugees are prevented from crossing a border, where they are subjected to armed attacks and where they are expelled from their country of asylum.

Article 35 of the 1951 UN Refugee Convention calls upon states "to cooperate with the Office of the United Nations High Commissioner for Refugees... in the exercise of its functions."(50) If that undertaking were to be more fully respected, then the disturbing decline in refugee protection standards witnessed of late could be halted and reversed, and UNHCR would not be confronted with the acute dilemmas which it has experienced in recent years.

Displaced Afghan women in Kabul © *S. Salgado*

3   Internal conflict and displacement

During the past decade, the concept of 'internally displaced people' has become a familiar feature of the humanitarian vocabulary. Indeed, the recent emergence of a new protection paradigm, focusing less exclusively on the situation of refugees in countries of asylum and more systematically on the plight of vulnerable populations in countries of origin, has pushed this issue to the top of the humanitarian agenda.

Commenting on this trend, the UN High Commissioner for Refugees has observed that "the scale and scope of this problem, the human suffering which underlies it, as well as its impact on international peace and security, have rightly made internal displacement an issue of great international concern."(1)

Despite the world's growing interest in the situation of internally displaced and other war-affected populations, many of the humanitarian issues associated with their plight remain to be resolved. Doubts have been raised with regard to the very concept of 'internally displaced people' and the wisdom of institutionalizing this notion in international law. Although a number of different international organizations have contributed to the welfare of internally displaced populations during the past few years, no single humanitarian agency has been given statutory responsibility for their protection. And, as this chapter explains, while multinational military forces have on a number of occasions been deployed to safeguard the security of citizens who have been displaced within their own state, such initiatives have not been particularly successful.

DEFINING INTERNAL DISPLACEMENT

Although the notion of 'internally displaced people' is now widely used by humanitarian agencies and policymakers, there remains a surprising lack of clarity about its precise meaning. The international community has not yet established a formal and legal definition of the term, and while a number of efforts have been made to fill this conceptual gap, many of the definitions offered have tended to be either too broad or too narrow, and therefore of limited value for either analytical or operational purposes.(2)

In this discussion, the term 'internally displaced people' will be used to denote those persons who, as a result of persecution, armed conflict or violence, have been forced to abandon their homes and leave their usual place of residence, and who remain within the borders of their own country. The complexity of this question is such, however, that a number of issues arising from this definition require some further discussion.

First, it must be emphasized that internally displaced people are to be found in a wide variety of circumstances. In the existing literature on this subject, internal displacement has most frequently been associated with highly visible and destructive armed conflicts such as those in Bosnia, Chechnya, Rwanda and Sri Lanka, where large numbers of people have been forced to flee at short notice and have congregated in specific areas. Such dramatic incidents have also understandably attracted the greatest degree of attention from the international media and humanitarian organizations.

3.1

Development-induced displacement

The World Bank estimates that between 90 and 100 million people around the world have been forcibly displaced over the past decade as a result of large-scale development initiatives such as dam construction, urban development and transportation programmes. An unknown number have also been uprooted by lower-profile forestry, mining, game park and land-use conversion projects. The scale of such displacement seems unlikely to diminish in the future, given the processes of economic development, urbanization and population growth which are taking place in many low and middle-income countries.

There is an inevitable clash of interests in the implementation of large-scale infrastructure projects. Governments, donor states and the international financial institutions tend to regard such projects as an unavoidable and ultimately beneficial part of the development process. Under the legal principle of 'eminent domain', states justify the expropriation of people's property on the grounds that such action is for the economic and political 'greater good' of the nation.

This perspective, however, does not take into account the views of those people most directly and adversely affected by such projects - almost invariably members of the poorest and most marginalized social groups. Indigenous populations, for example, form a large proportion of those affected. In India, which has one of highest rates of development-induced displacement in the world, 40 per cent of the 23 million people affected are tribal peoples.

Consequences of displacement

In a wide-ranging survey of the effects of development-induced relocation, World Bank expert Michael Cernea concluded that such displacement leads to various forms of impoverishment: landlessness, joblessness, homelessness, economic marginalization, increased morbidity, food insecurity, loss of access to common property and social disintegration. The impact of displacement on indigenous populations can be particularly severe in social and psychological terms, as it entails a severance of sacred ties to their land and culture.

The Organization for Economic Cooperation and Development, which brings together the states with the largest development assistance programmes, reaches similar conclusions. "Development projects that displace people involuntarily," it points out, "generally give rise to severe economic, social and environmental problems. Production systems are dismantled, productive assets and income sources are lost, and people are relocated to environments where their social and productive skills may be less applicable, and the competition for resources greater."

The relocation of 13,000 people during the construction of the Panatabangan dam in the Philippines provides one example of the far-reaching repercussions of development-induced displacement. Moved from a town that was due to be inundated as a result of the dam's construction in the early 1970s, local inhabitants were resettled on land that was ill-suited for cultivation. Their efforts to support themselves through agricultural production led to intensive environmental damage and eventually forced people to leave the land. As a result, they were obliged to compete for the few jobs available in the area, adding to the already high level of unemployment.

In order to eke out a living, the unemployed resorted to the illegal cutting of trees for the production and sale of charcoal, adding to the region's environmental

But the more diffuse and protracted situations of internal displacement associated with low-intensity conflicts of the type witnessed in Colombia and Peru, for example, have received far less attention from the international community.

Second, existing studies of internal displacement have also tended to focus on situations in which people flee spontaneously from life-threaten-

difficulties. Twenty years later, none of the displaced people have been able to repay their housing and personal loans; none of the farms which they were allocated are productive; most young people have left the area in search of work; and the landscape is ravaged by deforestation. According to one study, the construction of the dam and relocation of the population proved to be "a devastating medium of impoverishment."

In recent years, there has been a greater awareness of the problems associated with development-induced displacement and a growing recognition of the important human rights issues raised by this phenomenon. Such concern has been stimulated not only by the negative results of many relocation programmes, but also by the resistance which populations have mounted to their forced displacement.

The Kayapo people of Brazilian Amazonia, for example, formed strong alliances with environmental and human rights groups,

persuading the government and World Bank to abandon plans for the implementation of major dam and hydro-electric power projects on the Xingu river. But such protests have not always been so successful. Local and international efforts to prevent the construction of the Narmada dam in India, for example, failed to completely halt the project, while in Norway, the Saami people were unable to stop the construction of the Alta river dam.

Balancing interests

It would be unrealistic to argue for the abandonment of all development and infrastructure projects which require population displacements and resettlement. Safe water, irrigation systems, electricity supplies and transport links all have an important role to play in safeguarding human welfare and promoting sustainable economic growth. But such projects should evidently be designed and implemented in a manner which takes into account the interests of affected populations.

In response to this dilemma, the World Bank, which helps to finance up to ten per cent of all development projects which involve involuntary displacement, has introduced a resettlement policy. Its principles include a commitment to avoid displacement altogether or minimize its consequences when it does take place; to restore the living standards and earning capacities of affected populations and to improve them where possible; to ensure that resettled people share in the benefits of the project which has displaced them; and to promote the participation of affected populations in the resettlement planning process. The World Bank has also stated that it will not finance projects involving large-scale displacement unless the borrowing country adopts this policy and has established an appropriate legal framework for the resettlement process.

Despite this policy, which has been developed over the past 15 years, the World Bank continues to be criticized for its resettlement practice by

human rights organizations and environmental lobbyists. The Bank acknowledges that it has been only partially successful in implementing its own guidelines and recognizes that resettled populations rarely if ever succeed in regaining the standard of living they enjoyed prior to displacement. Examining these issues, one commentator observes that "turning good resettlement policy into good resettlement action is not easy: governments resist, managers equivocate and line agencies are not always willing to back up brave words with hard cash."

Nevertheless, as Michael Cernea has pointed out, the worst consequences of development-induced displacement are to be found in domestically rather than internationally financed projects. "Impoverishment and brutal violations of human rights," he states, "happen most frequently in programmes that are not subject to agreements on policy guidelines and to professional outside review."

ing situations, and to pay less attention to organized population transfers or relocations involving the use of force and other human rights violations.

Displacements of this type have been witnessed in many different parts of the world. In the first two months of 1997, for example, UNHCR recorded the arrival of some 114,000 displaced people in Kabul, all of whom had been ordered out of their homes and herded into the Afghan capital in order to facilitate the Taliban military offensive in the north of the country. In Bosnia, of course, organized population displacements formed a central part of the Serbian effort to create communally homogeneous areas. And in countries such as Burundi, Guatemala and Myanmar, compulsory relocation programmes have been systematically employed as a counterinsurgency technique, designed to prevent rebel and guerrilla movements from associating with - and mobilizing support amongst - the rural population.

It is not always easy, however, to draw a neat distinction between 'spontaneous' and 'organized' population displacements. In the Rift Valley of Kenya, for example, more than 250,000 Kikuyus and Luos were reported to be displaced in late 1993, ostensibly as a result of conflicts over land with the Kalenjin and Maasai people. But many observers believe that the clashes were politically inspired and designed to influence the electoral geography of the area.(3)

Third, unlike the definition of internal displacement offered by some other studies, that which is employed in this chapter generally excludes those situations in which people are obliged to move as a result of environmental disasters, development projects and infrastructural schemes. For although such people often suffer from material and psychological hardship, they may also continue to benefit from the protection of the state, and may even receive some form of compensation from it (see Box 3.1).

Exceptions to this rule, however, are not very difficult to find. During the mid-1980s, for example, the Ethiopian government moved many thousands of people from the northern highlands to the south-west of the country, employing varying degrees of coercion and inducement. Ostensibly introduced to remove people from an area afflicted by chronic problems of drought, famine and land degradation, this organized resettlement programme also served the purpose of depopulating an area inhabited by supporters of an armed opposition movement, the Tigray People's Liberation Front.

Fourth, the efforts of some analysts and advocates to establish internally displaced people as a discrete humanitarian category have to a considerable extent been undermined by the growing complexity of the problem of forced displacement. In some situations of armed conflict, eastern Zaire being the best-known recent example, internally displaced people are to be found living alongside refugees and members of the resident population, all of whom have an identical need for protection and assistance, even if their legal status is different.

Similarly, in countries where conflicts have come to an end, internally displaced people and refugees will typically move back to their homes at the same time, settle in the same communities and encounter the same reintegration problems. Finally, in areas such as former Yugoslavia and the Caucasus, where national boundaries are changing or contested, even the legal distinction between internally displaced people and refugees may be unclear, or interpreted differently by the parties to the conflict.

Fifth, while there is no doubt that a large proportion of the world's internally displaced people live in conditions of great danger, some doubts remain as to whether their needs are any different from those of other citizens who have been deprived of the protection of their state. Displacement is, of course, a very tangible and visible manifestation of human insecurity. But in situations of armed conflict and violence, the needs of displaced and non-displaced communities may be indistinguishable.

Indeed, people who are unable to escape from zones of active conflict - such as those trapped in the Chechen capital of Grozny or the Liberian town of Tubmanburg - are sometimes confronted with greater danger than those who are able to move. As one recent article has observed, around 40 per cent of UNHCR's beneficiaries in Bosnia were at one point people who had not been displaced. The conventional distinction between refugees, internally displaced people and war-affected populations, the authors conclude, "are conceptually vapid in a situation like the former Yugoslavia" (see Figure 3.1). (4)

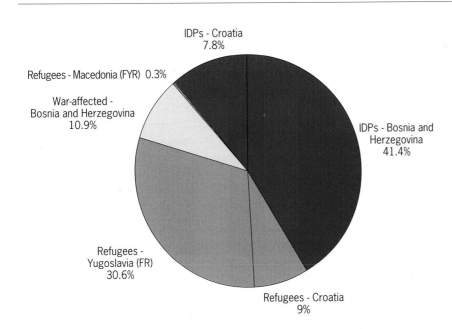

Fig. 3.1

People of concern to UNHCR in former Yugoslavia

IDPs - Croatia 7.8%

Refugees - Macedonia (FYR) 0.3%

War-affected - Bosnia and Herzegovina 10.9%

IDPs - Bosnia and Herzegovina 41.4%

Refugees - Yugoslavia (FR) 30.6%

Refugees - Croatia 9%

Statistics at March 1997

Sixth, despite the large amount of literature produced on the issue of internal displacement, relatively little thought has been given to the question of when a person ceases to be internally displaced. In the case of refugees, of course, this problem does not arise: when a refugee returns voluntarily to his or her homeland and assumes the rights and obligations of other citizens in that country, then that person can no longer be considered as a refugee. In the case of displaced people who have not crossed an international border, the issue is evidently more complex.

In general, there is a strong case to be made for the argument that internally displaced people do not necessarily have to return to their original place of residence in order to find a solution to their plight, as long as they benefit from the protection of the state and are able to enjoy a satisfactory degree of physical, material and legal security in the location where they have settled. In South Africa, for example, the number of internally displaced people is said by some sources to be in the region of four million, although this total includes those who have been uprooted or relocated over a period of 30 years, many of whom are now fully settled and integrated in their place of residence. The concept of internally displaced people - which is problematic enough in any case - clearly loses even more of its value when used in this indiscriminate manner.(5)

These definitional issues are not simply a matter of academic or intellectual interest. As the following sections of this chapter suggest, conceptual clarity is required for a number of different reasons: in order to assist with the collection of accurate statistics and other data on this humanitarian problem; in order to facilitate the establishment of legal standards and instruments for the protection of internally displaced people; and in order to ensure that organizational responsibility for this protective function is appropriately allocated, both at the national and international levels.

The scale and scope of the problem

It has not proven easy to ascertain the number and location of the world's internally displaced people. This is due not only to the definitional difficulties identified above, but is also the result of several institutional, political and operational obstacles. Unlike the collection of refugee statistics, a task undertaken by UNHCR, no single UN agency has assumed responsibility for the collection of figures on internally displaced populations.

The question of internal displacement is also a politically sensitive one. Governments are often unwilling to admit to the presence of such populations on their territory, indicative as they are of the state's failure to protect its citizens. Internally displaced people may themselves be reluctant to report to or register with the local authorities. Indeed, there is evidence to suggest that a large proportion of the world's internally displaced people live not in highly visible camps, but mingled with family members and

friends, often in urban areas where they can enjoy a higher degree of anonymity.

Finally, there are some very obvious obstacles to the collection of data
in areas affected by ongoing armed conflicts. In the combat zones of
Liberia, Somalia and Zaire, for example, the international presence is
minimal or non-existent, making it extremely difficult even to provide
rough estimates of the number of people who have been displaced. Thus
in Sierra Leone, the statistics have been based on food aid beneficiary lists,
and probably reflect only a fraction of the displaced population. In other
situations, such as Chechnya, internally displaced people are highly mobile, again making it very difficult to determine their exact numbers at
any moment in time.

Despite all of these definitional and methodological difficulties, there is a
broad international consensus that the global population of internally displaced people stands somewhere in the region of 25 to 30 million: up to 16
million in Africa, six or seven million in Asia, around five million in Europe
(predominantly former Yugoslavia and the Caucasus region) and up to three
million in the Americas.(6) Some of the most significant situations of internal displacement are presented in the accompanying map (see Map F).

Patterns of displacement

While the plight of the internally displaced has in recent years been the subject of regular discussion by humanitarian and human rights organizations,
surprisingly few field-based studies of this problem have been undertaken. It
is therefore not easy to draw any definitive conclusions about the dynamics of
internal displacement. On the basis of the available evidence, however, it is
possible to provide tentative answers to two specific questions. What are the
typical patterns of movement associated with internally displaced populations? And why do some people become displaced within their own country
while others move across an international border to become refugees in another state?

The dynamics of internal displacement, particularly in its more
'spontaneous' forms, are determined by a wide range of variables: the nature
of the threat affecting people's security; the escape routes available to them
and their proximity to international borders, urban centres and other places
of potential refuge; the financial resources and other assets which they possess; the location of their family, clan and community members; and the
availability of protection and assistance from both national and international organizations.

In the early stages of an armed conflict or situation of social violence, a
form of 'nocturnal displacement' is common, whereby individuals and families who fear an attack leave their homes during the night and return during
the day to farm the land and undertake other economic activities. At the end

Map F

Major situations of internal displacement worldwide

Bosnia and Herzegovina

By the beginning of 1997, close to a half of Bosnia's pre-war population of 4.4 million remained uprooted, around one million of them within the country. Many of the internally displaced, particularly Muslims, have been prevented from returning to their homes by the continuing hostility of other communities and the efforts of political leaders to establish ethnically homogenous territories.

Turkey

Large numbers of villagers have moved into the towns of south-eastern Turkey, where the country's armed forces have been engaged in a protracted conflict with Kurdish rebels. While precise figures are not available, the number of internally displaced people in the country has been estimated at between 500,000 and two million.

Liberia and Sierra Leone

The related armed conflicts in Liberia and Sierra Leone have led to a complex pattern of involuntary migration within and between the two countries. The prospects for Sierra Leone's estimated 800,000 internally displaced people deteriorated sharply in mid-1997, when the country's civilian government was overthrown by armed rebels.

Colombia

The number of internally displaced people in Colombia rose sharply in 1996 and 1997, reaching an estimated 900,000 by the middle of the latter year. This massive population displacement is the result of mounting political violence involving the country's armed forces, unofficial militia groups, rebel guerrillas and Colombia's powerful drug cartels.

Angola

Despite the establishment of a government of national unity early in 1997, up to 1.2 million people were still displaced within Angola at that time, unable to go home because of insecurity, banditry and the presence of land-mines in their home areas. In the central and eastern provinces of the country, war-affected populations continue to depend on international assistance.

Burundi

By the middle of 1997, as many as a million people had moved or been forced into camps in Burundi, where violence continued between the country's two principal ethnic groups. Many of these camps lacked the basic necessities of life and were the target of regular attacks by both government forces and by rebel soldiers.

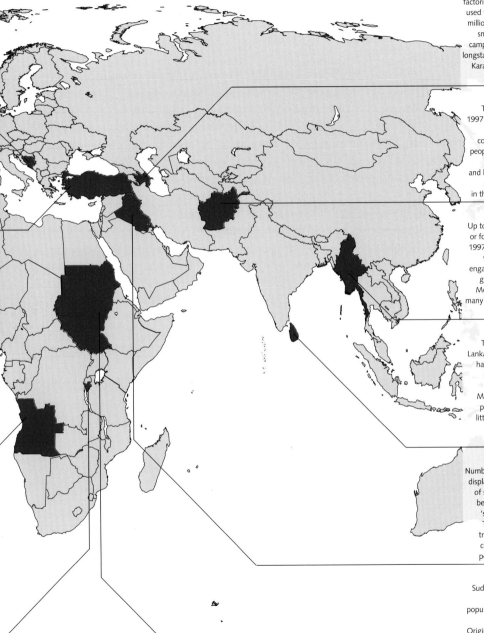

Azerbaijan
In Azerbaijan, schools, hospitals, unused factories and railway coaches have all been used to accommodate the country's half a million internally displaced people. Only a small proportion are accommodated in camps. The displacement is a result of the longstanding armed conflict over Nagorno-Karabakh, a largely Armenian-populated enclave within Azerbaijan.

Afghanistan
Throughout 1996 and the first half of 1997, continued fighting between Taliban forces and other political factions continued to displace large numbers of people within Afghanistan. Many villagers were also forced out of their homes and herded into Kabul. The total number of internally displaced Afghans stood in the region of 1.2 million by mid-1997.

Myanmar
Up to a million people had been displaced or forcibly relocated in Myanmar by early 1997, primarily in the east of the country, where the country's armed forces are engaged in a conflict with ethnic minority groups such as the Karen, Karenni and Mon. To escape the forced relocations, many members of these ethnic groups also crossed the border into Thailand.

Sri Lanka
The longstanding war between the Sri Lankan armed forces and Tamil separatists has created one of the largest and most protracted situations of internal displacement anywhere in the world. Many of Sri Lanka's internally displaced people - up to a million in total - enjoy little freedom of movement, particularly those living in the northern Jaffna peninsula.

Iraq
Numbering a million or more, the internally displaced population of Iraq is the product of several different phenomena: fighting between Kurdish parties in the northern 'safe area'; incursions into that area by Turkish, and to a lesser extent, Iranian troops; and the Baghdad government's continued campaign against the Shi'ite population in the southern marshlands.

Sudan
Sudan is generally acknowledged to have one of the largest internally displaced populations in the world: some four million in total, according to many estimates. Originating from the war-torn south of the country, up to two million of this number are thought to have made their way to Khartoum and other parts of the north. Many have been removed from the city and placed in special camps.

Most of this information is drawn from the *World Refugee Survey* 1997, US Committee for Refugees, Washington DC, 1997.
The countries featured on this map are representative, not exhaustive.

107

of 1996 in the Ugandan town of Gulu, for example, as many as 15,000 people were reported to be sheltering at night in the town's public buildings, fearing the atrocities which had been committed by a rebel group known as the Lord's Resistance Army. A similar pattern of displacement has been observed in countries such as Mozambique, Kenya, Colombia and Peru (see Box 3.2).

As a conflict intensifies, internal displacement is liable to assume a more permanent or semi-permanent form. In many situations, some family members will move away from the danger zones while others stay behind as long as possible or return periodically to plant, tend and harvest their land. In the more economically developed context of Bosnia, it was observed that women, children and the elderly would frequently flee first, leaving the able-bodied men to protect their homes and property. Alternatively, the breadwinners in a family or community may actually move out first, returning to collect other members of the population once they have found a relatively safe location where they can all take refuge.

As indicated earlier, a large proportion of the world's internally displaced people are to be found in cities and squatter settlements, where they are in many cases virtually indistinguishable from other rural-to-urban migrants. Such locations offer a number of advantages to the internally displaced: they are often relatively safe in comparison with the countryside, where most civil wars are fought; they usually offer a variety of different employment and income-generating opportunities, often in the informal sector of the economy; and they may provide better access to public services and relief agency programmes in areas such as health, education and food assistance.

A good example of this tendency is to be found in Liberia, where an estimated 1.3 million people have crowded into the areas protected by ECO-MOG, the West African peacekeeping force. In the neighbouring state of Sierra Leone, up to half a million displaced people made their way to the capital of Freetown at the height of the country's civil war in 1995. Similar scenarios have been witnessed in recent years in the urban centres of many war-torn states throughout Africa: Addis Ababa, Khartoum, Kisangani, Luanda, Maputo and Mogadishu, to give just a few examples.

Becoming an internally displaced person is often a first step in the process of becoming a refugee. With the exception of those who live very close to an international border (and those who have access to vehicles) people who have been forced out of their homes may have to walk for many days, or move in a number of stages, before they are able to seek asylum in another state.

Some displaced people, however, choose or are obliged to remain within their country of origin. In some situations - that of eastern Zaire in 1996-97, for example - the pattern of fighting may force displaced people (and displaced refugees) to move progressively into the interior of their country,

3.2

Internal displacement in Colombia

"Little noticed by the outside world, a humanitarian disaster is under way in north-western Colombia." As this April 1997 headline from *The Economist* indicates, the problems of internal conflict and displacement in that country have reached crisis proportions. In 1996 alone, 180,000 people were forced to flee from their homes, bringing the number of internally displaced people *(desplazados)* to over 900,000, one of the largest populations of its kind in the world. "While international concern and relief efforts focus on refugees in Africa and Asia," *The Economist* continues, "Colombia's *desplazados* receive little attention - not much, indeed, even from their own countrymen."

Internal displacement is not a new phenomena in Colombia. Indeed, the country has experienced several phases of displacement, each of which can be attributed to the same set of chronic problems: the absence of a strong and legitimate state; a deep-rooted culture of political violence and impunity; a highly inequitable distribution of wealth and power; and the consequent marginalization of large segments of society.

Dynamics of displacement

The first phase of displacement took place in the 1950s, when an estimated two million people were displaced from their land and up to 300,000 more were killed as a result of a bloody war between Colombia's two main political parties. This period, known as *La Violencia*, came to an end in the late 1950s, when the two parties established the National Front and agreed to alternate periods in office. By excluding other groups from political power, however, this arrangement led to widespread disaffection and the rise of guerrilla movements. During the 1970s, the state responded to the guerrilla insurgency with increasingly repressive measures. Local paramilitary groups were formed to counter the rebels, often with the support of the drug barons who controlled the trade in heroine and cocaine.

Since 1995, a number of authoritative reports by national and international bodies, including the United Nations and US State Department, have pointed to an intensification of the conflict in Colombia, a change in the dynamics of violence, a serious deterioration in the human rights situation and increased levels of forced displacement. Powerful alliances have been established between the drug cartels, the security forces and paramilitary groups, and in some instances between the drug cartels and the guerrillas. Opposition leaders, lawyers, teachers and peasants have all been selectively eliminated, through a systematic process which some commentators have described as 'social and political cleansing'. As Francis Deng observed in his 1996 report for the United Nations, "displacement is an instrumental part of the government's counter-insurgency strategy and of the guerrillas' increase of territorial control."

The problem of internal displacement is most serious in those parts of Colombia which have the highest levels of guerrilla and paramilitary activity. Increasingly, there is a merging of economic and military interests in these regions. Paramilitary groups forge alliances with wealthy landowners and drug barons in return for protection against guerrilla activities, while landowners and business entrepreneurs profit from the flight of peasant farmers, whose land they are able to purchase at a minimal cost. Such a pattern has been observed in the wealthy banana producing district of Uraba in north-west Colombia, where the convergence of paramilitary groups, guerrilla forces, narcotics and arms traffickers has led to a dramatic increase in the scale of the conflict.

Patterns of displacement

The victims of internal displacement in Colombia are predominantly peasants, many of them from the country's indigenous and black populations. Frequently, they find themselves caught in the cross-fire between guerrilla and counter-insurgency groups and are victimized by both sides. As a journalist has written in the British newspaper *The Guardian*, "left and right rarely meet in direct combat, preferring to settle their scores by tit-for-tat attacks on peasants seen as being associated with the other side."

A general pattern which has been observed throughout Colombia is the tendency for the *desplazados* to flee in small and unobtrusive family groups. According to a recent article in *Le Monde*, "people flee silently, individually and almost shamefully." Generally, the displaced move first to nearby areas, often working away from their homes during the day and returning at night. "Displacement produces a spiral effect," the article continues. "When there is conflict, the people

Map G

Colombia: areas of internal displacement

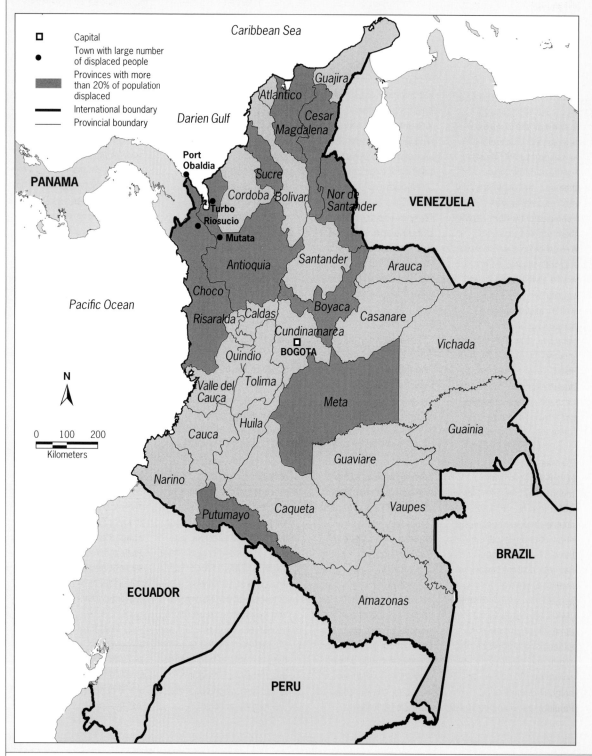

from the hamlets flee towards the villages, then from the villages towards the towns, and finally towards the capital. A certain solidarity forms amongst them: everyone who flees leaves his house open for those who follow."

In some of the worst affected regions, the displaced gather in makeshift camps, waiting for the situation to improve in their villages before they will risk returning home. Eventually, however, most of them flock to the already overcrowded shanty towns of Bogota and other cities, where conditions are both squalid and dangerous. As well as fearing reprisals and harassment from the security services, paramilitary and guerrilla groups, many of the internally displaced lack legal documentation and so are unable to exercise a full range of civic and political rights.

The vast majority of Colombians uprooted in recent years have remained within the country. Many are unable or unwilling to leave, due to the militarization of the border area and the natural obstacles to flight: rivers, mountains and jungles. In the first half of 1997, however, the deteriorating security situation in the border areas prompted a movement of some 2,000 people into the neighbouring state of Panama, as well as unknown

numbers into Ecuador and Venezuela. UNHCR, which had not been given access to the Colombian refugees by the middle of the year, has expressed its concern about their well-being and security. On two occasions - in November 1996 and April 1997 - the Panamanian authorities returned hundreds of refugees to Uraba, prompting UNHCR to criticise this action in public statements.

Responses to displacement

The problem of internal displacement in Colombia remains largely unaddressed at both national and international levels. In recent years, the Colombian government has adopted a series of measures and mechanisms to address the country's human rights problem. These have included the introduction of a new constitution and the establishment of a national ombudsman's office for human rights. Some assistance for internally displaced people is also provided through the national Solidarity and Emergency Fund of the Presidency. Unfortunately, however, many of these national initiatives appear to lack the staff, resources, autonomy and authority required to implement effective human rights policies or to respond to the needs of the internally displaced.

Non-governmental organizations (NGOs) and the Church play an important role in highlighting the plight of the internally displaced in Colombia. In 1995, for example, the Colombian Episcopal Conference completed a year-long project to assess the scale of internal displacement in Colombia. Although NGOs play a vital role in mediating between displaced people and the state, relations between the two are frequently strained. Sometimes treated with suspicion by the authorities and lacking both financial resources and technical expertise, the NGO community has tended to function in a fragmented and poorly coordinated manner.

Despite the presence of many UN and international agencies in Colombia, very few of them are directly involved in assisting the internally displaced. The International Committee of the Red Cross is one of the few. The UN High Commissioner for Human Rights has also established an office in the country.

Until recently UNHCR did not have a field presence in Colombia, and was not directly involved in providing assistance or protection to the victims of internal displacement. The deteriorating situation in the country, however, has led the organization to

reconsider its position, both in Colombia itself and in neighbouring countries of asylum. At the end of May 1997, UNHCR established an 'antenna' in Bogota to monitor developments in Colombia. UNHCR staff have also been present in Panama since the first Colombian asylum seekers started to arrive at the end of 1996. Finally, UNHCR continues to play an active role in various regional initiatives to address the problem of internal displacement, such as the inter-agency Consultative Group on Internally Displaced in the Americas.

According to recent reports, most of Colombia's displaced people would like to leave the camps and shanty towns and to go back to the countryside. But they will not do so until their safety is guaranteed. Until the conflict is brought to a halt, their future seems likely to be grim. As *The Economist* concludes, "traumatized and desensitized by violence, many will take to crime to support themselves, inviting further disapproval from a society, most of which understands little about their plight and cares less."

rather than seeking refuge abroad. In other situations, geographical and topographical considerations may stand in the way of external flight. The majority of the internally displaced in Peru, for example, originate from the central and eastern areas of the country, where they are hemmed in by mountains and situated a long distance from the country's borders.

In a number of recent crises, the departure of displaced populations has been blocked more by political than geographical obstacles. During the war in Bosnia, for example, people were prevented from leaving the country by travel restrictions and check points erected by the local authorities. In Sri Lanka, Tamils living in conflict zones have experienced severe constraints on their movement, imposed by armed rebels, the country's military forces and, at certain times, the Indian navy. A more dramatic case of obstruction occurred in 1991, when half a million fleeing Iraqi Kurds were prevented from seeking refuge in Turkey and were stranded in the mountainous border area.

Finally, internal and external flight options are often determined by simple considerations such as wealth, social connections, age and physical fitness. In Chechnya, for example, many ethnic Russians have remained behind in conflict zones, often because they are too old and weak to travel long distances and lack the social support networks that other members of the population can find in neighbouring republics. According to one expert on the region, the townspeople of Chechnya were more likely to become displaced than the rural population, because the latter were less dependent on services supplied by the state and were able to make use of more sophisticated survival strategies. (7) During the war in former Yugoslavia, it was very evident that wealthier members of the population could flee to Germany and other Western European states, whereas poorer rural families were far more likely to remain internally displaced.

Internal displacement and insecurity

Whatever the cause or pattern of their displacement, a characteristic which unites a large proportion of the world's internally displaced people is the insecurity of their lives. Many commentators have argued that internally displaced people generally find themselves in more difficult and dangerous circumstances than refugees, primarily because they remain under the jurisdiction of the state which is unable or unwilling to protect them. Given the low - and in many parts of the world declining - level of protection available to refugees and asylum seekers, such comparisons are not particularly helpful.

Even so, there is substantial evidence available to demonstrate the acute conditions of physical, material, legal and psychological insecurity experienced by many internally displaced people. At the same time, it remains the case that refugees are generally more likely to come to the attention of the international community and thus to receive some form of protection and humanitarian assistance than internally displaced people.

During 1994-95 in Burundi, for example, considerably greater international resources were allocated to programmes for Rwandese refugees than for internally displaced Burundi citizens, although the latter constituted some 10 per cent of the population. Similarly, during the crisis in eastern Zaire, particularly in its earlier stages, the Rwandese refugees generally received much more attention from the international community than displaced members of the local population.(8)

When people flee from a situation of violence and persecution, those who go into exile may well enjoy better protection than those who remain in their country of origin. As the incumbent UN Secretary-General observed in 1996, "it is inadmissible that those who have managed to cross the border should benefit from the rules of international refugee law, while, at times only several hundred metres away, those who were not able to leave their country remain unprotected."(9)

Such populations are frequently confronted with threats to their security and welfare throughout the process of flight and displacement. Like refugees, they are often obliged to abandon their homes at short notice, leaving their assets behind. The journey out of a combat zone and into a more peaceful area may itself be fraught with danger.

During the past decade, for example, some two million people from southern Sudan are believed to have made their way to central and northern parts of the country in order to escape from the civil war being fought in their home areas. Accounts from the region tell of older children being forcibly separated from their families, conscripted into armed groups and militia forces and even sold into slavery. Travelling on foot or on overcrowded trains with inadequate sanitation and scarce food and water, large numbers of displaced people have not even survived the journey to their intended destination.

Reports from countries which have (or have had) significant populations of internally displaced people - Afghanistan, Angola, Azerbaijan, Georgia, Liberia, Mozambique, Somalia and Sri Lanka, for example - also tell a consistent story of material destitution. Congregated in camps, squatter settlements, church compounds, warehouses or abandoned buildings, internally displaced people often have insufficient food and water and little or no access to the most basic public services. While many people in low-income countries are obliged to live in conditions of acute poverty, surveys have shown that mortality rates amongst displaced communities can be much higher than those of settled populations within the same country.(10)

Internally displaced people can also be exposed to more direct physical threats. In a number of countries, camps and settlements for displaced persons have been the target of attacks by the warring parties - a particular problem in situations where those camps are believed to accommodate military elements. One of the most tragic instances of this type occurred at the

Kibeho camp in Rwanda in April 1995, when thousands of internally displaced people (the exact number has not been established) were killed during a military operation designed to close down the camp and send its residents back to their places of origin.(11) Armed attacks on camps, settlements and so-called 'safe areas' accommodating the internally displaced have also occurred in countries such as Bosnia, Burundi, Chechnya, Lebanon, Liberia, Sudan and Sri Lanka, resulting in thousands of deaths and forcing many other people to flee for a second time.

Some of the world's internally displaced people enjoy little or no freedom of movement. As recent events in former Yugoslavia have demonstrated, intense pressure may be placed on internally displaced populations to return prematurely (and involuntarily) to their places of origin, so as to reclaim those areas for a particular ethnic or social group. Conversely, internally displaced and forcibly relocated populations may be confined to heavily guarded camps or 'strategic villages', a situation characteristic of the Central American wars of the 1980s, as well as the more recent conflicts in countries such as Myanmar and Peru.

The precise purpose of such relocation programmes is not always easy to determine. In early 1997, for example, large numbers of internally displaced people in Burundi, predominantly Hutu, were placed in camps on the instructions of the government. According to the authorities, this was required as a security measure to take them out of areas of armed conflict. Opponents of the government, however, alleged that the camps were being established to intimidate the Hutu population, to deprive a rebel movement of popular support and to establish 'free-fire zones' in the rural areas.(12)

A further factor which often reinforces the vulnerability of the internally displaced is their lack of legal documentation. The retention of some elements of the Soviet *propiska* or residence permit system in the Commonwealth of Independent States, for example, places internally displaced people in a particularly precarious position. Under this system, people who move to a new place of residence without official authorization and documentation can be denied access to public services and may even be detained by the authorities. Lack of legal documentation has also been cited as one of the major problems facing displaced populations in Central and South America, making it difficult for them to vote, register the births of their children, to gain access to public education, health services and the judicial system.

Finally, it should be noted that because they remain in their country of citizenship, internally displaced people do not escape from the kind of discrimination, harassment and rejection that refugees often experience when they settle in another country. Indeed, such antagonism is frequently expressed with equal if not greater force, especially in countries affected by communal conflicts. In Tajikistan, for example, members of the Garmi and Pamiri communities who have moved into the capital city of Dushanbe have experienced considerable discrimination when seeking access to housing and employment.

NATIONAL AND INTERNATIONAL INITIATIVES

In 1986, the Independent Commission on International Humanitarian Issues published one of the first analyses of the problem of internal displacement. "The international community's response to the plight of displaced people has been unsystematic," it observed. "New initiatives to assist the internally displaced are urgently needed."(13) Since those words were written, however, the issue of internal displacement has assumed a far higher international profile, a trend that has been manifested in a number of ways.

During the past decade, the number of international conferences, studies and reports on the issue of internal displacement has increased very significantly, as has the number of organizations with an analytical or advocacy role in relation to this subject.(14) In addition to UNHCR, these include the Brookings Institution, the Lawyers Committee for Human Rights, the Refugee Policy Group and the US Committee for Refugees, as well as international agencies such as the International Organization for Migration, the UN Development Programme and UNICEF. Most recently, the Norwegian Refugee Council has announced its intention to publish a 'global IDP survey' on an annual basis, an initiative which should help to provide a more systematic set of data on this issue.

For the past five years, the UN Secretary-General has retained a representative on internally displaced persons, a post filled by the scholar and former diplomat, Dr Francis Deng. In fulfilment of his mandate to examine the human rights issues raised by this problem, Dr Deng has visited a dozen countries with large populations of displaced people and reported regularly to the UN Human Rights Commission and the General Assembly. In addition, he has been instrumental in completing a study of legal standards pertaining to the internally displaced and has reviewed the current organizational arrangements relating to the protection and material welfare of this group of people.(15)

During the same period, an Inter-Agency Task Force on internally displaced people was established in Geneva, chaired by the UN's Department of Humanitarian Affairs, with the purpose of looking more closely at the issue of organizational responsibility and coordination amongst the international agencies concerned. There has been a lively debate on this issue during the past few years, both within and outside of the UN system, much of it revolving around the question of whether UNHCR or some other agency should assume statutory responsibility for the protection and welfare of internally displaced people. As a number of commentators have pointed out, there is currently a lack of consistency and predictability in the international community's response to this problem (see Box 3.3).(16)

3.3

Organizational responsibility for internally displaced people

According to many commentators, one of the most critical obstacles to the effective protection of internally displaced people, has been the unpredictability and inconsistency of the international response to the problem. Human rights expert Roberta Cohen, for example, suggests that the "selectivity and conditionality" of the response has often resulted in "limited and inconsistent coverage for the internally displaced, leaving large numbers with little or no protection and assistance."

While UNHCR has a statutory responsibility for the welfare of refugees, no single agency has been mandated to protect, assist and find solutions for the internally displaced. There are several reasons for this discrepancy.

The existence of an agency with specific responsibility for refugees is largely a reflection of the international dimensions of the refugee problem and the desire of states to regulate this issue by multilateral means. Internally displaced people, however, remain under the

jurisdiction of their own state. Even if a single agency were to be given a statutory role with regard to the internally displaced, many governments with significant populations of internally displaced people would undoubtedly resist its interference in their domestic affairs and reject its presence on their territory.

Although the refugee concept has been defined in international law, there is still no consensus about the notion of internally displaced persons - a term which is currently used to describe a very disparate and ill-defined group of people. While such conceptual confusion continues, it would be difficult for a single international agency to accept responsibility for them. According to some analysts, it would also be discriminatory for an agency to focus on the situation of the internally displaced to the exclusion of other people whose security and human rights are also at risk within their own country.

A single agency?

In the past there have been numerous calls for a single international agency to take responsibility for the internally displaced. But there is now a general consensus that such a proposition is unrealistic. In his presentation to the 1997 UN Commission on Human Rights, Francis Deng, who

was previously a proponent of a single agency, conceded that "the problem of internal displacement exceeds the capacities of any single organization." Furthermore, it is unlikely, in the current international climate, that states would accept the creation of a new UN agency with sole responsibility for internally displaced populations.

Most commentators agree that in the absence of a single organization with responsibility for this issue, effective collaboration and coordination are required to ensure that the needs of the internally displaced are met. The Inter-Agency Standing Committee, which brings together relief and development agencies within and outside of the UN system, has played an important role in this respect.

The most common inter-agency approach to situations of internal displacement is known as the 'lead agency model', whereby one organization is assigned responsibility for coordinating humanitarian action within a complex emergency, including activities on behalf of the internally displaced. This approach has been implemented in several recent emergencies. Operation Lifeline Sudan, for example, an initiative designed to assist internally displaced and war-affected

populations throughout the country, is an example of this arrangement. In the north of Sudan the UN Development Programme is responsible for coordinating the programme, whereas in the south of the country UNICEF plays the leading role.

In former Yugoslavia, UNHCR was designated as the lead agency, while in Cambodia, the World Food Programme has played this role in relation to internally displaced people. In Rwanda, however, the UN's Department of Humanitarian Affairs, through the UN Rwanda Emergency Office, has been responsible for coordinating an inter-agency response to the problem of internal displacement.

Despite these efforts, the international response to the problem of internal displacement continues to be unpredictable and deficient in certain aspects. While there is no doubt that the agencies cited above have the capacity and expertise to coordinate the delivery of humanitarian assistance, none except UNHCR has the protection mandate or experience required to safeguard the security of internally displaced people. Furthermore, such agencies are often hesitant about engaging in activities which might bring them into conflict with the national authorities, thereby jeopardizing their ability to implement other humanitarian or development programmes in the same country.

The two agencies which have been most consistently and visibly involved in situations of internal displacement and which can most effectively address the protection needs of internally displaced populations are the International Committee of the Red Cross (ICRC) and UNHCR. Both organizations have a long-established and internationally recognized protection mandate. And both agencies are familiar with the task of combining their protection function with the implementation of large-scale assistance programmes.

Since its formation in 1863, the ICRC has been providing protection and assistance to non-combatants affected by war and internal conflict, many of whom are internally displaced people. The ICRC, however, extends its services to all civilian victims of conflict, whether they have been obliged to move or not, rather than treating internally displaced people as a special category. Similarly, the ICRC does not work on the basis of a specific protection regime for internally displaced people. Instead, it oversees the implementation of the 1949 Geneva Conventions and their two Additional Protocols, which

provide protection for all civilians (including internally displaced people) in the context of international and non-international armed conflict.

As a result of its strict neutrality and unique status as the guardian of international humanitarian law, the ICRC has often found it possible to work on both sides of a conflict and to gain access to populations which are beyond the reach of other agencies. In Chechnya, for example, the ICRC was one of the few agencies permitted to work with displaced and war-affected populations within the republic itself, whereas UNHCR and other UN agencies were only allowed to work with displaced people in the neighbouring republics of Ingushetia, Daghestan and North Ossetia.

The role of UNHCR

While UNHCR has worked with internally displaced people for at least 25 years, its involvement with this group of beneficiaries has been sporadic in nature. Only in the 1990s has the organization been more regularly asked to extend its services to the internally displaced, a development which is symptomatic of the growing international interest in the prevention of cross-border population movements and the protection of forcibly

displaced populations within their country of origin.

As a recent UNHCR document has stated, "to the extent that refugee flows and internal displacement have the same causes, it makes little sense to deal only with the trans-frontier aspects of coerced population movements, either in responding to immediate humanitarian needs or in seeking solutions." The document continues by stating that "from the vantage point of UNHCR, as the international agency responsible for refugees, it is clearly preferable, where possible, to obviate the need for people to leave their country - and thus to become refugees - in order to find safety and to obtain vital humanitarian assistance."

In 1993, UNHCR established a set of guidelines to clarify the conditions under which the organization would undertake activities on behalf of the internally displaced. First, the guidelines observe that UNHCR is most likely to take primary responsibility for the internally displaced when such people are present in or going back to the same areas as returning refugees - a situation witnessed recently in countries such as Guatemala and Mozambique. Second, as exemplified in locations such as eastern Zaire and northern Afghanistan, UNHCR

may work with the internally displaced if they are living alongside a refugee population and have a similar need for protection and assistance.

Third, as in Bosnia, UNHCR may extend its services to the internally displaced in situations where the same factors have given rise to both internal and external population movements, and where there are good reasons for addressing those problems by means of a single humanitarian operation. Fourth and finally, UNHCR may become involved in situations of internal displacement where there is a potential for cross-border movement and where the provision of protection and assistance to the internally displaced may enable them to remain in safety in their own country. UNHCR's activities on behalf of displaced people within Sri Lanka fall into this final category.

Within the context of these guidelines, UNHCR has also established a number of more specific criteria which must be met if the organization is to become involved with an internally displaced population. These include: a specific request from the UN Secretary-General or the General Assembly; the consent of the state concerned and other relevant parties; the availability of funds, as well as adequate institutional capacity and expertise. In addition, the guidelines point out that any activities on behalf of the internally displaced should be compatible with organization's protection function, that they should not undermine the right of people to seek asylum in another state, and that UNHCR must enjoy unhindered access to the people concerned.

Lack of predictability

Despite the introduction of these guidelines, UNHCR's activities on behalf of internally displaced people have attracted a degree of criticism. On one hand, some commentators have suggested that the organization's criteria allow it to pick and choose the situations of internal displacement in which it wants to become involved, thereby perpetuating the lack of predictability in the international response. In eastern Zaire, for example, several non-governmental organizations have suggested that UNHCR was

too slow to extend its services to local Zaireans who had been displaced by the fighting at the end of 1996. Some observers have also questioned UNHCR's reluctance to become involved in assisting the internally displaced in Colombia and Peru, although the Secretary-General has now designated UNDP as lead agency in the latter state.

On the other hand, it has been suggested that by working with displaced populations in their own country, UNHCR encourages neighbouring and nearby states to close their borders to potential refugees, thereby undermining the institution of asylum. Such comments have been made in relation to the organization's operation in Bosnia, where UNHCR initially believed that its presence might mitigate the level of human rights abuse and thereby enable people to remain in their homes.

A number of states subsequently used the

organization's presence in the conflict zone as a pretext for the closure of their borders to Bosnian asylum seekers.

Furthermore, some commentators have argued that UNHCR's activities with internally displaced people in countries which are also hosting large numbers of refugees may undermine the protection of the latter group. If UNHCR advocates strongly on behalf of the internally displaced, it has been suggested, then the state's willingness to cooperate with the organization on refugee-related matters may be weakened. Others observers suggest that there is no contradiction between the organization's two protection functions. Ultimately, they suggest, both entail the promotion of the same human rights principles.

The question of organizational responsibility for internally displaced people clearly remains a prominent issue on the international humanitarian agenda. As the problem of

internal displacement increases, the need for UNHCR and other agencies to clarify and strengthen their role in this area becomes more urgent and important. Indeed, the impending reform and consolidation of humanitarian capacities within the United Nations provides the international community with an excellent opportunity to enhance its response to the plight of internally displaced people.

At the same time, however, it is important to recognize the limitations of multilateral action in situations of internal conflict and displacement, and ultimately to ensure that the principle of state responsibility is respected. As the UN High Commissioner for Refugees has observed, "UNHCR and other international organizations can play a supportive role, but they cannot substitute for governments in the protection of their own citizens."

Recent years have also seen a growing tendency amongst humanitarian or-ganizations to identify internal displacement as a distinct - if not an entirely discreet - problem in their public awareness efforts, fund-raising appeals and operational activities. A recent statement by the International Committee of the Red Cross (ICRC), for example, indicated that "over 80 per cent of the ICRC's budget is allocated to protection and assistance activities for civilians, in particular internally displaced persons."(17) Similarly, the UN High

Commissioner for Refugees has observed that "the similarity of the plight of the internally displaced to that of refugees has increasingly led UNHCR to extend its expertise to instances of internal displacement."(18) These instances are listed in Figure 3.2.

It would be inaccurate to suggest, however, that UNHCR's operational involvement with the issue of internal displacement is a particularly new phenomenon. A recent publication on this issue cites 15 cases between 1961 and 1991 in which the organization was involved with the internally displaced, most frequently in situations where they were living in or moving to the same areas as returning refugees.(19) These included, for example, the cases of Bangladesh (1971-72), southern Sudan (1972), Uganda (1979), Zimbabwe (1980) and Chad (1981). In addition, UNHCR has assisted the internally dis-

Fig. 3.2
UNHCR's involvement with internally displaced people by country

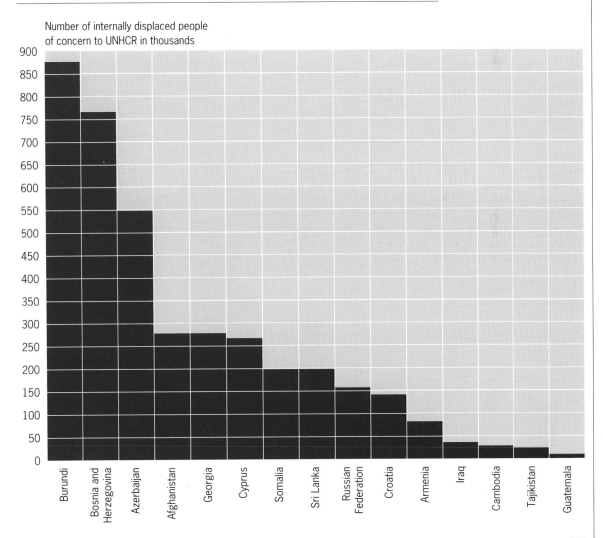

Number of internally displaced people of concern to UNHCR in thousands

placed in special programmes, unrelated to ongoing refugee or returnee assistance activities, such as that mounted in Cyprus after the division of the island in 1974.

What we are witnessing, therefore, is not the emergence of an entirely new problem, but rather a growth in the scale and geographical scope of the issue, coupled with a new awareness of its strategic and humanitarian significance (see Figure 3.3). With the recent upsurge in communal conflicts, the growing concern of states to avert or obstruct mass refugee outflows from such situations, and (until quite recently at least) the increased willingness of some influential states to intervene in areas of crisis and conflict, the issue of internal displacement has found a newly prominent place on the international humanitarian agenda.

Fig. 3.3

Number of countries with internally displaced populations, 1970-96

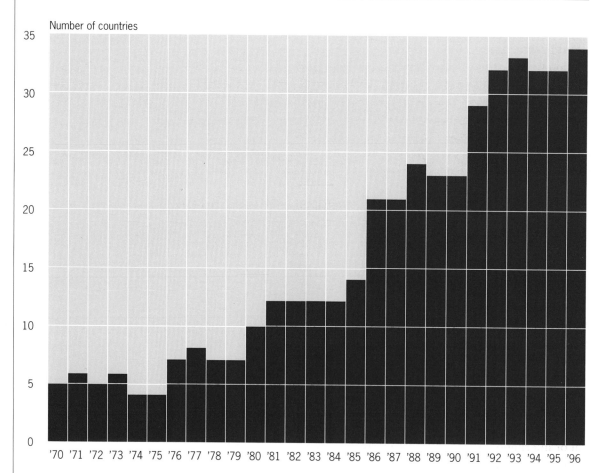

Number of countries

Source: S. Schmeidl, *International Forced Migration: Exploring a Refugee Early Warning Model*, Praeger, Westport, forthcoming

National protection capacities

During the past few years, UNHCR and other humanitarian organizations have placed increasing emphasis on the notion of state responsibility - a principle which stipulates that governments and other actors in countries of origin have a primary duty to act in a way that is conducive to the prevention and resolution of refugee problems. The same principle is of equal if not greater relevance to the problem of internal displacement, in the sense that internally displaced people remain under the jurisdiction of their own state, even if they do not benefit from its effective protection.

Some commentators have even suggested that an over-eagerness to promote international involvement in situations of internal displacement could have the unintended consequence of diluting the notion of state responsibility.(20) The restoration and strengthening of national protection capacities is thus an essential first step in the effort to safeguard the security of internally displaced people and to resolve the problem of internal displacement.

Recent discussions concerning the role of international organizations in relation to the internally displaced have tended to downplay the capacity of such populations to survive and safeguard their own welfare, even in the most difficult circumstances and in the absence of external assistance. In a number of war-torn states, many of the internally displaced and other war-affected populations have been obliged to rely on their own coping mechanisms, given the high level of disorder and the consequent absence of international organizations. But the precise nature of these mechanisms varies considerably from place to place.

In Somalia, for example, the clan-based militias and warlords have often been portrayed as the primary cause of the state's collapse and the consequent suffering experienced by the country's population. While there may be considerable truth in such observations, it must also be acknowledged that the clans provide their members with a degree of safety which they would not otherwise enjoy. Indeed, large numbers of people in Somalia have moved into the strongholds of their own clan for precisely this reason. As this example suggests, in many situations of internal conflict and displacement, state protection is replaced by armed self-defence.

Even so, recent experience has demonstrated that the institutions of civil society also have an important role to play in safeguarding the security of displaced people. The growth of self-help organisations in Liberia, for example, has been described as "one of the more positive phenomena to have emerged through the Liberian war."(21) Elsewhere, in the absence of official or international assistance, local religious, human rights and women's groups have taken the lead in mobilizing support for the internally displaced.

Viewpoint II

Preventing communal conflict
by David Hamburg

Human societies have a pervasive tendency to make distinctions between 'in-groups' and 'out-groups' in ways that justify violence. Whether they are established on the basis of religion, race, language, region, tribe or nation, such groups tend to foster deeply felt beliefs about their own superiority. At the same time, and as witnessed most graphically in the case of countries such as Rwanda and former Yugoslavia, such groups frequently feel that their survival is jeopardized by the presence of other social entities in the same territory and that their continued existence can only be guaranteed by the use of force.

The sense of belonging to a valued group is a fundamental part of our historical heritage. But there is no need to assume that this very natural sense of belonging must always be expressed in ways which are hateful and lethal towards others. On the contrary, it is reasonable to assume that the different social groups which are to be found within every state can learn to live peacefully together, resolving their differences by non-violent means.

What, then, can the international community do to help prevent communal conflict? As the recent example of Ethiopia and Eritrea suggests, secession or the partition of an existing country can sometimes provide an answer to this problem by enabling a social group with a highly developed sense of collective identity to establish its own nation state.

However, the situations in which this solution can be pursued are rare, and are in any case normally the product of armed struggles involving substantial loss of life. There is consequently a need to create the conditions under which different ethnic, religious and other groups can interact positively and harmoniously with each other. And for such mutual accommodation to be possible, a genuinely free civil society is required. There will always be a potential for deadly conflict in states where there is no equality of citizenship and where certain social groups are politically, economically and culturally marginalized. As UNHCR has learned through painful experience, states with such characteristics also tend to be the most seriously affected by massive refugee flows and other forms of population displacement.

The best safeguard against such events is the establishment of democratic institutions and capable governments. The international community must therefore find ways of contributing to the development of such indigenous capacities. This objective can be achieved in a variety of different ways - by assisting, for example, in the organization of free and fair elections and by supporting the establishment of written constitutions, independent judiciaries and impartial security services.

At the same time, and as already demonstrated in the countries of Eastern and Central Europe, the world's more affluent societies have an important role to play in fostering the growth of voluntary associations, non-governmental organizations, human rights institutions and independent mass media in

---

As one of the most important social institutions in South America, the church has played a leading role in publicizing the plight of the internally displaced. In Colombia, for example, the Episcopal Conference recently completed a major project to document the number of internally displaced people throughout the country. According to Francis Deng's report on the situation in Peru, "church organizations were among the first to provide the displaced with emergency assistance and to encourage them to organize."(22)

Sometimes local NGOs take great risks in providing assistance and advocating on behalf of the internally displaced, and by virtue of association themselves become targets of abuses and attacks by both government and rebel

countries which are emerging from long periods of authoritarian government.

The best approach to the prevention of deadly conflict is thus one that emphasizes local solutions to local problems, supported as necessary and where possible by external assistance. While such assistance will in many cases be provided by governments and international organizations, it should not only come from such sources. Many elements in the private sector also have an important contribution to make to the prevention of armed conflict: universities and educational institutions; churches and other religious bodies; scientists, journalists and the business community, to give just a few examples.

The United Nations and its specialized agencies have a special role to play in the tasks of conflict resolution,

democratization and institution-building. UNHCR, for example, which provides a unique window on the world's disasters, has in recent years attempted to develop a more proactive approach to the problem of forced displacement. As well as responding to emergencies, the organization has become increasingly involved in the task of averting communal conflict.

In the former Soviet states of Central Asia, for example, UNHCR has established educational initiatives and cultural programmes, with the intention of promoting tolerance, understanding and positive interactions amongst different social groups. In countries where civil wars have come to an end and where refugees have been able to go back to their homes - Cambodia, Mozambique and Nicaragua, for example - UNHCR and its operational partners have

also become increasingly involved in the establishment of local rehabilitation and reconstruction projects which encourage former enemies to work together and to develop common interests. In this way, it is hoped, the peacebuilding process can be reinforced and a recurrence of violence averted.

Many of these issues are currently being studied by the Carnegie Commission on Preventing Deadly Conflict, which was formed in 1994 with a membership of international leaders and scholars with long experience in the areas of conflict prevention, management and resolution. The Commission is based on a belief that a body of knowledge which is based on systematic research and which is put into action by trained and experienced practitioners could help to prevent mass violence, just as medical knowledge and public health

practice has helped to eliminate diseases that previously caused terrible epidemics.

Prevention is best thought of not only as avoiding undesirable situations and circumstances, but also as creating preferred alternatives. In the long run, we can be most successful in preventing communal conflict by both averting direct confrontations between hostile groups and by promoting democracy, economic reform, good governance and high human rights standards in fragmented states and divided societies.

A medical doctor and research psychiatrist, David Hamburg is co-chairman of the Carnegie Commission on Preventing Deadly Conflict and was formerly President of the Carnegie Corporation of New York.

parties. Members of the active women's organizations established in Chechnya, for example, have taken great personal risks in documenting human rights abuses and forwarding this information to Moscow-based and international human rights organizations.

It would be wrong to suggest that governments currently play no role in protecting, assisting or finding solutions to the problems of internally displaced people. Situations of internal displacement sometimes arise because the state is unable - rather than unwilling - to protect its citizens. In certain countries, moreover, national and local government structures have helped to strengthen the security and safeguard the welfare of the internally displaced.

Francis Deng suggests that "strengthening the capacities of governments to deal with the problem of internal displacement could prove an important step towards finding solutions in certain cases."(23) In dealing with the diverse situations of internal displacement, he observes, it is important to understand the problem in its national context and to see what can be done by both the government and the international community to remedy the situation. "If, during crises of internal displacement, governments are unable to discharge their responsibilities to provide their citizens with adequate protection... they are expected to invite, or at least accept, international cooperation to supplement their own efforts."(24)

Unfortunately, of course, governments and rebel groups are not always ready 'to invite, or at least accept' international involvement on behalf of the internally displaced. Indeed, in situations of armed conflict or ethnic persecution, and in wars where population displacements are an objective of the combatants or a military strategy employed by them, the potential for national protection may be very limited.

In the worst cases, governments and rebel forces may deny the existence of internally displaced populations or obstruct the work of relief organizations, thereby placing the people concerned beyond the reach of the international community. Referring to this problem in a recent statement to the UN Commission on Human Rights, Francis Deng reported that hitherto, his work had focused on countries that were receptive to his fact-finding mission. "I believe," he continued, "that we have passed this selective phase of the challenge; the role of the international community in providing protection and assistance to the internally displaced is no longer debatable."(25)

In an attempt to address this increasingly important item on the humanitarian agenda, considerable thought has recently been given to the legal, operational and even military action required to safeguard the security of internally displaced and war-affected populations. These issues are considered in the remaining sections of this chapter.

The development of legal standards

Several analysts have pointed out that the development of an international legal framework for the protection of internally displaced people is needed to establish standards of treatment that governments and other actors can be encouraged to observe.(26) There are, however, three principal schools of thought on this matter: those who argue that the best approach lies in the development and dissemination of existing international human rights and humanitarian law; those who claim that there is a need for new legal instruments or standards, akin to international refugee law but specifically focused on the protection of internally displaced people; and those who call for a more radical and comprehensive legal framework, covering all forms of forced displacement.

As the recognized guardian of international humanitarian law (sometimes known as 'the laws of war') the ICRC is perhaps the most influential representative of the first school of thought. In a review of this issue, the ICRC emphasizes that the Geneva Conventions and their Additional Protocols already make provision for the protection of the internally displaced during periods of armed conflict. "As internally displaced persons are in principle civilians, they are protected before, during and after their displacement by all the rules that protect civilians in an armed conflict situation."(27) According to an ICRC staff member, "even in times of war, civilians should be able to lead as normal a life as possible. In particular, they should be able to remain in their homes; this is a basic objective of international humanitarian law." (28)

The preceding observation is quite easily illustrated by reference to Protocol II of the Geneva Convention, which deals with 'the protection of victims of non-international armed conflicts', and which includes the following provisions:

- Article 4, which states that "all persons who do not take a direct part or who have ceased to take part in hostilities... are entitled to respect for their person, honour and convictions and religious practices. They shall in all circumstances be treated humanely, without any adverse distinction..."

- Article 13, which states that "the civilian population and individual civilians shall enjoy general protection against the dangers arising from military operations," and that "acts or threats of violence, the primary purpose of which is to spread terror amongst the civilian population, are prohibited."

- Article 14, which states that "starvation of civilians as a method of combat is prohibited. It is therefore prohibited to attack, destroy, remove or render useless, for that purpose, objects indispensable to the survival of the civilian population, such as foodstuffs, agricultural areas... crops, livestock, drinking water installations and supplies..."

- Article 17, which states that "the displacement of the civilian population shall not be ordered for reasons related to the conflict..." "Civilians," it continues, "shall not be compelled to leave their own territory for reasons connected with the conflict."

According to the ICRC, there is a danger that the introduction of new legal standards for internally displaced people will weaken or narrow the scope of these and other norms. By concentrating on the treatment of people once they have been uprooted, such standards might also divert attention from the need to avert displacements in the first place. "The suffering experienced by displaced persons must not undermine faith in the rules whose violation has prompted the displacements." In conclusion, the

ICRC emphasizes that "efforts should focus on improving respect for international humanitarian law, rather than on the establishment of new rules for the specific category - moreover very difficult to define - of displaced persons."(29)

Adopting guiding principles

In an attempt to ascertain the value of existing international human rights, humanitarian and refugee law in relation to the internally displaced, the Secretary-General's representative on the issue, Dr Francis Deng, has completed a detailed study of this question. Undertaken over a three-year period by a team of legal experts and institutions, the study was completed in 1996.(30)

In brief, Dr Deng's review concluded that the current international legal provisions do not cover all situations of internal displacement and often fall short of providing adequate protection to the affected populations. Most notably, it points out, while international humanitarian law is applicable in situations of armed conflict it does not apply in the context of internal tensions and disturbances, nor in situations of social and communal violence.

At the same time, Dr Deng identifies a number of other areas in which existing international law seems inadequate. These include, for example, the provision of personal documentation to internally displaced people; the issue of compensation for property which has been lost during displacement; the right of displaced people to receive humanitarian assistance; and the absence of guarantees ensuring the right of internally displaced people to return to their usual place of residence and to be protected against forcible return to situations of danger.

Three other weaknesses in the existing framework of legal protection must also be pointed out. First, given its primary concern to regulate the behaviour of states and government institutions, international law is limited in its application to actors such as rebel groups or warlords. Second, it is sadly the case that some states have not ratified the key human rights treaties, nor the Geneva Conventions and their Protocols. Third, many provisions of international human rights law can in any case be suspended when a national emergency has been declared - precisely the circumstances which generate the largest movements of internally displaced people.

On the basis of these and other considerations, Francis Deng concludes that initiatives are required to fill the gaps in the existing legal framework and to address more directly the particular protection needs of the internally displaced. Along with other analysts, he suggests that such an initiative should take the form of an international declaration, statement of principle or code of conduct, consolidating new and existing standards in a single document.(31)

As well as specifying protection standards during the period of displacement, the document would underscore the right of people not to be arbitrarily uprooted and would thereby have a preventive impact. At the same time, it would establish principles and guarantees relating to the return of displaced people to their areas of origin, and thus deal with the post-displacement phase. Such principles would be directed to governments and rebel forces alike and would be non-derogable in all circumstances.

Alternative legal approaches

While states and other actors digest and consider Dr Deng's proposals, the debate concerning the legal protection of internally displaced people shows no sign of diminishing. According to some commentators, the international community's current interest in the plight of the internally displaced is a manifestation of its declining commitment to the institution of asylum and the established principles of refugee protection. If new standards of treatment for the internally displaced are established, states will argue that uprooted populations can find adequate protection in their country of origin, and can legitimately be prevented from crossing an international border.

Analysts have also argued that it may be misguided to institutionalize the category of 'internally displaced person' and to develop a legal framework on the basis of that category. First, internally displaced people might actually suffer as a result of becoming more visible and being given a status which is different from other citizens. As suggested earlier, large numbers of internally displaced people are reluctant to present themselves to their national authorities and move to areas where they can retain a degree of anonymity.

Second, there is a sense in which the effort to establish a dedicated legal framework for internally displaced people might obstruct the development of a holistic approach to the issue of forced displacement in all its complexity and different manifestations. What is needed, some commentators suggest, is a comprehensive set of norms, standards and rules, which apply to all situations of displacement and which would be of particular relevance to complex emergencies, where refugees, returnees, the internally displaced and the local population frequently find themselves together in the same location.(32)

Amongst other things, an instrument of this type would prohibit all forms of forced displacement and reaffirm the right of threatened populations to seek asylum abroad. It would elaborate protection principles for both internally and externally displaced populations, including their right to protection and assistance and their right to return in safety to their usual places of residence. Such an approach, it has been suggested, would place the protection of forcibly displaced people in the broader context of prevention and solutions - a strategy which has been strongly supported by UNHCR in recent years.(33)

Whatever their precise content, legal frameworks and international instruments cannot by themselves protect forcibly displaced populations. First, such frameworks and instruments must be widely disseminated, so their provisions are known to all those individuals and institutions whose policies, decisions and actions have a bearing on this issue. Second, those individuals and institutions must act in accordance with these instruments - objectives that require an intensive process of education, training and public information.

Third, international laws and standards (like domestic laws and standards) must be supported by deterrents. Institutions and individuals who are responsible for the human rights violations which provoke forced population displacements must know that they cannot act with impunity. It is for this reason that UNHCR and many other humanitarian organizations have welcomed the recent establishment of international tribunals for individuals suspected of war crimes and crimes against humanity in Rwanda and former Yugoslavia.

THE MEANING AND MODES OF PROTECTION

What exactly does 'protection' mean in situations of internal displacement? In the context of refugees, there is a clearly established framework of international protection which includes core elements such as the principle of non-refoulement, the right of refugees to enjoy physical and legal security in their country of asylum, as well as their right to return to their homeland in conditions of safety and dignity. Ultimately, the framework of refugee protection exists to safeguard the well-being of people who are outside of their own country and who are unable to avail themselves of the protection which a state should provide to its citizens.

The situation is more complex in the case of the internally displaced, by virtue of the fact that such people remain under the jurisdiction of the state, despite its evident unwillingness or inability to guarantee the security of its citizens. The protection of internally displaced people and other victims of violence within their own country thus raises in a very direct manner the question of state sovereignty. To what extent can humanitarian organizations substitute for an absence of national protection, even if the government and other actors involved consent to their presence? And if such consent is not forthcoming, do the United Nations and other multilateral actors have the right - or the capacity - to intervene in an assertive or coercive manner?

There is now a growing recognition that the international community has in some senses attempted to avoid these difficult issues by concentrating excessively on the provision of emergency assistance to internally displaced and war-affected populations, while giving inadequate attention to their physical security. As one scholar has concluded, "humanitarian aid is often conceived of as a matter of delivering humanitarian supplies: food, shelter and medicine. What easily gets neglected is the central importance of protection."(34)

Recognizing the inadequacy - and even the immorality - of policies which favour emergency assistance at the expense of human rights protection, there is now a growing awareness of the need for a more balanced approach to this issue. "Humanitarian action", the UN High Commissioner for Refugees has affirmed, "is not only about the delivery of relief but first and foremost about ensuring the basic human rights, security and protection of the victims on all sides of a conflict."(35)

In its contribution to the debate, the ICRC also stresses the complementarity of these activities and the need to adopt a holistic notion of security, incorporating its physical and material dimensions. "The distinction between activities qualified as assistance and those considered as protection is often an artificial one," the ICRC observes. "To deliver relief supplies and make certain that they reach the people they are intended for is also a form of protection."(36)

UNHCR's experience has demonstrated that with a strong and well organized field presence, humanitarian organizations can play a valuable role in the protection of displaced and threatened populations. Thus an internal review of UNHCR's operations in former Yugoslavia concluded that "UNHCR's involvement kept innumerable displaced and war-affected people alive, and in some instances averted population displacements by preventing - or at least moderating - the abuses committed by the warring parties. By sharing information with the media and other members of the international community, UNHCR also alerted the world to the process of ethnic cleansing and focused global attention on other atrocities."

Another internal review of a less well-known operation, in the Central Asian republic of Tajikistan, made some similar observations. "When serious incidents have been reported to UNHCR, staff have taken prompt and frequently successful action to address abuses. UNHCR's role in protecting returnees and internally displaced persons has undeniably helped to avert large-scale movements to the cities as well as the forced relocation of the internally displaced back to their region of origin." Emphasizing the question of presence, the evaluation states that "some of the operation's success must be attributed to the quick establishment of a highly mobile and field-oriented operation."

UNHCR and the ICRC are not, of course, the only organizations to undertake such activities. One of the most significant recent developments in this area is to be seen in the deployment of UN human rights monitors and field officers, under the auspices of the High Commissioner for Human Rights and other components of the UN system. The impact and effectiveness of such efforts, however, remain to be fully assessed.

There is an emerging consensus that MINUGUA, the UN's human rights verification mission in Guatemala, represents one of the more successful initiatives of this type, due to a combination of factors: the positive evolution of the country's peace process and consent of the parties concerned; the strong support given to MINUGUA by other states in the region and the international community as a whole; the strength of the mission's field presence, which involved more than 200 international personnel, spread throughout the country; and the mission's involvement not only in human rights verification, but also in the process of strengthening national structures such as the judicial system and the institutions of civil society.(37)

By way of contrast, the UN's human rights mission in Rwanda has been obliged to function in a much more difficult and dangerous operational environment, with the result that its achievements have, most observers would agree, been far more modest. Epitomizing the serious problems confronting this mission, five members of the human rights team were murdered in the area of Cyangugu in February 1997, an incident which obliged the UN to withdraw its staff members from a large part of the country.

Humanitarian access

In countries where the structures of state have collapsed and armed conflict is taking place, the protection of internally displaced people and other civilians is an enormously difficult undertaking. The parties to the conflict may well prevent humanitarian organizations from establishing a presence in conflict zones. As in Bosnia, where starvation was used as a weapon of war, access may be obstructed in order to prevent the delivery of humanitarian relief. As in eastern Zaire, access may be denied as a means of preventing humanitarian organizations from carrying out protection and monitoring activities in areas where deadly human rights violations are occurring. If such organizations are allowed to operate, it may only be so that the supplies they bring with them can be plundered, employed to support the war effort or used to mobilize the support of the civilian population. In many recent conflicts, of course, even the distinction between combatants and civilians has proved difficult to make, given the extent to which whole societies have become mobilized for war.

In these circumstances, humanitarian action is likely to be dependent on some form of negotiated access with the warring parties. It may also involve the establishment of an agreed code of conduct or declaration of principles, so as to minimize the risk of political manipulation, to protect the security of humanitarian personnel and to preserve the ethos of impartiality which guides their work.

International efforts to gain access to displaced and vulnerable populations have in practice assumed a variety of different forms: the establishment of 'humanitarian corridors' or 'corridors of tranquillity', enabling the delivery of relief to war-affected areas; the creation of 'open relief centres' where the local population can take refuge when they are threatened by fighting; and the negotiation of temporary cease-fires with the warring parties, enabling humanitarian organizations to provide emergency assistance or to undertake immunization campaigns. Perhaps the most concerted effort to apply such techniques to a situation of internal displacement is to be found in the activities of Operation Lifeline, a United Nations initiative in Sudan (see Box 3.4).

Despite negotiations and agreements, however, humanitarian agencies often find it extremely difficult to reach and assist - let alone to protect - populations which have been displaced by armed conflict. The work of humanitarian organizations in Chechnya, for example, has been obstructed by all parties to the conflict, while UNHCR has been authorized to work only with displaced people in neighbouring parts of the Russian Federation.

In Liberia, humanitarian organizations have been constantly obliged to suspend their operations, due to the intensity of the conflict and the regularity with which their offices, vehicles and relief supplies have been plundered by the combatants. In both Bosnia and Somalia, constant negotiations, political pressure, and even some trade-offs were required to ease the passage of humanitarian assistance through the network of roadblocks established by the parties to those conflicts.

Commenting on such circumstances, the UN High Commissioner for Refugees has openly acknowledged the limitations of humanitarian action undertaken by civilian organizations and has raised the issue of whether more assertive forms of action and intervention are required. "The threat of force, and the will to use it, becomes indispensable where consensual arrangements have no chance of success." "Enforcement," she continues, "is a critical issue. It may complicate the arduous efforts of conflict mediators. It may undermine neutrality and engender risks for impartial humanitarian action. But are strict neutrality and effective protection not often incompatible? Humanitarian responses should serve first of all the protection of people."(38)

MILITARY INVOLVEMENT AND THE SAFE AREA CONCEPT

Since the beginning of the 1990s, the international community (normally but not exclusively in the form of the UN Security Council) has on a number of occasions deployed multinational military forces in armed conflicts, with the objective of protecting or assisting displaced and war-affected populations within their country of origin. In an effort to meet these objectives, two basic strategies have emerged. First, such forces have been used to pro-

3.4

Operation Lifeline Sudan

Operation Lifeline Sudan (OLS) was launched by the United Nations in 1989 to bring assistance to internally displaced and other populations affected by the civil war in Sudan. The operation is based on the principle of neutrality. At its inception, OLS was unique in its efforts to assist civilian populations on both sides of the conflict, regardless of their location and on the basis of need, by negotiating access with the warring parties. Recent reviews of the programme suggest, however, that the principles upon which OLS was based are facing some major challenges.

Sudan has been in an almost continuous state of civil war for the past 40 years. Ostensibly a struggle for power between the Islamic, 'Arab' north and the Christian and pagan south of the country, the conflict is also rooted in the unequal distribution of power and resources during the colonial period. Despite numerous peace agreements and cease-fires between the government and opposition movements in the south, the conflict remains unresolved. Indeed, it has worsened in recent years, not least

because of the division of the Sudan People's Liberation Army (SPLA), the rebel army, into four different factions. Each of these factions has its own leader and controls different parts of the south, thereby increasing the levels of strife and insecurity in the area.

Untold destruction

The civil war has taken a heavy toll on the country's civilian population. Millions of people have been displaced, both within and outside Sudan. Thousands of lives have been lost, and there has been untold destruction of the country's infrastructural and agricultural resources. Supported by a consortium of international aid agencies and donors, Operation Lifeline Sudan was established under UN auspices to meet the needs of civilians affected by the war.

Although the operation was originally intended to bring humanitarian assistance, mainly in the form of food aid, to displaced and war-affected populations throughout Sudan, the programme was split into a northern and southern sector soon after it started in 1989. The northern sector is coordinated from Khartoum by the UN Development Programme (UNDP), in cooperation with the Sudanese government. Assistance in the south is provided mainly in opposition-controlled areas, coordinated

by UNICEF from a base in northern Kenya. The World Food Programme and other international and non-governmental agencies are responsible for implementing the programme in both sectors.

The principle of negotiating access to war-affected and displaced civilians on both sides of the conflict, with the consent of all the warring parties, is one of the main characteristics of OLS. Most commentators agree that the programme in the south has generally been successful in this respect. At the beginning of the programme, aid agencies negotiated temporary cease-fire agreements between the warring parties so that 'corridors of tranquillity' could be established and used to channel assistance to people in need. Later, however, when this system proved too rigid for the volatile nature of the conflict, a more flexible 'open corridors' approach was developed, entailing continuing dialogue with the warring parties.

Finally, in response to deteriorating security problems in the south and the death of four aid workers, the agencies drew up some minimum standards of conduct, known as 'ground rules', with the rebel factions. As well as requesting the opposition movements to adhere to the humanitarian principles of neutrality and

free access, the agencies also required a commitment to the international standards found in instruments such as the UN Convention on the Rights of the Child and the Geneva Conventions. The ground rules have become an effective mechanism to monitor the conduct of the opposition movements and to exert pressure on them when violations against civilians occur.

Access to war-affected populations in the south has also been achieved as a result of the elaborate security and evacuation system coordinated by UNICEF. This system, which provides for the rapid removal of agency staff from emergency situations, has enabled relief organizations to establish operations in areas which might otherwise have been considered too dangerous. The evacuation system is also symptomatic of the effective working relationship which has been established between OLS and the rebel movements.

At least two million of the people displaced in southern Sudan are thought to have made their way to the north of the country, some 800,000 of whom are to be found in greater Khartoum alone. The government has responded to this huge problem through compulsory relocation and resettlement schemes, intended to stem the movement of the displaced people to the country's urban centers.

In contrast to the south, the northern sector of OLS has remained largely under the influence of the government, which has placed serious restrictions on the areas in which OLS can function and on the choice of implementing partners for the operation. Furthermore, as the coordinating agency for OLS in the north, UNDP faces a conflict of interests between its on-going development work, which it undertakes in association with the government, and its responsibility for war-affected and displaced populations. A recent evaluation of OLS concludes that these difficulties have compromised the operation's ability to respect one of its stated principles, namely to deliver relief "to all needy populations regardless of their locations." "The continuing crisis among war-displaced populations in greater Khartoum", argues the review, "represents the greatest failure of OLS in the northern sector."

Crisis of legitimacy
Operation Lifeline Sudan is thus facing a crisis of

Map H

Operation Lifeline Sudan: logistical network

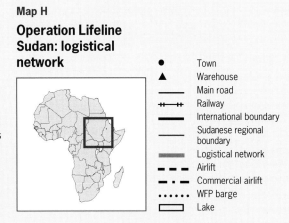

●	Town
▲	Warehouse
——	Main road
+—+—+	Railway
▬▬	International boundary
——	Sudanese regional boundary
▬▬	Logistical network
- - -	Airlift
-·-·-	Commercial airlift
······	WFP barge
▭	Lake

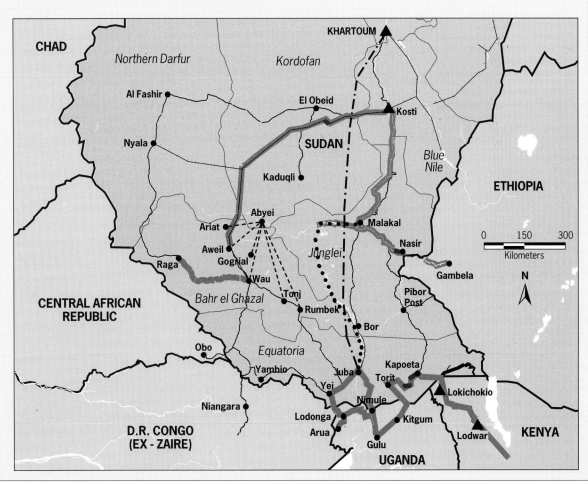

133

legitimacy. The government has become increasingly concerned about the autonomy of the programme in the south, and has attempted to exert its control on that sector through bans on internal flights and regulations concerning the activities of NGOs. On several occasions it has even called for the closure of the operation. At the same time, factional fighting amongst the southern movements has resulted in a serious deterioration in the security situation in the area, further restricting humanitarian access to the civilian population.

In the north, on the other hand, assistance has been limited to the distribution of food aid. Minimal attention has been paid to protecting the human rights and security of war-affected and displaced populations. According to some critics, the United Nations and OLS have sacrificed the principle of neutrality in the north so as to facilitate its access to war-affected populations in the south. As the recent evaluation concludes, "the equivocal autonomy of the southern sector has been purchased at the expense of war-affected populations in the north."

In the light of such findings, some commentators have questioned the future viability of OLS. Should the operation continue, they ask, if it is unable to respect the very principles of free access and neutrality on which it was established? According to Larry Minear of the Humanitarianism and War Project, the operation has become "a prisoner of the conflict itself." "Providing assistance under conditions which seriously compromise its integrity," he continues, "represents a mockery of humanitarian action."

tect humanitarian activities and to facilitate the delivery of emergency assistance - an approach adopted in Somalia from 1992-94, throughout the war in former Yugoslavia and in eastern Zaire during the 1994 Rwandese refugee crisis.(39)

Second, multinational forces have been used to implement what has become known as the 'safe area', 'safety zone' or 'safe haven' strategy. In general terms, this entails the use of such forces to insulate and protect a given geographical area from a surrounding situation of armed conflict and violence, thereby safeguarding the security of people who are living in or returning to that zone. (40)

The concept of specially protected areas for civilians in times of armed conflict is actually a long-established one. Under international humanitarian law, combatants are prohibited from attacking areas which have been reserved for the care of civilians and soldiers in need of medical attention. The Geneva Conventions also contain some little-known provisions whereby the parties to a conflict can formally agree to the establishment of 'non-defended localities', 'safety zones' or 'hospital zones', that is to say, neutral and demilitarized areas where civilian populations can find safety, security and assistance.

While a number of different 'safe areas' have been established since the beginning of the 1990s, it is important to note that none of these initiatives complies with the principles of consensuality and demilitarization which underpin the arrangements provided for in the Geneva Conventions:

- In 1991, a US-led coalition of states established a safe area in northern Iraq, with the intention of providing protection and assistance to more than 1.5

million people, the majority of them Kurds, who had been attacked by the country's armed forces and who had fled towards Iran and Turkey.

- In 1993, the UN Security Council declared six government-held enclaves in Bosnia to be safe areas, under the protection of the United Nations and the NATO alliance, so as to safeguard their inhabitants from attack and to ensure that they received the humanitarian assistance which they needed to survive.

- In 1994, a 'humanitarian protection zone' was established in south-west Rwanda, in the context of a French-led military intervention known as Operation Turquoise. Authorizing this initiative, the Security Council approved "the establishment of a temporary operation under national command and control, aimed at contributing, in an impartial way, to the security and protection of displaced persons, refugees and civilians at risk."(41)

In principle, of course, there is a great deal to be said for a strategy which is intended to provide internally displaced and other war-affected populations with a greater degree of security, and which enables uprooted populations to return to their homes. In practice, however, the consequences of establishing the safe areas described above have been mixed.

Safe areas: an assessment

In northern Iraq, the allied military intervention obliged the Iraqi army to halt its attacks on the Kurdish population and enabled UNHCR and other humanitarian organizations to establish a large-scale emergency assistance, repatriation and reintegration programme. As a result, a large proportion of the people who had been displaced by the military offensive were able to go back to their homes, a process which also averted the creation of a large and potentially long-term refugee problem in the neighbouring states.

During the past five years, however, the non-consensual way in which the safe haven was established and the absence of any recognized authority in the area has had several adverse consequences. Residents have had to contend with a stringent economic blockade imposed by the Baghdad government, which has itself been subjected to sanctions by the Security Council. Living conditions in the area, now a 'no-fly zone' patrolled by allied aircraft, have consequently been very difficult for the population .

In some parts of northern Iraq, people have been caught in the crossfire between rival Kurdish militias. In March 1995, some 35,000 Turkish troops moved into the area to conduct an offensive against Kurdish guerrillas, an operation which obliged the western powers to suspend their protective air flights over the safe haven. As a result of this military intervention, humanitarian activities in the safe haven also had to be temporarily halted, thousands of Iraqi citizens were displaced from their homes, and UNHCR was obliged to relocate more than 2,500 Kurdish refugees living in the area. Since that time, the area has been the target of further interventions by Turkey, as well as Iranian and Iraqi government forces.

The record of the safe area initiative in Bosnia, most commentators agree, was far from satisfactory. Commenting on this initiative, the UN Secretary-General observed that "when the consent and cooperation of the parties has been forthcoming... the presence of UN observers and patrols has enabled the monitoring of cease-fires, stabilized surrounding confrontation lines and improved security by resolving localized disputes or outbreaks of fighting."(42)

In practice, however, this 'consent and cooperation' rarely existed. The six safe areas were under constant siege and intermittent bombardment by the Bosnian Serbs, jeopardizing the safety and the dignity of the residents. As the former chief of UNHCR's Bosnia operation wrote in 1994, "surrounded by enemy forces, without basic shelter, medical assistance or infrastructure, isolated and living under sporadic shelling or sniper fire, these areas are becoming more and more like detention centres, administered by the UN and assisted by UNHCR."(43)

As the Secretary-General acknowledged, the safe areas in Bosnia were not only dangerous, but were also drawn into the logic of the war. "What is happening now," he observed in May 1995, "is that certain safe areas are used by the two parties to the conflict to sustain their confrontation."(44) Established without the consent of the Bosnian Serbs, and used as military bases by the Bosnian government forces, the safe areas actually provoked attacks on the residents and relief personnel they were intended to protect. Eventually, two of the safe areas - Srebrenica and Zepa - fell to the Bosnian Serb forces, an event which led to the death, disappearance and dispersal of many thousands of people.

Reporting to the United Nations on the outcome of Operation Turquoise, the French government suggested that the creation of a 'humanitarian protection zone' in south-west Rwanda had four principal achievements to its credit: halting the massacres which were taking place in the area; providing protection to the population there; allowing humanitarian activities to be launched; and assisting in the collection of information about human rights abuses. Other commentators have suggested that the outflow of refugees from this part of the country to the neighbouring state of Zaire was also reduced as a result of the military operation.(45)

The French NGO Médecins sans Frontières (MSF), however, has been less positive in its assessment, arguing that Operation Turquoise was "too little and too late." The genocide, MSF suggests, was halted not by the military intervention, but by the advance of the Rwanda Patriotic Front, which was soon to form the country's new government. While acknowledging that

Operation Turquoise "saved a few thousand lives and helped stabilize population movements within Rwanda," the French agency argues that the security zone established in south-west Rwanda "also gave shelter to the militias and perpetrators of the massacres."(46) When Operation Turquoise came to an end, moreover, those people who had been able to remain in the country as a result of the international presence ultimately chose to flee. Despite these criticisms, and whatever the motivation of the operation, the French intervention was the only real response to the UN Secretary-General's repeated calls for international action in Rwanda.

Humanitarian action and military intervention

In addition to the specific issues raised by the safe area initiatives in Iraq, Bosnia and Rwanda, a number of more general observations can be made with regard to this strategy.

First, although phrases such as safe area, safe haven and security zone are now regularly used by governments, international organizations and academic analysts, they have hitherto been employed in a very loose manner. Little effort has been made to define these concepts or to identify the criteria and standards which should be met when safe areas are established. As former UN Secretary-General Boutros Boutros-Ghali commented in relation to the Security Council's resolutions on Bosnia and Herzegovina, "the problem with safe areas is first of all that we have not received a definition of what is meant by a safe area." (47)

Second, without clear criteria and standards, the safe area concept is liable to be used in a misleading way, as a declaration of intent rather than an accurate statement of fact. For, as indicated above, the inescapable truth is that the so-called safe areas established in recent years have not been safe at all for many of the people living in them. Moreover, while ostensibly designed to strengthen the security of civilian populations, local military forces have continued to operate in each of the safe areas established during the past few years.

A third issue associated with the safe area strategy is the threat which it can pose to the principle of asylum and the right of freedom of movement. The creation of the safe haven in northern Iraq was a direct result of Turkey's unwillingness to admit the fleeing Kurds, a decision which had left thousands of people stranded - and dying - in the mountainous border area. In former Yugoslavia, the freedom of people to leave the safe areas was constrained both by the Bosnian Serb siege and by the Bosnian government's reluctance to allow the departure of the population in areas remaining under its control. At a more general level, it is quite evident that the international community's interest in the safe area concept has to a considerable extent been prompted by the growing reluctance of states to admit large numbers of refugees.

Fourth and finally, there is an evident need for safe areas to be established on the basis of an unambiguous mandate. Ideally, such areas should conform to the strict principles enshrined in the Geneva Conventions: civilian and demilitarized areas, established with the full consent of all the parties concerned. While this model of the safe area has rarely been implemented in recent years, a somewhat similar approach has been seen in Sri Lanka, where UNHCR has been instrumental in the establishment of 'open relief centres'. These are temporary sanctuaries where internally displaced people can obtain emergency assistance in a relatively safe environment, pending a stabilization of the situation in their usual area of residence.(48)

Given the brutal nature of many of the world's most recent internal and communal conflicts, the conditions required for the establishment of 'Geneva Convention safe areas' seem unlikely to be fulfilled. The level of animosity between the warring parties, their determination to gain control over people and territory and their disrespect for international humanitarian law may mean that consensual arrangements are simply not feasible. Safe areas of a non-consensual nature may therefore be required if civilian populations are to be protected.

If they are to be effective, then it is essential for such areas to be supported by the credible threat or use of force against external attack. As recent experience in Bosnia, Somalia and the Great Lakes region of Africa suggests, how-

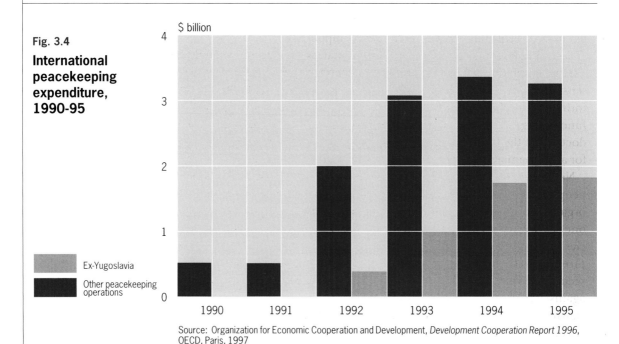

Fig. 3.4

International peacekeeping expenditure, 1990-95

Ex-Yugoslavia

Other peacekeeping operations

Source: Organization for Economic Cooperation and Development, *Development Cooperation Report 1996*, OECD, Paris, 1997

ever, the political will needed for this condition to be fulfilled may not always be forthcoming, especially if it requires states to commit their ground forces in an ongoing armed conflict. Indeed, there is now a growing consensus that the kind of 'humanitarian intervention' witnessed in the first half of the 1990s is unlikely to be repeated in the second half of the decade (see Figure 3.4).(49)

At the same time, it has become evident that safe areas must form part of a comprehensive political strategy, designed to bring a conflict to an end and to ensure that the state in which the safe area has been established is ultimately able to assume responsibility for the protection of its own citizens. As one scholar has observed, this is another reason why the safe area concept is highly unlikely to be implemented on a regular basis. "Safe areas produce a *de facto* secession," he argues, "which may be one of the strongest political obstacles to their employment."(50) Thus in northern Iraq, for example, while the allied coalition certainly wished to protect the Kurds and to exert pressure on the Baghdad government, it did not want to challenge the principle of Iraqi sovereignty. Indeed, the Security Council resolution which paved the way for the creation of a safe area in northern Iraq explicitly reaffirmed the UN's commitment to the territorial integrity of the country.

Almost inevitably, on those rare occasions when non-consensual safe areas are established, then humanitarian agencies will be invited and encouraged to work alongside the military, in order to provide assistance to the protected population. Indeed, a recent Canadian proposal envisaged the establishment of a 'United Nations rapid reaction force', incorporating military, humanitarian, civil affairs and human rights components.

According to some commentators, humanitarian organizations should resist the temptation to become involved in coercive operations and non-consensual safe areas, on the grounds that "enforcement is itself incompatible with the neutrality of humanitarian activities and is likely to undermine their functioning."(51) While this argument is supported by the long-established doctrine of the ICRC, it is perhaps not possible (or in some cases desirable) for all humanitarian organizations to adopt this position.

Neutrality may be undesirable if it obstructs the effective protection of people whose lives are at risk. It may also be impossible for a humanitarian organization such as UNHCR, given its membership of the UN system. As one scholar has stated, "it is undeniably difficult for the UN, and for agencies within the UN system, to maintain impartiality when the system is by nature involved in a wide range of political decision-making, and when its security responsibilities may lead it to advocate enforcement measures against a particular party." "With respect to many conflicts," he concludes, "fairness in exercising judgement... may be a better guide to policy than impartiality."(52)

In the context of efforts to safeguard the security of internally displaced and war-affected populations, the judgment exercised by humanitarian organizations should be derived from a number of basic principles.

First, while recognizing that geopolitical considerations will inevitably influence the decision to establish - or not to establish - a safe area, humanitarian organizations must be satisfied that such an initiative has a primarily protective purpose. Second, protective efforts should not violate the right of people to leave a situation of danger and to seek sanctuary elsewhere, whether in another country or another part of their own state. Third, the right of internally displaced people to return to their previous or usual place of residence should be upheld, while recognizing that it may not always be possible to realize this right in situations where the borders of a state and its ethnic composition have been changed in the course of a conflict.

Finally, internally displaced people should not be pressurized to go back to any area against their will. It is not acceptable for displaced people to be returned to locations which are still affected by armed conflict or violence. Furthermore, if future population displacements are to be averted, then the premature return of people to areas where their security cannot be assured is clearly inadvisable.

Replanting the land in Ixcan region, Guatemala.   *UNHCR/B. Press*

4   **Return and reintegration**

Since the beginning of the 1990s, armed conflicts have come to a formal end in several different parts of the world, bringing a new degree of security to the populations concerned and enabling large numbers of displaced people to return voluntarily to their homes. At the same time, growing numbers of refugees have been obliged to go back to their country of origin, either as a result of pressures exerted by the host government or as a consequence of deteriorating conditions in the areas where they have settled.

The circumstances confronting such returnees are often fraught with difficulty. Countries which have experienced armed conflict and communal violence are frequently characterized by deep social divisions, chronic political instability, widespread physical devastation and high levels of psychological trauma. As a result, they are precariously perched between the hope for continued peace and the danger of a return to war.

There is a symbiotic relationship between the return and reintegration of displaced people and the peace-building process. Unless uprooted populations can go back to their homes and enjoy a reasonable degree of security in their own community, the transition from war to peace may in some situations be delayed or even reversed.

As this chapter explains, however, the return and reintegration of displaced people can only be sustained if a variety of other tasks are carried out: the establishment of a representative government, the restoration of basic education and health services, the demobilization of soldiers and the revitalization of the national economy, to give just a few examples. One of the most important items on the humanitarian agenda is to ensure that these activities are undertaken in an effective and coordinated manner, thereby averting the threat of renewed violence and forced population displacements.

PATTERNS OF RETURN

Large numbers of people have been forced to abandon their homes and seek safety elsewhere in recent years. But large numbers of displaced people have also been able to go back to their own country and community. At the beginning of 1996, the UN High Commissioner for Refugees announced that no fewer than nine million refugees had gone home during the preceding five-year period - a substantial increase over the figure recorded for the years 1985-1990, when around 1.2 million refugees repatriated.

The growth in the scale of repatriation since the beginning of the 1990s has been due in large part to the resolution of several longstanding regional

Map I
Major returnee populations worldwide

Bosnia and Herzegovina
Almost half of Bosnia's 4.4 million citizens were uprooted during the 1992-95 war. Many refugees and displaced people are now making their way back to their homes, some voluntarily and others because their countries of asylum have insisted that they repatriate. Reintegration seems certain to be a long and difficult process, given the country's continuing political tensions and economic problems.

Eritrea
The repatriation of Eritrean refugees has been disappointingly slow since the country gained its independence six years ago - largely as a result of the country's economic devastation and disagreements about the level of international support required to return and reintegrate those refugees who remain in Sudan. Even so, up to 200,000 Eritreans were believed to have repatriated by the beginning of 1997.

Guatemala
The Guatemalan peace process has enabled well over 20,000 refugees to repatriate from Mexico since the early 1990s. Those who have returned, however, continue to experience many difficulties, not least of which is access to land. According to some estimates, around 65 per cent of the country's land is owned by little more than two per cent of the population.

Chile
During the 1970s and early 1980s, thousands of Chilean citizens fled to other parts of the world to escape from human rights violations and the country's authoritarian system of government. Since the return to democracy at the end of the 1980s, many of these exiles - a large proportion of whom were educated and professional people - have made their way back to their homeland.

Angola
UNHCR has drawn up several plans for the return and reintegration of Angolan refugees, the largest numbers of whom are to be found in Zaire, Zambia and Congo Brazzaville. Unfortunately, the continued instability of the country and a shortage of funds has prevented these plans from being implemented. Even so, around 60,000 refugees are estimated to have returned independently to Angola in 1996.

Rwanda
Rwanda has witnessed a succession of massive repatriation movements in recent years: the return of some 700,000 long-time refugees, primarily from Uganda, following the victory of the Rwandese Patriotic Front in 1994; the repatriation of more than 700,000 refugees from conflict zones in eastern Zaire in 1996; and the return of an additional 600,000 refugees from Tanzania in 1996-97.

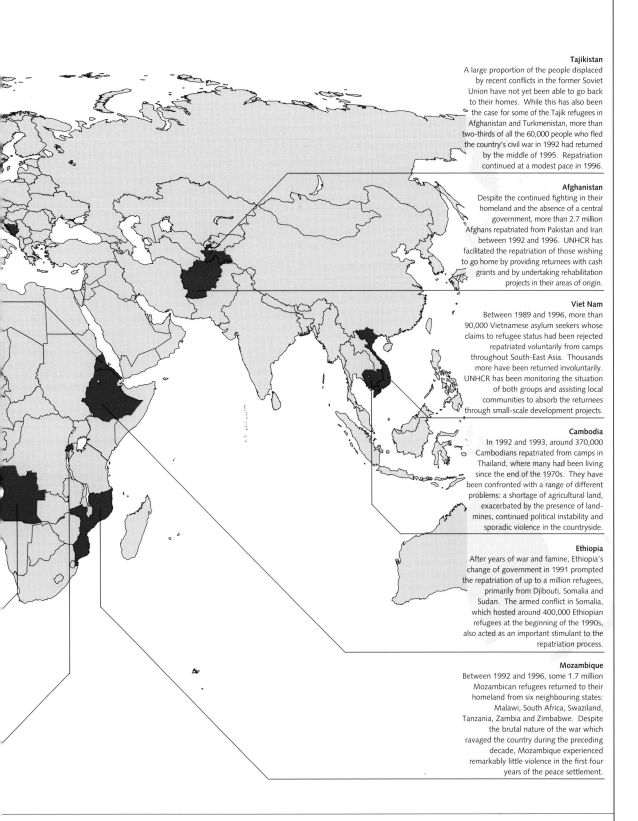

Tajikistan

A large proportion of the people displaced by recent conflicts in the former Soviet Union have not yet been able to go back to their homes. While this has also been the case for some of the Tajik refugees in Afghanistan and Turkmenistan, more than two-thirds of all the 60,000 people who fled the country's civil war in 1992 had returned by the middle of 1995. Repatriation continued at a modest pace in 1996.

Afghanistan

Despite the continued fighting in their homeland and the absence of a central government, more than 2.7 million Afghans repatriated from Pakistan and Iran between 1992 and 1996. UNHCR has facilitated the repatriation of those wishing to go home by providing returnees with cash grants and by undertaking rehabilitation projects in their areas of origin.

Viet Nam

Between 1989 and 1996, more than 90,000 Vietnamese asylum seekers whose claims to refugee status had been rejected repatriated voluntarily from camps throughout South-East Asia. Thousands more have been returned involuntarily. UNHCR has been monitoring the situation of both groups and assisting local communities to absorb the returnees through small-scale development projects.

Cambodia

In 1992 and 1993, around 370,000 Cambodians repatriated from camps in Thailand, where many had been living since the end of the 1970s. They have been confronted with a range of different problems: a shortage of agricultural land, exacerbated by the presence of land-mines, continued political instability and sporadic violence in the countryside.

Ethiopia

After years of war and famine, Ethiopia's change of government in 1991 prompted the repatriation of up to a million refugees, primarily from Djibouti, Somalia and Sudan. The armed conflict in Somalia, which hosted around 400,000 Ethiopian refugees at the beginning of the 1990s, also acted as an important stimulant to the repatriation process.

Mozambique

Between 1992 and 1996, some 1.7 million Mozambican refugees returned to their homeland from six neighbouring states: Malawi, South Africa, Swaziland, Tanzania, Zambia and Zimbabwe. Despite the brutal nature of the war which ravaged the country during the preceding decade, Mozambique experienced remarkably little violence in the first four years of the peace settlement.

The countries featured on this map are representative, not exhaustive.

145

conflicts that originated in the cold war years: Cambodia, El Salvador, Ethiopia, Mozambique, Namibia and Nicaragua, to give some of the most prominent examples (see Map I). During this period, large numbers of refugees have also returned to Afghanistan, where the initial struggle against the Soviet invasion of 1979 has been transformed into a more complex conflict between a variety of different political, military and tribal groups, many of whom continue to receive substantial external support.

During the past two years, large numbers of refugees have continued to go back to their countries of origin, taking the total number of returnees in the 1990s to well over the ten million mark (see Figure 4.1). In the 12 months which followed the signing of the Dayton peace accord in December 1995, around 250,000 displaced Bosnians were able to return, if not to their previous homes, then at least to their former areas of residence. In the second half of 1996, around 720,000 Rwandese refugees repatriated from eastern Zaire, while some 485,000 returned from Tanzania. Elsewhere in Africa, in the first half of 1997, the repatriation of some 150,000 Malian Tuaregs from Mauritania and other neighbouring states was also proceeding.

By the beginning of 1997, UNHCR was providing some form of protection or assistance to just under three million returnees around the world. Given the hope that large-scale repatriation movements will soon be able to take place in countries such as Eritrea, Liberia, Sierra Leone and Somalia, this figure seems unlikely to diminish in the immediate future.

Fig. 4.1

Major repatriation movements in 1996

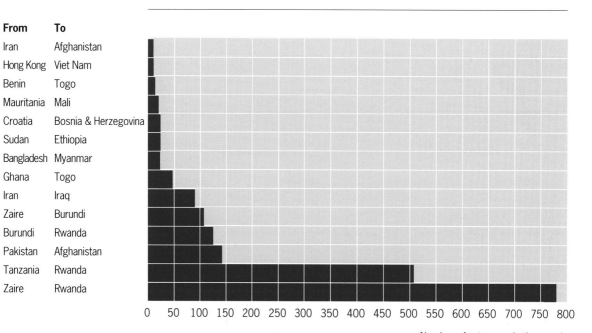

From	To
Iran	Afghanistan
Hong Kong	Viet Nam
Benin	Togo
Mauritania	Mali
Croatia	Bosnia & Herzegovina
Sudan	Ethiopia
Bangladesh	Myanmar
Ghana	Togo
Iran	Iraq
Zaire	Burundi
Burundi	Rwanda
Pakistan	Afghanistan
Tanzania	Rwanda
Zaire	Rwanda

0 50 100 150 200 250 300 350 400 450 500 550 600 650 700 750 800

Number of returnees in thousands

The statistics presented above provide a useful indication of the changing pattern of refugee repatriation over the past decade. It should be noted, however, that these figures usually refer only to refugees in the legal sense of the term. With the notable exception of Bosnia, they exclude the very large numbers of internally displaced people who have also been able to go back to their previous place of residence. In Mozambique, for example, around 1.7 million returning refugees were registered by UNHCR between 1992 and 1996. While precise statistics are not available, at least twice as many internally displaced Mozambicans are believed to have gone back to their homes during the same period. Given the declining number of refugees throughout the world and the rapidly growing scale of internal displacement, it seems likely that returning exiles will in future represent an even smaller proportion of the people wishing to make their way home at the end of an armed conflict.

Like refugee exoduses, repatriation movements take place in diverse political and socio-economic circumstances. They also vary substantially with regard to a range of other variables: the number of people involved; the speed of their return; the extent to which it takes place on a voluntary basis; the way in which the repatriation is organized; and the conditions which the returnees encounter on arrival in their area of origin. Despite their heterogeneous nature, it is possible to identify three dominant and interconnected characteristics of recent repatriation movements, each of which has important implications for the task of returnee reintegration and the broader peacebuilding process. These are discussed in the sections which follow.

Repatriation under duress

Despite a well-established international principle that refugee repatriation should take place on a "wholly voluntary basis" and in "conditions of safety and dignity," it is quite clear that a large proportion of the world's recent returnees have repatriated under some form of duress.(1) As Chapter Two explained, such duress has in many instances been deliberate, exercised by host governments, host communities and other actors, with the specific intention of forcing refugees to go back to their homeland. Sadly, the principle of non-refoulement, which prevents refugees from being returned to countries where their life or liberty would be at risk, has been flouted on a regular basis during the past few years.

 In many other situations, refugee returns have been induced by a more general deterioration of conditions in the country of asylum, whether as a result of social and political violence, declining economic opportunities or reductions in international assistance. As a recent study of repatriation movements in North-East Africa suggests, many returnees are perhaps more accurately described as "refugees from refuge." "There has been little that is either voluntary or safe about the returns discussed in this book," the editors point out. "Most of them have been a consequence of a deteriorating situation in areas of exile, including, in some cases, military action against the displaced groups."(2)

Such circumstances have given rise to a phenomenon known as 'repatriation emergencies', in which large numbers of refugees abandon their country of asylum and return to their country of origin, often to areas which are ill-prepared to absorb such large numbers of new arrivals. The return of around 700,000 Rwandese refugees in little more than a week at the end of 1996, forced out of eastern Zaire by the advance of the rebel forces, provides a particularly dramatic example of this phenomenon.

Repatriation during conflict

Recent experience has demonstrated that refugees frequently go back to countries which are not fully at peace. As one expert on this issue has written, "most repatriations occur during conflict, without a decisive political event such as elections or a peace agreement and without a major change in the regime or the conditions that originally caused flight."(3)

In many cases, refugees return to situations of conflict and instability because they are repatriating under duress or because they feel that it is in their best interests to repatriate, even if conditions are not completely safe at home. Significant numbers of Nicaraguan refugees repatriated from Honduras before the *contra* war was over, for example, partly because of the growing insecurity which prevailed in their camps and partly because their material expectations of life in exile had not been met.(4) As this example suggests, repatriation movements often represent the outcome of a careful decision-making process, whereby individuals, households and communities weigh up the relative benefits of moving or staying put.

The considerations which influence the decision to repatriate may not always be immediately apparent to the external observer. Afghanistan, for example, has experienced an almost uninterrupted period of armed conflict since the Soviet withdrawal in 1988, and yet large numbers of refugees have continued to leave the security of Pakistan so that they can go back to their homes. For many of the Afghans, it would appear, the absence of a stable central government is not a major disincentive to repatriation, as long as they can go back to a part of the country controlled by a faction which can offer them some protection.

The decision to repatriate under conditions of conflict can also be influenced by more explicitly political considerations. The repatriation of Salvadoran refugees from Honduras, for example, was largely completed before peace had returned to their homeland and despite the overt hostility of the authorities towards the returnees. As a study of this repatriation movement has explained, the refugees' decision to return *en masse* to a country where they were not wanted was in fact a carefully calculated gesture of resistance to the incumbent regime. "They went home because they believed that the moment had come when, as organized communities in El Salvador, they could contribute to the political struggle against the government and military," the study concludes. (5)

Self-organized returns

A third characteristic of many recent repatriation movements is to be found in the extent to which they are planned by refugees themselves, even amongst exiled populations which lack the highly structured and politicized leadership that was present in the case of El Salvador.

In recent years it has become common for refugee analysts and practitioners to refer to 'organized' and 'spontaneous' repatriations - the former referring to movements undertaken with international funding and the active involvement of UNHCR, and the latter referring to movements which take place in the absence of such support. It has become equally common for such observers to note that internationally organized repatriation movements, involving the use of UNHCR registration procedures, transport facilities and reception arrangements, have become something of a rarity.

In situations such as the one that UNHCR encountered in Cambodia, where funding was not a particular problem and where substantial numbers of people had to be repatriated very quickly in order to meet an electoral deadline, an organized repatriation may be both possible and desirable. (6) More frequently, however, the resources required for a movement of this type are not available. In addition, the refugees themselves may be unwilling to wait for a UNHCR repatriation programme to be established or may simply prefer to go home the way that they arrived: under their own steam. Thus in June 1996, a UNHCR report on Afghanistan observed that some three million refugees had returned to the country during the preceding three years. "This movement was achieved without the aid of an organized cross-border logistics operation, without comprehensive repatriation and reintegration assistance from UNHCR, and without the presence in areas of return of major rehabilitation and reconstruction efforts by UN development agencies." (7)

While there is substantial evidence to support the argument that internationally organized returns are a rarity (according to one estimate they represent only ten per cent of all refugee returns) the notion of 'spontaneous repatriation' is not particularly helpful. (8) It obscures the extent to which displaced people who have gone home independently may nevertheless benefit from some form of international reintegration assistance once they are back in their own community. In addition, the concept of spontaneous return obscures the extent to which displaced households and communities organize their own return and reintegration - a process that can start even before they have abandoned their homes. In Rwanda, for example, it is reported that many refugees buried tools in the ground and hid their supply of seeds when they left for Tanzania and Zaire, so that they would have access to some basic agricultural inputs if they were able to repatriate in the near future.

More typically, of course, displaced populations plan their return and reintegration once they have reached a place of safety. As observed in a recent UNHCR report on the Mozambique repatriation, "during their time in exile, the refugees made careful plans to minimize the difficulties they would encounter and the risks they would have to take when they finally returned to their homeland."(9)

As the conflict within their homeland subsided, refugees who were living in camps made extra efforts to accumulate some capital, whether by trade, casual labour or by saving and selling some of their rations. At the same time, certain family members - usually adult and adolescent males - went back home for short periods of time, in order to establish their claims to land, to make contact with friends and family members and to take construction materials across the border. In many instances, these temporary returnees would also begin to clear their farm land and to put up simple shelters where they could stay on their next cross-border visit.

In general, Mozambican refugee households preferred to repatriate in stages, the most vulnerable members moving last, so that they could make best use of the services available in their country of asylum and benefit from the preparations which had already been made for them in their homeland. Those who had managed to find some kind of employment in their asylum country also tended to delay their return, thereby maximizing the amount of cash they had at their disposal when they finally took up permanent residence in their own country.

Studies in countries such as Afghanistan, Cambodia, Chad, Eritrea and Sudan tend to confirm the hypothesis that such strategies are not only a universal feature of the repatriation process, but that they - rather than the type of assistance provided by humanitarian organizations - play a primary role in facilitating the reintegration of displaced populations.(10) Unfortunately, much of the recent discussion on the issue of returnee reintegration has tended to ignore this important fact.

The studies mentioned above also indicate that international borders have far less significance for many refugees than they do for external observers. Indeed, in areas which have a long history of population displacement, in regions inhabited by nomads and pastoralists, and in areas where ethnic groups straddle an international border, concepts such as 'country of origin', 'country of asylum', 'refugee' and 'returnee' may have little meaning for the people concerned (see Box 4.1). (11)

4.1

The Tuareg repatriation

Little noticed by the international community, a substantial repatriation movement has been taking place in the heart of the Sahara desert. The refugees concerned are going back to some of the harshest living conditions to be found anywhere in the world.

The Tuaregs are nomadic pastoralists who live across the Sahelian belt in Algeria, Burkina Faso, Libya, Mauritania, Mali and Niger. The largest Tuareg populations are to be found in the latter two countries, 750,000 of them living in Niger and 500,000 in Mali. Distinguished by their Berber origins and nomadic way of life, the Tuareg have remained ethnically, racially and linguistically distinct from the majority population of the societies in which they live. As a result of their refusal to assimilate and their fierce desire to preserve their culture, they have often clashed with the governments of the region. Now, however, many of those who were displaced during earlier periods of armed conflict are making their way home.

Economic decline

In pre-colonial days the Tuareg were a wealthy and powerful people. But aggressive colonization, economic decline and environmental disasters have all eroded their influence. Many have been forced to abandon their nomadic way of life and have moved to the outskirts of cities, where they survive by means of casual work and begging.

Throughout the Sahel, but most notably in Niger and Mali, the Tuaregs have called for greater autonomy and in some cases for self-government. In the early 1990s, militant Tuareg groups in Mali started to carry out armed attacks against government forces stationed in the north of the country. Despite the signing of a peace agreement

Map J

Tuareg repatriation to Mali and Niger

□ Capital
● Town
(ฑ) UNHCR office
➤ Main repatriation movements
▓ Major returnee area
⌂ Refugee site
Λ Refugee camp
▬ International boundary

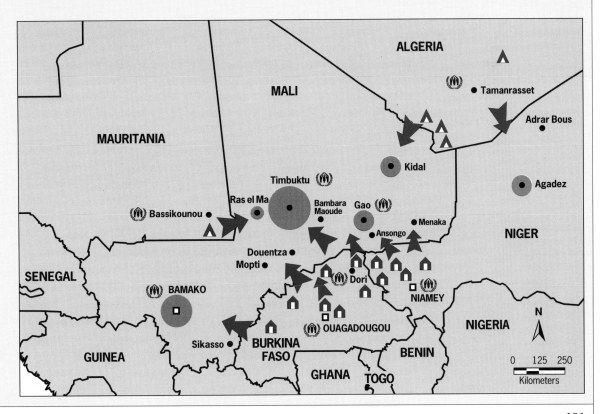

between the insurgents and the government in January 1991, the attacks continued until the president was removed from power later that year. By this time, thousands of people, most of them Tuaregs and Moors, had fled from military reprisals and summary killings and crossed the border into Algeria, Mauritania, Burkina Faso, Niger and Senegal.

In 1992, with the help of international mediation, a pact was signed between the Malian government and the major Tuareg rebel groups. As well as declaring a mutual cease-fire, the agreement also provided for the enrolment of former rebels in the army or civil service and the establishment of development programmes in the northern provinces of the country. Unfortunately, very few of these proposals were actually realized and fighting resumed in 1993. It was only in 1994 that the government really started to implement the pact, thus returning some peace and stability to the north of the country and enabling plans for the repatriation of the refugees to proceed.

During the same period, a similar rebellion by a coalition of armed Tuareg opposition groups took place in northern Niger. As in Mali, the government responded with harsh military reprisals, which forced up to 20,000 Tuaregs to flee into Algeria and Burkina Faso. After several thwarted attempts, a peace agreement was finally signed by both sides in April 1995. The fighting continued sporadically throughout 1995, however, as certain rebel groups refused to accept the settlement.

The situation began to improve following a round table conference between the government, rebel groups, local authorities, traditional chiefs and the donor community in October 1995. As a result of these discussions, all sides agreed to support the peace process. Concrete plans were also put into place for the rehabilitation of pastoral zones and the implementation of development programmes in northern Niger. In March 1997, the government began to introduce an amnesty for all prisoners who had been involved in the armed conflict, and the cease-fire between both sides was finally respected. Since then, there has been a marked improvement in security conditions in the north of the country and plans for the repatriation of refugees and internally displaced people have begun.

Assistance package

The repatriation of the Malian refugees started in November 1995, and by March 1997 around 100,000 refugees had returned to that country. In May 1997, UNHCR estimated that a further 60,000 Malian refugees remained in exile, many of them in Niger. The great majority of Malian refugees have returned to their homes independently, with a smaller number repatriating in UNHCR convoys. Whatever means they use to return, former refugees are entitled to an assistance package which includes items such as tents, mosquito nets and food. On returning to their home areas, the refugees also receive a settlement grant.

Despite the signing of various agreements and the launch of funding appeals, plans for the repatriation and reintegration of some 10,500 Nigerien refugees, most of whom are in Algeria, are proceeding at a slower pace than in Mali. Although conditions in the northern provinces of Niger have improved, the political, security and economic situation in the region is still fragile, and UNHCR and the government are keen not to

PROBLEMS OF RETURN

Repatriation and reintegration are ostensibly the most positive aspects of the refugee problem. When compared with the trauma of flight and the uncertainty of exile, the journey back home can certainly be a joyful experience. At the same time, however, one should not be too sentimental about the circumstances of the returning refugee. For as one aid agency worker has observed, returnees "are displaced people of a special kind. They experience not one but two relocations; one when they flee and another when they return to their own country. Each relocation is accompanied with a loss of the

aggravate such problems with a rushed and poorly planned repatriation movement. In fact, an earlier repatriation programme to Niger, established in 1989 for refugees who had fled to neighbouring countries in the 1980s, actually aggravated the political situation by rasing expectations that were subsequently not fulfilled.

In both Mali and Niger, the refugees are returning to areas which have been ravaged by conflict, civil strife, drought and environmental degradation. The economy of those areas has been shattered, the infrastructure is in a state of disrepair, there is an almost total absence of government services and development activities have ground to a halt. The majority of refugees are nomadic livestock herders, with a smaller number of them engaged in other economic activities, such as crop

production, masonry and carpentry. While some of the refugees have been able to return with a few animals, the majority of those who were living in refugee camps have lost all their livestock and other means of livelihood. They are therefore returning with no independent means of support.

A main priority for all the Tuareg returnees is the availability of water. As one Malian refugee explained to the journal *Jeune Afrique*, "for us, the Tuaregs, water is life. When we have water, we can look at our feet and we don't have to keep looking at the sky." To meet this important need, UNHCR has allocated around 40 per cent of its programme funds to the construction and rehabilitation of water sources. In addition, resources have been provided to restock the refugees' herds, to distribute seeds, tools and other agricultural inputs, to train

refugees in appropriate irrigation techniques and to establish micro-credit and income generation projects for both women and men.

Another priority for many of the refugees is access to education for their children, many of whom were not able to attend school while they were living in exile. UNHCR's assistance activities therefore include the repair and construction of school buildings and the provision of school furniture and classroom materials. Unfortunately, the response to UNHCR's appeal for funds for this little-known repatriation programme has been very poor.

The repatriation and reintegration process is further complicated in both Mali and Niger by the simultaneous return of both refugees and internally displaced people. The mixed nature of the returnee population and their nomadic lifestyle have required

UNHCR and its operational partners to adopt a flexible and community-based approach. UNHCR's assistance programmes, for example, make no real distinction between former refugees, returning displaced people and the resident population, as the needs of these different groups are all essentially the same.

Despite the difficulties which they have encountered on returning to their own country, many refugees have been able to rebuild their lives and livelihoods in Mali. As a result, they are now encouraging their families and friends to return as well. "We still have brothers and sisters in Mauritania," a refugee named Mohamed ag Hamani explained to the magazine *Jeune Afrique*. "I have written to their community leader to encourage them to come back. It is important that they are sure that it is really me who has written."

means of livelihood, such as land, jobs, homes and livestock. And each relocation marks the start of a tough restoration process."(12)

A similar point is made in a study of returnees in Chad. "For the refugees who had received assistance in exile," it observes, "the return could be more difficult than the experience of exile itself. In place of the semblance of stability and physical security established in camps, where the major problems of survival were adequately met, a host of problems, uncertainties and dangers awaited the refugees on their return to their home country."(13)

What exactly are the problems, uncertainties and dangers which confront refugees and internally displaced people when they return to their own community? In order to answer this question in a structured manner, the definition of human security and insecurity presented in the first chapter of this book provides a useful analytical framework.

Physical insecurity

The most obvious and immediate problem confronting returnees is that of physical insecurity. During the past few years, it has become increasingly common for analysts to talk about 'post-conflict societies', referring to those situations in which the parties to an armed conflict have formally agreed to a cessation of hostilities. In reality, however, the transition from war to peace is often a long and difficult one, characterized by lingering tensions, sporadic and localized violence and the ever-present threat of a return to war.

It would be misleading to suggest that the dangers confronting returnees are completely different from those experienced by other citizens in a wartorn state. Like other members of society, returnees may have to survive in a situation where the rule of law hardly exists, where banditry and violent crime are rife, where demobilized soldiers prey on the civilian population and where light weapons are available to most of the population (see Box 4.2).

Nevertheless, recent experience in different parts of the world suggests that former refugees and displaced people may be exposed to particular risks when they go back to their homes. In Burundi, for example, Hutu returnees, coming back involuntarily from neighbouring Tanzania, have been attacked and killed by members of the Tutsi-dominated armed forces. In Myanmar, returnees arriving home with cash grants and assistance items provided by UNHCR have been singled out for theft and extortion. And in Cambodia, where there is a serious shortage of agricultural land, some returnees have found it necessary to settle on and farm those areas which are most heavily infested with land-mines.

In Bosnia, physical assaults have been targeted at former refugees and displaced people in a very systematic manner, and with the explicit purpose of preventing their return and reintegration. As a report by the Open Society Institute suggests, "despite a halt in the fighting, the struggle continues to establish ethnically homogenous entities. The main actors are now merely utilizing other means."(14) Those means include stoning and shooting returnees, attacking them with clubs and iron bars, setting fire to their homes, bombing the roads and bridges that lead to their villages and preventing them from exercising any freedom of movement. In October 1996 alone, the NATO-led Implementation Force confirmed 191 instances where the homes of actual or potential returnees had been wilfully destroyed, in direct contravention of the Dayton peace agreement.

Social and psychological security

Irrespective of the level of violence, returnee situations are frequently characterized by high levels of social tension and psychological insecurity. If they go home under duress, refugees will almost inevitably feel insecure about their future. If they repatriate voluntarily, they may have developed unrealistic expectations about the situation they will find when they get back to their place of origin. In countries where ethnic boundaries have shifted, where large numbers of land-mines have been laid, or where land-use patterns have changed, former refugees and displaced people may not even be able to return to the place which they consider to be their home.

Returnees often find it difficult to adapt to the way of life in their homeland, especially when they have lived in exile for many years and have adjusted to the semi-urban lifestyle of a large refugee camp. For young people who have been born and raised in a country of asylum, 'going home' may entail a particularly high degree of dislocation.

In some situations - Cambodia being a prime example - the initial settlement of returnees has been greatly facilitated by the support they have received from friends and relatives in the resident population. In other instances, however, rather than receiving a warm welcome from their compatriots, returnees have found that they are treated with suspicion or even contempt by people who did not become refugees. Moreover, in situations where large numbers of refugees and displaced people suddenly return to a devastated area, the new arrivals and the resident population may soon find themselves in competition for scarce resources such as land, water, wood, jobs and income-generating opportunities. In such difficult circumstances, returnees may also find that they are considered to enjoy an unfair advantage. In parts of Chad, for example, researchers found that "jealousies aroused by the material goods and money the returnees were perceived to have gained through exile disrupted the delicate balance of social relations."(15)

Such tensions have assumed a particularly acute form in Rwanda, which has recently experienced two distinct repatriation movements: the return of up to 800,000 Tutsi refugees from Uganda, following the victory of the Rwandese Patriotic Front (RPF) in 1994; and the return of over a million refugees from Zaire and Tanzania in 1996, predominantly Hutus who had left the country as a result of the RPF advance. Today, these two groups of returnees (not to mention those people who have remained in Rwanda throughout the turmoil of the past three years) find themselves living alongside each other, and in many instances laying claim to the same houses and land.

Legal security

A less evident but equally important form of insecurity experienced by returnees arises from their legal status and access to judicial procedures. Three issues are of particular importance in this respect: citizenship, documentation and property rights.

As Chapter Six explains, citizenship is an essential component of human security. Without an effective nationality, individuals and groups of people have no state to provide them with protection. It is therefore a matter of concern that some returnees may not even be recognized as fully-fledged citizens of the country to which they repatriate. In Myanmar, for example, this situation has arisen because the returning refugees - members of a Moslem minority group commonly known as the Rohingyas - are simply not recognized as citizens by the country's authorities. Significantly, the flight of around 250,000 Rohingyas to Bangladesh in 1991-92 was preceded by a very

4.2

The scourge of light weapons

In recent years, considerable international attention has been paid to the problem of land-mines and the destructive impact which they can have on societies which are attempting to recover from protracted periods of armed conflict. The issue of small arms, however, has attracted considerably less interest, despite the potential of such weapons to disrupt the peacebuilding process, to prevent the re-establishment of the rule of law and to impede the reintegration of displaced populations.

Light weapons are characterized by their accessibility, durability and utility. Because they can be carried by individual combatants, they are easy

to transport, smuggle and hide. Their size and relative technological simplicity make them cheap and easy to produce. As they become more widely available, prices are driven down, making them accessible to a much wider cross-section of groups and individuals.

In many parts of Africa today, an AK-47 automatic rifle can be procured for a sum equivalent in value to that of a goat or a bag of maize. Once purchased, small arms usually require little in the way of maintenance or spare parts. Moreover, only minimal training or expertise is required to use them. A relatively small quantity of light weapons can cause significant destruction, even in the hands of inexperienced, irregular and under-aged soldiers.

Supply and demand

The widespread availability of light weapons is a reflection

of some important changes in the global balance of supply and demand. Economic hardship, declining external aid and mounting debt have inhibited the transfer of larger conventional weapons to many developing countries. But growing social unrest and other challenges to state authority have dramatically increased the demand for small arms.

At the same time, in the face of declining domestic demand and a glut in production capacity, the arms industries in both NATO and former-Warsaw Pact countries have been looking for new overseas markets. Technology transfers have also given many low and middle-income countries the capacity to manufacture small arms for the first time, further increasing the number of suppliers in the global arms market.

Arms merchants have successfully exploited the

emergence of transnational commercial institutions and the weakness of existing regulatory mechanisms to create a sophisticated black market in small arms. In many cases, arms merchants utilise the same networks which are used to market other illegal goods, particularly drugs. When wars draw to a close, unwanted weapons are often sold on to nearby countries which are also gripped by armed conflict.

The trade in light weapons has had a range of negative consequences for people around the world. Armed societies are insecure societies. Once certain members of society begin to resolve disputes and secure a livelihood through the use of violence, then others are obliged to protect themselves in the same manner. In Colombia, for example, small arms have become a defining feature of the country's current civil

similar exodus in 1978-79, demonstrating the chronic insecurity of a community which lacks the rights of citizenship.

A more widespread problem experienced by returnees is a lack of official documentation such as identity cards and birth certificates. In an industrialized state, the loss of such documents may represent a temporary inconvenience rather than a long-term source of insecurity. But in a country such as El Salvador or Guatemala, where political tensions still exist and where the country's archives have been destroyed, a lack of documentation may place a person at risk of arrest or harassment and prevent them from voting, finding a job, gaining access to credit and moving freely around their own country.

strife. There are now estimated to be one million legal and five million illegal weapons in the country, resulting largely from a convergence of political terrorism and drug-related violence.

The arming of adolescents and children in many recent conflicts is evidently storing up social and political problems for many years to come. Will the thousands of uneducated Liberian, Sierra Leonean, Somali and Sudanese boys who have grown up carrying a rifle ever be able to support themselves through peaceful economic activities?

Control and limitation
Despite the scale of the small arms problem, states have been slow to subject such weapons to any form of control or limitation. In part, this stems from a lack of information and consensus amongst policymakers. Because the international

community has until recently focused its attention on weapons of mass destruction and on larger conventional weapons, relatively little is known about the commerce in small arms. Indeed, much of the evidence relies on fragmentary and anecdotal sources of information. In addition, many governments share the assumption that it is impossible to control the flow of light weapons to conflict-affected countries, given the massive stocks and numerous suppliers which already exist, and the ease with which they can be transferred from one part of the world to another.

Small arms transfers are not included in the major mechanism for controlling the arms trade - the UN register of conventional arms - which is principally concerned with the threat that large weapons systems pose to international or regional stability, rather than

the security of people in war-torn states. While the register could potentially play a role in monitoring the flow of small arms, such an initiative would still not address the issue of illicit arms transfers. Thus while the effort to curb the trade in light weapons is a necessary step in controlling the proliferation of small arms, it is not sufficient in itself.

The disarmament and demobilization of combatants after armed conflicts have come to an end is another important issue which must be addressed, which has direct consequences for the return and reintegration of displaced populations and the transition from war to peace. One reason for the limited success of recent initiatives in this area appears to stem from an over-emphasis on the collection and destruction of weapons and the inadequate attention paid to the integration of

soldiers into active civilian life. As one study perceptively notes, "success in disarming and demobilizing soldiers... depends on the extent to which warring parties and individual combatants believe that their physical and economic security will not be adversely affected by relinquishing arms and abandoning what for many is not just a profession, but also a way of life."

As demonstrated by the progress made in relation to the banning of land-mines, there is tremendous scope for governments and other actors to address the proliferation of small arms as well as the problem of post-conflict demilitarization. Effective initiatives in this area could do much to bring a greater degree of security to the members of war-torn societies and to avert the recurrence of armed conflict and population displacement.

Finally, there has in recent years been a growing recognition of the need for returnees to have secure title to the property which they left behind and the land on which they depend for their livelihood. In a number of countries which have experienced recent repatriation movements - Cambodia, Eritrea, Guatemala, Mozambique and Rwanda, for example - the question of land has become a source of increasing controversy. In some cases, this is because the land has been commercialized, allowing indigenous elites and foreign investors to gain control of the potentially most lucrative areas. In other cases, the land issue has come to the fore as a result of demographic growth, the degradation of the soil, declining agricultural productivity and the settlement of the land by other groups of people.

Whatever the origins of the problem, it is evident that returnees can find themselves in a particularly disadvantaged position when it comes to the distribution of land and the registration of land titles. Female-headed households tend to experience particular difficulties in this respect, partly because they are often socially and economically marginalized, and partly because the land tenure laws in many countries do not even recognize the right of women to enjoy secure access to land.

Material insecurity

Although different in many ways, some basic similarities can be found in the situation of war-torn countries such as Afghanistan, Bosnia, Cambodia and Mozambique. In all of these cases, thousands of refugees and displaced people have gone back to areas which have been laid waste by armed conflict. Most of the houses, shops and warehouses there have been systematically looted or destroyed. Agricultural land, irrigation systems and other elements of the infrastructure have fallen into disuse. Marketing, banking and credit systems have all broken down. Local production and commercial activity has collapsed, depriving the population of jobs and income-generating opportunities. To the extent that entrepreneurial activities are taking place, they may be illegal in nature. Sadly, it would appear, smuggling, illicit timber and mineral extraction, drug production and prostitution are the route to easy money in a war-torn state.

Despite their resourcefulness and the reintegration strategies which they invariably devise, the people who return to such circumstances are often hard pressed to survive. While the problem of the 'dependency syndrome' has almost certainly been exaggerated in much of the literature on refugees, there is little doubt that some of the people who have become accustomed to the services provided in organized camps find it difficult to adjust to the realities of life without international assistance.

Those difficulties can assume numerous different forms. When refugees repatriate under duress, they may arrive in their homeland at a point in the agricultural cycle which makes it impossible for them to plant crops in time for the next harvest. As suggested earlier, returnees may find it difficult to establish a claim to the land or property which they left behind when they fled. And if they are offered some land to establish a new settlement, it is likely to be in the least attractive areas, where the soil is poor in quality, where markets are inaccessible and where public services are non-existent.

Finally, it should be noted that returnee populations often include a disproportionate number of people, such as widows and members of female-headed households, who are poorly placed to establish new livelihoods when they return to their country of origin. Studies undertaken in Cambodia three years after the completion of the repatriation from Thailand, for example, suggested that up to 40 per cent of the returnees were living a precarious, hand-to-mouth existence. Prominent amongst this number were those who had no access to land and those in households with a high ratio of dependants to economically active members.(16) For returnees such as these, the process of reintegration is likely to be a long and arduous process (see Box 4.3).

REPATRIATION AND THE PEACEBUILDING PROCESS

The concepts of returnee reintegration and peacebuilding are frequently used but rarely defined. For the purposes of this analysis, reintegration can be regarded as a process which enables formerly displaced people and other members of their community to enjoy a progressively greater degree of physical, social, legal and material security. In addition, reintegration entails the erosion - and ultimately the disappearance - of any observable distinctions which set returnees apart from their compatriots, particularly in terms of their socio-economic and legal status. Peacebuilding, on the other hand, refers to the process whereby national protection and the rule of law are re-established. More specifically, it entails an absence of social and political violence, the establishment of effective judicial procedures, the introduction of pluralistic forms of government, and the equitable distribution of resources.

The question of returnee reintegration has in recent years become one of the most important items on the international humanitarian agenda, attracting the attention not only of relief, development and human rights organizations, but also senior political and military decision-makers.(17) One of the first manifestations of this trend came in 1987, when the leaders of the Central American countries came together in an attempt to resolve the armed conflicts which had devastated the region during the previous decade. Calling for an integrated and regional approach to the problem, the declaration issued at that summit meeting explicitly acknowledged that "there can be no lasting peace without initiatives to resolve the problem of refugees, returnees and displaced persons."(18) Significantly, since that declaration was drafted, almost every major peace agreement concluded around the world, whether in Bosnia, Cambodia, Mozambique or Namibia, has included specific provisions relating to the return of displaced populations.

How exactly can repatriation and reintegration contribute to the peace-building process in war-torn societies? This question can be answered with reference to a number of interlocking issues.

4.3

Women in war-torn societies

"Many women who lost everything and who are heads of households for the first time are faced with the difficult responsibility of trying to rebuild their lives while providing food, shelter and school fees for themselves and their surviving relatives. Regardless of their status - Tutsi, Hutu, displaced, returnees - all are facing problems because of the upheaval caused by the genocide, aggravated by their generally disadvantaged status as women." Those are the words used by Human Rights Watch to describe the situation of women in Rwanda at the end of 1996.

While genocidal killings of the type which took place in Rwanda are mercifully rare, the difficulties experienced by the women of that country are by no means unique. In any society where an armed

conflict has come to an end and where displaced people are going back to their homes, women are confronted with particular challenges. Acknowledging the importance of this topic, the UN High Commissioner for Refugees observed in 1991 that "relatively little had been documented on the specific issues facing women returning to their homes after years of exile." Six years later, that statement holds true; there is still a dearth of research on the situation of female returnees and other women in war-torn societies. At the operational level, however, some important initiatives have been taken in this area.

The Bosnia Women's Initiative

Economic recovery in post-war Bosnia is proving to be a slow process, and for every sector of the population, access to income-earning opportunities is a major concern. For displaced and returnee women, a large proportion of whom are widows and single heads of households, the economic situation is particularly

difficult. Many were financially dependent on their spouses before the war and they consequently have no marketable skills or entrepreneurial experience. Others who are of rural origins and who are unable to go back to their home areas face considerable problems in adapting to life in a town.

Visiting Bosnia in the aftermath of the war, a team of experts, some of them from the US-based Women's Commission for Refugee Women and Children, concluded that displaced and returnee women required much better access to vocational, literacy and skills training programmes, as well as banking and credit facilities. Without such services, they would not become economically independent. Acting upon these findings, in 1996, UNHCR established the Bosnia Women's Initiative (BWI) with the help of a major grant from the US government. The organization then began a detailed process of consultation with the many women's groups which had

sprung up in Bosnia during and after the conflict, so as to gain a better understanding of their needs and aspirations.

Administered from the UNHCR office in Sarajevo, the BWI initially focused all of its efforts on income-generating projects. But this approach was challenged by many Bosnian women, who argued, in the words of one Gorazde woman, that "the trauma of these people is not over with the last bullet." Responding to such comments, the project selection committee, comprised of representatives from UNHCR, the US government, the World Bank and Bosnian women, extended the range of the programme to include counselling and psychosocial rehabilitation projects.

In its first year of operation, the BWI has sponsored a wide range of activities, including the provision of legal training and advice to Bosnian women on issues such as land, property, employment and pension rights, as well as family law.

First, in the words of a recent World Bank discussion paper, "as long as significant portions of a society's population are displaced, the conflict has not ended. There can be no hope of normalcy until the majority of those displaced are able to reintegrate themselves into their societies."(19) As this statement suggests, refugee movements and other forms of forced displacement are an aberration. They are symptomatic of a situation in which the

The latter is of particular importance as there has been a disturbing increase in the incidence of domestic violence since the war came to an end. The programme also attempts to address some of the particular legal, social and political problems experienced by women with husbands from a different ethnic group. In addition, BWI funds have been used to establish health projects, day care facilities for children and the elderly, as well as a women's community radio project. One of the most celebrated BWI projects is the Gorazde cow bank, which has provided 40 women from that town with a cow, so that they can produce their own milk and cheese. The women are obliged to return their cow's first calf to the project, but are free to keep or to sell any additional calves, thereby enabling them to generate some additional income.

While it is still too early to provide a full assessment of the BWI, independent observers have already argued that this approach should be extended to other war-torn countries. The Open Society Institute's *Forced Migration Monitor*, for example, has recommended that a similar initiative be launched in Croatia, with a particular emphasis on the situation of displaced, widowed, elderly and sick women. "With some additional refinement," the report concludes, "the BWI may become a model for emulation, perhaps in the countries of the former Soviet Union".

Women in Rwanda

Rwanda is one country where the BWI approach has already been emulated. Although the social and economic context of the two countries is evidently quite different, many Rwandese women, like their Bosnian counterparts, have also suffered severe psychological and physical trauma as a result of recent events. As many as 5,000 Rwandese victims of rape are believed to have given birth since the 1994 genocide. Much larger numbers of women have been widowed and are now struggling single-handedly to support large numbers of dependants. The generally disadvantaged status of these women, as well as their lack of education and skills, oblige them to eke out a very precarious existence.

Modelled on the programme in Bosnia, the Rwanda Women's Initiative (RWI) was established at the end of 1996. The programme is administered by UNHCR and funds are channelled through the Ministry of Gender, Family and Social Affairs as well as several women's organizations. It is targeted primarily at widows, women heads of household, single mothers, victims of sexual violence and foster families. In the first few months of its existence, the RWI has funded a range of different activities, including a brick-making project and a tailoring school for widows in the Umutara and Kigali prefectures and an assistance programme for families who have fostered orphans of the genocide. Again, self-sufficiency is the objective; rather than being provided with free food, families are provided with a goat and the necessary veterinary drugs, so that the beneficiaries can supplement both their diet and their income.

As in Bosnia, the legal status and legal rights of Rwandese women are a primary UNHCR concern. Under customary local law, women are unable to inherit land or property, and married women cannot engage in commercial activities or employment without the authorization of their husbands. Such practices pose enormous difficulties for women who are the sole providers for their families. Recognizing these problems, the government is currently revising those laws which discriminate against women, with support and advice from UNHCR. At the same time, UNHCR is working with the government to provide legal training to local authorities and to women's associations. While such activities evidently cannot remove the physical and psychological scars of the country's recent history, they could play a small part in building the foundations of civil society.

state is unable to protect its citizens and in which different groups of citizens are unable to live in peace alongside each other. The voluntary repatriation and reintegration of people who have been uprooted by violence is thus an important manifestation of the process whereby national protection is restored and human security reinforced.

Because it represents a very tangible form of progress, the voluntary return of displaced people can have an important impact on public confidence in the peacebuilding process. As UNHCR has observed in a previous publication, "experience in several conflict-affected countries has demonstrated that for ordinary men and women, the safe return of friends and relatives who have been living in exile for many years is often a more meaningful and moving experience than any number of formal peace agreements and UN resolutions."(20)

Conversely, the transition from war to peace may be disrupted, and public confidence in the peacebuilding process undermined, if formerly displaced people are unable to reintegrate successfully into their own society. When returnees find it impossible to establish new livelihoods and are obliged to depend on humanitarian assistance; when they are unable to gain access to agricultural land and have to move into an urban squatter settlement in order to eke out a living; when they experience harassment from the authorities and discrimination from their compatriots; and when they resort to violent protest in order to make their voice heard, then the prospects for a sustainable peace are inevitably weakened.

Second, repatriation plays an important part in validating the post-conflict political order. When they choose voluntarily to go back to their homeland, refugees are, quite literally, voting with their feet and expressing confidence in the future of their country. More specifically, as demonstrated by the experience of countries such as Cambodia, Mozambique and Namibia, pre-election repatriation programmes can bring an important degree of credibility to internationally supervised elections.

Providing refugees with the opportunity to go home and to express their political preference is inherent in the concept of a free, fair and democratic election. It also legitimizes the outcome of the ballot. If, in the cases mentioned above, large numbers of citizens had been excluded from the ballot because they were living in exile, then the results of those elections might easily have been rejected by one or more of the parties involved, leading to renewed political chaos.

Third, the return and reintegration of an exiled population may be a precondition for peace in situations where refugees are politically and militarily active. No government can realistically be expected to sign a peace agreement with an opposition movement which insists on keeping a large and hostile force outside the borders of the country. Thus while the Khmer Rouge and other Cambodian factions maintained their camps on the Thai border; while SWAPO (the Namibian liberation movement) kept its army and supporters exiled in Angola; while the Nicaraguan *contras* continued to operate from bases in Honduras and Costa Rica; and while the former Rwandese army and militia forces maintained their bases in eastern Zaire, the peacebuilding process could make little progress. In each of these cases, the return of the refugees and their separation from the military represented an important step in the transition from war to peace.

Fourth and finally, the return of displaced populations can make an important contribution to the economic recovery of war-torn states. Indeed, repatriation may even be a prerequisite for that objective to be achieved. As one analyst suggests, "in many conflict countries, the displaced represent a high enough percentage of the total population to undermine any attempt at development... When 10 to 15 per cent of the population is not where they belong and their future residence is unpredictable, the design of social services, agricultural extension systems and other basic programmes is problematic at best."(21)

There is, of course, a less positive side to the coin, in the sense that a large and sudden influx of returnees can impose a substantial burden on the area where they settle, leading to increased competition for scarce resources and the threat of social conflict. This is particularly the case in situations where refugees have been forced to leave their country of asylum and have consequently been unable to make adequate preparations for their return and reintegration. Even so, there is also considerable evidence to suggest that when former refugees and displaced people go back to their homes, they frequently contribute to the peacebuilding process by revitalizing the local economy.

The Horn of Africa provides three good examples of the positive impact which returnees can have upon the areas where they settle. In the Ogaden region of Ethiopia, one observer reports, "the returnees act as a catalyst for development. In the rural areas it is the returnees who are spearheading ideas for change." "This new willingness and confidence to change," he continues, "is not confined to men. Returnee women have been in the forefront of opening new businesses and play a leading role in the long-distance trade in goods from Somaliland and Djibouti."(22)

According to another report, the Eritrean town of Alebu has been transformed by an influx of returnees from neighbouring Sudan. "Alebu has changed with remarkable speed from a barren place to a thriving town with around 6,000 inhabitants, numerous shops, hotels, grinding mills, a school, a clinic and hundreds of trees, shooting up between the houses."(23) Similar findings are reported from north-east Somalia, where an influx of former refugees and displaced people is said to have "contributed positively to the initial recovery process in the region. In many places the newcomers have become a dynamic force for recovery, constructing new dwellings and contributing to the local economy as they adjust to their new circumstances."(24)

As these examples suggest, returnees in the world's poorer countries may not bring a great deal of financial or physical capital with them when they arrive in their country and area of origin. But they often possess a considerable amount of human and social capital: skills, experience and survival strategies which they have acquired in exile; family, clan and community networks which can be activated once they have returned; and a collective determination to rebuild their livelihoods and communities.

If their impact is to be maximized and sustained, however, the efforts made by returnees to re-establish their livelihoods must take place within a conducive environment. To quote again from the World Bank's discussion paper, "reintegrating refugees into their home communities is a matter of highest priority in any reconstruction programme... The simple movement of groups of displaced people from one area to another without long-term plans to support their sustainable reintegration risks destabilizing the peace."(25) The next section examines the changing way in which UNHCR has attempted to provide such support.

RETURNEE REINTEGRATION: UNHCR'S CHANGING ROLE

The role of UNHCR in the return and reintegration of displaced populations has changed significantly since the organization was established in 1951. For the first 30 years of its existence, the question of repatriation played a relatively small part in the organization's activities, due in large part to the fact that most of the world's refugees came from communist states. Consequently, it was considered both inconceivable and undesirable by the western powers (UNHCR's principal donors) that those refugees should choose to go back to their homes.

This situation began to change somewhat in the 1960s and 1970s, when the focus of the global refugee problem began to shift from Europe to Africa, Asia and other low-income areas. Even so, repatriation remained a relatively low-profile issue, for at this time, most of the states which received large numbers of refugees were still willing to grant them asylum on an open-ended basis.

When refugees did go back to their homes in large numbers, as they did in the case of countries such as Algeria, Angola, Mozambique and Zimbabwe, it was generally in the context of successful anti-colonial struggles or after a fundamental change in the political situation in the country of origin. In such circumstances, returnees were considered to be the responsibility of the government of the country of origin, supported where necessary by development organizations rather than a refugee agency such as UNHCR.

These considerations led UNHCR to play a clearly circumscribed role in the repatriation and reintegration process. As far as protection was concerned, the agency's primary function was to verify that refugees were return-ing to their own country on a voluntary basis, and to encourage countries of origin to establish and respect amnesties for returning refugees. With regard to assistance, UNHCR regularly provided refugees with transport to their homeland, as well as a repatriation assistance package consisting of items such as foodstuffs, blankets, cooking equipment and tools.

In general, however, the organization did not seek (nor was it encouraged to pursue) a more extensive part in the task of returnee reintegration, let alone the broader peacebuilding process. Thus even as recently as 1990, a UNHCR policy paper stated that the organization's post-repatriation protec-tion and assistance activities "should not be envisaged as extending beyond three to six months."(26)

Over the past decade, the effectiveness of this approach to the return of displaced populations has been called into question by a number of factors. First, as indicated earlier in the chapter, the scale and geographical scope of the reintegration problem has expanded substantially since the beginning of the 1990s. With so many refugees returning to their homes, the difficulties which they encounter, and the problems associated with their presence, have become increasingly visible (see Figure 4.2).

Second, while those difficulties are not entirely new, they have certainly in-creased in intensity. Rather than returning voluntarily to countries where there has been a fundamental change of political circumstances, many refu-gee populations have in recent years gone home under duress and to countries which remain socially, economically and politically fragile, even if the fighting has formally come to an end. In such circumstances, it has been recognized, the limited forms and amount of assistance traditionally provided by UNHCR may not be sufficient to ensure the effective reintegration of returnees.

Third, it has become increasingly clear that in the aftermath of an armed conflict, the needs of returning refugees may not be any greater (and in some cases may even be less) than those of people who have been internally displaced or otherwise affected by the war. In such circumstances, assistance which is specifically targeted at former refugees and which brings no benefits to the population at large may well become a source of social tension and conflict.

Fourth, the earlier assumption that government bodies and development organizations would cater for the broader rehabilitation needs of returnee-populated areas has generally proven to be unfounded. The authorities of most war-torn countries (if such authorities exist at all) usually lack the finan-cial, logistical and administrative capacity required to undertake such activ-ities. And even if they do have access to resources, they may not wish to invest them in the peripheral border areas where the largest numbers of returnees are typically to be found.

Experience has demonstrated that development organizations are poorly placed to compensate for the absence of governmental capacity. The UN

Development Programme (UNDP), for example, tends to focus on long-term development issues, working at the national level through government structures. It is not institutionally well equipped to undertake the speedy and local-level rehabilitation activities which are required when large numbers of people suddenly return to areas which have been devastated by war.

Fifth, while host governments and donor states were previously reluctant to endorse an expansion of UNHCR's activities in the area of returnee reintegration, that situation has been reversed with the emergence of new approaches to the problem of forced displacement. As suggested in previous chapters, states are increasingly weary of the refugee problem, and are eager (in many cases, too eager) to promote the early repatriation of refugees.

Recognizing the extreme fragility of many war-torn societies, the international community now understands that the effective reintegration of for-

Fig. 4.2

Annual returnee totals, 1975-96

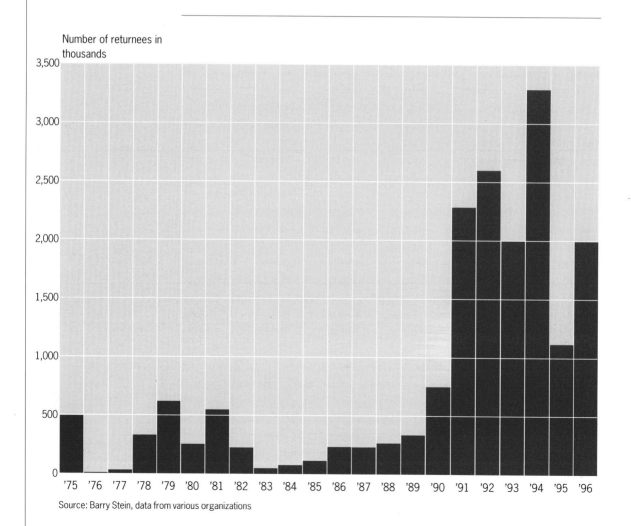

Number of returnees in thousands

Source: Barry Stein, data from various organizations

mer refugees has an important part to play in preventing the recurrence of violence and population displacements. There is consequently a broad consensus that UNHCR should not restrict its activities to the task of refugee protection and assistance, but that it should undertake a broader range of activities, both in countries of asylum and in countries of origin. The task of refugee repatriation and reintegration, of course, provides an important link between the two.

As a result of these different factors, UNHCR has in recent years become much more extensively involved in the task of returnee reintegration. During the past few years, the organization's annual spending on repatriation programmes has increased substantially (see Figure 4.3). The following sections examine three of the primary ways in which these resources have been used.

Fig. 4.3

Percentage of UNHCR expenditure on refugee repatriation 1975-96

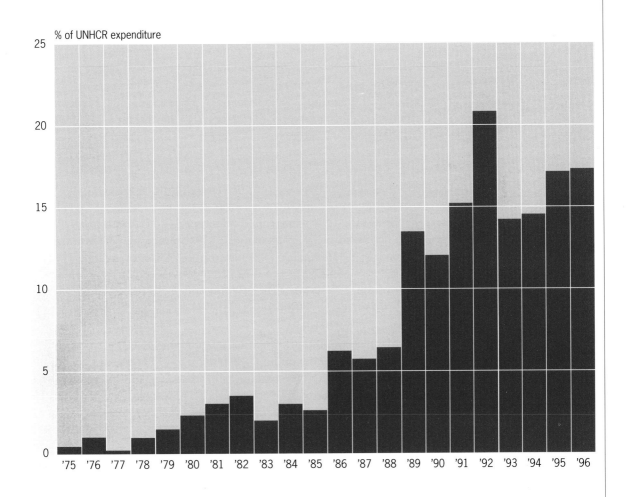

% of UNHCR expenditure

Peace-plan operations

On a number of recent occasions, UNHCR has played an integral part in comprehensive peace-plan operations undertaken by the United Nations. Largely unknown until the late 1980s, this new form of peacekeeping operation has had two principal objectives: to facilitate the implementation of cease-fires and peace agreements signed by the warring parties; and to consolidate the transition from war to peace through the election of new governments.

Sometimes referred to as 'multidimensional peacekeeping operations', these initiatives have involved the different components of the UN system in a wide range of activities: demobilizing the combatants, disposing of their weapons and removing the land-mines which they have laid; assisting governments to introduce constitutional and administrative reforms; registering voters and organizing free and fair elections; and assisting refugees and displaced people to go back to their homes.

While UNHCR has played a supporting role in several of these activities, the organization's primary responsibility has naturally been with the last, namely refugee repatriation. By assisting with the repatriation of refugees, UNHCR has tried to maximize the number of returnees who have been able to participate in the electoral process. And by undertaking reintegration and rehabilitation projects in returnee-populated areas, the organization has attempted to bring a degree of stability to communities which are struggling to absorb large numbers of new arrivals.

Such are the objectives which have guided UNHCR's activities in a number of recent peace-plan operations: Namibia, which involved the repatriation of more than 42,000 exiles, not only from neighbouring states but also from many other countries around the world; Cambodia, where UNHCR was responsible for the return and initial reintegration of around 370,000 refugees who had been living in Thailand; and Mozambique, which witnessed the return of some 1.7 million refugees from six different asylum countries between 1992 and 1996. Most recently, UNHCR has also been asked to play a leading role in the Bosnian repatriation and reintegration effort, which forms an essential part of the peace-plan operation set in motion by the Dayton accords (see Box 4.4).

The peace-plan operations which have been completed since the end of the 1980s have not been without their difficulties. The parties concerned have not always respected the commitments they have given to the international community - a problem which in the case of Angola led to a serious setback in the peacebuilding process and blocked the large-scale repatriation programme which UNHCR had planned to launch. Nor has it always been easy to coordinate the military and civilian elements of these operations, often because of their tendency to work to different timetables; while the military prefers to make a quick exit once a formal transition to peace has been accomplished, civilian activities in areas such as reintegration and reha-bilitation require longer-term planning and implementation. Even so, it is difficult to disagree with former UN Secretary-General Boutros Boutros-Ghali, when he referred to the "conspicuous success" of the peace-plan oper-ations undertaken during his term of office.(27)

Human rights protection and the rule of law

UNHCR repatriation programmes have always included a human rights pro-tection element, a function that was emphasized by the organization's gov-erning body in 1985. "The High Commissioner," the UNHCR Executive Committee asserted, "should be recognized as having a legitimate interest for the consequences of return... Within the framework of close consulta-tions with the state concerned, [UNHCR] should be given direct and unhin-dered access to returnees, so that [it] is in a position to monitor fulfilment of the amnesties, guarantees or assurances on the basis of which the refugees have returned."(28)

Since that statement was made, the protection activities undertaken by UNHCR in the context of large-scale repatriation programmes have changed in a number of ways. First, while UNHCR continues to monitor the welfare of returnees, the organization now undertakes this task in a more in-tensive and systematic manner, and over a longer period of time than was previously the case. Second, while returnees continue to be UNHCR's main preoccupation, there has been a growing recognition that the organization's protection role cannot be limited to one sector of the population.

Myanmar provides a useful illustration of both these points. In that coun-try, around 55 international and local UNHCR staff members continue to monitor the situation of more than 200,000 former refugees who have repa-triated from Bangladesh, even though a large majority of that number returned more than two years ago. Moreover, in addition to its work on be-half of the returnees, UNHCR monitors the well-being of the Rohingyas as a whole, given their precarious status in the country and their vulnerability to forced displacement. In this respect, it should be acknowledged that human rights abuses in Myanmar and movements of Rohingyas to Bangladesh have continued to take place during the past two years.(29)

Third, UNHCR has in the past few years begun to play an active role in an entirely new area, known as 'legal and judicial capacity-building'. This role has again been endorsed by the organization's governing body. As the Executive Committee agreed in 1996, "for states to fulfil their humanitarian responsibilities in reintegrating returning refugees... an effective human rights regime is essential, including institutions which sustain the rule of law, justice and accountability." In this connection, the Committee called upon UNHCR "to strengthen its activities in support of national legal and ju-dicial capacity-building."(30)

4.4

Return and reconstruction in Bosnia

During 1996 and 1997, UNHCR faced enormous difficulties in trying to implement what has turned out to be one of the most contentious provisions of the Dayton Peace Agreement: the return of refugees and displaced people to their homes in Bosnia and Herzegovina. By mid-1997, 18 months after the Dayton agreement brought the conflict in that country to a formal end, there were still up to 900,000 people displaced within the country and another 900,000 living as refugees in other states.

The military provisions of the peace agreement, such as the separation of the former warring sides, were swiftly and quite smoothly implemented by the NATO-led Implementation Force (IFOR), later renamed the Stabilization Force (SFOR). But Annex 7 of the agreement, which was intended to undo the process of ethnic cleansing and to restore the multi-ethnic composition of the country by facilitating the return of displaced populations, could only be implemented in a limited measure.

Right to return
By mid-1997, an estimated 300,000 people, including

both refugees and internally displaced people, had returned to their homes in Bosnia - a significant figure, but far below UNHCR's initial projection of half a million returnees in 1996 alone. Regrettably, the return of many other people was blocked by the leaders of Bosnia's divided communities, some of whom openly pursued in peace the same policy of ethnic separation which they had previously pursued during the war.

As a result of the Dayton agreement, two political and administrative 'entities' have been established in Bosnia: the Bosnia-Croat Federation and the Republic of Srpska. Many officials, most notably those in the latter entity, openly refused to fulfil the commitments they had made under the agreement, which explicitly gave all Bosnian refugees and displaced people the right to return home.

A similar attitude prevailed in certain areas controlled by Bosnian Croats. In some cases, houses rebuilt at a great cost under UNHCR's shelter programme were subsequently destroyed in an attempt to prevent minority returns. In other cases, the return of refugees to areas where they would be part of an ethnic minority met with a violent response, with attacks on returnees and on members of the resident minority population. In general, the

situation of minorities and the attitude toward minority returns has been considerably better in areas controlled by the Bosniacs.

In an effort to bridge the gap between the once hostile ethnic groups and to make minority returns possible, UNHCR introduced a number of confidence-building measures: bus lines running between the two entities, for example, and assessment visits by potential returnees to their places of origin. The bus lines - 14 of them by mid-1997 - proved to be extremely successful and were used every week by many thousands of people. In a divided country where there were no telephone connections between the two entities and where the vehicle registration plates of one were not recognized by the other, the UNHCR buses were often the only way for the people of Bosnia to stay in touch with each other.

A major obstacle to the return of displaced Bosnians has been the shortage of habitable accommodation throughout much of the country. It is estimated that 60 per cent of Bosnia's housing was either damaged or destroyed during the war. One of UNHCR's main programmes during 1996 and 1997 was a shelter project, entailing the repair of housing in urban and rural areas, as well as a gigantic glazing project in Sarajevo and the

former enclave of Gorazde, where most of the windows had been shattered as a result of the war. Hundreds of thousands of people benefited from these schemes. In Sarajevo, UNHCR and the City Development Institute also renovated 1,200 publicly owned apartments in different parts of the city, on condition that the original owners, members of minority groups, were allowed to return and reclaim their pre-war accommodation.

Much needed as it is, the shelter project cannot be a substitute for the major reconstruction effort required if Bosnia and Herzegovina is to absorb the many refugees and displaced people who are yet to go home. As a result of the war, the country's population is now much smaller and physically weaker than it was prior to the dissolution of Yugoslavia. Large numbers of highly qualified people have left, and are perhaps the refugees who are least likely to return. Few people have proper jobs, and unemployment is estimated at between 65 and 75 per cent. Almost half a million demobilized soldiers now have to adapt to civilian life.

War damage
While it is impossible to estimate the total amount of war damage in Bosnia, it is clear that the cost of reconstruction will run into many billions of dollars. And yet the country's *per capita*

gross national product has shrunk by more than two-thirds since 1990, while industrial production stands at less than 20 per cent of its pre-war level.

The scope and pace of reconstruction, however, as well as the willingness of donors to provide funds for it, depends largely on the ability of the two entities to piece the country together and to form joint institutions such as a central bank. Sadly, a major donor conference on Bosnia had to be postponed several times because of the failure of the two entities to

make sufficient progress in this respect.

A final problem hampering the return of displaced people in Bosnia has been the presence of millions of land-mines (no exact figures are available) in many rural areas of the country. Despite enormous pressure from the international community, Bosnia's former warring factions have been extremely slow to address this issue. Mine clearance has also been hampered by the lack of local expertise in this area, the absence of accurate mine field records and the

country's severe winters, when much of the ground is frozen and covered with snow.

Until the land-mine threat is removed, it seems likely that much of the country, which relies heavily on its agricultural sector, will remain a dangerous and economically stagnant wasteland. Moreover, while rural areas remain inaccessible, the cities will be overburdened with people and unemployment will be high, exacerbating the country's existing social and political tensions.

Map K

The new states of former Yugoslavia

	Capital
•	Town

International boundary
Provincial boundary
Republic boundary
Eastern Slavonia
Republika Srpska
Muslim-Croat Federation
UNHCR bus lines

In Rwanda, for example, UNHCR has provided logistical support and office equipment to the Ministry of Justice and other elements of the judicial system. The organization has organized local-level seminars on legal and human rights issues, focusing on relevant topics such as arrest procedures. Given the dearth of legal expertise in the country and the huge number of court cases arising from the genocide, the exodus of Rwandese refugees and their subsequent repatriation, efforts have also been made to support the teaching of law in the country's universities. As one UNHCR document explains, "the aim of this assistance is to further assure equal access to legal redress for returnees, long-term residents and new settlers alike."(31)

In Tajikistan, UNHCR has provided training and technical support to judges, government officials, law enforcement agencies and lawyers' associations, with the intention of building up an effective and impartial network of judicial institutions, especially in the main returnee-receiving regions of the country. In addition, working in cooperation with the Organization for Security and Cooperation in Europe, UNHCR has arranged for the publication of basic legal texts, and their distribution to judges, prosecutors, universities and libraries.

This is not to suggest that government officials and other actors are always able or willing to practice the legal principles and human rights standards to which they are exposed. Rwanda, for example, has experienced a great deal of violence since the new administration came to power in 1994, much of it provoked by members of the former army and militia forces. The methods used to counter these attacks have been criticized by many commentators, who allege that excessive and extra-legal force has been used by the authorities.(32) Moreover, by mid-1997, UNHCR was unable to undertake its monitoring function in several parts of the country due to the prevailing insecurity.

Tajikistan has also experienced some difficulties in matching principles with practice. The government has, for example, introduced a very ambitious law, intended to ensure that returning refugees are able to get back the land and jobs which they had before they left the country. "Unfortunately," Human Rights Watch reports, "this laudable legal regime has been impossible to implement," due to a lack of resources and the reluctance of some local authorities to implement the laws.(33) Even so, UNHCR's protection efforts amongst returnees in Tajikistan do appear to have had some positive results. Human Rights Watch, for example, reported in May 1996 that "many returnees in southern Tajikistan felt that the incidence of human rights abuses dropped significantly when UNHCR maintained a visible presence in their village."(34)

Economic and social reintegration

Finally, in its efforts to mitigate the serious economic and social difficulties encountered by returnees and other people in war-torn societies, UNHCR has recognized the need to provide assistance in a form that goes beyond the traditional repatriation assistance package and short-term food distribution programme. More specifically, the organization has pioneered the use of 'quick impact projects', small-scale initiatives that can be implemented at modest cost, with considerable speed and with the participation of the local community.

While there is no such thing as a typical quick impact project (QIP), such initiatives normally include the reconstruction of schools and health centres, the installation of water wells and handpumps, as well as the repair of roads, bridges and other elements of the infrastructure. Originally devised by UNHCR in Central America, the largest programme of QIPs to date has been undertaken in Mozambique, where UNHCR financed just under 1,600 projects between 1993 and 1996, most of them budgeted at less than $40,000. Around 55 different organizations were contracted to implement these projects, including international and local voluntary agencies, government departments, other UN and bilateral agencies.

One objective of QIPs is to provide an immediate injection of resources into areas which have been devastated by war and which are confronted with the need to absorb large numbers of returning refugees and displaced people. In this way, UNHCR has sought to compensate for the very limited capacity of state structures to undertake urgent rehabilitation activities and to alleviate some of the hardship which returnees inevitably experience when they first return to their homes. By implementing projects which are of benefit to the population as a whole, which require the participation of the local community, and which require former enemies to work together, the organization has also attempted to avert any conflict between the new arrivals and the resident population.

At the same time, QIPs have been devised with longer-term objectives in mind. In principle at least, they are intended to assist communities in their efforts to create and take advantage of local development opportunities, thereby enabling them to enjoy a greater degree of material security. By linking QIPs with the broader and longer-term reconstruction activities of government departments, development agencies and financial institutions, UNHCR has also tried to ensure that its reintegration efforts provide a basis for sustainable growth in returnee areas.

While QIPs have generally proved quite successful in meeting their immediate objectives, they appear to have been less effective in attaining their longer-term goals. As a number of recent evaluations have indicated, there is a fundamental tension between speed and sustainability in UNHCR's new approach to returnee reintegration. Implemented very quickly but with relatively little planning or preparation, doubts have been raised about the cost-effectiveness of QIPs and the extent to which they are viable once UNHCR has left the scene.(35)

In many instances, UNHCR's reintegration activities have been planned at too late a date, with the result that the organization has been unable to establish the necessary linkages with longer-term development agencies by the time that its own programmes have come to an end. At the same time, recent evaluations suggest, UNHCR activities in countries of asylum and countries of origin have been inadequately coordinated. Indeed, relatively little thought has been given to the way in which the organization's refugee assistance programmes might contribute to the eventual return and reintegration of exiled populations.

SUPPORTING THE TRANSITION FROM WAR TO PEACE

UNHCR's involvement in activities such as returnee monitoring, legal capacity-building and the implementation of quick impact projects has an important part to play in facilitating the repatriation and initial reintegration of displaced populations. But it would be naive to pretend that such efforts have a determining or long-term influence on the ability of returnees to enjoy a secure and stable life within their own country. As the UN High Commissioner for Refugees has observed, "activities for the reintegration of returnees are only a small, if important, part of the sum of post-conflict rehabilitation needs. But the future welfare of returnees and the peace of any country as a whole will depend on how those other needs are met." (36)

Those other needs are wide-ranging. According to one recent study, the peacebuilding process incorporates a dozen different but interlocking tasks: strengthening the capacity of official institutions; holding free and fair elections; monitoring and promoting human rights; addressing the problem of accountability for previous human rights violations; building a strong civil society; demobilizing combatants; removing land-mines and unexploded ordnance; reforming the security services; restoring education and health facilities; assisting war-stricken children; reviving agricultural production; rebuilding the physical infrastructure; and instituting macro-economic policy reforms. What is more, all of these peacebuilding activities must be carried out simultaneously if displaced populations are to be effectively and sustainably reintegrated in their own society. (37)

There is good reason to think that the transition to peace in war-torn societies may prove even more difficult in the future than it has in the recent past. While they appeared to be intractable at the time, the armed conflicts in countries such as Cambodia, Ethiopia, Mozambique, Namibia and Nicaragua were quite readily resolved once the period of superpower rivalry was over. And while all of these countries have experienced various difficulties during the past three or four years, none of them has yet slipped back into large-scale violence.

Given their deeper social roots and more overtly communal character, recent and current conflicts in regions such as the Balkans, the Caucasus,

Central and West Africa may prove far more difficult to bring to a definitive end. It also remains to be seen whether, at a time of increasing preoccupation with their domestic affairs, the world's more powerful states will be prepared to invest the political and financial resources required to underpin the peacebuilding process in these troubled parts of the world.

Since the middle of the 1990s, UNHCR and many other organizations have devoted a great deal of attention to the problems of peacebuilding. As a result, there now exists a considerable body of knowledge about the transition from war to peace and the ways in which that process can most effectively be supported.(38) While it is beyond the scope of this book to examine every aspect of this complex issue, a number of key lessons can be learned from the international community's recent efforts to bring armed conflicts to an end and to safeguard the security of the affected populations.

Diverse and differentiated strategies

First, there is no blueprint for peace. Looking at war-torn societies such as Afghanistan, Bosnia, Guatemala, Rwanda and Mozambique, it is quite apparent that the circumstances which lead to, sustain and eventually bring an end to civil wars and communal conflicts are extremely diverse. Peacebuilding strategies must reflect this diversity and be carefully tailored to the situation at hand. They must also be based upon a rigorous analysis of the circumstances which have led to violence. For as several experts have observed, the primary purpose of the reconstruction process must be to avert a recreation of the conditions which produced the conflict in the first place.(39)

The importance of a differentiated approach can be illustrated with regard to the issue of impunity. Influenced to a large extent by recent events in Bosnia, Rwanda and South Africa, there has been a growing tendency for commentators to suggest that without truth and justice there can be no reconciliation - and therefore no peace - in a war-torn society. This may be true in many cases, but it should not be a uniform principle. When the Mozambican peace agreement was established, for example, the country's political leaders agreed not only to declare a general amnesty but also to forego the opportunity of establishing a 'truth commission' of the type created in South Africa, El Salvador and a number of South American states. Given the absence of revenge and recrimination witnessed in Mozambique - a remarkable phenomenon in view of the atrocities which occurred during the war - this can only be regarded as a wise decision.

Foresight and early planning

Second, effective peacebuilding requires foresight and early planning. Even when a country is still at war, steps can be taken to support the transition to peace. Assistance programmes for refugees and internally displaced people, for example, can be designed in a way that discourages dependency and which provides the beneficiaries with skills which will support their eventual return and reintegration. A good example of this approach is to be seen in the land-mine awareness training that UNHCR and other organizations have provided to refugees from countries such as Afghanistan, Cambodia and Mozambique. Efforts can also be made to promote democratic values, human rights principles and a 'culture of peace' amongst the citizens of war-torn states (whether living in exile or in their own country), a particularly important function in the case of children and adolescents who have grown up in the midst of conflict.

Planning for the process of reintegration and reconstruction should also begin at a much earlier stage than has customarily been the case. Effective

Viewpoint III

Justice and reconciliation: the South African experience
by Frene Ginwala

The transition from apartheid to democracy in South Africa, through a relatively peaceful process of negotiations, is viewed by many as little short of miraculous. Just over a decade ago there were gloomy predictions about the situation in South Africa. The mission of a group of eminent Commonwealth leaders in May 1986 was aborted following military raids by South African commandos on Botswana, Zambia and Zimbabwe. Yet less than 18 months thereafter, the first tentative discussions between the African National Congress

(ANC) and the apartheid regime had begun.

There were a number of essential ingredients that made these negotiations possible and which facilitated their success.

When shorn of political rhetoric, the differences between the contending parties were not so antagonistic that a solution would have required either of them to come away from the negotiating table empty-handed. The inevitable victors (i.e. the party with the overwhelming support of the population) had a desire for an inclusive solution rather than any intention to exclude the minority from the polity or the country.

The relative strengths of the main antagonists were such that a fight to the finish would have been prohibitively costly, and for the ruling

National Party would have been politically unsustainable, as it would have destroyed the core objective it was seeking: economic power. The parties were conscious of their relative strengths, and of the implications of a fight to the finish. This awareness made negotiations a viable option, and gave the parties the political will to enter into discussions. An imperative developed for the two main parties to work jointly towards a resolution of the conflict.

The attitudes of the ANC were shaped by processes and developments that took place before the negotiations formally began. From 1987, white South Africans began reaching out to the ANC in exile in a search for possible solutions to the conflict. This was the starting point of the process of reconciliation - the search for what the other

side was thinking and believed in, and the reassurance that this provided. This exchange made it clear that there would continue to be a place for whites in South Africa, and that their language and culture would be respected and protected.

Initially, negotiations sought to secure an agreement for early elections. But elections were not possible in the abstract. The ANC accepted an agreement that an 'interim' constitution would be negotiated, while the National Party accepted that a final constitution would be adopted by democratically elected members of parliament.

This had two consequences. First, by negotiating a constitution we had to be precise; general agreements on principle were more likely to be renounced. Precision planning requires accurate information, and even in countries which are still at war, it is normally possible to collect a substantial amount of data about the situation in areas which have been devastated by conflict. In fact, it is with precisely this objective in mind that UNHCR and UNDP have recently devised a process known as 'district development mapping'. First undertaken in Mozambique, the objective of this exercise is to build up a detailed and regularly updated picture of all the development needs and opportunities which exist in potential areas of return. Looking to the future, far greater efforts should also be made to understand the repatriation strategies devised by displaced people themselves and to ensure that they are effectively supported by agencies working in both countries of asylum and in countries of origin.

---

ensured that everyone knew what was being agreed. The National Party felt secure as they were still in power and their supporters became accustomed to the idea of political change.

Second, it was easier to make concessions in negotiating an interim constitution as these could be reviewed later. It was therefore also easier to sell these concessions to one's supporters. In the minds of the people of South Africa, therefore, a transition began even as the process of negotiations continued.

The negotiation process was an inclusive one - 26 parties were involved in total and there were large teams of negotiators, not just one or two leaders. Negotiations were held in public so they could be followed in the media. This allowed the public to debate issues and

get used to the changes that were being discussed.

A decision on the issue of 'justice and amnesty' was postponed, albeit unconsciously. The National Party insisted that returning exiles had to apply for temporary indemnity against prosecution whilst the negotiations proceeded. A decision was effectively deferred until after the conflict was resolved.

For the ANC, Nuremberg-style trials were initially an option. But the very fact of the negotiations process meant that such trials were not possible. You cannot negotiate with someone and at the same time say that at the end of the process you will try them for crimes they have committed.

For the National Party, prosecution of members of the liberation movement was

also an option. But at the negotiations they sought a blanket amnesty as a means of closing the door on the past. We did not believe that perpetrators of human rights violations could grant themselves amnesty; only a democratically elected government could do so. The interim constitution therefore provided for an amnesty to be granted by the new government. As it was to be a Government of National Unity (GNU), the National Party accepted this as they would be a part of that GNU and felt that they could influence the process.

It was the GNU that proposed the establishment of a Truth and Reconciliation Commission. In keeping with an inclusive and reconciliation-based approach, our focus was not on exacting retribution for the past or on meting out individual justice. Our focus

was on the victims, not the perpetrators; our concern was to heal the nation and to ensure that such atrocities should not be allowed to happen again. For all of these objectives, the knowledge of exactly what happened and why it had happened was essential. This is imperative to facilitate forgiveness.

Dr Frene Ginwala is speaker of the South African parliament, co-founder of the Women's National Coalition and deputy-head of the ANC Commission on the Emancipation of Women.

Combining speed with patience

A third principle of peacebuilding is the need to combine speedy action with patience. The end of an armed conflict inevitably raises high hopes. Once the fighting has died down and uprooted populations have made their way home, people will expect their circumstances to improve very rapidly and in a tangible manner: through better access to education and health services, for example, as well as improved security and greater freedom of movement.

It is imperative to ensure that such expectations are at least partially fulfilled. It is equally important to ensure that the dividends of peace are shared fairly amongst different sections of the population. If they are not, there is a very real risk that old conflicts will be revived and that new tensions will surface, thereby delaying or reversing the peacebuilding process.

While speedy action is required in the aftermath of an armed conflict, it would be quite wrong to assume that there are any quick fixes in the transition from war to peace. Even when cease-fires have been introduced, peace agreements signed, combatants demobilized, refugees repatriated and democratic elections held, it can take a great deal of time to re-establish the nexus between citizens and the state.

If it took many years to reconcile the nations of post-second world war Europe, then it may take at least as long (certainly much longer than the one or two-year mandate usually given to the UN's peace-plan operations) to establish a degree of trust between groups of people who have inflicted terrible abuses on each other. It is also unrealistic to expect the transition from war to peace to progress in a unilinear manner. As witnessed most clearly in cases such as Afghanistan, Angola, Liberia and Sierra Leone, there will almost certainly be setbacks, whether in the form of new political crises, fresh outbreaks of violence and population displacement or an upsurge in criminal activity. Such setbacks must be the occasion for an intensification and a reorientation of the peacebuilding effort, rather than a pretext for a reduction or withdrawal of international support.

Generous and sustained financial support

Fourth, and as a logical consequence of the preceding statement, peacebuilding requires generous and sustained assistance. Given the deliberately destructive nature of contemporary warfare, post-conflict reconstruction is an enormously expensive undertaking. As societies which have experienced long periods of warfare are not in a position to fund this process themselves, and as private investors have little interest in infrastructural rehabilitation and the restoration of basic public services, the world's more affluent states must shoulder a large part of the burden. Moreover, this burden should not simply fall on traditional donor countries such as Canada, Japan, the USA and the states of Western Europe. Those newly industrialized countries which have recently enjoyed the most spectacular rates of economic growth - some of which have themselves benefited from international assistance in the past - should also play a more active role in mobilizing resources for reconstruction.

Those resources are required over an extended period of time. During the past few years, large sums of money have been allocated to peace-plan operations, repatriation operations and demobilization programmes for former combatants. But donor interest in peacebuilding processes tends to diminish too quickly. As one commentator has written, "despite a virtually universal consensus that fragile peace arrangements must be consolidated by means that visibly improve the security, well-being and confidence of the former adversaries and victims of conflict, international funding invariably declines far too soon after the ceasefire is in place."(40)

This statement is echoed by the UN High Commissioner for Refugees. "When there is no impending emergency, it is difficult to generate resources for what is perceived as - and often is - a risky and drawn-out process of rebuilding war-torn societies." It is for this reason that UNHCR has called for the creation of a new international funding arrangement for post-conflict reconstruction, designed to make resources available in a more predictable manner and to bridge the traditional gap between short-term humanitarian relief and longer-term development assistance. "Until now," the High Commissioner continues, "relief and development programmes have been treated as two significantly different ways of supporting people and countries in distress, leading to a dual structure in aid management which does not facilitate rehabilitation."(41) It is therefore of some significance that the World Bank has recently established a trust fund for post-conflict reconstruction, as well as a specialized new unit, dedicated to this issue.

Effective coordination

Effective coordination constitutes a fifth principle of peacebuilding. For without such coordination, there is always a risk that some elements of the peacebuilding process will be overlooked, that other activities will receive a disproportionate amount of attention, and that initiatives taken by one actor may contradict the efforts of another.

Unfortunately, recent experience suggests that effective coordination is easier said than done. This is partly because of the sheer number of institutions involved in the transition from war to peace. Thus in Bosnia, up to 240 international NGOs alone are believed to have set up a presence in the country, although nobody can establish a very accurate figure! But the problem of coordination also derives from the diversity of the organizations which are involved in the peacebuilding process.

UNHCR's involvement in the single task of returnee reintegration, for example, has required the organization to develop a working relationship with a range of different partners. To participate in comprehensive peace-plan operations, the organization has had to collaborate with the political components of the United Nations and the peacekeeping forces of member states. By developing an extended role in the area of returnee monitoring, UNHCR has been drawn into a new relationship with the UN's Centre for Human Rights and human rights field missions such as those established in Guatemala, Haiti and Rwanda.

UNHCR's efforts to implement QIPs and to link those projects to longer-term rehabilitation activities have naturally involved UNDP and international financial institutions such as the World Bank. Above all, perhaps, the task of reintegration has required UNHCR to work intensively with the national and local authorities in war-torn states.

Even if all these actors share a general interest in the transition from war to peace and the protection of human security, it would be unrealistic to imagine that their priorities are identical or even compatible. To give just one example, the World Bank and other financial institutions are primarily concerned with laying the foundations for long-term economic growth, an objective they have pursued by urging the governments of war-torn states to introduce market-oriented reforms and structural adjustment programmes. But as many aid organizations have pointed out, the short-term impact of such measures may be to increase unemployment, reduce wages, cut public services and provoke social or political unrest - conditions which are hardly conducive to the reintegration of returnees. (42)

While such institutional differences cannot simply be wished away, they can at least be managed and mitigated. At the global level, there is a particular need for organizations which are working together in reintegration and peacebuilding programmes to develop a much better understanding of each other's mandate, objectives and working methods, as well as their strengths and limitations. UNHCR's early and unrealized expectations of UNDP, for example, were based upon a general ignorance of the latter organization.

There are several steps which could be taken to avoid such problems: regular high-level coordination meetings; joint research and evaluation activities; a more systematic exchange of information and ideas; joint training initiatives as well as staff exchange and secondment programmes. There is also considerable scope for the establishment of inter-agency coordination units. In Central America, for example, the creation of a UNHCR/UNDP Joint Support Unit, staffed by personnel from both agencies, is widely recognized to have contributed to the successful implementation of CIREFCA, a regional programme focusing on the return and reintegration of displaced populations. (43)

The different actors involved should also treat the peacebuilding process in a more holistic manner than has commonly been the case. This is an issue which the member states and agencies of the UN system have discussed at considerable length in recent times. While the results of this process remain somewhat nebulous, an important principle has at least been established: the need for an agreed strategy which enables the government concerned, donor states, multilateral and non-governmental organizations to pool their resources and to ensure that the efforts of these different actors support, rather than contradict, each other.

International and national responsibilities

Sixth and finally, peacebuilding processes should carefully balance the principles of international solidarity and state responsibility. There are, of course, many ways in which external actors - particularly the world's more affluent countries - can support the reintegration of returnees and the broader transition from war to peace. They can provide the resources required to repatriate and reintegrate large numbers of displaced people. They can deploy the military forces required to demobilize an army and decommission its weapons. They can help to register voters and organize democratic elections. And they can pursue economic, foreign and human rights policies which encourage war-torn states to respect the rights of their citizens.

Such contributions, however, will be of little value unless they are matched by efforts to develop the indigenous capacities of war-torn states. Nor will they be effective unless they are accompanied by a genuine willingness on the part of national and regional leaders to promote social tolerance, to ensure that disputes are resolved in a peaceful manner and to be held accountable for their actions.

Unfortunately, in countries such as Afghanistan, Bosnia, Liberia and Somalia, some of the people who wield the greatest power evidently have nothing but contempt for such values. As a result, the return and reintegration of displaced populations and the transition to peace in general seem likely to be fraught with difficulties. More positively, however, it is worth recalling cases such as El Salvador, Eritrea, Ethiopia, Mozambique, Nicaragua and South Africa, countries where political leadership has been exercised in a largely responsible manner, enabling the peacebuilding process to move forward more smoothly and rapidly than many observers anticipated.

Setting out for Miami: Cubans at sea   © M. Meybourg/Signum

5 The asylum dilemma

Since the middle of the 1980s, more than five million people have submitted requests for refugee status in Western Europe, North America, Japan and Australasia. They have not received a particularly warm welcome. Confronted with growing social problems at home, and claiming that many of these asylum seekers are actually economic migrants, the governments of the industrialized states have introduced an array of different measures intended to prevent or deter people from seeking refuge on their territory.

Superficially, these measures appear to be having their intended effect; the total number of asylum applications submitted in the wealthier regions of the world has diminished quite significantly in the past few years, even though the global scale of forced displacement has continued to grow. But this outcome has been achieved at considerable cost: a decline in the standard of protection available to refugees; the diversion of the asylum flow to other parts of the world; and a substantial increase in the scale of human trafficking.

There is an evident tension between the right of people to seek and to enjoy asylum in another country and the right of states to regulate the arrival and admission of foreign nationals. While that tension is not easily resolved, it could at least be mitigated. This chapter identifies some of the ways in which states and other actors could address the asylum dilemma, focusing particularly on the notion of temporary protection. The analysis stresses the need for initiatives in this area to be consistent with humanitarian standards. The human rights of asylum seekers, it argues, must always be respected, whatever the validity of their claim to refugee status.

ASYLUM FLOWS: RECENT PATTERNS AND TRENDS

The term 'asylum seeker' refers to a person who requests refugee status in another state, normally on the grounds that they have a well-founded fear of persecution in their country of origin, or because their life and liberty is threatened by armed conflict and violence. The countries which receive the largest number of individual asylum applications are to be found primarily in the more affluent regions of the world: Western Europe and North America. But many states in Central and Eastern Europe, South-East Asia, Latin America, the Middle East and Africa are also in the process of establishing structures and procedures that will allow them to examine the asylum applications of people who arrive individually or in small numbers.

While the terms are frequently used synonymously, 'arrivals' and 'applications' should actually be differentiated. In many situations, people submit claims to refugee status in countries where they are already resident, whether as a student, businessperson, tourist, migrant worker or illegal immigrant. The total number of asylum applications received by any country in a given year is thus invariably larger than the number of people who request refugee status upon arrival there.

The category of 'asylum seeker' is a somewhat ambiguous one, in the sense that it includes some people who will ultimately be recognized as refugees, some whose claim will be rejected, and others who will be given some kind of residence permit, even if they are not formally granted refugee status. Until their claim has been examined all asylum seekers must be considered as 'presumptive refugees'. They are consequently protected by the principle of non-refoulement, which forbids states from returning people to countries where they might be at risk of persecution. Those asylum seekers who have passed through a refugee status determination procedure and whose claims have been definitively rejected, however, become subject to the normal immigration regulations of the state concerned.

The category of asylum seeker is also ambiguous in the sense that people who may automatically be considered as refugees if they moved to a neighbouring state might be regarded as asylum seekers when they travel further afield and seek admission to a country with individual asylum procedures. Thus the 750,000 Liberians who have crossed the border into Côte d'Ivoire and Guinea have all been granted refugee status on a *prima facie* basis. But of the 20,347 Liberians who applied for asylum in 15 Western European states between 1991 and 1995, only 214 were accorded refugee status.(1)

In some situations, changes in official admissions policy may convert what was once considered to be a refugee flow into a movement of asylum seekers. Throughout the first half of the 1980s, for example, the countries of South-East Asia automatically granted refugee status to the Vietnamese boat people arriving on their territory. In the second half of the decade, however, those countries introduced 'screening' procedures, requiring new Vietnamese arrivals to prove that they had a well-founded fear of persecution in their homeland.

Asylum applications: some facts and figures

As mentioned earlier, between 1985 and 1995, more than five million asylum applications were registered in the industrialized states. At the end of this period, at least 900,000 of them still had pending claims to refugee status, with the USA accounting for about half of the cases awaiting adjudication. It seems doubtful that such high figures will be maintained in the future, however, as the total number of asylum applications submitted in the industrialized states has dropped significantly since 1992, when it reached a peak of over 800,000.(2)

In order to gain a better understanding of recent asylum trends, it is necessary to examine the figures on a regional basis (see Figures 5.1, 5.2, 5.3 and 5.4). Turning first to Western Europe, the number of asylum applications grew from under 170,000 in 1985 to more than 690,000 in 1992. The numbers have steadily declined since 1993, however, reaching about 250,000 in 1996. While the number of applications submitted in Germany has declined from its peak in 1992, when some 438,000 claims were lodged, the country continues to receive about half of all the asylum applications in Western Europe.

As far as North America is concerned, the number of asylum applications in the region shows a generally upward trend: from 28,000 in 1985 to 173,000 in 1995. The USA accounted for most of this number, with asylum requests going up from 20,000 in 1985 to nearly 148,000 in 1995. The trend is different again in Asia and Oceania. After peaking in 1991 at 17,000, the number

Fig 5.1

Asylum applications in Western Europe, North America and Oceania, 1987-96

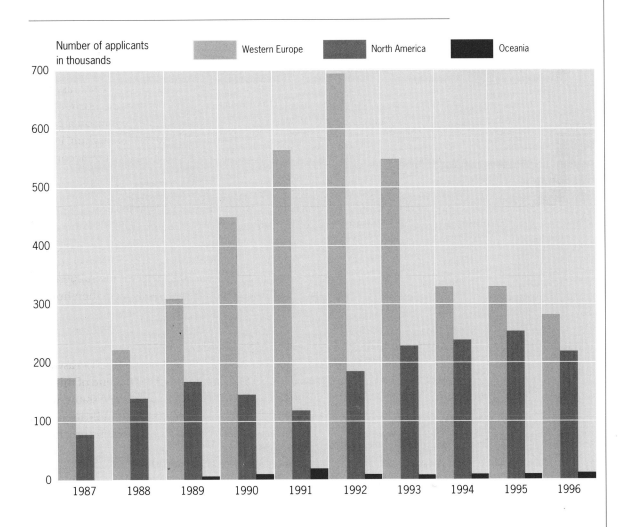

Fig 5.2

Asylum applications in Western Europe
by country of origin in 1996

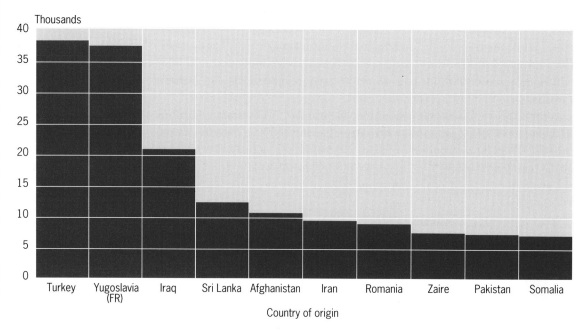

Thousands

Country of origin

Fig 5.3

Asylum applications in North America
by country of origin in 1996

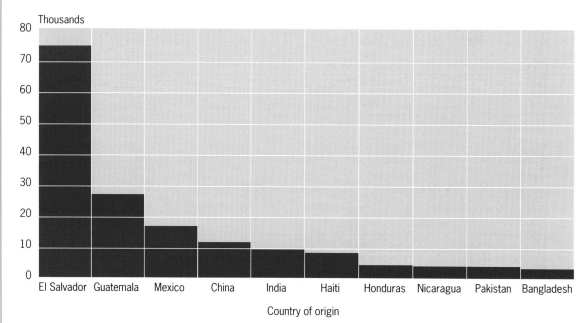

Thousands

Country of origin

of asylum applications submitted in Australia has since stabilized at around 4,000 or 5,000 a year. New Zealand received just 343 asylum applications in 1993, but this figure had increased to 1,310 by 1996. Of all the world's major industrialized states, Japan deals with the smallest number of asylum applications: around 150 in 1996.

Recognition rates

The notion of the 'recognition rate' refers to the proportion of asylum seekers who are actually granted refugee status. Between 1991 and 1995, 2.4 million applications for asylum were made in Europe. Of this number, some 212,000 - around 11 per cent of the cases decided - were successful. An almost identical proportion were allowed to remain for humanitarian reasons. In all, therefore, just over 20 per cent of asylum seekers in Europe were granted some form of protection between 1991 and 1995. In North America, the recognition rate has been much higher than the European average. It was

Fig. 5.4

Asylum applications: major receiving countries in 1996

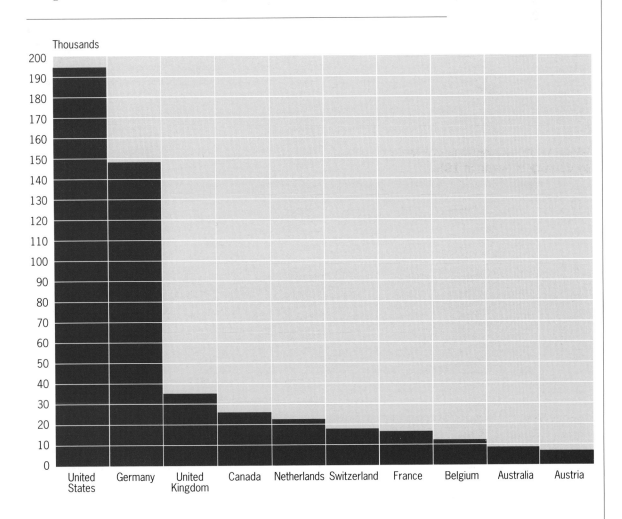

about 70 per cent in Canada in 1994 and 1995 and just over 20 per cent in the USA in 1995.

The relatively small proportion of asylum seekers who are granted either refugee status or humanitarian status - particularly in Europe - has given rise to conflicting interpretations (see Figure 5.5). For those who wish to impose stricter immigration controls, the low and declining recognition rate in the industrialized states is evidence of large-scale abuse of the asylum system. According to this belief, the majority of asylum applications are fraudulent, submitted by people who wish to migrate for economic reasons but who have no other means of gaining admission to these states. For many humanitarian organizations and analysts, however, the current recognition rates are a reflection of the increasingly restrictive refugee and immigration policies pursued by the world's most affluent societies.

Fig. 5.5

Refugee recognition rate: selected European countries, 1987-96

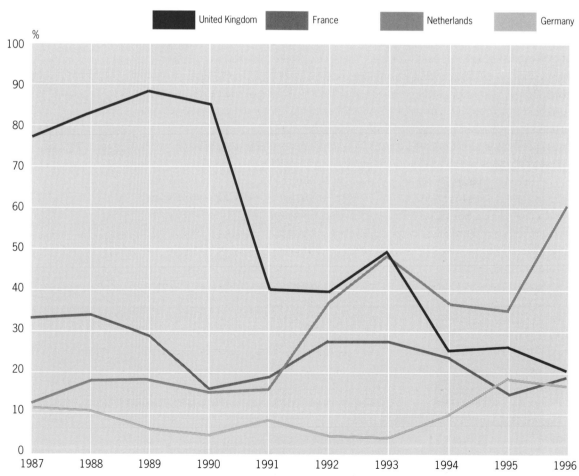

Figure shows total recognition rate for asylum applicants, including 1951 Convention recognition rate and humanitarian status. Figure does not include former Yugoslav citizens granted temporary protection

As suggested already, asylum seekers are not found exclusively in the industrialized states. Throughout most of the world, UNHCR and the national authorities have to respond to the arrival of individuals or small groups of people from other countries who want to claim refugee status: Angolans in Brazil, Afghans in India, Iranians in Thailand and Iraqis in Jordan, to give just a few examples.

With the dismantling of the apartheid regime, South Africa has become one of the most important destinations for asylum seekers amongst the low and middle-income countries. In early 1997, between 750 and 1,000 people were submitting claims for refugee status in the country each month, the largest numbers from Argentina, India, Nigeria, Somalia, Pakistan and Senegal. By May 1997, the country had a backlog of around 13,000 applications waiting to be processed. Of the 10,600 claims examined during the previous three years, only six had been granted full refugee status, while an additional 3,300 had been granted temporary residence permits. (3)

STATE RESPONSES TO THE ASYLUM ISSUE

In the 1950s and 1960s, relatively few asylum seekers and refugees from the low-income countries made their way to the world's wealthier states. The only large-scale movements into Western Europe, for example, took place as a result of the Hungarian uprising in 1956 and the Czechoslovak crisis of 1968. As a result of the post-war economic boom, moreover, foreign labour was in high demand, allowing large numbers of people from poorer countries to move to the wealthier states.

While much larger numbers of non-European refugees arrived in the industrialized states in the second half of the 1970s, primarily from countries in Indo-China and South America, most of them were admitted by means of organized resettlement programmes. It was not until the early 1980s that asylum seekers from countries in Africa, Asia, the Middle East and Central America began to arrive independently and in significant numbers. At around the same time, growing numbers of asylum seekers from the communist countries of Central and Eastern Europe also began to arrive in the west. Confronted with these flows, by the middle of the 1980s, almost all of the industrialized states expressed the opinion that they were experiencing an 'asylum crisis', often overlooking the fact that the real asylum crisis was to be found in the world's poorer regions, where the refugee population was increasing at an unprecedented rate.

The migratory context

To understand why the industrialized states reacted with such alarm, the broader migratory context has to be taken into account. The increased scale of the asylum flow which began in the late 1970s came just at a time when many of these countries were taking steps to curtail immigration. The long period of economic growth which followed the second world war had come to an end. As a result, the demand for unskilled and migrant workers was falling, while domestic unemployment was growing. It was also becoming increasingly clear at this time that those migrants who had been recruited from other parts of the world - even those recruited on a temporary basis such as the Turkish guest-workers in Germany - were unlikely to go home. Indeed, they were being joined by their family members.

The situation in traditional settlement countries such as the USA, Canada and Australia was somewhat different, in the sense that these states continued to admit large numbers of foreign nationals, both through regular immigration progammes and by means of special refugee and humanitarian quotas. Even so, such states were also perturbed by the growing number of people who were arriving on their territory in a spontaneous and independent manner, and who were able to jump the usual immigration queue by submitting claims to refugee status.

If the opportunities for immigration were diminishing in the 1980s, then the pressures to migrate from the world's poorer countries were mounting. In many such states, economic stagnation or decline went hand in hand with political instability, social violence and armed conflict. At the same time, the rapid expansion of the global communications network, the declining cost of international air transport and the presence of diaspora communities in the wealthier states gave a growing number of people both an incentive and the means to leave their own country and to seek asylum in another part of the world.

In the circumstances described above, it was becoming increasingly difficult to make a clear distinction between those asylum seekers who were fleeing from threats to their life and liberty and those who wanted to escape the poverty of their homeland. By the second half of the 1980s, asylum seekers had become increasingly confused with other immigrants in the official and public mind - a situation that was assiduously exploited by governments and political parties wishing to increase their electoral support.

The fear of mass immigration was reinforced in the final years of the decade, when the collapse of communism led to a belief that massive numbers of people would move out of the former Soviet bloc. In the event, such fears proved to be unfounded, due in large part to the lack of a westward migratory tradition in many of the communist states and the consequent absence of the social networks which made it relatively easy for many Africans, Asians and Central Americans to take up residence in the industrialized states. The importance of such networks was underlined after 1992, when large numbers of asylum seekers from former Yugoslavia began to arrive in Western Europe. It was no coincidence that many made their way to Germany, a country which in previous years had employed substantial numbers of Yugoslav migrant workers.

The world's more prosperous countries were thus left with a substantial problem on their hands. Throughout the 1980s, these states had struggled - and largely failed - to keep pace with the growing number of asylum applications which they received. The cost of processing these applications, and the sums of money involved in providing housing, social services and welfare benefits to asylum seekers, also became a growing concern to many governments. According to one estimate, the major industrialized states spent around $7 billion on these functions in 1991 alone. (4) At a time of budgetary austerity, the desire of governments to reduce such expenditure competed very strongly with their commitment to the principles of refugee protection.

RESTRICTIVE ASYLUM PRACTICES

Since the beginning of the 1980s, the industrialized states have individually and collectively introduced a wide range of measures relating to the arrival, admission and entitlements of people who wish to claim refugee status on their territory.

In an attempt to limit the number of asylum seekers at source, the governments of the industrialized states have extended visa requirements to the nationals of many countries that produce - or which threaten to produce - significant numbers of asylum seekers and irregular migrants. Sanctions, usually in the form of fines, levied on a *per capita* basis, have also been imposed upon airlines and shipping companies responsible for the arrival of passengers who lack the necessary papers (see Box 5.1). In an associated initiative, stringent pre-boarding documentation checks have been introduced in countries of origin and transit, focusing again on travellers from countries that produce significant numbers of asylum seekers. At the same time, asylum seekers leaving their own country by boat (Cubans, Haitians and Albanians being the most prominent examples) have been interdicted at sea and returned to their country of origin, or held on another territory until their status has been determined.

A further battery of measures has been introduced in relation to travellers who have managed to reach their intended destination. In some cases, new arrivals have been prevented from disembarking and have been sent straight back to their own or another country. Certain states have established detention centres at international airports, erroneously claiming that people who are held in such facilities have never been admitted to their territory. More commonly, governments have introduced fast-track asylum procedures with limited or non-existent rights of appeal, intended to facilitate the speedy removal of people who are deemed to have 'fraudulent' or 'manifestly unfounded' claims to refugee status.

States have devised the notion of 'safe countries of origin' in order to assist with the identification of asylum seekers who have manifestly unfounded claims and to channel them into accelerated asylum procedures. Acting again on both an individual and collective basis, governments in Western Europe have determined that the citizens of certain countries are unlikely to have a genuine claim to refugee status because persecution is rare in those states.

This is not to be confused with the 'safe third country' concept, whereby a state assumes the right to refuse admission to an asylum seeker if he or she has arrived via a country where their claim to refugee status might have been

5.1

Carrier sanctions

There is nothing new about the notion of imposing financial penalties and other sanctions on transport companies which disembark passengers who lack a valid passport or visa. Traditional countries of immigration such as Australia, Canada and the USA, for example, have had such legislation in place since the 1950s. In recent years, however, this practice has been extended to many other parts of the world.

The countries of Western Europe began to introduce carrier sanctions in the second half of the 1980s, at a time when the number of asylum applications submitted in those states was growing rapidly. By 1997, all the European Union (EU) member states except Ireland had introduced carriers' liability legislation of some sort or another, as had Switzerland.

Two European conventions actually stipulate that signatory states must implement carriers' liability legislation: the Schengen Convention on the abolition of checks at common frontiers, which came into force in March 1995 and which has been signed by all EU countries except Denmark, Ireland and the UK; and the Draft Convention on the Crossing of External Borders, which has yet to be opened for signature.

Carrier sanctions are not, however, a purely western or a northern phenomenon. In fact, they have now been introduced by countries in every part of the world: Argentina, Croatia, Dominican Republic, Guatemala, Iran, South Korea, Oman, the Philippines, South Africa, Turkey and the United Arab Emirates, to name just a few. Many other states which have not yet introduced formal carrier sanctions schemes nevertheless oblige transport companies to meet the costs of detaining or deporting passengers who arrive

without proper documentation.

Immigration control

One effect of carriers' liability legislation has been to draw airline companies and their ground staff into the process of immigration control - a function for which they were initially not well prepared. In order to address this problem, and to help airline companies avoid the financial penalties which they were incurring, the national immigration authorities of several states have provided training and technical support to airline personnel. As a result, carriers now subject travellers and their documents to more rigorous and frequent scrutiny, not only when they check in but also immediately before boarding an aircraft.

Although airlines have long protested that it is inappropriate and unfair to impose such tasks upon them, they have been obliged to accept these responsibilities as the price

of doing business in those countries which have introduced carrier sanctions. Given the penalties which they can incur, the airlines also have a strong financial incentive to prevent the embarkation of anyone who lacks the necessary passport or visa. The sums of money involved are substantial. The British government, for example, imposes a *per capita* fine of around $1,600 for passengers with incorrect papers. Between 1987 and 1995, airlines and other transport companies were charged a total of $140 million by the UK authorities, of which $85 million was actually paid.

States which have introduced carriers' liability legislation generally maintain that without such laws, the number of people arriving on their territory without valid documents would have been much higher. In that sense, carrier sanctions have had their intended effect. At the same time, however, these sanctions have had negative

submitted.(5) An associated initiative is to be seen in the introduction of 'readmission agreements'.(6) Under the terms of these agreements, asylum seekers can be deported from their country of final destination to their preceding country of transit, often in return for some form of financial assistance. Such accords do not generally include a commitment that the merits of an asylum seeker's claim will be considered upon readmission.

Germany is a prominent protagonist of this approach, having concluded readmission agreements with Bulgaria and Romania in 1992, with Poland in

consequences for the principles of refugee protection and human rights standards more generally.

Victims of persecution
First, states have a legitimate interest in controlling the movement of people onto their territory and have a right to curtail those forms of migration which assume illegal and irregular forms. But this right is tempered by obligations towards the victims of persecution, set out in international conventions such as the 1951 UN Refugee Convention and its 1967 Protocol, as well as the 1984 Convention against Torture. Carrier sanctions, which have been consciously employed by states as a means of avoiding those obligations, are not consistent with international refugee and human rights law.

Airline companies are neither qualified nor permitted to judge whether potential passengers are leaving their own country because their life or liberty is at risk, and

yet people in this situation may well have to flee at short notice and without the necessary papers. As a report to the Council of Europe commented in relation to the British legislation, "the Carriers' Liability Act has made it more difficult for asylum seekers to reach the United Kingdom, since it is in most cases impossible for a person fleeing persecution to obtain a valid passport and other legal documents."

Second, carrier sanctions have led to a growth in the production and use of forged documents. Indeed, the demand for such documents has helped to finance the burgeoning industry of human trafficking. In many cases, moreover, travellers who succeed in boarding a plane with forged documents destroy them during the flight so that they cannot be returned to their place of departure, thereby creating additional problems for the immigration authorities in the country of destination.

Finally, as well as the inconvenience which they

In 1996, more than half of all the fines imposed on the Dutch airline KLM involved travellers who had destroyed their documents.

Third, as a result of carrier sanctions, a growing number of people who have managed to leave their own country have nevertheless found themselves trapped halfway through their journey. The Sheremetyevo-2 transit zone at Moscow airport, for example, has held up to 20 passengers at any one time over the past five years, all of them prevented from boarding an aircraft to their intended destination because they do not possess the necessary papers. Given the nationalities of the people who have found themselves in this situation - most of them are from Somalia, Afghanistan, Iraq, Angola and Zaire - there is a very good chance that their number has included people with a valid claim to refugee status.

involve for airline staff and travellers, carrier sanctions lead inevitably to discrimination. While white passengers from the major industrialized states may be assumed to possess valid documents, members of ethnic minorities and citizens of developing and refugee-producing countries are far more likely to be treated with suspicion.

It is now highly unlikely that those states which have introduced carrier sanctions will choose to abolish them. Efforts must therefore be made to ensure that such controls are implemented in as equitable a manner as possible. At the very least, states should apply sanctions only if the carrier has shown negligence in checking documents, and should impose no fine at all in relation to passengers who submit an asylum claim which is subsequently accepted for consideration.

1993 and with the Czech Republic in 1994. Now that Germany has declared all of its neighbours to be either safe countries of origin or safe third countries, it has effectively renounced responsibility for considering the asylum request of any person arriving in the country by land without a valid visa.

Other measures have been introduced in relation to people who have already entered the asylum procedure, often with the effect of discouraging them from pursuing their claim. Practices such as the withdrawal of social welfare and legal aid entitlements, the introduction of restrictions on the right to work and education, and the protracted detention or imprisonment of asylum seekers all fall into this category.

Finally, the last decade has witnessed a growing tendency for governments (and even the courts) to interpret the criteria for refugee status in an increasingly restrictive manner. In some instances, it has been argued that asylum seekers should not be granted refugee status on the grounds that they had an 'internal flight alternative'. In other words, rather than leaving their homeland in order to seek asylum abroad, they should have sought safety in another part of their own country. In other instances, asylum seekers have been denied refugee status on the grounds that only states (rather than non-state actors such as warlords, rebel movements and unofficial militias) can be agents of persecution.

Most commonly of all, the industrialized countries have tended to insist that asylum seekers must demonstrate that they have been singled out for persecution if they are to be granted refugee status, and have used this principle to deny recognition to claimants originating from countries that are affected by more generalized forms of violence. As UNHCR has pointed out before, the drafters of the 1951 UN Refugee Convention did not intend the refugee definition to be interpreted in this restricted manner.(7)

THE HIDDEN COSTS OF CONTROL

As the statistics presented earlier suggest, the restrictive measures introduced by the industrialized states over the past decade appear to have had their intended effect. During that period, the problem of forced displacement has generally grown in scale and the number of international migrants has increased. And yet the world's wealthier states seem to have succeeded in limiting - and in many cases reducing - the number of asylum seekers arriving on their territory.

As a later part of this section will argue, while superficially successful, the measures introduced by governments in the more affluent states have had a number of negative consequences. Before going on to elaborate this critique, it is first necessary to make some general observations about the nature of the asylum dilemma.

First, as UNHCR has pointed out elsewhere, "the starting point for any serious approach to this issue must be that states and societies have a legitimate interest in regulating the movement of people into their territory."(8) The crux of the matter, therefore, is not whether governments have a right to impose controls on the arrival and admission of foreign nationals, but the extent to which those controls are consistent with international refugee law and humanitarian norms.

Second, it would be unfair to give the impression that the industrialized states are uniformly hostile to asylum seekers and refugees, and equally inaccurate to suggest that the institution of asylum has been irrevocably undermined in those countries. Canada, for example, has pursued a notably progressive refugee policy in recent years, as manifested in the country's recognition of claims to persecution on the basis of gender (see Box 5.2). As explained in Chapter Two, the Nordic countries and Switzerland have played a leading role in the resettlement of refugees with special needs and who, for one reason or another, cannot remain safely in their first country of asylum. And while Germany's decision to insist on the early return of Bosnian refugees has been criticized by UNHCR and other organizations, that country's generosity in providing temporary protection to well over 300,000 people from former Yugoslavia (far more than any other country) must be recognized.

More generally, it should be noted, large numbers of people continue to find some kind of asylum in the industrialized states. Indeed, the number of asylum seekers who were granted refugee status or some other form of protection in 1996 - around 140,000 - is very similar to the figure recorded in 1985, although the proportion of applicants being granted asylum has evidently declined.

Third, a critique of recent state policies in the area of asylum policy should not be read as an endorsement of the *status quo ante*. By the late 1980s, the asylum systems of the industrialized countries were evidently in need of reform. Considerable numbers of people without any need for international protection were clearly seeking entry to such states by submitting claims for refugee status. Existing structures and procedures were failing to cope with the demands made upon them. Abuses were certainly taking place. In Western Europe, for example, irregular migrants were able to go 'forum shopping' or 'asylum shopping', phrases used to describe the actions of people who moved from country to country, submitting successive (and in some cases simultaneous) claims to refugee status. It had also become evident by this time that only a small proportion of the applicants whose claims had been fairly rejected actually went back to their country of origin. Public confidence in the asylum procedure was consequently very low, a situation which did no favours at all for either asylum seekers or refugees. Both were regarded with suspicion.

Threatening human security

While the preceding considerations are sometimes overlooked by participants in the asylum debate, they do not detract from the fact that the restrictive measures introduced by the world's wealthier countries have had a number of negative consequences for the protection of refugees. In certain respects, moreover, in attempting to limit the number of asylum seekers arriving and remaining on their territory, these states have actually damaged their own interests.

First and foremost, the actions of the industrialized states have jeopardized the security of actual and potential asylum seekers. Visas, carrier sanctions and pre-boarding checks are blunt instruments. As well as impeding the movement of illegal and irregular migrants, they have almost certainly ob-

5.2

Gender-related persecution

Under the terms of the 1951 UN Refugee Convention, asylum seekers can be granted refugee status if they are able to demonstrate a well-founded fear of persecution in their country of origin "for reasons of race, religion, nationality, membership of a particular social group or political opinion." Persecution related to a person's gender or sexuality is therefore not explicitly mentioned in the principal international refugee instrument.

Over the past 15 years, however, there has been an increased recognition of the need to interpret the notion of persecution in a manner which is sensitive to issues of gender. In 1985, for example, the European Parliament called on states to grant refugee status "to

women who suffer cruel and inhuman treatment because they have violated the moral or ethical rules of their society." According to the European Parliament, women who have been treated in this manner constitute a "particular social group" and should therefore be granted asylum under the 1951 Convention. While the issue has not received the same degree of attention, there is also a growing awareness that men who transgress the norms of their society - homosexuals in certain countries being the obvious example - can also be persecuted on the grounds of being a member of a particular social group.

Obstacles to protection

Female asylum seekers who have experienced gender-related persecution are confronted with some significant obstacles in their efforts to obtain international protection. In their asylum interviews, women who have been subjected to abuse may find it too embarrassing

and humiliating to discuss with strangers, especially if they are men. The government officials who conduct such interviews may be primarily concerned with 'traditional' forms of persecution and be inadequately sensitive to gender-related issues such as sexual violence and forced marriages.

In contrast to those experienced by most men, the threats and dangers which confront many women tend to take place within a domestic context - a 'private' area which is sometimes regarded as being beyond the reach of international law. A closely related problem derives from the common belief that certain practices affecting women are sanctioned by culture or religion and therefore cannot constitute persecution, even if they violate universal human rights standards. It is therefore of some significance that the UN Declaration on the Elimination of Violence against Women

requires states to exercise due diligence to prevent, investigate and punish acts of violence against women, perpetrated not only by the state, but also by "private persons."

On the basis of recent legal cases involving asylum seekers, gender-based persecution can be said to assume six principal forms. The first and perhaps best established can be described as harsh or inhuman treatment for the transgression of social norms. A woman who transgresses the norms of her society may do so out of choice and as a result of deeply-held convictions. But such transgressions can also take place in circumstances over which the woman has no control. A rape victim who is threatened with prosecution and punishment for adultery would constitute such a case.

Second, persecution can take the form of sexual violence. Although women are

structed the flight of people who have a genuine fear of persecution in their own country and who are unable or unlikely to obtain refuge in a neighbouring state.

The measures introduced to impede movement after departure and to obstruct admission to the wealthier countries have also had negative effects. One disturbing feature of the current scenario is that of 'refugees in orbit' - asylum seekers who are shuttled from one country to another, trying to find a state which will assume responsibility for examining their claim to refugee status. It had been claimed that the safe third country notion would put a

particularly exposed to this form of persecution, both male and female children, as well as male prisoners, can be terrorized in this way. In Bosnia, for example, sexual violence was used as a systematic weapon of war, intended to intimidate and punish certain sections of society and to provoke their flight.

A third and somewhat controversial form of gender-related persecution is that of female genital mutilation or excision. Genital mutilation is a practice which few females seek to resist or flee, largely, perhaps, because it usually involves pre-pubertal girls. Obviously, the question of persecution does not arise in situations where women embrace or even tolerate a particular practice, however abhorrent it may appear. But in situations where it is imposed on a woman against her will and where the authorities are unable or unwilling to provide that

person with protection, then female genital mutilation could provide the basis for a claim to refugee status.

Fourth, on the issue of birth control, UNHCR has taken the view that national family planning policies cannot be regarded as inherently persecutory. When such policies are implemented in a non-discriminatory manner, when they are promoted on the basis of common welfare, and when respect for human rights is maintained, they can be considered as a legitimate state practice. However, as recognized in the Programme of Action from the 1994 Cairo Population Conference, all couples and individuals have a basic right "to make decisions concerning reproduction free of discrimination, coercion and violence."

The existence of family planning policies must therefore be distinguished from the methods used to implement them. Compliance may be sought by

persuasion, through methods such as education, publicity campaigns and economic incentives. But where coercive and intrusive methods are used, including forced abortions and involuntary sterilizations, a woman or man might legitimately claim to have a fear of persecution.

Sexual orientation

The punishment and mistreatment of people on the basis of their homosexuality has come to be regarded as a fifth form of gender-related persecution as it pertains to the roles which men and women are expected to play in society. Indeed, UNHCR has long held the view that a well-founded fear of persecution due to homosexuality can be a basis for the recognition of refugee status. Homosexuals are manifestly a "particular social group" in the meaning of the 1951 Convention, as a person's sexual orientation is a fundamental and arguably unchangeable part of his or her identity.

A sixth area of gender-related refugee jurisprudence is that of domestic violence, although this is a relatively new issue, which has formed the basis for successful asylum requests in only a small number of countries. Domestic violence becomes an asylum issue primarily in situations where the abuse attains a certain level of severity, and where the authorities are unable or unwilling to provide any protection to the person or people concerned.

In recent years, a number of countries, most notably Australia, Canada and the USA, have introduced guidelines for the assessment of asylum requests involving gender-related persecution. The intention of these guidelines is not to create new grounds upon which refugee status can be sought, but to clarify the interpretation of the refugee definition, not least by recognizing the specific forms of persecution encountered by women.

stop to this problem by making a single state - the first 'safe country' reached by the asylum seeker - responsible for examining their application. The evidence, however, suggests that the recent panoply of restrictive measures has not only failed to eliminate this relatively longstanding problem but has also created a new one in the form of 'chain deportations': the repeated removal of an asylum seeker from one state to another, on the grounds that he or she could have submitted a claim to refugee status in the previous country of transit.

Such incidents evidently add to the physical and psychological strain experienced by asylum seekers and place them at risk of being deported to their country of origin or to another country where they might be at risk. At the same time, the chain deportation phenomenon increases the total amount of time, effort and resources which states are obliged to expend on their asylum systems - precisely the opposite intention of the countries concerned.(9)

While one of the usual criteria for deeming a third country 'safe' is its accession to the 1951 UN Refugee Convention, it is also clear that the countries to which asylum seekers have been deported are not often as well equipped to consider claims to refugee status as those from which they have been removed. As the European Council on Refugees and Exiles has pointed out, "the complex web of readmission agreements is currently transferring much of the responsibility for assisting persons in need of protection to Central, Eastern and Southern Europe, where mechanisms of refugee protection and assistance are often less well developed."(10) In May 1997, for example, the Open Society Institute reported that Lithuania and Belarus were negotiating a readmission agreement which would enable the return of asylum seekers from the former to the latter state, even though Belarus was not a signatory to the international refugee conventions.(11)

Even if they are not prevented from leaving their homeland, and even if they are not turned back when they seek admission to their intended country of refuge, asylum seekers continue to experience unnecessarily high levels of insecurity. Much of this insecurity is of a psychological nature, derived from the length of time it takes for states to examine an asylum request. In Western Europe, for example, the procedure takes an average of three years, during which time the asylum seeker is obliged to live in a legal and social limbo.(12)

Increasingly, however, the insecurity experienced by asylum applicants is also assuming physical and material forms. As indicated earlier, even if they are not detained or imprisoned with common criminals - as too many asylum seekers are - then they are liable to find that their access to basic needs such as shelter, food and medical care is severely restricted. In the UK, for example, the withdrawal of welfare entitlements in 1996 caused widespread public disquiet and was challenged in the courts. In the course of these legal proceedings, one judge stated: "I find it impossible to believe that parliament intended that an asylum seeker, who was lawfully here and could not lawfully be removed from the country, should be left destitute, starving and at risk of grave illness and even death because he could find no-one to provide him with the bare necessities of life."(13)

Displacing the problem

The restrictive measures introduced by the world's more prosperous states have not resolved the asylum problem, but have merely diverted it. Initially, such diversions tended to take place from one of these countries to another. Thus in 1994, when the introduction of new asylum regulations caused a 60 per cent drop in the number of applications submitted in Germany, the number submitted in neighbouring Netherlands increased by around 50 per cent.

Now that all of the industrialized states have introduced stricter refugee policies, the asylum problem is resurfacing in other parts of the world. On one hand, as indicated earlier, UNHCR offices in low and middle-income countries which are readily accessible by air report a steady increase in the number of asylum seekers arriving from other continents. On the other hand, the combination of tight admission controls and readmission agreements has led to a substantial increase in the number of asylum seekers who have gone to - and who are frequently stranded in - the countries of the former Soviet bloc.

According to some estimates, there are now around 700,000 illegal and transit migrants in the Commonwealth of Independent States (CIS), of whom 500,000 are to be found in the Russian Federation alone. Of this number, around 180,000 are believed to be living in the Moscow area. Only a small proportion of this number, however, have approached UNHCR with a request for refugee status (see Box 5.3).

Encouragingly, some CIS countries and, more recently, the Baltic states of Estonia and Lithuania, have ratified the 1951 UN Refugee Convention and have passed national refugee legislation. But the institutional capacity to implement this legislation is underdeveloped and frequently imperfect. As a result, asylum-seekers from outside the CIS region often lack protection, have no legal status, do not benefit from social welfare services and may not even have access to refugee status determination procedures.

The growth of human trafficking

There is now a growing consensus that the restrictive asylum practices introduced by many of the industrialized states have converted what was a relatively visible and quantifiable flow of asylum seekers into a covert movement of irregular migrants that is even more difficult for states to count and control. There is also widespread agreement that such irregular movements are increasingly arranged and organized by professional traffickers. (14) These developments are intimately related to the geographical diversion discussed in the preceding section; it is no coincidence that the routes which traffickers use most frequently include those states in which large numbers of asylum seekers and other migrants find themselves stranded.

Traffickers are active in most parts of the world, primarily helping people to move to Western Europe, North America and Japan. Migrants from Asia, Africa and the Middle East are generally moved by ship, plane and truck to

5.3

Asylum seekers in the Russian Federation

During the past five years, more than three million people have made their way to the Russian Federation from other states. This influx consists of a number of different groups: Russian-speakers returning to their ancestral homeland, primarily from countries in Central Asia; non-Russians from the 'near abroad' (former Soviet states) many of them fleeing from armed conflicts in the Caucasus; illegal immigrants and transit migrants, the largest number of them from China; and asylum seekers from Africa, Asia, the Middle East and other parts of the world, known to the Russian people as the 'far abroad'.

During the past five years, around 40,000 asylum seekers from the far abroad have approached the UNHCR

office in Moscow for advice and assistance. Around 2,300 new cases were registered in 1996. By far the largest number - around 65 per cent of the total - are from Afghanistan, many of them people who were associated with the Soviet-backed regime which governed Afghanistan throughout the 1980s. In general, they have been educated in Russia and are familiar with the Russian language and culture. In that respect they differ from most of the other asylum seekers: around 7,000 people from countries such as Angola, Ethiopia, Iraq, Rwanda, Somalia, Sri Lanka and Zaire. Around 70 per cent of the asylum seekers registered by UNHCR in Moscow are adult males, and most are to be found in either Moscow or St Petersburg.

It is almost certainly true to say that few of these asylum seekers wanted or intended to remain in Russia for any length of time. Most arrived with the intention of moving on to Western Europe or

North America, either legally or by using the services of a trafficker. In practice, however, the increasingly restrictive admission policies of the industrialized states often makes it impossible for them to fulfill this ambition. As a result, a growing number of people who intended simply to transit through Russia find that they are obliged to remain there for a protracted period.

Law on refugees

In principle, the Russian Federation has taken some important steps towards the establishment of a legal and administrative structure related to the refugee and asylum issue. The country acceded to the 1951 UN Refugee Convention in 1992 and in the following year introduced a law on refugees, dealing with non-Russian nationals, and a law on forcibly displaced persons, pertaining to people with a claim to Russian citizenship. In 1993, the Russian government established a Federal Migration Service to deal with refugee-related

issues, and in 1995, a presidential decree was issued, giving effect to a constitutional provision on the granting of asylum to victims of persecution.

In practice, however, the impact of these laws and structures has been limited. Since the beginning of 1994, asylum seekers from the Commonwealth of Independent States and Baltic States have been able to register their requests for refugee status. In 1996, almost 20,000 people were recognized as refugees. Asylum seekers from the far abroad, however, have been treated somewhat differently.

Russia is not well placed to respond to the recent arrival of asylum seekers from other parts of the world. The country has never had to cope with such people before and its citizens are unused to having foreigners living in their midst. Russia has a host of domestic problems to deal with, not least of them the influx of ethnic Russians

relatively 'soft' entry points in Western Europe: from Morocco into Spain, from Albania into Italy or Greece, from the Czech Republic into Germany, and from the Baltic States into Scandinavia. The main gateways to the USA and Canada are through Central America, Mexico and the Caribbean, while Taiwan and Thailand are amongst the principal entry routes for irregular migrants being trafficked to Japan, Europe and North America.

China appears to be the most important single source of trafficked migrants, followed by South Asia. Afghanistan, Iraq, Nigeria, Somalia, Sri

---

from the former Soviet states, as well as an acute shortage of resources.

Government officials readily acknowledge, moreover, that the country's original intention in signing the 1951 Refugee Convention was to attract international assistance for the incoming ethnic Russians, rather than to assume responsibility for asylum seekers from Africa, Asia and the Middle East. The fact that many of the new arrivals do not even want to stay in Russia, and the fact that many of the Afghan asylum seekers are thought to have communist sympathies, reinforces the tendency for their problems to be ignored.

Those problems are numerous. Once they get into the country, asylum seekers are rarely deported, largely because the authorities lack the resources required to carry out deportations. But asylum seekers have been refused admission at Moscow's Sheremetyevo-2 airport, and have either been sent back to

their country of origin or to their last port of call.

Identity documents
In general, citizens of countries in the far abroad have not been able to register an asylum application with the Russian authorities. As a result, they cannot regularize their status in the country, gain access to public services, obtain a temporary residence permit or an identity document. They are consequently at a grave disadvantage when apprehended by the Moscow police, who are known to target foreigners and dark-skinned people during their patrols of the city.

Most asylum seekers who come into contact with the authorities are also hindered by the fact that they speak little Russian, do not understand the country's complex legal and administrative system, and do not have access to the network of voluntary agencies, lawyers and human rights organizations that are found in the states of Western

Europe. Not surprisingly in these circumstances, very few asylum seekers from the far abroad have been granted refugee status in Russia: around 80 people in total, most of them from Afghanistan and Ethiopia.

Since establishing a Moscow office in 1992, UNHCR has been assisting the Russian authorities to cope with the different population influxes which the country has experienced. In addition, the organization has provided assistance to people displaced within the Russian Federation as a result of the Chechnya conflict.

With regard to asylum seekers from the far abroad, UNHCR had had three primary concerns: to encourage and assist the government to establish a properly functioning procedure for the examination of asylum claims; to develop a network of lawyers, human rights organizations and non-governmental organizations which can provide advice and

support to people who are submitting an asylum request; and to offer practical forms of assistance to individual asylum seekers, especially those who are least able to cope with the difficulties of life in Russia.

Despite such efforts, the situation of asylum seekers in the Russian Federation seems unlikely to change substantially in the immediate future. In a society which is still trying to come to terms with the tumultuous political and economic changes of the past decade, and in a state which is preoccupied with other forms of migration and mass displacement, new arrivals from the far abroad are not a very high priority. Moreover, with the increasingly restrictive asylum and immigration controls introduced by states to the west, including new efforts to combat human trafficking, the opportunities for asylum seekers to move on from Russia and to seek refugee status elsewhere could well diminish.

Lanka and Sudan are among the countries whose nationals are most regularly trafficked. Significantly, all of these countries are affected by violence and human rights abuses and all of them feature prominently in the list of countries whose citizens seek asylum in Western Europe and North America. Indeed, recent studies of the trafficking business indicate that many, if not most, of the migrants concerned intend to apply for asylum on reaching their intended destinations. (15)

For the clients of these trafficking organizations, physical insecurity and financial exploitation are constant risks. As the penalties for trafficking have grown, the conditions for migrants have worsened. Having paid a substantial sum of money to move illegally across international borders, people are kept confined in ships' holds for long voyages, penned up in unsanitary conditions with little food or water. Drownings in unseaworthy boats, and suffocation in containers or hidden compartments in trucks, are among the harrowing stories that are increasingly reported from almost every part of the world.

The covert nature of trafficking inevitably means that it is drawn into the criminal world. Stealing and forging travel documents, work and residence permits have become an important industry. To get people across borders, it is often necessary to pay bribes to the police, immigration officers and local government officials. Migrants who manage to reach their intended destinations, usually after much exploitation and many privations, often find that they have to turn to crime to pay off their debts to traffickers; this may mean transporting or selling drugs for criminal organizations. The trafficking of women and children for prostitution is another clear link between the criminal underworld and the irregular movement of people.

The restrictive measures of the industrialized states have thus driven migration underground, prompting it to assume forms that pose a growing threat to the very societies that such practices were intended to protect. While precise statistics on this issue are inherently difficult to collect, there is reason to believe that people who would have a perfectly good claim to refugee status now no longer bother to submit an asylum application, fearing that they might be apprehended, detained and ultimately deported. The net result of the asylum and migration policies discussed above has thus been an expansion of the marginalized, excluded and criminalized underclass in so-called developed societies.

Hostility to refugees and asylum seekers

Although it is difficult to measure, there can be little doubt that public hostility to refugees has increased in much of the industrialized world. When asylum seekers are routinely labelled as 'bogus' by politicians and the press, and when would-be refugees are obliged to make use of irregular and illegal migration routes, then it is hardly surprising that they should be regarded with a degree of suspicion and hostility by the societies in which they hope to settle. Such sentiments have found expression in a host of different ways: from everyday prejudice and discrimination to murderous attacks on hostels inhabited by asylum seekers. According to some commentators, the constant suggestion that asylum seekers are illegal immigrants and 'welfare cheats' has created a fortress mentality in the industrialized states, legitimizing intolerance towards all ethnic minorities and marginalized groups.(16)

As well as reinforcing the inherent insecurity experienced by most asylum seekers, such hostility has also blighted the prospects of those who are eventually recognized as refugees. With such a difficult start in their adopted society, it is hardly surprising that many refugees find themselves socially and economically marginalized. Some states - the Nordic countries and the Netherlands, for example - have certainly made strenuous efforts to equip refugees with the skills they need to become productive members of their new society. But in too many of the industrialized states, they have been left to sink or swim.

One of the most troubling aspects of the restrictive asylum policies pursued by the industrialized states is to be found in their impact on refugee protection standards in other parts of the world. The countries of Europe and North America, it must be emphasized, were largely responsible for establishing UNHCR and for drafting the 1951 UN Refugee Convention. Such countries also continue to think of themselves as the standard-bearers for human rights principles and humanitarian standards. And yet these very same countries have taken a lead in challenging the spirit - if not the letter - of the 1948 Universal Declaration of Human Rights, which states that everyone has the right to seek and to enjoy asylum from persecution. In June 1997, for example, the European Union (EU) accepted a Spanish proposal, which could make it impossible for the citizen of one EU state to seek asylum in another, an initiative which has been criticized by UNHCR.

These developments have not gone unnoticed in the world's poorer countries, where the overwhelming majority of refugees and displaced people are to be found. Indeed, as Chapter Two pointed out, the governments of such countries now routinely refer to the asylum policies of the industrialized states as a means of legitimizing their own efforts to restrict the number of people seeking refuge on their territory.

ASYLUM RIGHTS AND TEMPORARY PROTECTION

What can be done to address the asylum dilemma? Introducing additional restrictive practices (if such remain to be invented) is evidently not the way forward. As the preceding section explained, the impact of such measures is simply too negative, whether seen in terms of the security of refugees or the security of states. A more constructive approach is required, addressing the whole range of issues involved in the movement of asylum seekers from one part of the world to another. The real test of such an approach must be the extent to which such measures safeguard human rights and are consistent with humanitarian standards - rather than the extent to which they reduce the number of people submitting claims to refugee status.

It must be acknowledged at the outset of this discussion that there are no easy means of resolving the asylum dilemma. Few if any of the policy proposals presented in the final sections of this chapter are new, and all of them are characterized by problems and limitations. If implemented in a consistent and coordinated manner, however, this package of measures would go some way towards improving the current situation.

Refugee protection principles

"It was in Europe that the institution of refugee protection was born, and it is in Europe today that the adequacy of that system is being tested," the UN High Commissioner for Refugees has observed. (17) As authors of the international law relating to refugees, governments in Europe and other affluent regions have a historical and a moral responsibility to uphold the right of asylum. If they do not, then protection standards in other parts of the world will almost inevitably decline.

A similar point has been made by another refugee expert. "Although no right to receive asylum yet exists in international, regional or municipal law," he writes, "a willingness to provide asylum is the litmus test for the commitment by affluent states to human rights. Affluent states cannot expect other, more vulnerable nations to execute demanding reforms or improve human rights conditions and at the same time claim that it is beyond their own substantial means to sustain a commitment to asylum." (18)

In practice, this entails much more than simply giving rhetorical support to the principles of international refugee and human rights law. First, it means eschewing restrictive interpretations of the 1951 UN Refugee Convention, such as the proposition that only states can act as agents of persecution.

Upholding access to asylum procedures is a second precondition for upholding the principle of asylum. As described earlier in this chapter, a great deal of effort has been expended by the industrialized states in the attempt to prevent asylum seekers from even setting foot on their territory. Technically, it is true, some of the measures employed to reach this objective are not specifically banned by the international refugee instruments. But as restrictive practices of this kind make no distinction between legitimate and unfounded claimants, they are clearly contrary to the spirit of the 1951 Refugee Convention.

A third area where reforms are required concerns the notions of safe countries of origin and safe third countries, as well as the related question of responsibility for examining asylum requests. The safe country of origin notion is an inherently dangerous one, as there is an evident potential for persecution to occur in any state, however democratic its constitution. The notion of safe countries of origin is also susceptible to political manipulation. Once they have established a list of nations which fall into this category, the world's more affluent states may be tempted to include their closest allies and most important trading partners.

As far as safe third countries are concerned, there is an evident value in arrangements which limit the ability of asylum seekers to apply for refugee status in one country after another. Governments have argued - and some legal experts agree - that asylum seekers should in principle submit their claim to refugee status in the first country they reach which has fair and effective determination procedures. But this should not take precedence over every other consideration.

Some asylum seekers have substantive connections with a particular country, whether through past residence, the presence of family members or through linguistic or cultural ties. Such connections, which in general are quite easy to verify, may make integration much easier for asylum applicants who are eventually granted refugee status. They may also help to reduce the social welfare costs incurred by the receiving state. As one commentary has suggested, "in sum, between the two extremes of allowing claimants multiple or unlimited choice of where to apply for asylum and providing them with no choice whatsoever, lies a middle ground that allows asylum seekers a single choice based on their ability to demonstrate pre-existing links."(19)

If asylum seekers are to be turned away from certain states on the grounds that they failed to apply for asylum in their previous country of transit, then it is imperative to ensure that high standards of protection are available in the place to which they are returned. It is certainly not acceptable to deport an asylum seeker to another country on the simple grounds that it has acceded to the 1951 UN Refugee Convention. The state concerned must also have demonstrated the capacity to fully implement that convention and to respect the international human rights instruments.

Asylum procedures

Turning next to the situation of people who have entered the refugee determination procedure, states should place much greater emphasis on the quality of the first instance interview and decision which they grant to asylum seekers. If these are of a high standard, undertaken fairly and thoroughly by properly qualified personnel, then there is likely to be less need for states and asylum seekers to become involved in lengthy appeals and legal proceedings. Regrettably, the 'front-line' staff employed by many governments - the officials whom asylum seekers first encounter when submitting their application for refugee status - are not always adequately equipped or trained to make such important decisions. States should take immediate steps to remedy this problem.

Decisions on asylum applications should also be made on the basis of an accurate understanding of conditions in countries of origin. It is for this reason that UNHCR's Centre for Documentation and Research has developed *Refworld*, a regularly updated CD-Rom and website, containing a huge quantity of information about the political and human rights situation in most countries of the world.(20) There is also a need for states to develop their own human rights information centres, such as those which exist in Canada and the USA, which have established publicly verifiable databases of information, drawn from a broad range of official and other sources. Making the information used in decision-making available to all of the parties involved would enhance the quality, speed and perceived fairness of the process.

During the past decade, states have regularly copied each other in the formulation and implementation of new restrictive measures. In fact, they have established a multitude of intergovernmental fora with precisely this purpose in mind. Regrettably, much less attention has been paid to identifying examples of good state practice which might usefully be replicated in other countries.

In this respect, some particularly useful lessons can be learned from examples such as the Danish asylum model.(21) Since the mid-1980s, Denmark has introduced a succession of useful reforms to its refugee determination procedures. Responsibility for initial asylum interviews was reallocated from the border police to a civilian body, the Aliens Directorate. The impartiality of the procedure was strengthened by authorizing a non-governmental organization, the Danish Refugee Council (DRC), to interview asylum seekers who were deemed by the Directorate to have manifestly unfounded claims. The DRC was authorized to veto the Directorate's decision, thus enabling the applicant concerned to enter the asylum procedure. Accuracy of interpretation and a better record of gathering case information were also improved through the employment of different interpreters by the DRC and the Directorate.

As a result of these reforms, both the government and refugee advocates agree, the impartiality and efficiency of Denmark's asylum procedures have been enhanced. The DRC's participation has helped to shield asylum decisions from foreign policy concerns, and has facilitated the identification of people who are at special risk. At the same time, the direct involvement of an independent body has legitimized the asylum procedure and has made it easier for the authorities to remove those people whose applications are manifestly unfounded.

While other states may balk at the idea of involving a non-governmental organization in an area which touches very directly on the issue of national sovereignty, such an approach clearly merits a much wider consideration. Indeed, systematic efforts should be made to ensure that the best practices of states with well-established asylum systems are emulated in countries which are now dealing with refugee issues for the first time. It is for this reason that a growing proportion of UNHCR's activities in low and middle-income countries are devoted to the establishment and reinforcement of national determination procedures by means of training programmes, the dissemination of information and other capacity-building measures.

While thoroughness should never be sacrificed to speed, all of the parties to any asylum decision have an interest in it being taken with the minimum of delay. Indeed, the so-called asylum crisis could probably have been avoided if the industrialized states had taken much earlier steps to establish effective and expeditious determination procedures. In this respect, there could be useful lessons to learn from the USA, where the Immigration and Naturalization Service has recently succeeded in reducing the waiting period for asylum decisions and has made substantial inroads into the country's huge backlog of pending cases.

Standards of treatment

When the 1951 UN Refugee Convention was established, little thought was given to the situation of people with pending claims to refugee status. Indeed, the Convention focuses almost exclusively on the rights and obligations of recognized refugees. It is for this amongst other reasons that asylum seekers in the industrialized states receive widely differing standards of treatment with regard to social welfare benefits, access to public services, the right to work, housing entitlements and conditions of detention.

To address this neglected problem, UNHCR, the states concerned and other interested parties should develop a set of agreed standards, applicable to people who are waiting for their status to be determined. Such standards should evidently discourage governments from introducing some of the more oppressive restrictive measures witnessed in recent years, particularly the withdrawal of social welfare benefits and the detention of asylum seekers. With regard to the latter issue, for example, bond or bail systems might be explored as an alternative to detention. Similarly, the establishment of relatively open but monitored reception centres might be considered as an alternative to the imprisonment of asylum applicants who are thought likely to abscond.

The heavy demands that asylum seekers can make on public resources and services should not be discounted, particularly in those lower-income countries which are beginning to receive substantial numbers of asylum seekers for the first time. But again there are alternatives that might be explored. Particular efforts could be made to determine whether non-governmental organizations, voluntary agencies, religious institutions and refugee community groups could make a contribution in this area, freeing state resources for those asylum seekers whose needs cannot be met in any other way. To facilitate such an approach, the official structures dealing with asylum issues should hold regular consultations with the institutions of civil society. In too many states, opinions on the refugee question have become dangerously polarized and politicized. This situation is in the interests of no-one, except, perhaps, those who would impose further restrictions on the right of asylum.

The role of temporary protection

There is nothing in international refugee law that obliges states to accommodate refugees if the circumstances which forced them to leave their homeland have been eradicated. As one expert on this issue has written, "protection is linked with the persistence of the causes of persecution. It is provided for a limited period of time."(22) On the basis of this principle, many developing countries admit refugees to their territory on a temporary basis, making it clear that the people concerned will be expected to go home when it is safe for them to do so. This has, for example, always been the position of the Pakistani authorities with regard to the exiled Afghans on its territory, for many years the largest refugee population in the world.

Until quite recently, people who have been granted refugee status in the industrialized states have normally been allowed to stay and settle permanently in their country of asylum, even if there has been a fundamental and durable improvement to the human rights situation in their homeland. There was a tentative move away from this approach in the 1980s, when the industrialized states began to grant various forms of 'humanitarian status' to asylum seekers who were in need of international protection, giving them a temporary right to remain in the country. This arrangement, it was felt, might facilitate the eventual repatriation of the people concerned. In practice, however, most of the people who were granted humanitarian status have been allowed to stay in their country of asylum on a long-term basis, often because of their inability or unwillingness to go home and the reluctance of the industrialized states to initiate deportation proceedings against people who had started to integrate in their society.

The policies pursued by the industrialized states took a decisive turn as a result of events in former Yugoslavia. In 1992, the number of asylum applications submitted in Western Europe reached an all-time high, placing heavy pressure on the asylum procedures of the countries concerned. At precisely the same time, substantial numbers of people from former Yugoslavia began to arrive in the region, escaping from the escalating war in the Balkans.

It was against this background that in July 1992, the UN High Commissioner for Refugees urged states to grant temporary protection to asylum seekers from former Yugoslavia, pending the time when the war had come to an end and they could go back to their own country. In the period which followed the High Commissioner's request, around 15 states, primarily in Western Europe, agreed to implement the temporary protection proposal. Altogether, more than half a million people have benefited from this arrangement, the largest number of them in Germany (see Figure 5.6).

Perhaps the most important benefit of the temporary protection approach has been that it provided immediate security to a large number of people whose lives and liberty were at risk, and spared them the anxiety associated with a long and complex refugee status determination procedure. Given the traumatic circumstances that forced people to flee from former Yugoslavia, the advantage of this arrangement cannot be overestimated.

At the same time, the temporary protection proposal has relieved states of the need to examine many thousands of individual asylum applications - a time-consuming and expensive process - and has enabled them to adopt a more generous asylum policy than might otherwise have been the case. Publicly and politically, the admission of former Yugoslav citizens became more acceptable because of the understanding that they would repatriate once conditions had improved at home. In this sense, as the UN High Commissioner for Refugees has observed, "temporary protection is an in-

Host country	Number of refugees
Germany	345,000
Yugoslavia (FR)	253,377
Croatia	288,000
Austria	80,012
Sweden	63,530
United States	38,000
Canada*	38,000
Slovenia	33,370
Switzerland	26,667
Australia**	24,000
Netherlands	23,500
Denmark	22,810
France	15,000
Norway	12,000
Italy	8,430
Macedonia (FYR)	7,210
United Kingdom	6,000
Belgium	5,884
Czech Republic	5,360

Fig. 5.6
Refugees from Bosnia and Herzegovina by host country

Statistics at March 1997
Table includes only host countries with more than 5,000 refugees
* This figure includes persons resettled from other countries in the region
** As at 31 December 1996

strument which balances the protection needs of people with the interests of states receiving them."(23)

The temporary protection principle has also had some broader benefits in terms of defending the principles of international protection in a situation of mass influx. As indicated earlier, the industrialized states have in recent years tended to apply restrictive definitions of the refugee concept. People from countries affected by war and generalized violence, those states have argued, should be granted protection only if they can demonstrate that they have been singled out for persecution. With the introduction of temporary protection, however, those same states have acknowledged a broader humanitarian obligation to provide a place of safety to people who have fled from a war-torn state.

Finally, temporary protection has helped to reassert the principle of international responsibility sharing. By admitting a substantial number of refugees from former Yugoslavia, the countries of Western Europe provided a concrete demonstration of their commitment to the principle of international protection and thereby provided a positive example to actual and potential host countries in other parts of the world. If the European states had not provided protection to people from Bosnia and other parts of former Yugoslavia, the whole of the international refugee regime would have been seriously undermined.

A number of important lessons can be learned from the international community's experience with asylum seekers from former Yugoslavia. First, it is evident that temporary protection is not in itself a solution to refugee problems and that this approach should not be applied in an isolated manner. If it is to have a real value, temporary protection must form part of a comprehensive international strategy, designed to deal with both the causes and the consequences of a refugee-producing conflict. In practice, this means that states must make vigorous and collective efforts to bring that conflict to an end, including, if necessary, the introduction of economic sanctions, the deployment of multinational forces and, when all other efforts have failed, coercive military action. At the same time, a comprehensive approach requires the effective provision of protection and assistance to those war-affected populations who are unable to leave the conflict zone and, once the conflict has come to an end, a properly coordinated and generously funded effort to promote reconstruction, reconciliation and justice in the country of origin.

A second lesson to be learned from recent experience is that people with temporary protection must be treated in a manner which is compatible with internationally accepted human rights principles and humanitarian standards. Although temporary protection is intended to be provisional and essentially short-term, people who benefit from this arrangement should evidently be granted a formal legal status, clearly defined residence rights, as well as access to adequate housing, welfare benefits, health care, psycho-social support and family reunification arrangements. The children of asylum seekers who have been granted temporary protection must receive a proper education, including mother-tongue language classes, during their time in exile.

The rights and benefits accorded to people with temporary protection must be progressively improved if it becomes necessary for them to stay longer in their country of asylum than was initially expected. Housing, welfare and work entitlements that are suitable for a few weeks or months, for example, may not be appropriate for a stay of several years. Such improvements do not necessarily contradict the principle that people with temporary protection should eventually go back to their own country. According to one school of thought, refugees who have been able to earn some money, receive an education and live a relatively normal life in their country of asylum may actually be better equipped and more prepared to repatriate than those who have been left in limbo for a protracted period of time.

As its name suggests, temporary protection should not be extended indefinitely. At a certain point in time, alternative long-term options must be examined for people who are unable to go back to their country of origin. As UNHCR has suggested in a paper submitted to its Executive Committee, "if return remains impossible after a prolonged stay of no more than five years, states should review the situation of temporarily protected persons, with a view to reducing their psychological uncertainty and to identifying long-term solutions for them."(24) Such solutions might include integration in the country of asylum, resettlement in a third country, or voluntary relocation to a secure area in the country of origin.

The third conclusion to be drawn about the temporary protection approach is that great care is needed in facilitating or encouraging the return of populations with temporary protection, not least because a proportion (and in the case of the Bosnians, a majority) of the people concerned might have qualified for refugee status if they had been able to apply for it on an individual basis. Both legally and ethically, therefore, such people must benefit from the principle of non-refoulement. It is for this reason that UNHCR has argued against the involuntary return of Bosnians originating from areas of the country where they would be a member of the ethnic minority.

Temporary protection should be brought to an end if there is a fundamental change in the circumstances that caused people to flee. But even then, repatriation should initially proceed on a voluntary basis. Any individual still claiming to have a fear of persecution, or who has been so traumatized by past events that he or she feels unable to go home, must be given an opportunity to present their case to the authorities. Individuals who require continued protection in their country of asylum must evidently be allowed to remain for as long as necessary.

While the temporary protection approach does not exclude the involuntary repatriation of people who no longer need to seek safety in another country, considerable caution must be exercized in this area. As UNHCR has affirmed in relation to the deportation of Bosnians with temporary protection, it is impermissible for people to be returned to places where their lives or liberty would be at risk, where violence and human rights violations are still occurring and where the necessities of life are unavailable.(25) In situations where forms of ethnic cleansing have taken place, moreover, it may eventually be necessary for people to go back to a new location within their country of origin, rather than their previous place of residence. Relocations of this type should be undertaken with the consent of the people concerned and with adequate preparation in the areas where they have opted to settle.

Viewpoint IV

Violence, displacement and asylum in Europe
by Otto Graf Lambsdorff

Poring with the despair over the tormented history of Europe, German writer Hannah Arendt arrived at the most poignant definition of the modern refugee: one who has lost his citizenship and whose effective statelessness "deprives him of expression within an action upon a common world, thereby losing all significance."

Arendt's Europe has changed a great deal. The good news is that we no longer face a divided continent, where the 'iron curtain' inflicted so much distress on those who happened to be on the wrong side. But the return of so many of our brethren to the common European fold, and the sudden enlargement of our continent, has created a wholly new configuration for all those who work on refugee problems.

Traditional policies of asylum ("as in the past, the safest mechanism when all other human rights protection fail," in the words of the UN High Commissioner for Refugees) are now being challenged. At a time when mass population displacements appear to be overtaxing the available public resources, asylum has become a highly sensitive issue in many European states. And this development has in turn threatened the continent with higher barriers against (and lower standards of protection for) those who wish to seek asylum in the region.

The inescapable need which emerges from the new European configuration is an agenda for action which revolves around four key concepts: prevention, harmonization, temporary protection and return.

Decisive policies to address the root causes of mass displacement are required because the risks of violent conflict remain very real, particularly along the central, eastern and southern confines of our continent. Such policies, which are clearly in Europe's strategic interests, should not be designed to obstruct the departure of people from situations of violence or persecution, but should aim to establish the rule of law within states, as well as a respect for the legal rights and citizenship status of individuals and minority groups.

Clearly, the only stable anchor for an effective policy of conflict prevention is the European Union (EU). Indeed, with the Maastricht agreement, the EU has sought to place a common asylum and migration policy at the heart of its agenda, as well as a programme of assistance to potential new members in the central and eastern parts of the continent.

But as we know, the process of harmonizing European asylum policy is not without its pitfalls. Different attitudes often prevail among the EU's 15 member states. Germany, for example, having borne the burden of hundreds of thousands of asylum seekers throughout the 1980s and early 1990s, eventually felt obliged to make fundamental changes to its laws and rules of entry. The risk now is that the EU member states will settle for the lowest common denominator in terms of their

UNHCR's caution in relation to the involuntary return of people with temporary protection also derives from the organization's awareness that such repatriation movements are likely to act as a destabilizing factor in war-torn societies. This issue has arisen not only in Bosnia, but also in relation to the US government's efforts to repatriate Central American asylum seekers whose temporary right of residence has expired. El Salvador, for example, receives an estimated 12 per cent of its gross national product - its largest single source of income - from the remittances of people living in the USA.

According to the Salvadoran government, the mass repatriation of its citizens would not only deprive the country of this income, but would also create a massive and socially explosive unemployment problem. Clearly, the industrialized states would be ill-advised to insist upon the return of people

obligations to refugees. The harmonization process remains on the whole highly desirable, but the EU and its members must do all in their power to prevent it from resulting in ever declining standards of protection.

Contrary to recent initiatives, we should not make it impossible for the citizen of one EU state to seek asylum in another. As UNHCR has rightly pointed out, such a decision would undermine the legitimacy and global relevance of international refugee law, and set a precedent which other regional groups - the Commonwealth of Independent States, for example - may well feel tempted to follow.

The countries of Western Europe have an important part to play with regard to the countries of Central and Eastern Europe and the Baltic states, which are now themselves becoming places of immigration for people from other parts of the world. More specifically, the European Union and its member states should help such countries to establish the legal and administrative structures required to examine individual asylum applications in an effective and humane manner.

However daunting they may be, the challenges to Europe's traditional policies of asylum should be put in some perspective. It was, after all, the European states which did so much to formalize the notion of refugee protection - first in the days after the first world war, through the work of High Commissioner for Refugees Fridtjof Nansen, and then with the Geneva Conventions and the UN Refugee Convention in the wake of the second world war. At that time, the countries of Western Europe were confronted with flows of displaced people which had to be measured in millions, even tens of millions. Today, however, the number of asylum seekers in Europe, totalling only a few hundred thousand each year, is actually falling. Clearly, it is our historical obligation to see that Europe manages today's asylum issues in a way that is consistent with our past and without yielding to vocal but marginal xenophobic tendencies which belie the continent's very soul.

In its efforts to address this challenge, Europe has devised a new and powerful concept: that of temporary protection. This quintessentially pragmatic tool provides a means of ensuring protection to those who need it and safeguarding the principles of refugee law, without overwhelming the asylum procedures of the countries concerned. More than 500,000 people from former Yugoslavia have benefited from this approach to the refugee problem, the largest number of them in Germany.

As well as providing a means of avoiding the refoulement or expulsion of people who are in need of asylum, the temporary protection approach incorporates another key concept: that of return. It is, perhaps, the ultimate yardstick of any successful refugee policy that it eventually allows those who have been forced to abandon their homeland to resume a normal life as citizens within their own state.

Dr Otto Graf Lambsdorff is a member of the German Federal Parliament and a former Federal Minister of Economic Affairs. He is also European Chairman of the Trilateral Commission.

with temporary protection if such a repatriation movement were to lead to renewed unrest in the country of origin and further population displacements.

ASYLUM AND MIGRATION: THE BROADER ISSUES

The effort to protect the right of asylum in the industrialized states must start with the rights of asylum seekers. This was the message conveyed by the UN High Commissioner for Refugees when she spoke at Washington's Holocaust Memorial Museum in April 1997. "Speak up for human rights," she told the audience. "Insist that the rights of refugees and asylum seekers are respected. Work against the imprisonment of asylum seekers. Maintain social services for refugees."(26)

In addition to these activities, which impinge directly on the rights and welfare of asylum seekers, there are a number of broader tasks which must be accomplished if the asylum dilemma is to be effectively addressed. This section examines those tasks, focusing on issues such as the role of public opinion, the return of rejected cases, the regularization of migration flows and the reduction of migration pressures in countries of origin.

Changing public opinion

The so-called asylum crisis in the industrialized states is to a large extent rooted in ignorance and fear. Politicians and the public in such countries often fail to make any distinction between refugees, asylum seekers, legal and illegal immigrants. They feel that their societies are being flooded by people who make little or no contribution to the life of their country. And, despite all of the restrictive measures introduced in recent years, the public seems to have lost confidence in the efficacy of the asylum systems established by their governments.

This phenomenon is not just a characteristic of the industrialized states. In South Africa, for example, there is a significant backlash against the arrival of people from other countries. "There is," one commentator writes, "a blunt and increasingly bellicose mythology targeted at non-South Africans living in the country." In the popular imagination, they "take jobs, commit crimes, depress wages, spread AIDS, and smuggle arms and drugs."(27)

Credible public information has an important part to play in puncturing some of the commonly held myths about refugees, thereby de-dramatizing and depoliticizing the asylum debate. The public in receiving countries should be properly informed about the number of asylum seekers arriving on their territory. The concern that these numbers are unmanageable should be dispelled. To begin with, it would be helpful to point out that the granting of refugee status to some 10 per cent of all applicants does not mean that the remaining 90 per cent are 'bogus', as many commentators and politicians maintain. As discussed earlier, a substantial proportion of asylum seekers are granted some kind of humanitarian status even if they are not recognized as refugees.

More could be done to make the public aware of the positive contribution that refugees can make to their host country, not just economically, but also socially and culturally. Care has to be exercized on this issue, however, if the distinction between refugees and other migrants is to be maintained: asylum seekers should be admitted to countries because they are in fear of their lives and in need of protection, not because of the economic contribution they may make to the society where they settle. As a further means of building public support for generous asylum policies, steps should be taken to explain the principle of responsibility sharing, pointing out that the world's poorest states continue to provide refuge to the vast majority of forcibly displaced people.

A more sympathetic environment could also be established by means of measures to promote the social and economic integration of recognized refugees. The idea that refugees are unproductive and a drain on public resources is in many senses a self-fulfilling prophecy. If, in the interests of economy, refugees are deprived of the means to adapt to their new country (language skills, vocational training, employment counselling and secure housing) then it is hardly surprising that they should encounter problems in becoming full and self-supporting members of society. In this respect, there is a particularly important (but too often neglected) role to be played by the refugee associations and community organizations which invariably spring up in cities with exiled and immigrant populations.(28)

The return of rejected cases

Better procedures for the repatriation of unsuccessful asylum seekers must also be developed if politicians and the public are to have greater confidence in the systems used to examine claims to refugee status. The treatment of rejected cases is undoubtedly problematic, even in situations where asylum seekers have had their cases examined in a fair and thorough manner, and where it is evident that they have no compelling reason to remain in their intended country of refuge.

According to some commentators, up to 80 per cent of rejected asylum seekers in the industrialized states stay on after the rejection of their claims, often because the authorities consider that it is too costly or difficult to apprehend and deport them.(29) Without legal status or a legitimate means of livelihood, such people cannot help but be propelled into the underworld of illegal employment and crime. Other observers dispute the suggestion that states are shying away from the deportation of rejected cases, pointing to the example of Germany, which deported more than 33,500 people in 1994, a year in which the country received just over 127,000 new asylum applications for refugee status.(30) The treatment of rejected cases is thus another dimension of the asylum issue in which state practice varies considerably from country to country.

Wherever the truth lies in this matter, the treatment of rejected cases is an important factor in establishing the legitimacy of refugee determination procedures. If such individuals are allowed to remain in the country where their application has been turned down, public confidence will inevitably be undermined. As a result, *bona fide* claimants may suffer. In cases where the return of rejected cases is warranted, the procedure employed to remove them should evidently be as safe, humane and transparent as possible. An unsuccessful asylum seeker has no fewer human rights than any other person, and no less an entitlement to be treated in a dignified manner. Regrettably, these principles have not always been respected by the affluent states.

There is a good humanitarian case to be made for providing a very modest amount of assistance to rejected asylum seekers who are deported to their country of origin or who return voluntarily to their homeland. In fact, receiving states might offer a slightly more generous sum of money to those who go back of their own accord, and who therefore spare the state the considerable expense involved in involuntary removals.

In order to allay the fears which are frequently expressed by asylum seekers and human rights organizations, arrangements should be made to monitor the welfare of rejected cases once they have gone back to their homes. UNHCR has, for example, played an extensive role with regard to unsuccessful asylum seekers who have returned to Viet Nam, an arrangement established in the context of the Comprehensive Plan of Action for Indo-Chinese Refugees (CPA).(31) UNHCR has also played a more limited role in relation to rejected asylum seekers who have been returned from Switzerland to Sri Lanka. While such activities are inherently sensitive in nature and fall somewhat beyond the organization's usual mandate, they have an important part to play in resolving the asylum dilemma.

Finally, it must be emphasized that countries of origin have an obligation to facilitate the return of nationals who have unsuccessfully sought asylum in another country. Unfortunately, there have been too many recent cases in which governments have refused to accept this responsibility (often on quite spurious grounds) thereby making it even more difficult to address the asylum question.

Regularizing population movements

Many commentators hold the view that the increase in asylum claims during the 1980s and early 1990s resulted largely from the closure or curtailment of regular migration channels into the industrialized states.(32) If that is correct, then it follows that an orderly reopening of such channels might relieve some of the migration pressure which exists in less developed states and help to disentangle asylum seekers from the flow of economic migrants. Other commentators, however, challenge such assertions. Some asylum advocates dispute the notion that substantial numbers of economic migrants have been using the asylum door as a means of entry, pointing to the fact that many refugee claimants come from countries which are not only poor, but which are also affected by violence and human rights violations.(33)

Others suggest that the people who have been seeking asylum in the industrialized states - whether or not they have well-founded claims to refugee status - are not the kind of migrants who would or could successfully make use of regular migration channels. The experience of countries such as the USA, Canada and Australia, which continue to have relatively large immigration programmes, lends weight to the latter argument, as the volume of asylum applications in those countries has followed broadly the same trend as in Europe.(34) Despite such reservations, the regularization of migration is increasingly regarded as a useful means of tackling the asylum question. Indeed, UNHCR has played a leading role in developing the notion of 'migration management', and has already put this principle into practice in several different parts of the world.(35)

Perhaps the earliest form of migration management undertaken by UNHCR is to be seen in the Vietnamese Orderly Departure Programme (ODP) which dates back to the late 1970s. In brief, the purpose of the ODP has been to provide Vietnamese citizens with a safe and legal means of leaving their own country, thereby averting the need for them to embark upon a risky and expensive boat journey to other states in the region. Well over half a million people have participated in the programme, most of them going to the USA and Australia. The migration agreement signed between the USA and Cuba in 1994 represents another form of orderly departure programme, although UNHCR has not been involved in this initiative (see Box 5.4).

Both the Vietnamese ODP and the US-Cuba migration agreement have been somewhat neglected by refugee and migration scholars, a somewhat surprising omission given their innovative character. A systematic examination of the orderly departure notion, focusing particularly on the implications of such an approach for the principles of refugee protection, would be of considerable value.

At the same time, additional thought should be given to the idea of processing asylum applications within countries of origin, as the USA has done to a limited extent in Haiti. The potential problems of such a system are quite evident. To what extent will people who have a well-founded fear of persecution be prepared to make themselves known to a foreign embassy or international processing centre? How many people without any need for international protection would attempt to take advantage of such arrangements? And how many states would be prepared to tolerate the establish-

5.4

Cuban and Haitian asylum seekers

For asylum seekers wishing to leave authoritarian and poverty-stricken states in the Caribbean, the USA represents a natural and nearby place of refuge. As the following analysis indicates, the USA has in recent years responded to the arrival of such asylum seekers with a wide variety of measures: interdiction at sea and involuntary return, in-country and shipboard asylum processing procedures, the establishment of 'regional safe havens' and migration management agreements with countries of origin. The objective of all these different measures has been largely the same, however: to limit the number of people arriving spontaneously on US territory and seeking admission there.

The case of Cuba

For most of the past three decades, Cubans have sought - and received - refuge in the USA. From 1959 until 1994, the USA operated a more or less open-door policy towards asylum seekers from Cuba, reflecting Washington's deep hostility to the communist government of Fidel Castro.

In the past few years, a number of developments have prompted the US government to abandon this longstanding policy: the end of the cold war and the consequent disappearance of the communist threat; a growing sense that the USA is losing control of the immigration and asylum problem; and a recognition by Washington that the authorities in Havana have the capacity to create substantial problems for the USA by the simple means of allowing large numbers of Cuban citizens to set sail for Florida.

All of these considerations came into play in 1994, when, as a result of deteriorating economic conditions, the number of Cubans making their way to the USA by boat and raft (commonly known as *balseros*) increased very rapidly. Many of the rafters were intercepted by the Cuban authorities, a policy which led to the drowning of several *balseros*, a number of violent boat hijackings and to anti-government riots. When the Cuban government responded to these events by lifting its restrictions on departure from the island, large numbers of people

Map L

Cuba, Haiti and the USA

◻   Capital

●   Town

▬   International boundary

began to prepare for the hazardous journey to Florida.

Faced with an impending influx of Cuban rafters, the US government announced in August 1994 that those who were picked up at sea by the Coast Guard would no longer be taken to Florida. Instead, they would be held at the US naval base in Guantanamo Bay, which is located on the same island as Cuba, and at another holding centre in the Panama canal zone.

The following month, US and Cuban negotiators reached an agreement on measures to stem the number of people trying to reach US territory by sea. The agreement contained four main provisions. First, the US confirmed its earlier decision to end the longstanding practice of allowing automatic entry to Cubans arriving on its shores. Second, the two countries agreed that the Cuban authorities would take action "to prevent unsafe departures using mainly persuasive means." Third, the Clinton and Castro adminstrations expressed a joint commitment to take effective measures against Cubans involved in the hijacking of ships and aircraft. Finally, the US government agreed to issue entry visas to 20,000 Cubans a year, thereby allowing them to leave their homeland by regular means. While it was not written into the agreement, it is widely

believed that the two countries also reached an understanding that the longstanding US trade embargo enforced upon Cuba might be eased if Havana introduced political and economic reforms.

Welcoming the agreement, President Bill Clinton observed that it would "help to ensure that the massive flow of dangerous and illegal migration will be replaced by a safer, legal and more orderly process." In this sense, the US-Cuba accord epitomized the current concerns of the industrialized states in relation to asylum and migration issues: their fear of uncontrolled population flows; their desire to channel 'irregular' and 'spontaneous' migration into more predictable and organized movements; and their belief that countries of origin should themselves play a part in the management of international migration.

By the beginning of 1995, the number of departures from Cuba by sea had fallen dramatically, but more than 30,000 rafters were still being held at Guantanamo Bay and in Panama. In May 1995, the US and Cuban governments agreed that most of the rafters still held at Guantanamo would be admitted to USA - reversing the earlier decision that they would not be allowed to enter. Despite objections from parts of the

Cuban-American community, the Clinton administration also announced that in future, rafters who were rescued or intercepted at sea would normally be returned to Cuba following a brief onboard screening procedure. Cubans who wished to enter the USA would then have to participate in the regular migration programme established by the 1994 accord, or approach the US Interests Section in Havana to apply for refugee status.

In late 1996, after another deterioration in relations between the two states had led to a suspension of negotiations, an understanding was reached over the return of those Cubans who succeeded in making their own way to US territory without a valid visa. From December 1996, they were to be treated like other illegal immigrants and would be subject to deportation.

US refugee and human rights organizations have been highly critical of the treatment of Cuban asylum seekers and the implications of the migration agreement, particularly the continuing restrictions on departure from Cuba and Havana's refusal to allow humanitarian organizations to monitor the treatment of rafters who have been returned to the country. Such concerns were reinforced in early 1997, when six Cubans who had been intercepted by the US

Coast Guard and handed over to the Cuban authorities were sentenced to long prison terms for trying to leave the country in a hijacked boat. The Cuban authorities, however, pointed out that the prison sentences were justified by the violent nature of the hijacking - the type of incident that the agreement with the USA was specifically designed to eliminate. By early 1997, more than 500 Cubans had been sent back to their homeland under the terms of the 1994 accord.

Haitian boat people

Haitian boat people, who have been arriving by boat on the shores of Florida since the early 1970s, have traditionally been treated differently from the Cuban *balseros*. Unlike the Cubans, who were until recently welcomed as refugees from a communist regime, consistent efforts have been made to interdict the boat people at sea, to deny them asylum in the USA, and to return them to Haiti.

Such policies can be explained by reference to a number of factors: Haiti's traditional support for US foreign policy and its role in the containment of Cuban communism; the belief that Haitians were leaving their homeland for economic rather than political reasons; the relative ease with which Haitian boat people could be intercepted and returned, unlike the much larger movement of asylum seekers and migrants across the Mexican border; and, according to many commentators, racism. Unlike the Cuban asylum seekers, a racially mixed group of people, the Haitian boat people were almost exclusively black.

In September 1981, an agreement was established between the USA and the government of Haiti, establishing a cooperative programme of interception and return. Interdictions by the US Coast Guard began almost immediately, and continued after the fall of the Duvalier regime in 1986. By September 1991, when the democratically elected government of President Aristide was overthrown, the Coast Guard had intercepted 443 vessels and interdicted 23,551 Haitians, of whom just 28 were admitted to the USA and allowed to apply for asylum.

The number of departures declined considerably during Aristide's brief tenure of office, but the outflow of Haitians increased in 1991 after the military coup that overthrew him. With the political, human rights, economic and environmental situation in the country deteriorating, nearly 10,000 Haitians were interdicted by the Coast Guard in 1991 and another 31,400 in 1992. Up to 30,000 more fled across the border to the Dominican

Republic. In November 1991 the US courts placed a temporary restraint on repatriation and a screening facility was set up at Guantanamo Bay. In the six months which followed, 34,000 Haitians were interdicted at sea and taken to the naval base. Some 10,500 were found to have a plausible asylum claim and were taken to the USA.

In May 1992, with the presidential election approaching, Washington issued an order ending asylum screenings and directing the repatriation of all Haitians who were interdicted at sea. The only recourse for Haitian asylum seekers was now to be an in-country refugee processing programme. Around 1,300 of the many Haitians who subsequently submitted applications to this programme were admitted to the USA. UNHCR was critical of the interdiction and return policy, pointing to the violence and human rights abuses which had taken place in Haiti since the overthrow of Aristide, and the dangers to which Haitians would be exposed if they were returned to their own country.

Despite such criticisms, direct returns to Haiti continued until May 1994, when another change of policy was prompted by the continuing outflow of boat people (nearly 25,000 were

apprehended by the US in 1994), the renunciation of the 1981 migration accord by president-in-exile Aristide, and continuing criticism of the interdiction policy within the USA. In June 1994, the US started to process the asylum applications of Haitians on board a hospital ship moored in Kingston, Jamaica. But when 11,000 Haitians were interdicted in a fortnight, the new facility was almost immediately overwhelmed.

This development prompted another policy shift, with the US government declaring that Haitians who were intercepted at sea would again be sent to the 'safe haven' at Guantanamo Bay. More than 21,000 Haitians were accommodated there from July 1994, until the US-led military intervention in Haiti in September 1994, which removed the military junta and restored President Aristide to power. After Aristide's return from exile in October 1994, 17,000 Haitians repatriated voluntarily from Guantanamo Bay to Haiti, and 4,000 others were sent back against their will. Since that time, the number of Haitians making their way to the USA by boat has declined considerably. In the last six months of 1996, for example, only 13 were intercepted.

As the preceding narrative indicates, US policy towards

Cuban and Haitian asylum seekers has undergone a succession of rapid changes. On many occasions, it would appear, the government has found itself caught between a number of divergent pressures: the nature of its relations with the states concerned, its obligations under international refugee law; and the competing demands of different domestic constituencies. Ultimately, however, the most important determinant of recent policy towards the Cubans and Haitians has been the country's desire to prevent the unpredictable and irregular arrival of people upon its shores. As US migration experts Michael Teitelbaum and Myron Weiner have observed, "with the end of the cold war, many Americans have come to regard the prevention of illegal migration and large-scale refugee flows as a major foreign policy objective."

ment of in-country processing systems, which are tantamount to an admission that persecution is taking place on their territory? Despite such obvious difficulties, a more detailed review of this approach to the asylum issue is also overdue.

A final means of regularizing the transnational and transcontinental movement of people is to be found in the form of information campaigns, targeted at potential migrants and asylum seekers. The impetus to migrate is often based on ill-founded perceptions of the conditions and opportunities that exist in the world's more affluent countries, as well as a poor grasp of the risks that migration (particularly in its irregular forms) often entails. Information programmes can help to dispel such misconceptions.

More specifically, such initiatives can fulfill a number of different functions: informing potential migrants about any regular migration opportunities that exist; warning them about the dangers they may face if they put their fate into the hands of traffickers; advising them about changes in the refugee and asylum policies of receiving countries; and providing them with details of the likely consequences of submitting a manifestly unfounded claim to refugee status. Information campaigns of this kind are a modest antidote to the rosy images of life in the affluent states which are disseminated by the mass communications industry. They should not be used as a means of preventing the flight of people who have a genuine need for international protection, and must therefore be honest, impartial and accurate in their content.

Information campaigns of this type have already been pursued by UNHCR and the International Organization for Migration (IOM), primarily in countries such as Albania, Romania and Viet Nam, where earlier movements of refugees have been succeeded by the departure of irregular migrants. Radio, television, newspapers and posters have been amongst the media used. It is difficult to assess the impact of such campaigns as their success can only be determined by the absence of migration, a phenomenon which is impossible to measure. Even so, in terms of their cost-effectiveness, not to mention their consistency with humanitarian principles, programmes of this kind have some evident advantages over the interdiction, detention and deportation of unsuccessful asylum seekers.

Action in countries of origin

International efforts to address the 'root causes' of forced and voluntary migration from the lower-income countries have a long and somewhat chequered history. While the record of achievement in this area might not be particularly impressive, serious attempts are evidently required to deal with the political, economic and environmental problems that prompt people to leave their own country and to seek asylum elsewhere. The intention should not be to dissuade or prevent people from moving to another country; historically, migration has proven to be one of the most powerful and positive forces in human development. But action is required to render people more secure in their own society, so that they migrate out of choice, rather than necessity.

Common sense suggests that an improvement in the economic performance of countries of origin should help to remove or at least diminish some of the pressures which induce people to migrate and to submit an asylum application in another state. Well directed investment, more liberal trading arrangements, a reduction of the debt burden and intelligently used aid can all help to raise living standards and provide the people of low-income countries with better public services.

Even so, such strategies do not represent a panacea to the asylum and migration issue. There is now considerable evidence to suggest that economic growth raises expectations and provides people with the resources which they need to migrate. Such short-term outcomes do not invalidate the 'development in place of migration' strategy, but they do point to the need for this strategy to be pursued over a considerable period of time.

Analysts differ on the question of how long it takes for increased living standards to be reflected in declining rates of international migration. One of the more optimistic commentaries suggests that "immigration countries should be comforted by how little - not how much - wage and job gaps must be narrowed to deter migration." Once the wage differential is down to a factor of four or five, and once there is a popular expectation that income differentials will continue to narrow, then, "economically-motivated migration practically ceases."(36) While this conclusion may seem over sanguine, recent evidence from countries in South and South-East Asia suggests that states with good rates of economic growth can be transformed very rapidly from countries of emigration to countries of immigration.

If there is some ambivalence about the positive impact of economic interventions on the propensity of people to migrate, there is little doubt about the negative consequences of the economic policies which have been imposed on many low and middle-income states. The policies of structural adjustment and economic liberalization advocated by many industrialized states and the international financial institutions have undoubtedly prompted migratory movements throughout Africa, Asia, Latin America and the former communist bloc.

The unintended consequences of macro-economic policy clearly need to be more firmly grasped by decision-makers whose main concern lies outside the realm of migration and asylum policy. In fact, there are already signs that this is happening. A recent study undertaken by the IOM and the UN Conference on Trade and Development (UNCTAD), for example, recommends that governments should undertake 'migration audits' before making decisions about overseas investment, trade and development. The report also makes the sensible suggestion that research should be undertaken in countries that have made the transition from being migrant-sending to migrant-receiving states, so as to identify the forms of economic intervention which have the greatest impact on people's propensity to move.

Just as economic interventions are now being considered more carefully with regard to their migratory consequences, so too are international efforts in the areas of human rights and conflict prevention. Again, however, the evidence of success is mixed. The process of democratization in the former communist states and other regions - the declared foreign policy objective of the western powers during the cold war years - has in its early stages been accompanied by declining levels of human security for the populations concerned.

This outcome should not, of course, discourage efforts to promote democracy and the improvement of human rights standards; indeed, such efforts must form the centrepiece of any attempt to avert and resolve situations of forced displacement. The international community should be aware, however, that democratization does not usually proceed in a unilinear fashion, and that in the short term at least, it may involve crises which generate new population movements.

States which receive significant numbers of refugee claimants could make far greater efforts to ensure that actions which they take in other policy domains are consistent with their approach to the asylum issue. To give one obvious example, if the richer states really want to make it possible for people in the less developed regions to live safely in their own country, then they should not sell arms to regimes which are intent on persecuting their citizens and expelling minority groups.

An interesting example of this more coordinated approach can be seen in Sweden, where an all-party commission was established with the precise purpose of examining the linkages between the country's refugee, immigration, development cooperation and foreign policies. "One overall objective for a cohesive global refugee policy," the Refugee Policy Commission reported, "should be that international cooperation actively contributes to the underlying causes of refugee movements and forced emigration." "At the same time," it observed, "those who are compelled to take flight must receive protection and assistance."(37)

The impetus to seek asylum is inevitable in a world where people experience vastly different levels of physical and material security. While those disparities persist, people will continue to move - by whatever means possible and whatever obstacles are placed in their way - from poorer and less stable states to countries where their basic rights are more likely to be protected. It is for this reason that the institution of asylum must be scrupulously upheld.

Uncertain status: displaced people in the Russian Federation.   *UNHCR/T. Bolstad*

6   Statelessness and citizenship

The Universal Declaration of Human Rights unequivocally states that "everyone has the right to a nationality" and that "no-one shall be arbitrarily deprived of his nationality." But many thousands of people across the globe lack the security and protection which citizenship can provide.

A substantial proportion of the world's stateless people are also victims of forced displacement. In some instances, individuals and communities are deprived of their nationality by governmental decree and are subsequently expelled from the country which they consider to be their home. In other situations, stateless people are obliged to flee because of the persecution and discrimination which they experience. And having left the country where they have lived for most or all their lives, stateless people may subsequently find it impossible to return.

Statelessness is not only a source of human insecurity and a cause of forced displacement, but may also pose a threat to national and regional stability. As this chapter indicates, citizenship disputes have become an important feature of the contemporary world, generating tension and even violence between different states and communities. Humanitarian organizations have a valuable role to play in averting such situations, protecting stateless people and finding just solutions to their plight. Ultimately, however, the problems of statelessness and disputed nationality can only be effectively addressed through the actions of states themselves.

NATIONALITY AND CITIZENSHIP

Citizenship is a fundamental element of human security. As well as providing people with a sense of belonging and identity, it entitles the individual to the protection of the state and provides a legal basis for the exercise of many civil and political rights. People who lack a nationality may find it difficult or impossible to engage in a range of activities that citizens take for granted. If an individual is to enjoy the automatic right of residence in a country, carry a passport and benefit from diplomatic protection while abroad, then citizenship is indispensable. In many situations, nationality also enables people to find employment, to make use of public services, to participate in the political process and to have access to the judicial system.(1)

Nationality is not granted indiscriminately, but is generally based upon factors such as a person's place of birth, parentage, or the relationship they have established with a state through long-term residence there. In legal terms, such ties provide the 'genuine effective link' between the individual and the state. For the vast majority of people around the world, that link is easily established and readily acknowledged by the authorities of the state concerned. In situations where these conditions do not pertain, however, problems of statelessness are likely to emerge.

Under international law, a stateless person is one "who is not considered as a national by any state under the operation of its law."(2) This definition is helpfully concise and to the point. But it is also a very limited and somewhat legalistic definition, referring to a specific group of people known as *de jure* stateless persons. It does not encompass the many people, usually described as *de facto* stateless persons, who are unable to establish their nationality or whose citizenship is disputed by one or more countries. This chapter uses the notion of statelessness in its broader sense, to denote all those people who lack what has become known as an 'effective nationality', and who are consequently unable to enjoy the rights that are associated with citizenship.(3)

Statelessness, whether of the *de jure* or *de facto* variety, has many causes. An individual may lose his or her nationality and fail to acquire a new one as a result of an extended stay abroad or through marriage to (and subsequent divorce from) a person of a different nationality - a problem which affects a disproportionate number of women. Although it is the fundamental right of every child to acquire a nationality, children who are born to stateless parents or refugees - or who are born out of wedlock - may be denied citizenship.

Individuals may also find themselves stateless because of faulty administrative practices, the failure or refusal of a state to ensure the registration of births, or because of conflicts in the nationality laws of different countries, particularly when one adheres to the principle of *jus sanguinis* (citizenship on the basis of descent) and the other adheres to the principle of *jus soli* (citizenship on the basis of the place of birth). Finally, a person may voluntarily renounce their nationality and fail to acquire a new citizenship before that renunciation takes effect. In recent years it has also been known for asylum seekers to become or remain stateless by choice, so as to enhance their prospects for admission to one of the more prosperous countries.

Situations of statelessness involving larger numbers of people tend to arise in a number of different circumstances. Governments may amend their citizenship laws and denationalize whole sections of society in order to punish or marginalize them or to facilitate their exclusion from the state's territory. The formation of new states, resulting from decolonization or the disintegration of a federal polity, may leave thousands or even millions of people stateless or with a disputed claim to citizenship. Large-scale statelessness may also arise in the context of mass expulsions and refugee movements, especially when the population concerned has lived in exile for many years without acquiring the citizenship of their asylum country.

The revival of international interest

During the cold war - a period of relative stability in the configuration of states - the problem of statelessness was generally regarded as a minor one, affecting just a small number of people who fell into the interstices of the international system. As a result, the issue failed to attract a significant amount of attention from governments or humanitarian organizations.

International conventions on statelessness were established in 1954 and 1961, but, for reasons that will be explained later, few countries chose to accede to these legal instruments. In 1975, UNHCR was entrusted with certain responsibilities in relation to stateless people. For the next 15 years, however, the organization devoted relatively little time, effort or resources to this element of its mandate.

Commenting upon this situation in 1988, the Independent Commission on International Humanitarian Issues (a body co-founded by a former UN High Commissioner for Refugees) observed that "UNHCR has remained somewhat indifferent when it comes to the fate of the stateless. The term 'stateless person' hardly ever appears in UNHCR publications - a fact which, together with the doctrinal vacuum in this particular area, only serves to heighten a general indifference towards a problem which should rather inspire in human terms the same compassion as that shown to refugees."(4)

Since that comment was made, the problem of statelessness has forced its way onto the international humanitarian and security agenda as a result of several related factors: the rise of ethnic consciousness in certain parts of the world; the increased incidence of communal conflict; the associated disintegration of several federal polities; the fear of large-scale population movements involving stateless people; and the tightening of immigration controls throughout most of the industrialized world.

At the same time, the international community's changing approach to the problem of forced displacement has prompted UNHCR and other humanitarian organizations to address the issue of statelessness in a more urgent and systematic manner. Three specific trends have contributed to this outcome: the new emphasis which is being placed on human rights in countries of origin and the prevention of mass exoduses; the growing recognition that countries of origin must play a primary role in averting and resolving situations of forced displacement; and the somewhat belated recognition that voluntary repatriation is in most instances the most appropriate solution to refugee problems. As a UNHCR staff member has observed, had voluntary repatriation been more actively promoted in earlier years, then the organization "would have been required to concentrate on nationality and citizenship issues much sooner, as a key element in the repatriation of stateless refugees."(5)

The relevance of history

The recent time of turbulence in international affairs can in many senses be compared with the period of imperial collapse which followed the first world war, and the period of state dissolution and formation which occurred in the aftermath of the second global conflict.

The disintegration of the Austro-Hungarian, German and Ottoman empires in the wake of their defeat in the first world war led to the establishment of new states such as Czechoslovakia, Hungary and Yugoslavia, the restoration of the former state of Poland, and the simultaneous adjustment of many international borders in the area directly or indirectly affected by the conflict. This process of state formation was accompanied by a number of large-scale population movements, including the transfer of populations on the basis of their ethnic and religious identity. Some five million people moved - or were moved - in this way, a process which evidently required the states concerned and the international community as a whole to address some complex citizenship questions.

US President Woodrow Wilson, perhaps the key figure of the post-war peace process, had little doubt about the relationship of nationality issues to the broader problem of regional and international security. Referring to the effort to create stable states through the redrawing of international borders and the transfer of populations, Wilson commented that "we are trying to eliminate those elements of disturbance, as far as possible, that may interfere with the peace of the world."(6)

Ironically, of course, the subsequent two decades were characterized much more by violence than by peace, culminating in a second world war that generated a new wave of expulsions and population displacements, many of them involving people who had lost or been stripped of their nationality. Analyzing these events in her seminal study of the period, Hannah Arendt observed that "since the peace treaties of 1919 and 1920, refugees and the stateless have attached themselves like a curse to all the newly established states on earth."(7)

Although some of these people were able to return to their homes almost as soon as the war had ended, the problems of displacement and statelessness persisted. With the borders of Europe being redrawn once more, up to 15 million Germans from Czechoslovakia, Hungary, Poland, the Soviet Union and Yugoslavia were forced to move to Austria or Germany. The Soviet Union's annexation of the eastern part of the interwar Polish state resulted in the massive transfer and expulsion of Ukrainians and Poles, many of the latter settling in areas which had been newly acquired from Germany and from which the native population had been expelled. These and other movements involved not only the displacement of people, but also necessitated a transfer of nationality and citizenship rights.

While the post-war configuration of European states had begun to assume a degree of stability by the end of the 1940s, the same period witnessed a new spate of upheavals in other parts of the world, leaving a further legacy of statelessness amongst the populations involved. These events included, for example, the decolonization and partition of India in 1947 and the subsequent movement of Hindus and Muslims between India and Pakistan; the conflict over Palestine and the creation of Israel in 1948, creating a Palestinian diaspora in the Middle East and beyond; and the Chinese revolution of 1949, which led to the establishment of a communist government on the mainland and a nationalist government on the island of Taiwan, both of them claiming to represent the Chinese state. All of these tumultuous events raised important questions about the citizenship status of the populations concerned - questions which in many cases have not yet been fully resolved.

In Bangladesh, for example, some 240,000 Biharis (primarily non-Bengali Moslems who fled from India during the partition of 1947 and who supported West Pakistan during the 1971 secessionist struggle) continue to live in camps, waiting for the day when they can take up residence and citizenship in Pakistan.(8) Despite the progress that has been made in the Middle East peace process, the current and future citizenship status of many Palestinian refugees remains to be determined. And in early 1997, efforts were still being made to find a solution for a small number of ethnic Chinese boat people in Hong Kong, whose claim to refugee status had been rejected and who were refused readmission to Viet Nam, on the grounds that they had a stronger link to China or Taiwan.(9)

As these and other examples demonstrate, the question of nationality is an unusually sensitive one, going to the heart of a country's sovereignty and identity. It is for this reason that disputes over citizenship so frequently prove to be intractable and become the source of tension and conflict, both within and between states.

New dimensions of statelessness

History has demonstrated that the problems of statelessness and disputed or ambiguous nationality are normally associated with periods of profound change in international relations. It is therefore not surprising that the past few years have witnessed a significant increase in the incidence of such problems.

Since the end of the 1980s, serious situations of statelessness have arisen in almost every part of the world, with the primary exception of the Americas (see Map M). For analytical purposes, such situations can be divided into two broad categories: those involving ethnic or minority groups which do not enjoy full or undisputed citizenship of the countries where they live; and those associated with the dissolution of multinational or multiethnic federal states and the formation of new political entities.

Map M

Major situations of statelessness and disputed nationality worldwide

The Baltic states
When the Baltic states gained their independence from the Soviet Union at the beginning of the 1990s, citizenship issues quickly found their way to the top of the political agenda. In Latvia and Estonia, large numbers of Russians who had been resident in those countries for many years found that they had been rendered effectively stateless following the introduction of new nationality laws.

The Czech and Slovak republics
Czechoslovakia was dissolved in 1992 and each of the two successor states introduced their own citizenship legislation. Large numbers of people, especially members of the Roma or gypsy community, found themselves threatened with statelessness as a result of problems in the formulation and implementation of these laws.

Former Yugoslavia
The question of nationality has been just one of the many problems to confront the people of former Yugoslavia since the early 1990s. The speedy disintegration of the country, the massive displacement of people during the war and the desire of some political leaders to obstruct the return of certain ethnic groups have combined to make the citizenship question a particularly important one.

Ukraine
Expelled from their homeland when Stalin ruled the Soviet Union, about quarter of a million Tatars have returned to the Crimea over the past decade. By the end of 1996, at least 60,000 - and possibly many more - of the returnees were waiting to acquire Ukrainian citizenship. Without it, they have not been able to vote and have lacked effective access to jobs and public services.

Zaire
The 1996 crisis in Zaire, which eventually led to the overthrow of the Mobutu government, had many different roots. Not least of these was the question of citizenship. When the regime attempted to strengthen its position by denationalizing and expelling large numbers of ethnic Tutsis in the east of the country, the affected population took up arms against the government and played a major part in its downfall.

The Palestinians
While accurate statistics are difficult to establish, there are thought to be some three million Palestinians who lack an effective nationality, making them the largest group of stateless people in the world. While this problem lies at the heart of the Arab-Israeli dispute, it remains to be properly addressed by the Middle East peace process.

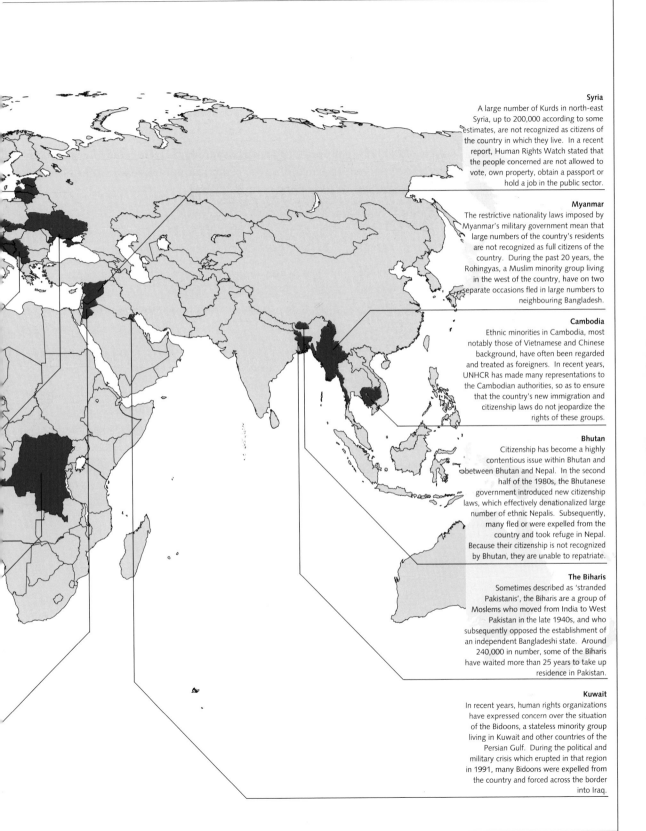

Syria

A large number of Kurds in north-east Syria, up to 200,000 according to some estimates, are not recognized as citizens of the country in which they live. In a recent report, Human Rights Watch stated that the people concerned are not allowed to vote, own property, obtain a passport or hold a job in the public sector.

Myanmar

The restrictive nationality laws imposed by Myanmar's military government mean that large numbers of the country's residents are not recognized as full citizens of the country. During the past 20 years, the Rohingyas, a Muslim minority group living in the west of the country, have on two separate occasions fled in large numbers to neighbouring Bangladesh.

Cambodia

Ethnic minorities in Cambodia, most notably those of Vietnamese and Chinese background, have often been regarded and treated as foreigners. In recent years, UNHCR has made many representations to the Cambodian authorities, so as to ensure that the country's new immigration and citizenship laws do not jeopardize the rights of these groups.

Bhutan

Citizenship has become a highly contentious issue within Bhutan and between Bhutan and Nepal. In the second half of the 1980s, the Bhutanese government introduced new citizenship laws, which effectively denationalized large number of ethnic Nepalis. Subsequently, many fled or were expelled from the country and took refuge in Nepal. Because their citizenship is not recognized by Bhutan, they are unable to repatriate.

The Biharis

Sometimes described as 'stranded Pakistanis', the Biharis are a group of Moslems who moved from India to West Pakistan in the late 1940s, and who subsequently opposed the establishment of an independent Bangladeshi state. Around 240,000 in number, some of the Biharis have waited more than 25 years to take up residence in Pakistan.

Kuwait

In recent years, human rights organizations have expressed concern over the situation of the Bidoons, a stateless minority group living in Kuwait and other countries of the Persian Gulf. During the political and military crisis which erupted in that region in 1991, many Bidoons were expelled from the country and forced across the border into Iraq.

The countries featured on this map are representative, not exhaustive.

Africa, Asia, the Americas and Middle East

The situations of statelessness and disputed citizenship which can be placed in the first of these two categories are generally to be found in the less-developed regions of the world. The ethnic and minority groups most directly affected by these problems in recent years include:

- up to 120,000 Nepali-speaking southern Bhutanese who are living as refugees in Nepal and India, and whose claim to Bhutanese citizenship is rejected by the authorities of that country;(10)

- the ethnic Vietnamese population of Cambodia, thought to consist of around five per cent of the country's 10 million people, and whose citizenship remains unclear in the country's current nationality legislation;

- up to 250,000 Bidoons (an Arabic expression derived from a phrase meaning 'without nationality'), long-term but stateless residents of Kuwait, many of whom are now to be found in Iraq and other countries in the Persian Gulf;

- around 60,000 black Africans from Mauritania living as refugees in the neighbouring country of Senegal, and whose claim to citizenship has been challenged by the Mauritanian authorities;

- up to 200,000 Kurds in Syria, many of whom became stateless as a result of a 1962 census which withdrew Syrian citizenship from people who had allegedly entered the country illegally from Turkey;

- the Rohingya people of western Myanmar, a largely stateless Moslem minority group consisting of some two million people, a small proportion of whom are accommodated in refugee camps in Bangladesh; and,

- the Banyarwanda and Banyamulenge peoples of eastern Zaire, ethnic Tutsis with a previously disputed claim to Zairean citizenship, estimated by many commentators to number in the region of 800,000.

While the situations described above are somewhat disparate in nature, a number of broad generalizations can be made with regard to such manifestations of statelessness. First, they tend to involve groups which are clearly distinguished from the rest of a country's population, whether as a result of their race, religion or ethnic origin. Second, they often involve communities which are regarded as a threat to the ruling elite or the majority population, either by virtue of their numbers or as a consequence of their perceived disloyalty to the state. And third, such situations normally arise in countries which lack a pluralistic political culture, and where minority groups are liable to be used as scapegoats by the state and other sections of society. Recognizing this link, the UN High Commissioner for Refugees has observed that "on the plane of rights, the prevention and reduction of statelessness is an important aspect of securing minority rights."(11)

The second of the two categories identified earlier - problems of statelessness associated with the break-up of multiethnic federal states - relates primarily to more developed regions of the world, and specifically to areas which are emerging from long periods of communist or socialist rule: the Commonwealth of Independent States (CIS), the Baltic states, former Yugoslavia, and the Czech and Slovak republics. As one analyst has suggested, with the end of the cold war and the disintegration of the communist bloc, an 'unmixing of peoples' is under way, bringing insecurity and uncertain citizenship status to substantial numbers of people.(12)

In numerical terms, the number of stateless people living in the former communist areas is almost certainly no greater than the number to be found in other parts of the world. And in humanitarian terms, the insecurity and hardship experienced by stateless people in the less-developed regions has in many instances been far more serious than that experienced by their European counterparts. Even so, it is quite evident that the international community's new interest in statelessness and nationality disputes has to a very large extent been generated by the fear of instability, conflict and population displacement in the geopolitically sensitive areas examined below.

The Commonwealth of Independent States

During its 75-year history, the former Soviet Union, a vast and ethnically heterogeneous state, experienced forced displacement and officially stimulated migration flows on a massive scale. Describing the ensuing problems for the Soviet successor states, one analyst has observed that "the breakup of the Soviet Union has transformed yesterday's internal migrants, secure in their Soviet citizenship, into today's international migrants of contested legitimacy and uncertain membership... In so doing, it has made the politics of membership and citizenship one of the most pressing issues confronting the successor states." (13)

A scholar from the region makes a broadly similar point, emphasizing that there has been nothing accidental about these developments. "The enforcement of ethnically selective citizenship and official language laws in societies with sizeable and culturally distinct communities has caused massive discontent and inter-ethnic tensions in Estonia, Latvia, Moldavia, Georgia, Ukraine and in Central Asia."(14)

When, in December 1991, Soviet citizenship ceased to exist, some 287 million people were left with or in need of a new nationality. One of the primary tasks for the 15 countries which emerged from the dissolution of the USSR was to define precisely who their citizens were, and to establish new rules for the granting of citizenship.

6.1

Forcibly transferred populations in the CIS

Amongst the many population movements currently taking place in the Commonwealth of Independent States (CIS) are those which are a legacy of forcible population transfers implemented during the Stalinist period. Several of these transfers have given rise to problems of citizenship and statelessness that still need to be resolved.

Between 1941 and 1944, large numbers of people, living mainly in the western part of the Soviet Union, were rounded up and forcibly transferred huge distances to Siberia or Central Asia. Most of the deportations were carried out during the second world war, amid accusations that the people concerned were disloyal, had collaborated with the Nazis, or presented threats to the Soviet war effort. The majority of the people moved were also members of ethnic minorities or nationalities, some of which had earlier been granted their own autonomous republics or regions.

The first and largest of these transfers affected the Volga Germans, who had settled in Russia since the end of the 18th century. In 1941, some 380,000 of them were forced into cattle wagons and shunted to Siberia or Central Asia by train. The forced transfer of seven other nationalities, totalling more than a million people, followed in 1943-44: the Karachai, Kalmyks, Chechen, Ingush, Balkars, Crimean Tatars and Meskhetians. More Soviet Germans were moved after the war from Ukraine to Central Asia. Others who were forcibly transferred during the Stalinist years included several hundred thousand Balts, Greeks, Koreans, Moldovans, Poles and Ukrainians.

With the political changes that took place in the 1950s after Stalin's death, some of this injustice was redressed, as the accusations against the deported nationalities were retracted. Some of the transferred peoples began to return, although not without experiencing great difficulties over issues such as access to land. However the right of return of the Crimean Tatars, Meskhetians and Volga Germans continued to be denied, even though they were cleared of treason charges in the 1960s. Since then, the situation of the Germans has been partly resolved by emigration agreements between the Soviet Union and the Federal Republic of Germany and later between the CIS and the reunited Germany. By the end of 1995, some 1,376,000 people had moved to the latter state.

The prospects for the other forcibly transferred peoples changed substantially with the demise of the Soviet Union. In April 1991, the parliament of the Russian Federation adopted a law on the rehabilitation of repressed peoples, which included the transferred peoples; and late in 1992, CIS countries signed the Bishkek agreement signalling their intent to deal with the restitution of the rights of forcibly transferred people. While the situation of most of these populations has been resolved - during the Soviet era and after - the situation of the Crimean Tatars and the Meskhetians is still not settled, giving rise to actual and potential problems of statelessness and disputed citizenship.

Crimean Tatars

About 250,000 Tatars have returned to the Crimea in Ukraine since 1988; an equal number are thought to remain outside their ancestral homeland, mainly in Uzbekistan. Their repatriation has been difficult, partly because of tensions between the returnees and the established ethnic Russian community, and partly because of difficult economic conditions and the consequent lack of resources. Between 1988 and 1992, the return was blocked by the local authorities, and the Crimean Tatars resorted to seizing land and establishing squatter settlements. Return and reintegration have also been hampered by the absence of a clear framework for confirming the Tatar returnees as citizens of the Ukraine.

The rate of repatriation has fallen substantially, from about 120,000 in 1990 to just 5,000 in 1995. Aware of the economic, citizenship and other problems the repatriates face, the Crimean Tatar leadership has focused on trying to secure the legal rights of those who have already returned rather than encouraging further return migration. The Tatar *mejlis* or council has urged the Ukraine authorities to grant citizenship immediately and pressed for measures to revive the Tatar language and culture.

Towards the end of 1996, estimates of the number of Tatars thought not yet to have acquired Ukrainian citizenship varied between 60,000 and 176,000. These people could not vote and lacked access to employment, housing, education, medical care and other services. The citizenship issue became an important source of dispute with the Ukrainian authorities, and indirectly a source of tension between the Tatars and the local ethnic Russian population.

While the Ukraine's 1991 law on citizenship was liberal and inclusive in its definition of the initial body of citizens - all those resident in Ukraine on the day the law came into effect - regulations for acquiring citizenship were more stringent, requiring renunciation of other citizenship, five years residence (except for those who could show their forebears were resident), sufficient Ukrainian language for conversation, a legal livelihood and acceptance of the Ukrainian constitution. Those Tatars arriving before 1991 were deemed citizens. But for later arrivals some of these conditions - particularly the language and means of existence requirements - were difficult to fulfill. Renouncing former citizenship was time-consuming, and in any case many wished to retain rights in Uzbekistan and other Central Asian republics where their relatives still lived. Many were also fearful that they might not secure Ukrainian citizenship after renouncing Uzbek citizenship. For some, following Soviet practice, securing a *propiska* or residence permit was the key to employment and social benefits, and was thought more important than citizenship.

Since 1996, UNHCR has been offering advice to those who wish to apply for citizenship, as well as examining the possibility of revising Ukraine's citizenship legislation to regularize the status of Crimean Tatars who have returned. Since the majority were still *de jure* Uzbek citizens towards the end of 1996, and Uzbek law stipulates that citizenship may be forfeited if residence abroad is permanent, there was some danger the Crimean Tatars might be rendered stateless if they were unable to secure Ukrainian citizenship. Changes in the Ukrainian citizenship law announced in April 1997, however, seemed to clear the way for a resolution of such problems.

Meskhetians
The case of the Meskhetians is different from the other deported peoples in several respects. First, they were not a recognized nationality like the others at the time of the deportation, and they had not been granted an autonomous territory within the Russian Republic. They only consolidated into a nationality after the deportation, from a number of disparate Turkic or Turkicised ethnic groups living in the south-western part of Georgia known as Meskhetia. Their ancestors had come under Russian rule when this area was annexed from Turkey early in the 19th century.

Second, the Meskhetians were never accused of collaborating with the German army, which did not come close to their territory; their deportation probably had more to do with Soviet designs on Turkey, removing a population with an ethnic and cultural affinity with a potential adversary. Third, the strategic importance of their territory - unlike those of the North Caucasus nationalities - militated against their restoration to their lands. Their plight drove the Meskhetians to develop a Turkic nationality, and they organized politically, comparing themselves to the Palestinians, but claiming worse treatment. Losing hope of restoration to their homeland, they turned, like the Germans, to emigration, with lukewarm support from Turkey.

More recently, while the plight of the Volga Germans and the Crimean Tatars has edged towards resolution, the repatriation of the Meskhetians has proved highly problematic, not least because they have experienced a series of secondary displacements. As a result of ethnic conflict in Uzbekistan, around 74,000 fled in 1990-91, of whom some 46,000 made their way to Azerbaijan, a country to which the Meskhetians have some close cultural affinities.

Although some tried to return to Georgia, that state has been unwilling to admit them, partly because of their Turkish background; partly because others, particularly Armenians, are settled in their former homes and Georgia is concerned not to antagonize Armenia by uprooting them; and partly because Georgia is already stretched by the presence of displaced people. Other Meskhetians have moved from Central Asia to the Russian Federation where they have suffered discrimination and harassment by both local populations and local authorities. Still others remain in Central Asia. They number some 200,000 to 300,000 in all, of whom up to 100,000 are now located in Azerbaijan.

The Meskhetians in Azerbaijan are split between those who are content to remain in the new republic and those (perhaps 50,000) who insist on returning to Georgia - either to within that republic or to their actual original homeland. The former are likely to be made citizens of Azerbaijan if they wish.

Azerbaijan has introduced legislation covering citizenship, the status of refugees and forcibly removed people, and the legal status of foreign citizens and stateless persons. UNHCR has argued for a liberal interpretation of citizenship to include those present at the time the Azeri Republic came into being. The organization has also suggested that all those whose 'genuine and effective link' is with Azerbaijan should be granted automatic citizenship, particularly where statelessness might otherwise result: this applies in particularly to minorities like the Meskhetians. But even if this is accepted, some of the legal provisions on citizenship may falter in implementation. For example, under the law on foreigners and stateless persons, the latter are entitled to apply for Azeri citizenship; however, as elsewhere in the CIS region, in practice one of the requirements for citizenship is to hold a residence permit, a condition which cannot be fulfilled by most stateless people.

Although those Meskhetians who moved to Azerbaijan should be eligible for Azeri citizenship, the majority suffer the consequences of undetermined or disputed nationality. Those in the Russian Federation and elsewhere in the CIS region may be even worse off. The Meskhetians are rather less well organized than the Tatars in pressing their case, which remains one of the outstanding injustices of the Soviet era.

In general, the 12 countries which now comprise the Commonwealth of Independent States (CIS) have chosen variants of the so-called 'zero-option', whereby all those people who were permanent residents when the new law entered into force were recognized as citizens, irrespective of their ethnic origins.

Because of the different rules and policies used by the successor states for the granting of citizenship to those people who were not permanently resident when their respective citizenship laws were adopted, some groups of people have encountered problems of statelessness. Amongst such people are the 'formerly deported peoples', who were forcibly transferred *en masse* during the period of Stalinist rule, and who had not managed to return to their place of origin before the Soviet Union disintegrated (see Box 6.1).

In 1997, for example, between 60,000 and 170,000 Crimean Tatars who had returned to Crimea from Central Asia after 1991 remained without citizenship. The same problem confronts some of the Meskhetian Turks who are dispersed in the Russian Federation, Ukraine and other CIS states.

While not always stateless in legal terms, much larger numbers of Russians, Ukrainians and Belarusians living outside of their ancestral homelands have been significantly affected by the events of the past six years. A politically, economically and culturally dominant group during the period of communist rule, the special status of the Russian-speaking Slavic diaspora has been undermined by the unexpected transformation of the region's political geography and the reaffirmation of national identities within the successor states.

Having lost the security which they once enjoyed, having become akin to foreigners in their country of permanent residence, and having in some instances been affected by communal tensions, large numbers have decided to move. According to the Russian authorities, between 1992 and 1996, some three million people migrated to the Russian Federation, mainly from

Central Asia and the Transcaucasus. Their reasons for moving were various: to improve their economic situation, to escape from armed conflict or to remove themselves from situations where they perceived a growing level of discrimination against them. Up to a third of these 'resettlers' have been recognized by the Russian authorities as forced migrants.(15)

The Baltic states

Of all the Russian diaspora - in 1991 more than 25 million people in total - those living in the Baltic states have been most directly affected by the issues of citizenship and statelessness. This phenomenon is the result of both demographic and political factors.

At the end of the 1980s, Russians comprised around 18 per cent of the total population living outside of the Russian Republic, the result of a longstanding migratory process that had been actively promoted during the Soviet period. But the Russian diaspora was not evenly scattered across the Soviet Union, over two-thirds of it being concentrated in Ukraine and Kazakstan. In Georgia, Azerbaijan and Armenia, the Russian share of the population amounted to less than seven per cent, whereas in the Baltic republics of Estonia and Latvia, the proportion stood in the region of one third (see Figure 6.1).

The migration of Russians into Estonia and Latvia, a movement which continued until the latter years of the Soviet Union, led to significant changes in the ethnic composition of these societies. In the period from 1939 to 1989, for example, the proportion of Latvians in the population of Latvia fell from around 75 per cent to just over 50 per cent. During the same period, the titular proportion of the population in neighbouring Estonia fell from 90 per cent to just over 60 per cent.

The particular salience of the Russian presence in the Baltic states is not simply a question of demography, but also a matter of political history. For

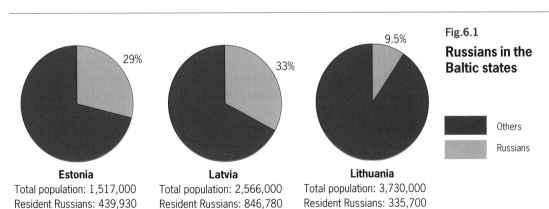

Fig.6.1

Russians in the Baltic states

■ Others
▨ Russians

Estonia
Total population: 1,517,000
Resident Russians: 439,930

Latvia
Total population: 2,566,000
Resident Russians: 846,780

Lithuania
Total population: 3,730,000
Resident Russians: 335,700

Source: *Forced Migration Monitor*, January 1997

Estonia, Latvia and Lithuania, unlike the other successor states of the Soviet Union, had all enjoyed a protracted period of independence after the first world war. Only in 1940 had the Baltic states been annexed and incorporated by the USSR, an event which had opened the door to mass deportations, large-scale Russian settlement and a corresponding belief amongst the 'indigenous' population that their society and culture was being diluted.

Given this historical context, it was not altogether surprising that on reasserting their national rights and eventually regaining their independence, the Estonian and Latvian authorities chose to introduce new nationality laws which granted citizenship only to those residents and their descendants who were citizens at the time of occupation in 1940. Complex naturalization procedures were established for people who took up residence after that date, a provision which had important exclusionary implications for most of the russophone Slavic population.

Not least of the conditions attached to citizenship was proficiency in the local language, a requirement which effectively barred many Russians from becoming citizens of the two reconstituted states. At the same time, substantial numbers of long-term residents have been excluded from the electoral process, prevented from taking up certain kinds of employment and barred from participating in privatization programmes. Consequently, in Latvia, out of a population of 2.6 million, over 700,000 people were left stateless, while in Estonia, a third of the 1.5 million population became non-citizens. By February 1997, fewer than 5,000 people had been granted Latvian citizenship through the new naturalization procedure.

These developments have had some important consequences, not only for the people concerned, but also for the broader issue of regional stability. Tensions have been generated between Russia and the Baltic states, while fears have been expressed that large numbers of stateless people will join the reflux to Russia, placing additional strains upon that country's already limited resources.

Former Yugoslavia

The significance and complexity of the citizenship issue in former Yugoslavia derives from three related phenomena: the disintegration of the Socialist Federal Republic of Yugoslavia (SFRY) at the beginning of the 1990s; the subsequent armed conflicts which occurred within and between the successor states; and the displacement of around four million people, both within and beyond the borders of former Yugoslavia, as a result of those wars.

In the legal regime of the SFRY, every Yugoslav citizen possessed both federal citizenship and internal citizenship of one of the six republics: Bosnia and Herzegovina, Croatia, Macedonia, Montenegro, Serbia and Slovenia.

But the latter form of citizenship had few practical implications. All citizens of the SFRY, irrespective of their republican nationality, enjoyed the same rights and were free to live and work on any part of the federal territory.

As all citizens of the SFRY held a republican citizenship at the time when the country disintegrated, and as the citizenship laws of the successor states all enshrined the principle of legal continuity, *de jure* statelessness has in general been avoided. In states which were affected by armed conflict, however, most notably Bosnia and Croatia, some people found themselves without a nationality because they could not prove their former republican citizenship and because municipal birth and nationality registers had disappeared or been destroyed.

While *de jure* statelessness may not have been a great problem, the application of the principle of legal continuity threatened to create a problem of *de facto* statelessness for the hundreds of thousands of people who were living outside of the republic of which they were now citizens. In short, they were at risk of becoming foreigners in their usual place of residence. Some successor states, such as Bosnia and the Federal Republic of Yugoslavia (Serbia and Montenegro) have taken steps to facilitate the naturalization of people who were living on their territory at the time of independence. However, many citizens of the former SFRY, particularly those in Croatia and Macedonia, as well as those who had fled abroad, have not been able to obtain an effective nationality.(16)

In 1995, a UNHCR publication reported that the citizenship problems of former Yugoslavia were political as well as legal in nature. "The main problem," it stated, "is that some of the newly established states have, by means of various legal devices, attempted to exclude from their nationality or at least delay the acquisition of their nationality by persons who have been residing in their territory for considerable lengths of time. Such cases have invariably involved persons belonging to an ethnic minority which is perceived as 'undesirable' from the point of view of the majority's nationalist faction."(17)

With the mutual recognition of the successor states and the signing of the Dayton accords (which include *inter alia* the 1961 Convention on the Reduction of Statelessness) a basis has been established for the resolution of the citizenship issue. In addition, a number of expert meetings on citizenship legislation have been held, enabling the Council of Europe and UNHCR to develop a set of recommendations that will allow the states concerned to address the problem of statelessness and to promote the right to an effective nationality for all former SFRY citizens. Even so, organizations such as the Open Society Institute have continued to express disquiet about this issue, especially its impact on already disadvantaged groups, such as ethnically mixed families, migrants, refugees and the Roma.(18)

The Czech and Slovak republics

From its emergence in 1918 until 1968, Czechoslovakia was a unitary state with a single citizenship. When the Czechoslovak Federation was created in 1969, however, two levels of citizenship were introduced: citizenship of the federation and citizenship (termed 'nationality' or 'internal citizenship') of the two constituent entities. In the context of international law, only citizenship of the federation was recognized and conferred any rights and duties. Internal citizenship held little meaning in practice.

When the country was dissolved in December 1992, each of the successor entities - the Czech Republic and the Slovak Republic - adopted new legislation to define both the initial body of citizens and the process whereby people could become naturalized citizens. The legislation of both countries defined their initial bodies of citizens by reference to the 'internal citizenship' of the former federation. As a result, many people with lifetime residence in the Czech Republic were nevertheless designated as Slovaks and *vice versa*. These people effectively became foreign citizens in their usual place of residence.

Whereas the Slovak legislation provided an unrestricted option of Slovak citizenship for all former federal citizens, the Czech legislation imposed three significant restrictions on the right to become a Czech citizen. An individual wishing to acquire Czech citizenship had to have been resident on the territory of the Czech Republic for at least two years, had to have been exempted from Slovak citizenship, and had to have a clean criminal record for the preceding five years. These restrictions applied regardless of the individual's connections with the Czech Republic.

Although the scope of the problem was not clear, cases of *de jure* and *de facto* statelessness certainly occurred as a result of this legislation. The problem was of particular relevance to the gypsy or Roma minority group in the Czech Republic, since most were born on Slovak territory or were descended from people born in Slovakia (see Box 6.2).

Along with other bodies, such as the Council of Europe, UNHCR expressed concern about the restrictions incorporated into the Czech citizenship law and called for solutions to the problem. In addition to the obstacles contained in the law, UNHCR pointed out, people were finding it hard to acquire Czech citizenship as a result of restrictive interpretations of the legislation, coupled with high administrative fees, burdensome paperwork and a lack of clear guidance and information.

In September 1996, UNHCR's Regional Bureau for Europe reported that there were "significant numbers" of *de facto* stateless persons in the Czech Republic, many of them wrongly assumed to be Slovak.(19) At the end of the year, however, the Czech parliament passed an amendment to the citizenship law, providing the Minister of the Interior with the authority to waive the clean criminal record requirement - an amendment which is now being vigorously exercised. At the same time, UNHCR has established a project with a local non-governmental organization to provide legal assistance and administrative guidance to more than 2,000 people who have faced difficulties in ascertaining their nationality, a significant number of whom are former prisoners, foster children and people with physical disabilities.

Human and humanitarian implications

The right to nationality or citizenship was once described by a member of the US Supreme Court as "the right to have rights." (20) As this comment suggests, citizenship provides the legal connection between individuals and the state, and thus serves as the basis for the realization and enjoyment of all other rights. It is therefore not surprising that stateless people have in many instances been denied those rights and have been obliged to live in conditions of acute legal, physical and psychological insecurity.

The desperate circumstances of stateless people have attracted the attention of many commentators over the years. A United Nations study on statelessness published in 1949, noted that "normally every individual belongs to a national community and feels himself part of it. He enjoys the protection and assistance of the national authorities. When he is abroad, his own national authorities look after him... The fact that the stateless person has no nationality places him in an abnormal and inferior position which reduces his social value and destroys his own self-confidence."(21) Two years later, Hannah Arendt observed that the tragedy of stateless people "is that they no longer belong to any community whatsoever," and that they are often forced into the role of outlaws, living on the margins of society, "without the right to residence and without the right to work."(22)

A paper completed in 1996 by UNHCR's expert on nationality issues indicates that little has changed since those observations were made. "Failure to acquire status under the law," she comments, "creates significant human problems. These problems can negatively impact many important elements of life, including the right to vote, to own property, to have health care, to send one's children to school, to work, and to travel to and from one's country of residence."(23)

In its analysis of the problem, the Independent Commission on International Humanitarian Issues draws particular attention to the linkages between statelessness, the right to freedom of movement and the broader problem of forced displacement. "The stateless are part of those unwanted people who are refused right of entry to countries or who are turned back at borders... If they are taken in, they often live in uncertainty for many years." "Nationality," the Commission continues, "is not only the right to a passport and material advantages. It also confers upon the individual an identity and the sense of belonging to a community - elements without which a person remains vulnerable and uprooted."(24)

6.2

The Roma of Central and Eastern Europe

The Roma or gypsies of Central and Eastern Europe have often been described as 'stateless' or 'border' people. Although they may not all be legally stateless, the citizenship status of many has been uncertain, as has their ability to exercise a full range of economic, social and political rights. Indeed, some commentators refer to the Roma as Europe's largest and most disadvantaged minority.

The history of the Roma has been one of migration. Most historians agree that the Roma left India between the 7th and 10th centuries, migrating to Europe via Persia and arriving in the Balkans between the 13th and 15th centuries. The majority of Roma settled in Central and Eastern Europe, although they have moved further west on three main occasions: in the 15th century following their initial arrival in Europe; in the 19th century after the abolition of gypsy slavery; and most recently in the late 1980s and early 1990s, following the collapse of communism.

Throughout their migratory history the Roma have never tried to establish a state of their own. They have settled instead in border areas, fiercely guarding their social and cultural identity. As a result, they have consistently been regarded and treated as outsiders. There are currently estimated to be some eight million in Europe. Exact figures are difficult to obtain, however, as many Roma are unregistered with the authorities or are not identified as such in national censuses.

State policies

Since their arrival in Europe, the Roma have been perceived by states as a problem to be resolved, whether by assimilation, containment, exclusion or expulsion. Between 1445 and 1856, gypsies in Transylvania (now Romania), were kept as slaves and excluded from citizenship rights, which were contingent upon the ownership of land. In other states, they were hunted down, imprisoned and killed.

History repeated itself in the 20th century, when the Nazi regime attempted to exterminate the gypsies. Initially the Roma were designated as 'social deviants'. As such, they were involuntarily sterilized and banned from marrying German citizens. Later they were incarcerated in concentration camps or *Zigeunerlager,* ostensibly on the grounds of crime prevention. By the end of the war, the gypsies were viewed not only as an 'undesirable social element' but also as an 'undesirable racial element'. As many as 500,000 are believed to have been put to death.

After the second world war, the communist regimes of Central and Eastern Europe attempted to assimilate,

Fig. 6.2

Estimated Roma populations in selected European countries

State	minimum	maximum
Albania	90,000	100,000
Belarus	10,000	15,000
Bosnia and Herzegovina	40,000	50,000
Bulgaria	700,000	800,000
Croatia	30,000	40,000
Czech Republic	250,000	300,000
Germany	110,000	130,000
Greece	160,000	200,000
Hungary	550,000	600,000
Macedonia (FYR)	220,000	260,000
Moldova	20,000	25,000
Poland	50,000	60,000
Romania	1,800,000	2,500,000
Russian Federation	220,000	400,000
Slovak Republic	480,000	520,000
Turkey	300,000	500,000
Ukraine	50,000	60,000
Yugoslavia (FR)	400,000	450,000

Source: J-P. Liegeois and N. Gheorghe, *Roma/Gypsies: A European Minority*, Minority Rights Group, London, 1995

rather than exclude or eliminate, their Roma populations. Viewed by the authorities as social misfits, countries such as Bulgaria, Czechoslovakia, Poland and Romania all made efforts to integrate the Roma into 'mainstream' society by means of forced settlement and employment programmes. Later, during the 1970s and 1980s, the government of Bulgaria took steps to abolish the special identity and culture of the Roma by requiring them to change their names and by prohibiting them from speaking their own language. If there was a positive aspect to these assimilationist policies, it was to be found in the insistence of the communist regimes that all citizens, including the Roma and other minority groups, should enjoy full citizenship status and civil rights.

The treatment and status of the Roma has in many ways deteriorated since the collapse of communism. New citizenship laws have been introduced throughout much of Central and Eastern Europe, which have often inadvertently (and in some cases deliberately) discriminated against the Roma. The criteria for obtaining citizenship in the Czech Republic, for example, were felt by many commentators, including UNHCR, to discriminate against the Roma.

As described elsewhere in this chapter, the new citizenship laws required any individual wishing to acquire Czech nationality to be fluent in Czech, to have been resident on Czech territory for at least two years, to have a clean criminal record for the preceding five years, and to have a document proving exemption from Slovak citizenship. Such criteria were difficult for many Roma to fulfill, due to their itinerant lifestyle and marginalized socio-economic status. Fears that the Czech Republic's citizenship law might render many Roma stateless have not materialized, however, due to legislative changes introduced by the authorities with the assistance and advice of UNHCR.

As well as experiencing such citizenship problems, the security of the Roma has been threatened in other ways. Many countries in Central and Eastern Europe adopted new constitutions after the fall of communism, recognizing the rights of specific minority populations. But the Roma were frequently excluded from such arrangements. More generally, the Roma have continued to experience social discrimination and victimization. An indication of this problem is to be seen in the failure of local officials, security services and judges to apprehend and punish the perpetrators of racist attacks on the Roma and their

property, examples of which have been reported in Bulgaria, Germany, Hungary, Poland, the Czech and Slovak republics.

Asylum amd migration

A common characteristic of almost all Roma communities across Europe is their nomadic lifestyle. Throughout their history, the Roma have moved continuously from one place to another, either by necessity or out of choice. For the Roma, migration has been both a defence against external aggression and discrimination, as well as a means of securing a livelihood. Indeed, one of the constant frustrations of European governments, both democratic and authoritarian, has been the unwillingness of the Roma to settle in one place and to engage in routine economic activities.

During the period of communist rule, the Roma of Central and Eastern Europe were limited in the extent to which they could move, due to strict border controls and the official sedentarization programmes to which they were subjected. But with the collapse of communism and the lifting of the iron curtain, they have been free to migrate once again. During the early 1990s, many thousands of Roma attempted to move into Western Europe, both to improve their standard of

living and to escape from harassment.

Confronted with the arrival of so many Roma, the countries of Western Europe have attempted to obstruct their arrival and return them to their country of origin or previous place of residence. Germany, for example, which received the largest number of Roma asylum seekers, has signed a succession of agreements with neighbouring states, facilitating the removal and readmission of unsuccessful asylum seekers.

An agreement signed in 1992 by Germany and Romania, for example, allowed for the "repatriation of German and Romanian nationals to their respective countries" with particular regard to "Romanian and German nationals who have entered one of these two countries illegally." In practice, the convention was primarily intended to address the question of Romanian asylum seekers in Germany, about 40 per cent of whom were believed to be Roma. As the citizenship of some Roma is unclear, however, and as others do not carry a passport or identity documents, the task of returning them to the states of Central and Eastern Europe has in many cases proved to be difficult.

The link with forced displacement

There are some intimate connections between statelessness, refugee movements and others forms of forced displacement. This section considers
three: displacement as a cause of statelessness; displacement as consequence
of statelessness; and statelessness as an obstacle to the resolution of refugee
problems.

Exiled communities and other uprooted populations are particularly vulnerable to statelessness, especially when their displacement is followed or accompanied by a redrawing of territorial boundaries. Several examples of this
phenomenon have already been cited: the Biharis of Bangladesh, the
Palestinians, and the formerly deported populations of the former Soviet
Union.

The CIS region provides some additional instances of the way that large-
scale displacement can arise in the context of forced displacement. The conflict between Armenia and Azerbaijan, for example, resulted in the forced
displacement of hundreds of thousands of people. As the USSR still existed
when the conflict began in 1988, these internally displaced people initially
retained their status as Soviet citizens. After 1991, however, they became
both stateless and refugees, due to the absence of citizenship legislation in
the two successor states.

A second and perhaps more significant linkage between forced displacement and disputed citizenship is to be found in the frequency with which
stateless and denaturalized populations are obliged to flee from their usual
place of residence. In the CIS region and other parts of the former communist bloc, the movement of people affected by citizenship problems has not
really assumed the dramatic form that some commentators had predicted
two or three years ago. The return of the Russians and other Slavic peoples
to their ancestral homelands can in some instances be regarded as a form of
forced displacement, especially when it has been provoked by targeted attacks on such groups and discrimination against them. More generally, however, it is perhaps best described as a migratory movement.

Elsewhere in the world, however, several groups of stateless people have
been directly involved in recent refugee movements, expulsions and internal
displacements.

Mauritania. In 1989-90, around 60,000 black Africans were expelled from
Mauritania to Senegal, where they were recognized as refugees and assisted
by UNHCR. The impasse for the 56,000 refugees who are still in Senegal centres on their insistence that the Mauritanian authorities repatriate them *en
masse,* return their land and issue them with new identity documents. For
their part, the Mauritanian authorities have maintained that those people
who were expelled from the country at the end of the 1980s were in fact
Senegalese nationals and that their Mauritanian identity documents were
fraudulent. (25)

Kuwait. In the late 1980s, the Kuwaiti authorities promulgated a series of measures that removed the Bidoon from the country's census rolls and stripped them of their civil identification cards, thereby depriving them of access to government jobs and social services. During and after the Iraqi occupation and Gulf War of 1991, 100,000 or more Bidoons left Kuwait and arrived in Iraq, some of them leaving as a result of mass expulsions. Following their departure, the US State Department reported in 1993, "the government prevented the return of the Bidoon who had left Kuwait, either willingly or by force... by delaying or denying their entry visas." Since that time, few have been allowed to return to their former country of residence. (26)

Myanmar. In 1991-92, some 250,000 Rohingyas, members of a Muslim minority group who are generally not recognized as citizens of Myanmar, fled from their homes and were accommodated in UNHCR-assisted refugee camps in Bangladesh. According to a report submitted by a Special Rapporteur of the UN Human Rights Commission, the exodus was occasioned by a military campaign which involved "extrajudicial executions, torture and ill-treatment, and forced labour and portering." These accusations have been rejected by the Myanmar authorities. (27)

Bhutan. Between 1990 and 1992, up to 120,000 Nepali-speaking people abandoned their homes in southern Bhutan and fled to Nepal and India. Around 90,000 of this number are accommodated in UNHCR refugee camps in Nepal. According to a UNHCR-sponsored report, the exodus was provoked by an attempt to withdraw Bhutanese citizenship from these people and to impose the very different culture and language of northern Bhutan upon them. These initiatives led to a series of demonstrations by the southern Bhutanese, followed by a "swift and harsh" response from the authorities, involving "arbitrary arrests, ill-treatment and torture." While the refugees have expressed their desire to return to Bhutan, the authorities there continue to deny that the majority of the refugees have a claim to Bhutanese citizenship, and therefore refuse to admit them. (28)

Cambodia. In 1993, around 35,000 ethnic Vietnamese - long-term residents of Cambodia who lack a clear status in the country's nationality laws - fled by boat after they had been subjected to a series of racially motivated attacks by Khmer Rouge soldiers. Most of this number fled into Viet Nam, while around 5,000 remained stranded on the Cambodian side of the border. According to a UNHCR publication, "all people of Vietnamese origin in Cambodia are vulnerable to racial violence, not only from the Khmer Rouge but also from other groups who may use anti-Vietnamese propaganda for political gains. The fact that the ethnic Vietnamese community cannot rely on regulations or legal documents makes them all the more vulnerable." (29)

Zaire. In 1996 and 1997, eastern Zaire was engulfed by an armed conflict which was to a large extent sparked off by a dispute over the nationality of ethnic Tutsis living in the area. The subsequent fighting, involving at least three different forces - Tutsi rebels, the former Rwandese army and the Zairean military - has provoked mass displacement amongst the local population and amongst the Rwandese refugees who fled to the area in 1994 (see Box 1.1).

Third and finally, if statelessness can be both a product of and lead to forced displacement, then the peaceful settlement of nationality disputes can play an important role in the task of resolving and averting situations of forced displacement. The exercise of an 'effective nationality' evidently enhances the attachment of individuals to a state and its territory. It reinforces their security and sense of belonging, and thereby contributes to the objective of enabling people to remain in - or return to - their usual place of residence.

Unfortunately, statelessness and nationality disputes continue to obstruct the search for solutions to refugee-related problems in several parts of the world. According to the Inter-Governmental Consultations on Asylum, Refugee and Migration Policies, in the CIS region and Eastern Europe, at least five different countries have refused to readmit rejected asylum seekers on grounds of their statelessness. And in Africa, Asia and the Middle East, a further 10 countries have declined to accept such rejected cases on the grounds that they did not recognize the people concerned as their nationals. In February 1997, moreover, Malaysia announced that it was unable to repatriate 8,000 irregular migrants originating from Myanmar, as the authorities of that country did not recognize their claim to citizenship.

More seriously, perhaps, nationality disputes continue to play an important part in several protracted situations of mass displacement, including those involving the Bidoons, the ethnic Vietnamese of Cambodia and the Palestinians (see Box 6.4). In the case of the southern Bhutanese, for example, the refugees in Nepal have expressed a desire to go back to their former country of residence, but have been unable to do so because their citizenship - and therefore their right to return - has not been recognized by the Bhutanese authorities. While the two states have held discussions on this and related issues, no solution has yet been found to the problem. As UNHCR has reported elsewhere, "the slow pace of progress of the Nepal-Bhutan government talks means that there is still some way to go before an end to the refugee crisis will be in sight."(30)

The slow pace of repatriation to Bosnia has also been attributed to the persistence of the citizenship problem in that country. "The displaced would be far more likely to return home," the Open Society Institute suggests, "if they felt protected under rights afforded to citizens. Likewise, a harmonized and balanced approach to citizenship in successor states would probably build confidence and reduce instances of new movements of people."(31)

NATIONAL AND INTERNATIONAL RESPONSIBILITIES

Statelessness is first and foremost a problem for states to resolve. In the refugee field, it has become an established principle that countries of origin have a primary duty to desist from actions that force people to abandon their homes and a corresponding obligation to create the conditions that will enable exiled populations to repatriate.

A similar principle of state responsibility must be fostered in relation to the problem of statelessness. Above all, governments must acknowledge, both formally and in practice, that they do not have a right to withdraw or withhold the benefits of citizenship from whole sections of the population who can demonstrate a genuine and effective link with the country.

Given the frequency with which governments have denaturalized and expelled their citizens, coupled with the protracted nature of so many citizenship disputes, an appeal to the notion of state responsibility might seem somewhat naive. It is therefore worth recalling that in the past few years a number of countries have managed to address the problem of statelessness in a positive manner.

In Lebanon, for example, more than 10,000 stateless persons, most of them from Middle Eastern minority groups (but not including the Palestinians) were granted citizenship in 1994-95 (see Box 6.3). In the Baltic state of Lithuania, where the Russian population is relatively small, an inclusive approach to the nationality issue has given all permanent residents the opportunity to become citizens of the country. As a result, the issue has not become a matter of significant political controversy. And in early 1997, the Hong Kong authorities granted British passports to around 8,000 people, many of them of Indian origin, who were at risk of becoming stateless following the handover of the colony to China.

Despite the nationality issues which have arisen with the dissolution of Czechoslovakia, the two successor countries have largely succeeded in sorting out the affairs of the former state. What is more, this objective has been achieved in a very short period of time and in a peaceful manner - in striking contrast to the violence and mass population displacements which have accompanied the dissolution of other federal states.

Significantly, both the Czech and Slovak states have both welcomed international involvement in their nationality problems. This approach has enabled UNHCR, the Organization for Security and Cooperation in Europe and the Council of Europe to assist in a number of ways: undertaking fact-finding missions; commenting on new nationality legislation; training civil servants who are responsible for citizenship issues; and assisting individuals whose nationality status is unresolved.

As this example suggests, statelessness is often a result of rapid political change and a lack of preparedness in the countries concerned. A similar situation has arisen in Azerbaijan and several other parts of the CIS region.

Map N

Palestinian refugees registered with UNRWA

□ Capital
● Town
— Boundary

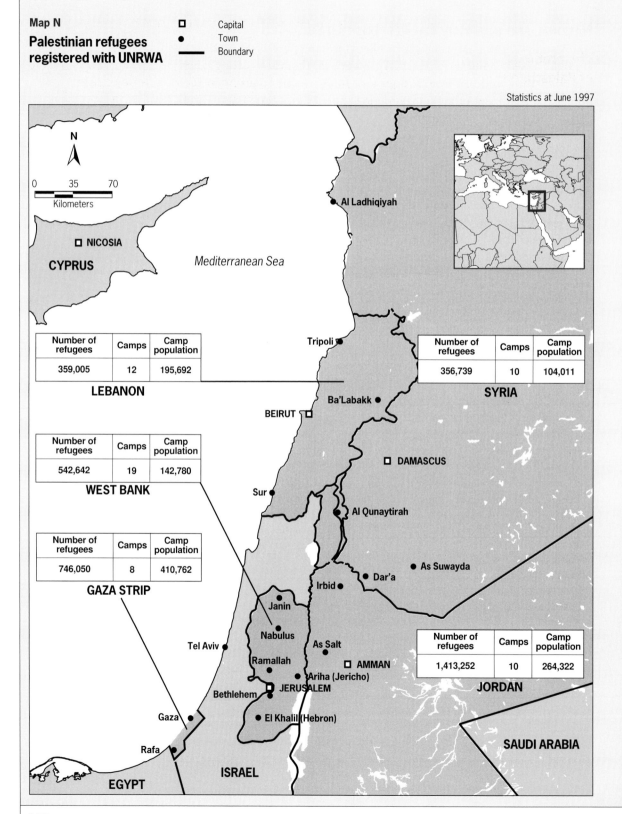

Statistics at June 1997

LEBANON

Number of refugees	Camps	Camp population
359,005	12	195,692

SYRIA

Number of refugees	Camps	Camp population
356,739	10	104,011

WEST BANK

Number of refugees	Camps	Camp population
542,642	19	142,780

GAZA STRIP

Number of refugees	Camps	Camp population
746,050	8	410,762

JORDAN

Number of refugees	Camps	Camp population
1,413,252	10	264,322

6.3

The problem of Palestinian nationality

As a result of the political and military upheavals which have taken place in the Middle East since the end of the second world war, millions of Palestinians have been obliged to take up residence in neighbouring territories, other parts of the Middle East and more distant parts of the world. Around half of the worldwide Palestinian population of 6.4 million are believed to be stateless, and many of those who have a nominal nationality are not able to exercise all of the rights enjoyed by other citizens.

The number of Palestinian refugees is itself a matter of great contention and lies at the heart of the Arab-Israeli dispute. When the state of Israel was proclaimed in May 1948, fighting between the Arab and Jewish populations of Palestine, a territory administered by Britain, was already taking place. The proclamation prompted the intervention of several Arab states and in the ensuing armed conflict, 700,000 or 800,000 Palestinians took refuge elsewhere, primarily in the West Bank, the Gaza Strip, Jordan, Lebanon and Syria. Around 150,000 stayed in Israel and became citizens of the new state.

According to many estimates, during the 'six-day war' between Israel and the Arab states in 1967, some 300,000 Palestinians moved from the West Bank to the East Bank in Jordan and to Syria, and from the Gaza Strip to Egypt and Jordan. In later years, substantial numbers of Palestinians were obliged to leave Jordan (1970-71), Lebanon (1982), Kuwait and other Gulf states (1990-92), and Libya (1995-96). A considerable number of Palestinians have thus been displaced on more than one occasion, a factor which has complicated the question of their nationality and legal status.

Rights of residence
The UN Relief and Works Agency for Palestine Refugees in the Near East (UNRWA) was established in 1948 to assist those Palestinians who had been displaced when the state of Israel was established. Almost three million Palestinians are currently registered with the agency, which operates in Jordan, Lebanon, Syria, Gaza and the West Bank.

UNRWA defines Palestinian refugees as those people, and their descendants, who lived in Palestine two years prior to the 1948 hostilities, and who lost their homes and livelihoods as a consequence of the conflict. UNRWA was not given a mandate to protect the Palestinian

refugees; that responsibility was implicitly left to the countries where they took refuge. Moreover, because they were already under the aegis of a UN agency, those Palestinians registered with UNRWA were effectively excluded from the mandate of UNHCR when it was established in 1951.

The legal status of the Palestinians varies according to both the date of their displacement (or that of their parents and grandparents) and according to their current place of residence. Some 850,000 Palestinians - those and their descendants who remained in the new state of Israel after 1948 - now have Israeli citizenship. An unknown number have also acquired the nationality of countries outside the Middle East. Of the Arab states accommodating Palestinian refugees, only Jordan has granted them citizenship on any substantial scale. The status of the remainder has proved at best ambiguous and has placed many Palestinians in an intolerable situation.

Those Palestinians who hold Israeli nationality are in many senses second-class citizens, with standards of education, housing, employment and social services that are generally inferior to those enjoyed by the rest of the population. Palestinians living in areas occupied by Israel experience considerably

greater difficulties. They have for many years lived in a state of limbo, with severe restrictions on their access to jobs, land and public services, their freedom of movement and the exercise of other human rights. According to the UN Commission on Human Rights, Palestinians in the occupied territories are also frequently subjected to collective punishments, in violation of the Geneva Conventions.

In the Arab states, the Palestinians benefit in principle from the 1965 Casablanca Protocol, which enjoined signatories to uphold the right of Palestinians to work, to enjoy full residency rights and freedom of movement within and among the Arab countries. Such rights, however, explicitly stopped short of formal citizenship, due to the importance which the Arab states attached to maintaining the identity of the Palestinians and their claim to a separate homeland. In later years, however, as the Palestinian nationalist movement came into conflict with the governments of the Arab states, the legal status of the Palestinians diminished. As a result, few Palestinians in the Arab world now enjoy a secure right to remain in their country of residence.

Travel represents another difficulty for many

Palestinians as no standard travel document has been established for them. Their entitlement to such documents consequently depends of a number of different factors, including their country of residence, date of arrival, marital status and means of support. The right of Palestinians to re-enter the country where they were born can also be jeopardized if the travel document which they are using expires while they are abroad.

Because of their problematic citizenship status, Palestinian refugees are particularly prone to expulsion. Those who have gone to the Gulf states and Libya, for example, are viewed in much the same way as other migrant workers, and are ultimately expected to return to their country of asylum, however long they have lived and worked in another country. Their vulnerability was highlighted during the Gulf Crisis of 1990-92, when up to 350,000 Palestinians were forced to leave Kuwait and other states in the Persian Gulf.

Some of the least secure Palestinians are those from the Gaza Strip, many of whom fled during the 1948 upheaval and again in 1967. While Gaza was administered by Egypt, they were issued with documents by that country. In practice,

however, such documents have been of little use for travel. Those who fled to Jordan were given two-year renewable documents which did not confer citizenship. Others moved on to the Gulf states or Libya.

The expulsion in 1995 of part of the 30,000 strong Palestinian community in Libya - most of whom had long been settled in the country - was ordered by the government to demonstrate its anger at the peace agreement established between Israel and the PLO. Some of the Palestinians affected by this order had previously lived in Lebanon and held travel documents from that country, but Lebanon refused to admit them. Some of those expelled from Libya managed to travel overland through Egypt to the West Bank or Gaza, or, after an even more tortuous journey, to Syria and Jordan. But up to a thousand were stranded in very poor conditions on the border between Egypt and Libya. Most of this number originated from Gaza and did not have documents allowing them to enter other states.

Following international pressure, the Libyan government eventually relented and allowed most of the stranded Palestinians back. But several hundred remained on the border, living in appalling circumstances. In April 1997 those remaining in

this no-man's land camp were forcibly removed by Libyan soldiers and sent to another location in eastern Libya.

Peace process

Despite these negative developments, the faltering Middle East peace process has offered a glimmer of hope that the issues of citizenship and statelessness can be resolved. Shortly after the time when most of the Gaza Strip and parts of the West Bank were handed over to the Palestinian Authority late in 1995, the Authority began to issue Palestinian passports to residents of the West Bank and Gaza. The documents allow travel outside the areas controlled by the Palestinian Authority, and have been recognized by more than 40 countries, including Israel, the US, Canada and the countries of the European Union. Continuing tensions in the area, however, mean that it is still very difficult for Palestinians to move between the Gaza Strip, the West Bank, Jerusalem and Israel, let alone further afield. Moreover, since the Palestinian Authority does not have sovereignty over any territory, such passports cannot confer citizenship on their holders.

Early in 1997, a draft law on Palestinian citizenship was being developed. Among the questions it may have to address is that of refugee status through male descent.

If refugee status or registration is to be taken as a criterion for defining Palestinian citizenship, many Palestinian women who are married to non-registered men and their offspring could well be excluded, thereby perpetuating their marginalized status.

According to one commentator, "the administrative structures and legislative basis inherited from the Soviet period proved both inadequate and insufficient. New policies and legislation had to be designed without any institutional experience or trained personnel."(32) In such situations, UNHCR and other international organizations evidently have an important role to play in helping the authorities to address the problem of citizenship.

The limits of sovereignty

Unfortunately, however, statelessness does not always arise in an accidental or incidental manner. Nor are states with substantial numbers of stateless people always willing to seek advice and support from the international community. In such situations, and particularly when governments take steps to denaturalize and expel whole sections of their population, more assertive forms of international action may ultimately be required.

Statelessness has important implications for the security of people and the realization of their human rights. Statelessness can provoke large-scale refugee movements and thereby place substantial burdens on countries of asylum. Statelessness is a source of regional instability and can even become a threat to international peace and security. The international community therefore has a wholly legitimate interest in its prevention and elimination. Sadly, it would appear, in some situations this objective may only be achieved by measures such as the introduction of economic or diplomatic sanctions, the suspension of preferential trading agreements and the public condemnation of the country concerned.

Many states would evidently resist such intervention, stating that they have a sovereign right to determine under their own law who are and who are not its nationals. While this is technically correct, the power of the state in this respect is by no means absolute or untrammelled. The 1930 Hague Convention, for example, the first international attempt to ensure that all people have a nationality, stipulated that states must act in accordance with "international conventions, international custom and the principles of law generally recognized with regard to nationality." Subsequent jurisprudence has reconfirmed the principle that the citizenship issue cannot be considered to fall within the sole jurisdiction of states.

Regional initiatives

Recent experience suggests that increased efforts should be made to articulate and implement the notion of state responsibility at the regional level. A good example of such initiatives is to be seen in an agreement amongst the CIS states, signed in Bishkek, Kyrgyzstan, in October 1992, on the situation of formerly deported populations.

Under the Bishkek agreement, signatory states undertook to settle the question of citizenship of deported people in accordance with national legislation, bilateral agreements and international law. Forcibly transferred people who returned to their prior places of residence were guaranteed the same political, economic and social rights as other citizens living in those locations.

The signatory states agreed to provide the documents necessary for formerly deported people to enjoy full social, economic and political rights. While for reasons indicated elsewhere the agreement has yet to be fully implemented (see Box 6.1), it can be taken as a statement of good intent among the states concerned to right a historical wrong and to resolve a potential problem of statelessness in a multilateral manner.

Another example of positive action at the regional level is the attention paid to nationality questions in the CIREFCA process, a five-year programme of activities introduced in 1989 to resolve the problem of forced displacement in Mexico, Belize and the Central American states. Reflecting the region's traditionally liberal approach to nationality issues, the plan incorporated a provision to guarantee citizenship to every child born in exile, whether in their country of asylum or in the state to which they eventually repatriated.

Treaties and regional accords on nationality issues have an admittedly chequered history, as demonstrated by the human suffering associated with the population exchanges and organized repatriations which followed the first and second world wars. It is for this reason that bilateral and regional initiatives on issues related to statelessness must be supported by an agreed framework of principles, conforming to recognized international standards.

The CIREFCA agreement, for example, was clearly underpinned by the widespread acceptance of the *jus soli* principle throughout the Americas region and its incorporation into Article 20 of the 1969 American Convention on Human Rights: "every person has the right to a nationality of the state in whose territory he was born if he does not have the right to any other nationality." The practical and human benefits of this approach are to be seen in Mexico, where children born to Guatemalan refugee parents have an automatic right to Mexican citizenship when they reach the age of 18 - as well as the right to claim Guatemalan citizenship if they decide to repatriate.

Europe provides another example of a region which is attempting to establish a regional framework of principles on issues relating to citizenship and statelessness. A European Convention on Nationality is currently being finalized. As well as reconfirming the right to a nationality and the right not to be arbitrarily deprived of citizenship, the draft convention prohibits nationality legislation which discriminates on ethnic and other grounds. It also requires every signatory state to facilitate the naturalization of stateless persons and refugees who are "lawfully and habitually on its territory," and, in cases of state succession, obliges successor states to take account of four different factors in defining its initial body of citizens: genuine and effective links, habitual residence, territorial origin, and the will of the individual.

As the establishment of the European Convention suggests, there is a developing area of international law relating to state succession - an issue which has particular relevance to the problem of statelessness in regions such as the CIS, the Baltic States, former Yugoslavia and the Czech and Slovak republics. Recent experience in these areas shows all too clearly that when federal polities collapse and new states take their place, significant numbers of people may find that they are unable to acquire citizenship in the territory where they have lived for the whole of their lives.

New states and restored states have to establish principles in order to determine their initial body of citizens, and to ascertain who might subsequently be granted citizenship. In international law, the general presumption is that all those people who have been nationals of a predecessor state have a genuine and effective link with the successor state. As one international authority on this issue has written, "sovereignty denotes responsibility, and a change of sovereignty does not give the new sovereign the right to dispose of the population concerned at the discretion of the government. The population goes with the territory."(33)

While other legal scholars have disputed this assertion, the emphasis which it places on the principle of state responsibility is clearly a valuable one. If a person has a significant connection with a newly established state, derived from factors such as birth, descent and long-term residence, then this connection should be acknowledged as being indicative of the right to citizenship.

STRENGTHENING THE LEGAL AND INSTITUTIONAL REGIME

With the growth of statelessness around the world and the growing awareness of its implications for national and regional security, the international community has in recent years been revisiting the international instruments related to questions of citizenship. The 1954 Convention relating to the Status of Stateless Persons and the 1961 Convention on the Reduction of Statelessness serve as important reference points for the current debate.

In brief, the former of these instruments was designed primarily to regulate the treatment of *de jure* stateless people who are not covered by the 1951 UN Refugee Convention, primarily in areas such as their legal rights, their access to work and welfare and their ability to acquire a nationality. The latter instrument, however, was intended to reduce the future number of stateless cases by addressing the problem at source.

As well as stipulating that *de jure* stateless children should be granted the nationality of the signatory state in which a parent had citizenship, the 1961 Convention attempts to avert those cases of statelessness resulting from a change of civil status, residence abroad or the voluntary renunciation of nationality. At the same time, the Convention prohibits signatory states from depriving people of their nationality on racial, ethnic, religious or political

6.4

Stateless and unregistered children

In most countries, babies are registered with the relevant authorities soon after they are born, enabling them to receive a birth certificate. Without such a certificate, it can be very difficult for a person to lay claim to a nationality or to exercise the rights associated with citizenship. Individuals who lack a birth certificate may, for example, find it impossible to leave or return to their own country, register as a voter or gain access to public health and education services.

The legal framework

Recognizing the importance of these issues, Article 7 of the 1989 Convention on the Rights of the Child states that every child "shall be registered immediately after birth and shall have the right from birth to a name, the right to acquire a nationality and, as far as possible, the right to know and be cared for by his or her parents." The convention continues by stipulating that signatory states "shall ensure the implementation of these rights in accordance with their national law and their obligations under the relevant international instruments in the field, in particular where

the child would otherwise be stateless." The Convention on the Rights of the Child has now been signed by 140 states, very few of which have entered any reservations to Article 7.

Several regional instruments have also reiterated a child's right to registration at birth and to a nationality, including Article 6 of the 1990 African Charter on the Rights and Welfare of the Child and Article 20 of the 1969 American Convention on Human Rights. Moreover, these instruments state that children should be granted the nationality of their place of birth if they do not have another nationality.

As discussed elsewhere in this chapter, nationality is normally granted on the basis of a person's place of birth (*jus soli*) or on the basis of their descent (*jus sanguinis*). There has been a tendency in the existing (and very sparse) literature on children and nationality to equate registration at birth with the right to a nationality. But the two are not always synonymous. Although the right of children to registration at birth is unequivocal, this does not always give them an automatic right to a particular nationality.

In those countries which grant citizenship on the basis of place of birth, as in much of the Americas, registration at

birth gives a child automatic rights to the citizenship of that country if he or she cannot claim citizenship by descent. However, in countries which grant citizenship exclusively on the basis of *jus sanguinis,* as is the case throughout most of Asia, registration at birth does not give a child a right to citizenship in their country of birth if the parents are not nationals of that state.

Children without a nationality

Despite the clear legal guidelines which exist in relation to a child's right to a nationality, there are many young people throughout the world who are effectively stateless. This can arise for a variety of reasons, the most important of which are summarized below:

- if nationality is granted on the basis of *jus sanguinis* and one or both of a child's parents are stateless or their nationality is disputed;

- if a child is born out of wedlock;

- if a child's birth is not registered because of the parent's failure to do so, because of flawed administrative practices or because the authorities refuse to register the birth;

- if a child is born in a refugee camp or to

parents who are refugees, asylum seekers or migrant workers, and if the birth is not registered with the authorities;

- if a child is born in a country of asylum and the registration of that birth is not accepted by the authorities in the child's country of origin; and,

- if a child is born during a civil or international war, or during a process of state dissolution, and the authorities are unable or unwilling to register the birth.

Although cases of stateless children have come to UNHCR's attention in countries across the world, the problem is particularly prominent in those areas which grant citizenship on the basis of *jus sanguinis* and where the nationality of one or both of the child's parents is disputed. This is the case in Bhutan, for example, where the 1985 Citizenship Act stipulates that children do not have a right to Bhutanese nationality if they are born to parents who are stateless or who are not entitled to Bhutanese citizenship themselves. Children born in Bhutan to non-Bhutanese nationals and who are unable to obtain the nationality of their parents are therefore rendered stateless. The citizenship status of those children born and registered in the Bhutanese refugee camps of Nepal is even less clear.

A somewhat similar situation has arisen in Myanmar. The Rohingyas, a Muslim minority group living in the west of the country, are generally not recognized as Myanmar nationals because of the country's very restrictive citizenship laws. The citizenship status of Rohingya children who were born in refugee camps in Bangladesh and who have returned to Myanmar is even more precarious.

The problem of stateless children is not restricted to those countries which provide citizenship on the basis of *jus sanguinis*. Unfortunately, children can also face difficulties in obtaining a nationality in countries which provide citizenship on the basis of *jus soli*. This usually occurs because the authorities of those countries are reluctant to register the births of certain children born on their territory. This has been a common problem for the children of refugees, asylum seekers and migrant workers in several countries in Central and South America, where the authorities have been reluctant to register their births for the very reason that this will give them an automatic right to citizenship.

In Honduras, for example, none of the children born in the Salvadoran refugee camps during the late 1970s and 1980s were registered with the authorities. Although the Honduran authorities were legally obliged to register all children born on their territory, in practice, the refugee camps were treated as if they had extra-territorial status.

A similar situation arose in the Guatemalan refugee camps of Mexico. Until 1993, the Mexican authorities refused to issue children born in those camps with birth certificates, despite domestic legislation obliging them to take such action. Following lengthy negotiations with UNHCR, the Mexican government finally decided in 1993 to retroactively provide birth certificates to all the children concerned - some 10,000 children in all, who, when they reach the age of 18, will be entitled to Mexican citizenship.

Asylum seekers in the Russian Federation have also been affected by this problem. According to Russian nationality laws, children born on Russian territory to non-Russian parents are considered to be Russian if the states of which their parents are nationals do not provide them with citizenship. Similarly, children born to stateless parents on Russian territory have the right to Russian citizenship.

In practice, however, non-Russian or stateless parents are unable to register the births of their children if they are not themselves legally resident in the country. As asylum seekers from countries outside the former Soviet Union find it almost impossible to regularize their status with the Russian authorities, and as many are unwilling to approach the embassy of their country of origin, their children can easily become stateless. Like stateless and unregistered children in other parts of the world, they are unable to attend school or seek medical assistance, and are more likely to be exposed to illegal adoption, trafficking and sexual exploitation.

Finding solutions

Despite the frequency with which such circumstances arise, there has been little concerted effort to address the problem of stateless children. Little research has been done on this issue and even the principal legal texts on statelessness pay little or no attention to it. One of the main challenges for UNHCR is to ensure that the births of children born to refugees and asylum seekers are properly registered with the authorities in the country where they are living. Measures are also required to ensure that the birth certificates issued to these children are recognized by their parents' country of origin.

UNHCR has participated in birth registration programmes on a number of recent occasions, most notably in Mexico, Honduras and El Salvador. When Salvadoran refugees began to go home in large numbers in the late 1980s, for example, the organization issued birth certificates to all children who had been born in the camps, based on medical records. These certificates were endorsed by the Salvadoran consul in Honduras, enabling the children to obtain citizenship of El Salvador when they returned to that country.

Finally, there must be a concerted effort to ensure that all those countries which have signed the 1989 Convention on the Rights of the Child, as well as relevant regional conventions, respect the fundamental right of a child to a name and nationality in their domestic legislation and administrative practices. According to UNICEF, some progress has already been made in this regard, most notably in Bolivia, Costa Rica, Ecuador, Nicaragua, Peru and the Philippines, where identity papers have been issued to thousands of children who were previously not registered.

grounds. The Convention does not oblige signatories to grant nationality to any stateless persons who enter its territory - only those who already have a strong connection with the state and for whom no other nationality is forthcoming.

Other international instruments dealing with the right to a nationality include the 1957 Convention on the Nationality of Married Women, the 1966 Covenant on Civil and Political Rights, the 1979 Convention on the Elimination of All Forms of Discrimination against Women, and the 1989 Convention on the Rights of the Child. The instruments concerning women seek to ensure that they enjoy equal rights to acquire, change or retain nationality, while those covering children are primarily intended to ensure that children have the right to be registered and to acquire a nationality from birth (see Box 6.4).

There is a general recognition that the international instruments on statelessness are characterized by a number of related weaknesses - problems which must be addressed now that this issue has found a more prominent place on the international humanitarian agenda.

The first of these weaknesses is to be found in the failure of the existing conventions to address the causes of statelessness in a sufficiently vigorous manner. As the Independent Commission on International Humanitarian Issues (ICIHI) has observed, "they have been formulated more from the point of view of a state's prerogatives and sovereignty than of individual human rights."(34) Thus while the forum that was established to draft the 1961 Convention was described as the 'UN conference on the *elimination or reduction* of future statelessness', the instrument itself was described simply as the 'UN Convention on the reduction of statelessness'. As a UNHCR staff member has suggested, "the focus on reduction, rather than elimination, is evident in the articles which aim at avoiding statelessness at birth, but neither prohibit the possibility of revocation of nationality under certain circumstances, nor retroactively grant citizenship in all cases to address current statelessness." (35)

The 1961 Convention also represented a compromise between states adhering to the principles of *jus soli* and *jus sanguinis*. Recognizing the advantages of the *jus soli* principle as a means of eliminating statelessness - an advantage which has been clearly demonstrated in the Americas region - the ICIHI has called for the introduction of a new international instrument, enshrining this principle as the sole criterion for the acquisition of nationality.

While it is evident that such a far-reaching suggestion would not attract the support of many states, a broader consensus could very usefully be established around the notion of a 'right of attachment' or 'genuine effective link', whereby citizenship is determined not by a single criterion, but by a combination of factors such as birth, residency and descent. The basis of this approach to the problem is the sensible assumption that statelessness could normally be avoided if individuals were guaranteed citizenship in the country to which they are most closely connected and attached. Interestingly, this was the very suggestion advanced in a landmark report on statelessness prepared by the International Law Commission in 1952. (36)

The role of UNHCR

The second weakness in the international community's efforts to eliminate and regulate the problem of statelessness is to be found in the very small number of states which have actually become signatories to the 1954 and 1961 Conventions - 44 and 19 respectively, compared with the UN's total membership of around 185 (see Figure 6.3). Significantly, more than 130 countries have signed the 1951 Convention relating to the status of Refugees or its 1967 Protocol, demonstrating a major difference in the attitude of governments to these closely related issues. Whereas the refugee problem concerns the situation of non-nationals, nationality issues are directly linked to the more sensitive matter of national sovereignty and membership of the state.

There is a broad consensus that the limited number of accessions to the conventions on statelessness is also a result of a third weakness in the current international arrangements relating to this problem: the absence of a body to supervise and promote these instruments. When the 1961 Convention on Statelessness was introduced, it foresaw the establishment of a body that might assist stateless people to present their naturalization claims to the appropriate authorities. When the Convention finally came into force in 1975, UNHCR was entrusted with this task. But no mention was made of UNHCR's competence with regard to the 1954 Convention, nor was UNHCR asked to assume any wider responsibilities in addressing the problem of statelessness.

In the past few years, however, recognizing the important links between statelessness, security and forced population displacements, the international community has encouraged UNHCR to adopt a more active role in this area. Thus the UN General Assembly has requested UNHCR "actively to promote accession" to the 1954 and 1961 Conventions on statelessness, "as well as to provide relevant technical and advisory services pertaining to the preparation and implementation of nationality legislation."(37)

In response to such requests, UNHCR has taken a number of practical steps to strengthen its efforts in this domain. These include, for example, the recruitment of a legal expert on the problem of statelessness, the preparation of an information package on the 1954 and 1961 conventions, the introduction of a staff training programme on citizenship questions, and the establishment of more systematic reporting procedures on nationality problems. In addition, UNHCR has reinforced its working relationship with a number of actors which are involved in this issue: UN organizations such as

Fig. 6.3

States parties to the 1954 Convention relating to the Status of Stateless Persons and the 1961 Convention on the Reduction of Statelessness

Country	1954 Convention	1961 Convention
Algeria	+	
Antigua and Barbuda	+	
Argentina	+	
Armenia	+	+
Australia	+	+
Austria		+
Azerbaijan	+	+
Barbados	+	
Belgium	+	
Bolivia	+	+
Bosnia and Herzegovina	+	+
Botswana	+	
Canada		+
Costa Rica	+	+
Croatia	+	
Denmark	+	+
Ecuador	+	
Fiji	+	
Finland	+	
France	+	
Germany	+	+
Greece	+	
Guinea	+	
Ireland	+	+
Israel	+	
Italy	+	
Kiribati	+	+
Korea, Republic of	+	
Latvia		+
Lesotho	+	
Liberia	+	
Libya	+	+
Luxembourg	+	
Madagascar	+	
Macedonia (FYR)	+	
Netherlands	+	+
Niger		+
Norway	+	+
Slovenia	+	
Spain	+	
Sweden	+	+
Switzerland	+	
Trinidad and Tobago	+	
Tunisia	+	
Uganda	+	
United Kingdom	+	+
Yugoslavia (FR)	+	
Zambia	+	
Total number	**44**	**19**

Situation at June 1997

the Centre for Human Rights, regional bodies such as the Council of Europe and the Organization for Security and Cooperation in Europe, and non-governmental agencies such as the Open Society Institute, to give just a few examples.

At the same time, UNHCR has been able to play an active role in a number of situations where problems related to statelessness and the acquisition of an effective nationality have arisen. In countries such as Azerbaijan, Cambodia, the Czech and Slovak republics and the Federal Republic of Yugoslavia (Serbia and Montenegro), for example, the organization has been engaged in an intensive dialogue with the authorities with regard to their nationality legislation.

In former Yugoslavia more generally, UNHCR is playing a central role in supervising and monitoring the implementation of the Dayton agreement's provisions on citizenship issues. And through its involvement in the CIS conference on refugees, UNHCR has sought to ensure that the problem of statelessness in the former Soviet Union is addressed at both a national and regional level.(38) In addition, UNHCR continues to provide protection and assistance to many groups of stateless refugees, and to help the many individual asylum seekers who are without a nationality or whose citizenship is disputed.

Looking to the future, UNHCR and its partners might be expected to play a more active and assertive role in a number of different areas, such as:

- encouraging governments to sign and respect the existing international conventions on statelessness;

- promoting the establishment of new international and regional agreements on the elimination of statelessness and the protection of stateless people;

- providing advice, training and technical assistance to governments, especially those of newly-formed states and those confronted for the first time with nationality problems;

- mediating between governments which have become involved in nationality disputes, and assisting groups of stateless people to find a solution to their plight;

- intervening with governments which are responsible for creating situations of statelessness or violating the rights of stateless people;

- bringing public attention to the problems of stateless people and acting as their advocates on the international stage; and,

- reaffirming the principle of state responsibility in relation to citizenship rights, and encouraging other elements of the international community to ensure that this principle is respected.

One of the most important tasks to be undertaken by UNHCR and its partners is to collect and analyze information relating to the numbers of stateless people around the world, their conditions of life and the problems which they most commonly encounter. For despite the steadily growing volume of literature on this subject, the real dimensions and human implications of the problem remain somewhat obscure.(39)

To give just one example of this difficulty, the US State Department, in its annual human rights survey, asserts that there are an estimated 85,000 stateless people in Sri Lanka. Known as 'estate Tamils', these are people of Indian origin who have not been able to establish their citizenship of either that country or their country of residence. In its annual protection report, however, UNHCR reports that only two cases of statelessness are known to the agency in Sri Lanka! Evidently, the two organizations are using divergent definitions of statelessness or have access to very different sources of information on the situation in that country.

Neither UNHCR nor the US Committee for Refugees (USCR) - the most authoritative sources of statistics on refugee-related issues - have been able to gather comprehensive data on the subject of stateless people, a situation which has arisen for a combination of different reasons: the ambiguities surrounding the very concept of 'stateless person'; the general reluctance of governments to collect or disseminate information on the matter; the limited operational involvement of UNHCR and other agencies with stateless populations; and the hitherto low priority accorded to this issue by the international community.

Those statistics which have been collected on the question of statelessness tend to be presented in different ways. In its year-end figures for 1995, for example, UNHCR lists 'stateless refugees' as a separate category, but includes 'stateless non-refugees' in a broader group of beneficiaries described as 'other people of concern to the organization'. In its *World Refugee Survey*, the USCR includes stateless people in its category of people 'in refugee-like situations', without distinguishing them from others in this group. Moreover, the USCR makes no attempt to present data on those stateless people who are not in refugee-like situations - the most elusive group of all.

The Inter-Governmental Consultations on Asylum, Refugee and Migration Policies has recently expressed its intention to investigate this issue and to undertake a survey of contemporary statelessness. UNHCR was also requested by its governing body, the Executive Committee, to report on the magnitude of statelessness at its October 1997 meeting. Responding to this request, the organization's statistical unit has added a section on statelessness to the questionnaire which is sent out every year to offices in the field. At the same time, UNHCR is cooperating with a number of non-governmental partners to build up a profile of statelessness in Central and Eastern Europe.

Hopefully, these exercises will provide the international community with a more accurate and detailed picture of statelessness in the years to come. Even so, given the practical and political constraints involved, it seems highly unlikely that the statistics on stateless people will ever compare with those which are available for more readily identifiable and quantifiable groups such as refugees, returnees and asylum seekers.

Citizenship and international security

The study of statelessness has historically been dominated by legal experts, with the result that much of the existing literature on the subject is somewhat technical and apolitical in nature. Responding to this situation, one commentator has suggested that the legal problems associated with nationality are in some senses "fairly artificial," and could be resolved without difficulty if states were prepared to cooperate with each other and to pursue more liberal citizenship policies. (40)

UNHCR's expert on nationality issues makes a somewhat similar point. In practice, she argues, it is not usually very hard to identify the state or states with which an individual has the closest link. "The difficulty," she asserts, "lies in the legislation, administrative practices and political decisions which fail to recognize basic principles pertaining to the right to a nationality." (41)

The unwillingness of governments to assume their proper responsibility in relation to the question of citizenship has some important implications for both human security and the security of states. Statelessness is a threat to peace and security because it is a manifestation of intolerance and prejudice, especially when it occurs as a result of mass denaturalization and with the intention of forcing people to abandon their homes. Citizenship, on the other hand, and the ability of people to realize the rights associated with nationality, provide an indispensable element of stability to life, whether at the personal, societal or international levels.

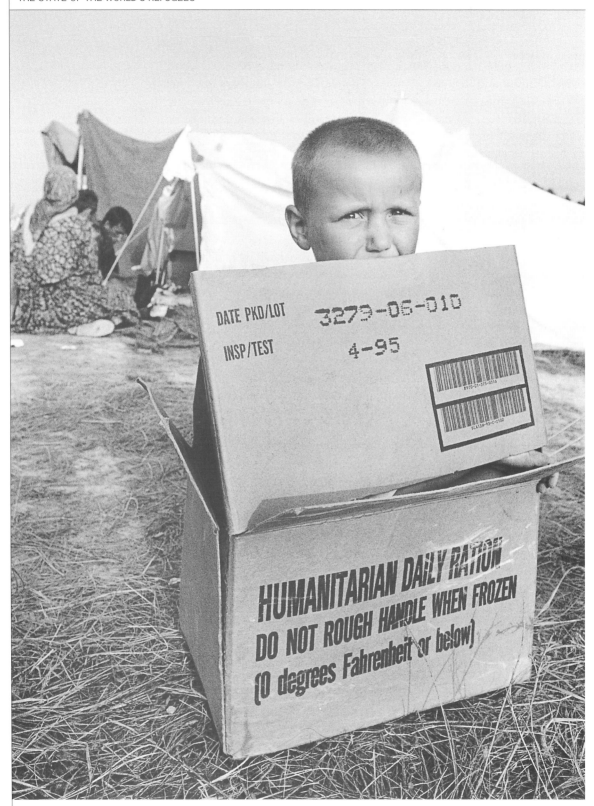

Tuzla airport, Bosnia and Herzegovina   © *C.Jungeblodt/Signum*

Conclusion **An agenda
for action**

As indicated in the introduction to this book, the past decade has witnessed a number of positive developments in international affairs: the democratization of many authoritarian states; the reduction of the global nuclear weapons arsenal; the resolution of several longstanding civil wars, and an improvement in the standard of living in many developing countries, to give just a few examples.

Some positive achievements have also been recorded with regard to the state of the world's refugees. During the past few years, millions of displaced people have been able to go back to their homes and to resume a more peaceful and productive life. Many states have continued to offer refuge to large numbers of people who have been obliged to flee their own country. And despite the widespread assumption that the world is suffering from 'compassion fatigue', there is actually considerable evidence to the contrary. In the words of the President of the International Committee of the Red Cross (ICRC), "never before in the history of mankind has there been such an outpouring of compassion to victims who are often far away, who are not members of our family or nation, but who nevertheless arouse a sometimes astonishing degree of solidarity because they are seen as belonging to the wider human family."(1)

It would be intellectually dishonest and morally irresponsible, however, to deny that the contemporary world is also characterized by some deeply disturbing trends. Indeed, the principal reason why there has been such an "outpouring of compassion to victims" in recent years is precisely because such large numbers of people have been victimized, whether by civil war, communal conflict or political persecution.

Looking to the future

What developments can be expected in the coming years with regard to the issues of human security, forced displacement and humanitarian action? While predicting the future is always a hazardous occupation, a number of tentative forecasts can be made with regard to these issues.

First, as indicated in the opening chapter of this book, while some analysts have suggested that the period of post-cold war turbulence could now be drawing to a close, this sanguine outlook is contradicted by the number of states around the world which are politically, socially and economically fragile, which are prone to internal armed conflict and which may well in future years be unable or unwilling to protect their citizens. The fragmentation of such states seems likely to be hastened by the ideologies of ethno-nationalism and communal separatism, which have proved in recent years to be such an effective means of political mobilization and manipulation.

In the attempt to bolster their own position and to intimidate their opponents, governments, rebel groups and warlords in weak states will resort to the tactics of terror: arbitrary arrests, disappearances and non-judicial executions, as well as the brutalization and exploitation of civilian populations. Following the pattern already set over the past decade, these abuses seem likely to generate a complex pattern of forced population displacements, including mass expulsions, compulsory relocations, refugee and asylum flows, as well as different varieties of ethnic and communal cleansing.

The decline of asylum

Second, it can be predicted with some degree of certainty that states will prove increasingly reluctant to open their borders to refugees and to provide them with effective protection. While some welcome exceptions to this rule can be anticipated, particularly in situations where the host society has ethnic, cultural or political affinities with the refugee population, the exclusionary attitude of states is now firmly established in both richer and poorer regions of the world.

Rather than offering refugees a place of safety for as long as they need or want it, states seem likely to introduce further restrictions on admission to their territory and to press for the early (and in some cases premature) return of refugees to their homeland. As a result of these trends, the number of internally displaced people around the world, and the ratio of internally displaced people to refugees, may well continue to increase.

The new caution

Third, unless they have strategic interests to protect (as they did in the Persian Gulf in 1991) the world's more powerful states will prove resistant to the notion of intervening in situations of internal conflict and displacement (as they have been in Rwanda and Zaire since 1994). Such caution was clearly in evidence in May 1997, when the UN Security Council held an unprecedented debate on the provision of humanitarian assistance to refugees and victims of war. At that meeting, a number of relief organizations called on states to provide military protection for humanitarian operations in high-risk situations, and to take the necessary action to separate civilian beneficiaries from armed combatants. "Humanitarian organizations should not be left alone to solve refugee situations that are clearly politicized or militarized," the UNHCR representative explained.(2)

The permanent members of the Security Council did not respond very positively to such suggestions. In the diplomatic language of an official UN press release, "speakers expressed concern over the difficulty of providing international military support for humanitarian assistance operations." In the more direct words of one news agency report, "key UN Security Council states gave a cool reception to calls for military protection... Permanent members and key donor states stressed that the issues were complex and needed to be considered in a realistic manner."

Three or four years ago, when the world's most affluent states began to express a new degree of caution in relation to the notion of 'humanitarian intervention', there was a widespread hope that regional organizations might assume a growing responsibility in the maintenance of peace and security and protection of humanitarian assistance. Such hopes do not seem likely to be realized in the immediate future, as many regional organizations lack the capacity to intervene decisively or effectively in situations of armed conflict. Doubts have also been raised about the wisdom of this approach, as regional organizations are sometimes dominated by states which have a direct interest in armed conflicts taking place in nearby countries.(3) Their involvement may therefore add to the instability of the situation.

The low-risk option

Fourth, while the permanent members of the UN Security Council and other influential states might well prefer to avoid any risky foreign engagements, their ability to ignore armed conflicts and emergency situations in other parts of the world will continue to be constrained by a number of related factors: the influence of the mass media; the power of public opinion; the activities of domestic constituencies and advocacy groups; and their own value systems. As a number of analysts have reminded us, notions such as charity, solidarity and common humanity are deeply embedded in the culture of many societies, making it difficult for them to turn their backs on the suffering of others when they are in a position to help them.(4) And it is precisely those sentiments which the media and advocacy groups are most assiduous in exploiting. The important question, then, is not only whether states will respond to situations of acute human suffering beyond the borders of their own territory, but how they will respond.

To extrapolate again from recent trends, it seems highly likely that in the absence of a willingness to intervene by other means, the world's more powerful states will continue to give pride of place to humanitarian assistance. Indeed, the arguments in favour of such an approach must appear overwhelming to many governments. Such assistance is financially and politically a relatively low-risk option. It satisfies the demands of the media and public opinion. It provides donor governments with some favourable publicity. And it can be used as a means of fending off demands for more decisive forms of political and military action. As a senior UNHCR official commented during the war in former Yugoslavia, "every time the question of settling the conflict came up, the donors responded by saying that they were going to give more money to the humanitarian effort."(5)

Humanitarianism discredited?

Fifth, if humanitarian assistance continues to be used as a substitute for other forms of action, then there is a serious risk that it will become increasingly discredited. Indeed, there is already considerable evidence to suggest that this process has already started.

In the early 1990s, particularly after the international response to the refugee crisis in northern Iraq, humanitarian action tended to be regarded in heroic terms - as an integral part of a new world order in which the needs of persecuted and threatened populations would take precedence over the dictates of state sovereignty. Perhaps a little carried away by these developments, aid and relief organizations themselves played a significant part in promoting the notion that humanitarian action could play a decisive role in national and international affairs.

By the middle of the 1990s, a new degree of scepticism was creeping into the analysis provided by many academics and practitioners. Drawing mainly on evidence from countries such as Bosnia, Liberia and Sierra Leone, a growing number of commentators now pointed to the 'unintended' and 'negative' consequences of humanitarian action. One expert, for example, concluded that "many international aid efforts are actually contributing to and reinforcing tensions and conflict. This occurs inadvertently and unintentionally... It represents no failure of goodwill, but rather a set of conditions and choices which interact to produce negative impacts."(6)

Most recently, influenced primarily by the violence in eastern Zaire, commentators have started to depict the impact of humanitarian action in even more negative terms, going so far as to suggest that it creates as many (if not more) problems than it solves. "Large numbers of refugees," wrote one journalist in July 1997, "menaced by starvation and disease, make for pathos and dramatic press that attracts aid dollars from international humanitarian organizations and foreign governments. The aid that flows to the camps where the refugees are gathered can be skimmed by militants based in the camps, as well as local businesspeople and military officials of the host government. The packed camps, protected by international sympathy and international law, provide excellent cover for guerrillas and serve as bases from which they can launch attacks."(7) While the article in question is a somewhat tendentious one, both empirically and analytically, its publication in the influential journal *Foreign Affairs* provides an indication of the kind of critique which is now reaching the public domain.

Charity and solidarity

Sixth, as well as becoming discredited, there is also a risk that humanitarianism will become increasingly fragmented in the coming years. Not surprisingly, perhaps, given the unprecedented operational challenges and ethical dilemmas which they face, humanitarian organizations are reaching quite different conclusions about their proper role and responsibilities.

According to one school of thought, the only legitimate function of humanitarian action is that of meeting urgent human needs, wherever they exist and on the basis of consent. In the words of the ICRC President, "humanitarian action deals only with the symptoms of crisis, not the crisis itself or its causes. It seeks only to relieve the victims of suffering, not to punish their tormentors. It is essentially an act of charity, which is not necessarily a guarantee of justice."(8)

UNHCR, which has a clear mandate to seek solutions to refugee problems as well as providing protection to uprooted populations, provides a second and more expansive interpretation of humanitarian action. In addition to relieving human suffering, the agency has suggested, "the presence and activities of humanitarian organizations can help to stabilize fragile situations and buy time and space for negotiations." "Far from being solely a question of international charity," the High Commissioner observes, "humanitarian action can support peace and reconciliation."(9)

A third school of thought is to be found amongst those agencies and analysts who would replace the whole notion of charity with the principle of solidarity. According to this view, the humanitarian imperative is to be on the side of victimized populations. And to be on the side of the victimized means more than providing assistance in a neutral and impartial manner. In the words of the advocacy organization African Rights, "some people may be fed or treated - an outcome not to be despised. But this is at the cost of addressing more fundamental political and human rights concerns." "The possibility of undertaking relief work on the basis of solidarity with victims should be considered," African Rights concludes. "Relief programmes would become explicitly political, on the side of the poor and vulnerable."(10)

Such contrasting philosophies should not be overplayed. They are by no means a new phenomenon, and they have rarely prevented different humanitarian organizations from working alongside each other in the operational arena. Even so, in a period when the efficacy of humanitarian action is being called into question, and at a time when there is growing competition amongst the agencies concerned, there is an evident risk that these differences will sharpen and will be exploited by states.

There is perhaps an even greater risk of division between operational humanitarian organizations and human rights advocacy agencies. While the ultimate goal of such agencies - the protection of human life, liberty and dignity - may well be the same, a clear distinction has emerged in their approach to this objective. As suggested in Chapter Two, UNHCR has tended to argue that it cannot simply withdraw from operations where it is assisting large numbers of needy people, even if the basic principles of refugee protection cannot be guaranteed. Human rights agencies such as Amnesty International and Human Rights Watch, however, have argued that such a position makes UNHCR an effective accomplice to the violation of its own mandate and the principles of international refugee law. Recent exchanges on this issue suggest that it may be difficult to reconcile these two perspectives. (11)

Beyond humanitarianism?

The predictions presented in the preceding sections paint a rather bleak vision of the future. If those forecasts hold true, more people around the world will be forced to abandon their homes but fewer will be able to find a safe refuge. The world's most powerful states will generally be reluctant to address the problem of internal conflict and state collapse. Public confidence in the efficacy of humanitarian action may wane, and humanitarian organizations could find themselves in growing disagreement about their objectives and operational principles.

To accept this scenario as a *fait accompli* would constitute the worst possible kind of defeatism. For the cost of doing nothing is too high. Armed conflicts, complex emergencies and forced population displacements are not only ethically unacceptable, but also represent an astonishing wastage of the world's human, social and physical resources. (12)

The cost of doing nothing is also too high in political terms. As events in the Great Lakes region of Africa have demonstrated so vividly, forced population displacements are not only a result of political instability, but can also create and perpetuate it. In the words of the UN High Commissioner for Refugees, "the challenge of the 21st century will be to ensure the security of people. Unless people feel secure in their own homes, the security of states will continue to be threatened." (13)

Prevention: a political and economic agenda

The preceding chapters of this book have set out a wide-ranging agenda for humanitarian action, the primary purpose of which is to safeguard the security of those people who have already been uprooted or threatened with displacement: refugees, returnees, internally displaced and war-affected populations, asylum seekers and stateless people. If it were to be effectively implemented, that agenda for action would provide these groups of people with a much better level of protection than they currently experience and enable them to live a more dignified life. But to what extent can humanitarian action also avert those situations of violence and armed conflict which oblige people to abandon their homes?

It would be misleading to answer that question in a wholly negative manner. Recent experience in regions such as the Balkans, Central America and Central Asia, for example, suggests that by establishing a presence in volatile situations, humanitarian organizations can in some instances moderate the behaviour of the parties to a conflict. By means of educational and information programmes, those agencies may also be able to foster a degree of tolerance and understanding in divided communities.

Humanitarian organizations have an essential role to play in alerting the international community to human rights violations. And in situations where wars have come to an end and displaced populations have gone back to their homes, such organizations can play a valuable role in the peacebuilding process, thereby averting a recurrence of armed conflict. But one should not pretend that such initiatives, however extensive in nature and however effectively implemented, can prevent the kind of violence which has been witnessed in countries such as Bosnia, Liberia, Rwanda or Somalia. As the High Commissioner for Refugees has acknowledged, "the prevention of the causes which force people to flee is a massive undertaking, going far beyond the capacity of UNHCR."(14)

The issue of conflict prevention has spawned a massive literature in recent years, and it is not the purpose of this conclusion to add substantially to that genre.(15) The following sections draw upon some of the most recent thinking on this question, identifying five of the most important issues which must be addressed by states, other political actors and the UN system as a whole if the objective of averting armed conflict and forced displacement is to be achieved.

1. Eliminating poverty

It is no coincidence that forced population displacements occur most frequently in societies where a large proportion of the population is suffering from absolute poverty or where the standard of living has suddenly declined. There are, of course, some lower income countries which have been able to maintain democratic systems of government, to uphold high human rights standards and to remain free of communal violence. But they are sadly few and far between. When large sections of a population are economically marginalized, when they develop expectations that can rarely be realized by legitimate means, and when they are obliged to compete against each other for a limited and in some cases dwindling pool of resources, violence in one form or another is a predictable outcome.

The elimination of poverty, and the sustainable economic growth which is required for that objective to be achieved, is also a far more effective (if less dramatic) means of safeguarding people's security than the provision of humanitarian assistance. Indeed, the 'silent emergencies' which are taking place in many societies around the world claim far more lives than those which are lost in civil wars or communal conflicts. As the late UNICEF Director James Grant pointed out, the international community took decisive action once it was known that half a million young Somali children had died in 1992 as a result of the war in that country. But the massive relief operation established in Somalia did nothing to save the lives of 13 million children in other states who died as a result of poverty in the same 12-month period.

While the elimination of poverty may appear to be a naive and unattainable goal, many leading experts in this field believe that such pessimism is not justified. "Eradicating absolute poverty in the first decades of the 21st century is feasible, affordable and a moral imperative," states the 1997 *Human Development Report*. While the strategy for poverty reduction will obviously vary from one country and region to another, the report suggests that there are six global priorities for action:

- empowering poor people and communities, so that they can participate in decisions that affect their lives, build upon their own strengths and gain access to assets that make them less vulnerable;

- achieving gender equality by ending discrimination against girls, ensuring that females have access to land, credit and job opportunities, and by taking action to end violence against women;

- promoting forms of economic growth which are 'pro-poor', particularly by means of policies which restore full employment, raise agricultural productivity, reduce inequalities and provide education and health for all;

- managing the process of globalization more carefully and with more concern for equity, so as to reduce the widening gap between 'winner' and 'loser' societies;

- ensuring the establishment of strong and legitimate states, which advance the interests of the poor, which foster the peaceful expression of people's demands, and which assume effective responsibility for the welfare of their citizens; and,

- providing special international support to the world's poorest countries, by means of debt relief, improvements to the quantity and quality of aid, and the opening of global markets for agricultural exports.

Implementing this ambitious agenda for poverty reduction and eradication will not be easy. But the costs of accelerated action must be measured against the costs of delay and inaction: continued economic stagnation and environmental degradation; further social conflict and political instability; and renewed instances of forced population displacement. As the *Human Development Report* concludes "no longer inevitable, poverty should be relegated to history - along with slavery, colonialism and nuclear warfare."(16)

2. Investing in peacebuilding

While equitable economic growth and sustainable human development are required in all of the world's poorer societies, special efforts are required to consolidate peace and bring political stability to countries which are emerging from periods of armed conflict. Without such action, there will always be a risk of a return to war.

As suggested in Chapter Four, peacebuilding requires a sustained commitment. From the experience gained in countries such as Bosnia, Cambodia, El Salvador, Mozambique, Namibia and Nicaragua, it has become clear that it is simply not enough for the international community to broker a peace settlement, to demobilize the combatants, to supervise an election and then to leave a war-torn country to its own devices.

Such an approach may produce a temporary suspension of the conflict, and may satisfy those members of the international community who believe in 'quick fix' solutions. But it will do little to address the injustices and inequities which have prompted the parties to take up arms in the first place. As the UN Research Institute for Social Development has pointed out, if that objective is to be even partially achieved, then a more comprehensive approach to the peacebuilding process will be required, combining long-term and coordinated efforts in the humanitarian, developmental, political and judicial domains.(17)

Of course, such efforts will require substantial resources and may appear to be unaffordable to donor states which are working within tight budgetary constraints. It is therefore essential that those countries recognize that they have a very direct and tangible interest in the stabilization of societies which have been ravaged by armed conflict.

First, if such societies erupt into violence again and if they are unable to meet their most basic material needs, then they can be expected to generate substantial numbers of refugees, migrants and asylum seekers, some of whom will inevitably make their way to richer and more stable parts of the world. If the industrialized states have a real desire to curtail such population movements, they should do so by making it possible for people to live securely in their own country, rather than by erecting physical and administrative obstacles to their movement.

Second, the investments made by the more powerful states into the future of those which are weaker has to be set against the costs which they will occur if war breaks out again. Imagine, for example, the billions of dollars which have been spent in emergency assistance, refugee relief and peacekeeping activities because of the conflicts in countries such as Angola, Cambodia, El Salvador and Mozambique. If the peacebuilding process in such states breaks down, donor governments will again be expected to foot the bill for any emergencies which occur.

Third, and perhaps most persuasively, states can serve their own economic interests by investing in peacebuilding processes. After the second world war, for example, the US government made enormous efforts to support the reconstruction of Western Europe, most notably by means of the Marshall Plan. And as one analyst has commented, by bringing political stability to the region and by providing an expanding market for American goods, the greatest beneficiary of the Marshall Plan was the United States itself.(18) A similar logic could and should be applied to other parts of the world. It is in the interests of all states to ensure that societies which have been scarred by war are able to develop thriving economies and to establish legitimate state structures.

3. Curtailing the arms trade

As the genocide in Rwanda demonstrated, you do not need sophisticated weapons to murder huge numbers of people. Even so, there is an emerging consensus that the high levels of social and political violence witnessed in many societies is sustained and reinforced (if not actually provoked) by the ease with which armaments can be procured.

It is sometimes suggested that the kind of weapons used in most contemporary conflicts are so easy to manufacture and distribute that any attempt to control them would be doomed to failure. While there is a degree of truth to this argument, it can also very easily become an excuse for doing nothing. And something can be done. First, the permanent members of the UN Security Council, four of whom account for no less than 86 per cent of all arms sales to developing countries, could set a much better example. As other states have demonstrated, it is perfectly possible to have a thriving economy without a large-scale armaments industry. Indeed, the enormous amount of resources devoted to the development of new weapons would give much better returns if they were invested in peaceful forms of scientific and technological research.

Second, while a great deal of effort has been made in recent years to disarm and demobilize the parties to conflicts once the fighting has come to a formal end, very little has been done to reduce the number of weapons in circulation in countries which are still at war or which are at risk of being engulfed by conflict. At the domestic level, efforts have been made by some of the industrialized states to establish amnesties for firearms and knives and other weapons, with the owners receiving a cash payment for any weapons they relinquish. It should not be beyond the international community's imagination to devise and finance schemes of this nature for societies in other parts of the world.

Third, progressive efforts must be made to outlaw the most destructive instruments of war and to curb the introduction of new weapons technology. While such objectives may appear idealistic, and while they certainly will not be achieved overnight, there is no excuse for not trying. A large number of states have already accepted the international ban on chemical weapons. The campaign against anti-personnel land-mines, initially led by the ICRC, is rapidly gaining support from politicians and the public. Wider restrictions on the manufacture, sale and use of deadly weapons must be a long-term goal.

4. Promoting democracy and human rights

The issues of democracy, human rights, armed conflict and forced displacement are inextricably linked. As the Carnegie Commission on Preventing Deadly Conflict has observed, "countries that govern themselves in a truly democratic fashion do not go to war with each other. Democratic governments do not ethnically cleanse their own populations, and they are much less likely to face ethnic insurgency... Precisely because, within their own borders, they respect competition, civil liberties, property rights and the rule of law, democracies are the only reliable foundation on which a new world order of international security and property can be built."(19)

This is not to propose that every political system should assume an identical form, nor to suggest that notions such as democracy and pluralism have an identical meaning in different cultural contexts. But it must not be forgotten that the most important international instrument regulating the relationship between citizens and states is explicitly referred to as the 'Universal' Declaration of Human Rights. One can therefore quite legitimately oblige all governments to respect its provisions, including, for example, the right to freedom of thought, opinion, expression, peaceful assembly and participation in genuinely free elections.

The question of how democracy and human rights might most effectively be promoted is, of course, a complex and sensitive issue, raising as it does the whole question of sovereignty and interference in the domestic affairs of states. In situations where countries are emerging from periods of authoritarian rule and wish to reform their own political and economic structures, external support and involvement may be welcomed. Many of the new (or restored) democracies in Africa, Latin America, Eastern and Central Europe, for example, have been eager to draw upon the experience of other states and the advice of international organizations such as the UN Centre for Human Rights. But there are other states - often those which are most affected by the problems of violence and forced displacement - which are less eager to seek such assistance.

The international response to such situations might assume a number of different forms. First, there is considerable scope for the use of positive incentives to encourage democratization and human rights observance. Diplomatic recognition, membership of international and regional organizations, and access to development assistance and trading agreements, for example, can all be made conditional upon the behaviour of states towards their citizens.(20)

Second, even in situations where states are resistant to change at the level of central government, there is often a great deal that can be done to introduce democratic principles and participatory practices at the local level. Humanitarian assistance operations, community development programmes and larger-scale aid projects should always be organized in a manner that promotes what the Global Governance Commission describes as 'neighbourhood values': liberty, justice, equity and mutual respect.(21)

Third, while recognizing that punitive measures may cause a backlash when they are applied to authoritarian states, the international community should not shy away from the use of diplomatic, economic and military sanctions in situations where governments are responsible for blatant violations of human and minority rights. As the Carnegie Commission on Preventing Deadly Conflict has pointed out, it is now possible to establish a very long list of countries where such pressures have induced governments to introduce democratic change. South Africa may be the best known example, but it is by no means a unique case.(22) At the same time, it is clear from the example of countries such as Burundi and Iraq that the imposition of sanctions can have a negative impact on the poorest and most vulnerable members of society, a consequence which must evidently be weighed in the balance when decisions are taken in this area.

5. Ensuring accountability

The notion of state responsibility has become a well established concept in the vocabulary of refugee organizations and analysts. A recent resolution adopted by UNHCR's Executive Committee, for example, "emphasizes the responsibility of states to ensure conditions which do not compel people to flee in fear..." "The essential condition for the prevention of refugee flows," it continues, "is sufficient political will by the states directly concerned to address the causes which are at the origin of refugee movements." (23)

Two comments are required in relation to such statements. First, it has become increasingly clear that the principle of responsibility must now be used in a more inclusive manner, applied not only to states but also to all of those other actors which play a significant part in national and international affairs: rebel groups, political leaders and parties, warlords and military factions, religious bodies and commercial enterprises, to give just a few examples. In the context of countries such as Afghanistan, Bosnia, Colombia or Liberia, it is simply not possible to understand - let alone avert or resolve - the problem of forced displacement without taking account of such actors and seeking to influence their behaviour.

Second, if the notion of corporate or collective responsibility is to have any real meaning, it must be underpinned by the principle of individual accountability. Refugee movements and other forms of forced displacement do not happen by chance. Nor are they the result of anonymous and abstract historical forces. They occur because certain individuals decide to violate the rights of others, to put the lives of those people at risk and to make it impossible for them to remain safely in their homes. Indeed, as previous chapters have pointed out, the displacement of civilians has in recent years become a direct objective of political and military decision-makers in certain parts of the globe.

As the world has begun to recognize following events in the Great Lakes region of Africa and former Yugoslavia, massacres and mass expulsions will continue to take place for as long as the perpetrators believe that they can escape from justice and punishment. The international war crimes tribunals established in relation to those situations have certainly experienced a range of problems, not least of which is their inability to try many of the most important suspects. But those difficulties should not be allowed to obstruct the establishment of a permanent international criminal court. As one author has written, "a culture which allows total impunity for the past is a culture which will not be able to prevent humanitarian disasters in the future." (24)

The continued relevance of asylum

The agenda for action presented above is an admittedly ambitious one. Even the most optimistic observer would acknowledge, for example, that abject poverty and the widening gap between rich and poor are unlikely to be eradicated in the foreseeable future. Billions of dollars have already been spent on peacekeeping and peace plan operations in countries where conflicts have diminished in scale or come to an effective end. But as the examples of Bosnia and Cambodia suggest, it is not easy to foster real democracy and high standards of governance in fragmented states and divided societies. And while human rights issues have certainly attracted growing international attention in recent years, progress in this area continues to be thwarted by many authoritarian governments, supported in too many instances by affluent states which are reluctant to sacrifice any lucrative trade and investment opportunities.

Given these constraints, as well as the unintended and negative consequences of humanitarian operations which are undertaken in zones of active conflict, there is an compelling need to restate the importance of asylum as a means of safeguarding human security.

There is now a disturbingly widespread assumption that refugee protection is a thing of the past, a phenomenon which has become irrelevant to states with the passing of the cold war. While there may be some truth in that assertion, it should not be forgotten that asylum continues to have a very direct relevance to people whose lives and liberty are at risk and who can only find any kind of security by seeking sanctuary in another country. As one refugee specialist has argued, "humanitarian assistance inside the country of origin is no guarantee of safety... As inconvenient as it may be, and as imperfect as conditions of asylum often were, we ought to return to the principles of refugee protection... Until permanent solutions can be found, keeping borders open to people in harm's way will save lives." (25)

Peace and tolerance

When it was written in 1945, the Preamble to the UN Charter enjoined states and citizens around the world "to practice tolerance and live together in peace with one another as good neighbours." The prevention of armed conflict, the maintenance of high human rights standards and the protection of refugees and other people who are at risk thus constitute the very purpose of the United Nations.

But what exactly is the United Nations? In recent years, there has been a tendency for both politicians and the public to associate the world body with the work of the Secretary-General and his staff, as well as specialized organizations such as UNHCR. But the United Nations is actually a far more inclusive entity, encompassing all of its member states and the billions of people who are citizens of those countries.

If the agenda for action presented in this book is to be effectively implemented, then greater effort and commitment will be required by all members of the international community, irrespective of their differing ideologies, cultural traditions and institutional mandates. Political leadership has a central role to play in this process. On too many occasions in the recent past, governments and other actors have interpreted the notion of 'national interest' in an unduly narrow and insular manner. As well as failing to acknowledge their broader responsibility to the protection of human welfare, they have also ignored the fact that their longer-term interests would actually be served by respecting and promoting the principles embodied in the UN Charter.

As the 21st century approaches, therefore, we must ensure that humanitarian organizations have the ability to respond quickly and effectively to complex emergencies and other situations in which people are forced to flee for their lives. But we must also recognize that such a capacity is of limited value unless it is accompanied by vigorous advocacy and longer-term action on behalf of victimized and dispossessed populations. In striving to develop and implement a humanitarian agenda, our ultimate goal must be to establish a world in which the current and coming generations of people can live together in peace, security and dignity.

Endnotes

Introduction
People in need of protection

1 This figure is highly speculative, given the absence of an agreed definition of 'forced displacement' and the difficulty of collecting accurate statistics on uprooted populations. The nominal figure of 50 million includes around 22 million people who are of direct concern to UNHCR, an additional 20 million internally displaced people for whom the organization has no responsibility, and around three million Palestinian refugees who are assisted by the United Nations Relief and Works Agency for Palestine Refugees in the Near East.

2 See, for example, Human Rights Watch, 'Uncertain refuge: international failures to protect refugees', report no. 9/1, New York, April 1997.

3 A. Roberts, *Humanitarian Action in War*, Adelphi Paper no. 305, International Institute for Strategic Studies, London, 1996, p. 79.

Chapter 1
Safeguarding human security

1 See, for example, Commission on Global Governance, *Our Global Neighbourhood*, Oxford University Press, Oxford, 1995; United Nations Development Programme, *Human Development Report 1994*, Oxford University Press, New York, 1994; and A. Roberts, *Humanitarian Action in War*, Adelphi Paper no. 305, International Institute for Strategic Studies, London, 1996.

2 Although this book employs the notion of 'international community' to denote the collective identity of states, the United Nations and other significant actors in international affairs, the severe limitations of this concept are acknowledged. The alternative proposed by some scholars - 'international society' - does not have a great deal of additional analytic value.

3 L. Rosenblatt, 'The challenges of humanitarian relief', *The Washington Times*, 30 December 1996. For an extended analysis of these issues and their interrelationship, see United Nations Research Institute for Social Development, *States of Disarray: The Social Effects of Globalization*, Geneva, 1995.

4 'Security Council Summit Meeting, New York, 31 January 1992', United Nations document, New York, 1992.

5 See, for example, K. Booth, 'Human wrongs and international relations', *International Affairs*, vol. 71, no. 1,

1995; and S. Hoffmann, 'The politics and ethics of military intervention', *Survival*, vol. 37, no. 4, 1995-96.

6 See 'The state in a changing world', World Bank website, <www-jazz.worldbank.org>.

7 G. Sorensen, 'Individual security and national security: the state remains the principal problem', *Security Dialogue*, vol. 27, no. 4, 1996.

8 *Human Development Report 1994*, *op cit*, p. 23.

9 The data in this section is drawn from *ibid*, and from the *1997 Report on the World Social Situation*, United Nations, New York, 1997.

10 *The Reality of Aid 1996: An Independent Review of International Aid*, Earthscan, London, 1996. See also 'Financial flows to developing countries in 1995; sharp decline in official aid; private flows rise', OECD press release, 11 June 1996.

11 For an attempt to provide a quantitative analysis of this issue see UNHCR, *The State of the World's Refugees: In Search of Solutions*, Oxford University Press, Oxford, 1995, pp. 147-152, and M. Weiner, 'Bad neighbors, bad neighborhoods: an inquiry into the causes of refugee flows', *International Security*, vol. 21, no. 1, 1996.

12 L. Diamond, *Promoting Democracy in the 1990s: Actors and Instruments, Issues and Instruments*, Carnegie Commission on Preventing Deadly Conflict, New York, 1995, p. 9.

13 V. Tishkov, *Ethnicity, Nationalism and Conflict in and after the Soviet Union: the Mind Aflame*, United Nations Research Institute for Social Development, International Peace Research Institute and Sage Publications, London, 1997, p. 274.

14 S. Ellis, 'Africa after the cold war: new patterns of government and politics', *Development and Change*, vol. 27, no. 1, 1996.

15 Human Rights Watch, *Playing the Communal Card: Communal Violence and Human Rights*, New York, 1995. See also Chapter Six of *States of Disarray, op cit*.

16 M. Kaldor, 'A cosmopolitan response to new wars', *Peace Review*, vol. 8, no. 4, 1996.

17 F. Jean and J-C. Rufin, *Economie des Guerres Civiles*, Editions Pluriel/Hachette, Paris, 1996.

18 The classic expression of this position is to be found in R. Kaplan, 'The coming anarchy', *The Atlantic Monthly*, February 1994.

19 C. Maynes, 'The new pessimism', *Foreign Policy*, no. 100, 1995.

20 'Human rights and massive exoduses: report of the Secretary-General', UN Commission on Human Rights,

document E/CN.4/1996/42, February 1996, on *Refworld* CD-Rom, UNHCR, Geneva, 1997.

21 F. Corley, 'Peoples on the move', *War Report*, no. 48, 1997, p. 22.

22 S. Ogata, 'Peace, security and humanitarian action', Alastair Buchan Memorial Lecture, International Institute for Strategic Studies, London, April 1997.

23 D. Rajasingham, 'The human rights dimension of population transfer in South Asia', UN expert seminar on the human rights dimensions of population transfer, Geneva, February 1997, UN document HR/SEM.1/PT/1997/WP3. See also *Regional Consultation on Refugee and Migratory Movements*, UNHCR, Colombo, 1995.

24 See M. Weiner, *op cit.*

25 'The lost boys of the Sudan', in UNICEF, *The State of the World's Children 1996*, Oxford University Press, Oxford, 1996.

26 M. Weiner, *The Global Migration Crisis: Challenge to States and to Human Rights*, Harper Collins, New York, 1995, p. 29.

27 S. Ogata, 'The United Nations at fifty: the humanitarian challenge', statement to the European Parliament, May 1995, on *Refworld* CD-Rom, *op cit.*

28 For a more detailed examination of this issue, see Chapter One of *The State of the World's Refugees: In Search of Solutions, op cit.*

29 J. Ayala Lasso, introductory statement at the UN Expert Seminar on the human rights dimensions of population transfer, Geneva, February 1997.

30 Quoted in E. Lederer, 'Report finds West less responsive to Third World crises', *The Washington Times*, 26 April 1997.

31 See E. Mortimer, 'Descent into chaos', *The Financial Times*, 9 April 1997; and 'The Albanian mess', *The Washington Post*, 21 May 1997.

32 Quoted in E. Penketh, 'Security Council cool to appeals for humanitarian enforcement', AFP despatch, 21 May 1997.

33 For a concise analysis of the issues raised by this trend, see A. Roberts, *op cit.*

34 The principal features of this paradigm are identified and examined in M. Duffield, 'Humanitarian intervention in Africa: adapting to separate development', *New Political Economy*, Summer 1997.

35 S. Ogata, 'Peace, security and humanitarian action', *op cit.*

36 A. Roberts, *op cit.* p. 9.

37 See, for example, B. Chimni, 'Solutions to the global refugee problem and the language of security: a disturbing trend', unpublished paper, 1997. For a case study which incorporates this critique, see M. Barutciski, 'The reinforcement of non-admission policies and the subversion of UNHCR: displacement and internal assistance in Bosnia-Herzegovina (1992-94)', *International Journal of Refugee Law*, vol. 8, no. 1/2, 1996.

Chapter 2
Defending refugee rights

1 Article I, 1951 UN Convention relating to the Status of Refugees, on *Refworld* CD-Rom, UNHCR, Geneva, 1997.

2 Article I, 1969 OAU Convention governing the specific aspects of refugee problems in Africa, *ibid.*

3 The 1951 Convention was essentially limited to refugees from Europe, whereas the 1967 Protocol extended the scope of the Convention to refugees from other parts of the world. In this chapter, references to the Convention should also be read as references to the Protocol.

4 Preamble, 1951 UN Refugee Convention, *op cit.*

5 Article II, 1969 OAU Refugee Convention, *op cit.*

6 Palestinians in the West Bank, Gaza, Jordan, Lebanon and Syria are normally assisted by the UN Relief and Works Agency for Palestine Refugees in the Near East, which was established prior to the creation of UNHCR. Palestinians outside of this area may come under the mandate of UNHCR.

7 For further details of these and other recent refugee movements, see US Committee for Refugees, *World Refugee Survey 1997*, Washington DC, 1997.

8 W. Van Damme, 'Do refugees belong in camps? Experiences from Goma and Guinea', *The Lancet*, 5 August 1995.

9 G. Kramer, 'Global refugee flow reported declining, along with prospects of safe haven', Reuters despatch, 19 May 1997.

10 S. Ogata, opening statement at the 47th session of the UNHCR Executive Committee, Geneva, October 1996, on *Refworld* CD-Rom, *op cit.*

11 S. Ogata, opening statement at the 46th session of the UNHCR Executive Committee, Geneva, October, 1995, on *Refworld* CD-Rom, *op cit.* .

12 Details of the incidents mentioned in this and the following paragraph - and UNHCR's reaction to them - are posted on the UNHCR Website, <http://www.unhcr.ch>.

13 See untitled UNHCR press release, 28 February 1997.

14 S. Vieira de Mello, 'The humanitarian situation in the Great Lakes region', statement to the Standing Committee of the UNHCR Executive Committee, Geneva, 30 January 1997; and 'Impact of military personnel and the militia presence in Rwandese refugee camps and settlements', paper submitted by the UN High Commissioner for Refugees to the Bujumbura Conference on Assistance to Refugees, Returnees and Displaced People in the Great Lakes Region, 15 - 17 February 1995.

15 Untitled UNHCR press statement, posted 21 December 1996 on ReliefWeb Website, <http://www.reliefweb.int/>.

16 S. Ogata, remarks at the UN Security Council, New York, 28 April 1997.

17 For examples of this phenomenon, see Human Rights Watch, 'Discussion paper: protection in the decade of voluntary repatriation', New York, September 1996.

18 UNHCR handbook, *Voluntary Repatriation: International Protection*, Geneva, 1996, p. 42.

19 'UNHCR protests forcible return of Rwandese refugees', UNHCR press release, 23 July 1996.

20 *World Refugee Survey 1997, op cit*, p. 13.

21 See Chapter Six for additional details.

22 Internal UNHCR memorandum, 17 October 1996.

23 P. Oakley, statement of the US representative to the 47th Session of the UNHCR Executive Committee, Geneva, 7 October 1996, posted on US State Department Website, <http://www.state.g.al/prm/961007.html>.

24 See UNHCR, *The State of the World's Refugees: In Search of Solutions*, Oxford University Press, Oxford, 1995 pp. 143-170, *passim*.

25 G. Kibreab, 'Environmental causes and impact of refugee movements: a critique of the current debate', *Disasters*, vol. 21, no. 1, 1997.

26 K. Jacobsen, *The Impact of Refugees on the Environment: A Review of the Evidence*, Refugee Policy Group, Washington DC, 1994.

27 H. Ketel, 'Tanzania: environmental assessment report of the Rwandese refugee camps and the affected local communities in Kagera region', UNHCR, Dar es Salaam, July 1994.

28 Médecins sans Frontières, 'Ethnic cleansing rears its head in Zaire', November 1996.

29 See, for example, UNHCR, 'Report of the advisory group on refugee policies in the African region', Geneva, May 1996.

30 'UNHCR concerned about restricted access to asylum in Europe', UNHCR press release, 20 June 1997.

31 Human Rights Watch, 'Uncertain refuge: international failures to protect refugees', Report no. 9/1(G), New York, April 1997, p. 20.

32 T. Weiss and A. Pasic, 'Reinventing UNHCR: enterprising humanitarians in the former Yugoslavia, 1991-1995, *Global Governance*, vol. 3, no. 1, pp. 50-51.

33 See N. Morris, 'Protection dilemmas and UNHCR's response: a personal view from within UNHCR', forthcoming, *International Journal of Refugee Law*.

34 S. Ogata, remarks at the UN Security Council, *op cit*.

35 See, for example, Human Rights Watch, *op cit*; Amnesty International, 'Rwanda: human rights overlooked in mass repatriation', report no. AFR47/02/97, January 1997, and 'Great Lakes region: still in need of protection: repatriation, refoulement and the safety of refugees and the internally displaced', report no. AFR02/07/97, January 1997; K. Lambrecht, *The Return of the Rohingya Refugees to Burma: Voluntary Repatriation or Refoulement?*, US Committee for Refugees, Washington DC, 1995.

36 UNHCR, 'Review of UNHCR's women victims of violence project in Kenya', Geneva, March 1996. See also Human Rights Watch, *op cit*, pp. 15-19.

37 UNHCR, 'Note on International Protection', UNHCR document no. EC/47/SC/CRP.26, Geneva, May 1997, p. 9.

38 'Refugee official calls for lifeline', *International Herald Tribune*, 5 November 1996.

39 This position is suggested in G. Goodwin-Gill, 'United Nations reform and the future of refugee protection', unpublished e-mail, 4 June 1997.

40 UNHCR. 'Note on the exclusion clauses', UNHCR document no. EC/47/SC/CRP.29, Geneva, May 1997, p. 6.

41 UNHCR handbook, *Voluntary Repatriation: International Protection*, Geneva, 1996, pp. 10-11.

42 UNHCR, 'Note on the cessation clauses', UNHCR document no. EC/47/SC/CRP.30, Geneva, May 1997.

43 S. Ogata, statement to the InterAction annual forum, Alexandria, Virginia, 5 May 1997.

44 See above, notes 17 and 35, for references to these situations. The Iraqi case differs from the others somewhat in the sense that most of the fleeing population did not cross the border into Turkey, and so were technically internally displaced people. See G. Rudd, 'Operation Provide Comfort: humanitarian intervention to save the Kurds in northern Iraq, 1991', US Army Center of Military History, Washington DC, 1992.

45 UNHCR Division of International Protection, 'Imposed return', Geneva, 1996, p. 4.

46 Refugee Policy Group, *Older Refugee Settlements in Africa: Final Report*, Washington DC, November 1985.

47 G. Kibreab, *State of the Art Review of Refugee Studies in Africa*, Uppsala Papers in Economic History, Uppsala University, 1991, p. 55.

48 Quoted in E. Ferris, 'Refugees: new approaches to traditional solutions', paper presented to the UNHCR conference 'People of Concern', Geneva, November 1996, p. 12.

49 S. Ogata, 'Managing and solving forced displacement: issues and dilemmas', remarks at the Carnegie Council on Ethics and International Affairs, New York, November 1996.

50 Article 35, 1951 UN Refugee Convention, *op cit*.

Chapter 3
Internal conflict and displacement

1 S. Ogata, 'Statement at a roundtable discussion on United Nations human rights protection of internally displaced persons', Nyon, February 1993, on *Refworld* CD-Rom, UNHCR, Geneva, 1997.

2 For a discussion of the definitional issue, see 'Analytical report of the Secretary-General on internally displaced persons', 1992, UN document E/CN.4/1992/23, p. 5; and E. Ressler, 'Reflections on the topic of internal displacement', unpublished paper, 1994.

3 R. Carver, 'Kenya: aftermath of the elections', *Refugee Survey Quarterly*, vol. 13, no. 1, 1994. See also Human Rights Watch, *Failing the Internally Displaced: the UNDP Displaced Persons Program in Kenya*, New York, 1997.

4 T. Weiss and A. Pasic, 'Reinventing UNHCR: enterprising humanitarians in the former Yugoslavia, 1991-1995', *Global Governance*, no. 3, 1997.

5 See, for example, US Committee for Refugees, *World Refugee Survey 1992*, Washington DC, 1995, p. 44.

6 F. Deng, 'Internally displaced persons: report of the Representative of the Secretary-General', 1995, UN document UN/E/CN.4/1995/50, para. 11, on *Refworld* CD-Rom, *op cit.*

7 V. Tishkov, 'Internal displacement: post-Soviet challenges', unpublished note, April 1997.

8 Ethnic cleansing rears its head in Zaire', Médecins Sans Frontières, November 1996.

9 B. Boutros-Ghali, UN Press Release SG/SM/5866, January 1996.

10 F. Deng, *op cit*, para. 14.

11 For a full analysis of the Kibeho incident see Joint Evaluation of Emergency Assistance to Rwanda, *The International Response to Conflict and Genocide. Study 2: Early Warning and Conflict Management*, 1996; and S. Kleine-Ahlbrandt, *The Protection Gap: The International Protection of Internally Displaced People: The Case of Rwanda*, Institut Universitaire de Hautes Etudes Internationales, Geneva, 1996.

12 'Un demi-million de deplacés au Burundi: deportation ou mesures de protection?', *Journal de Genève*, 7 March 1997. See also C. McGreal, 'Prisoners in their own tortured land', *The Guardian*, 14 July 1997.

13 Independent Commission on International Humanitarian Issues, *Refugees: The Dynamics of Displacement*, Zed Books, London, 1986, p. 127.

14 For a bibliography of recent literature on internally displaced people, see *Refugee Survey Quarterly*, vol. 14, no. 1-2, 1995.

15 For details of Dr Deng's activities and findings see F. Deng, *op cit*.

16 See, for example, R. Cohen, 'Protecting the internally displaced', *World Refugee Survey 1996*, US Committee for Refugees, Washington DC, 1996.

17 Statement by the ICRC representative at the Commission on Human Rights, Geneva, February 1993.

18 S. Ogata, 'Statement at a roundtable discussion on United Nations human rights protection of internally displaced persons', *op cit*.

19 UNHCR, *UNHCR's Operational Experience with Internally Displaced Persons*, Geneva, 1994.

20 E. Ressler, *op cit*.

21 Accord Conciliation Resources, *The Liberian Peace Process, 1990-1996*, London, 1996, p. 25.

22 F. Deng, 'Internally displaced persons: report of the Representative of the Secretary-General. Profiles in displacement: Peru', 1996, UN document E/CN.4/1996/52/Add.1, on *Refworld* CD-Rom, *op cit*.

23 F. Deng, 'Internally displaced persons: report of the Representative of the Secretary-General', 1995, UN document UN/E/CN.4/1995/50, para. 26, on *Refworld* CD-Rom, *op cit*.

24 *ibid*.

25 F. Deng, statement to the UN Commission on Human Rights, March 1997.

26 See, for example, R. Cohen, *op cit*.

27 'The ICRC and internally displaced persons', *International Review of the Red Cross*, no. 305, 1995, p. 185.

28 P. Lavoyer, 'Refugees and internally displaced persons: international humanitarian law and the role of the ICRC', *International Review of the Red Cross*, no. 305, 1995, p. 170.

29 *ibid*, p. 179.

30 F. Deng, 'Conclusions on the compilation and analysis of legal norms', 1996, UN Document E/CN.4/1996/52/Add.2, paras. 5-14, on *Refworld* CD-Rom, *op cit*.

31 See, for example, R. Cohen. *op cit*.

32 D. Petrasek, 'Internally displaced persons: the need for new standards', unpublished paper, UNHCR, Geneva, 1995.

33 See UNHCR, *The State of the World's Refugees: In Search of Solutions*, Oxford University Press, Oxford, 1995.

34 A. Roberts, *Humanitarian Action in War*, Adelphi Paper no. 305, International Institute of Strategic Studies, London, 1996.

35 S. Ogata, 'Humanitarianism in the midst of armed conflict', statement at the Brookings Institution, Washington DC, May 1994, on *Refworld* CD-Rom, *op cit*.

36 Statement by the ICRC representative at the Sub-Committee on International Protection, UNHCR Executive Committee, Geneva, May 1994.

37 S. Baranyi, 'The challenge in Guatemala: verifying human rights, strengthening national institutions and enhancing an integrated UN approach to peace', *Journal of Humanitarian Assistance*, website <www-jha.sps.cam.ac.uk>, posted January 1996.

38 S. Ogata, statement to a conference on humanitarian response and the prevention of deadly conflict, convened by the Carnegie Commission on the Prevention of Deadly Conflict and UNHCR, Geneva, February 1997.

39 The humanitarian issues associated with this strategy are discussed in detail in Chapter Four of *The State of the World's Refugees: In Search of Solutions, op cit*.

40 Several reviews of the safe area concept have been published. See, for example, L. Franco, 'An examination of safety zones for internally displaced persons as a contribution toward prevention and solution of refugee problems', in N. Al-Naumi and R. Meese (eds), *International Legal Issues Arising under the United Nations Decade of International* Law, Martinus Nijhoff, The Hague, 1995; K. Landgren, 'Safety zones and international protection: a dark grey area', *International Journal of Refugee Law*, vol. 7, no. 3, 1995; and B. Y. Sandoz, 'The establishment of safety zones for persons displaced within their country of origin', International Committee of the Red Cross, Geneva, 1994.

41 UN Security Council Resolution 929, 1994.

42 'Report of the Secretary-General on the implementation of the mandate of UNPROFOR', New York, May 1995, para. 16.

43 J. Mendiluce, 'War and disaster in the former Yugoslavia: the limits of humanitarian action', *World Refugee Survey 1994*, US Committee for Refugees, Washington DC, 1994, p. 14.

44 'Report of the Secretary-General on the implementation of the mandate of UNPROFOR', *op cit*, para. 23.

45 K. Landgren, *op cit*.

46 F. Jean, *Populations in Danger 1995*, Médecins sans Frontières, London, 1995, p. 41. For another critical account, see A. Destexhe, *Rwanda and Genocide in the Twentieth Century*, Pluto, London, 1995, pp. 51-55.

47 B. Boutros-Ghali, UN Press Briefing SG/SM/5633, May 1995.

48 W. Clarance, 'Open relief centres: a pragmatic approach to emergency relief and monitoring during conflict in a country of origin', *International Journal of Refugee Law*, vol. 3, no. 2, 1991.

49 See A. Roberts, *op cit*, pp. 19-31, and *The State of the World's Refugees: In Search of Solutions, op cit*, pp. 139-141.

50 B. Posen, 'Military responses to refugee disasters', *International Security*, vol. 21, no. 1, 1996, p. 94.

51 K. Landgren. *op cit*, p. 455.

52 A. Roberts, *op cit*, pp. 55 and 84.

Chapter 4
Return and reintegration

1 For an examination of these principles, see UNHCR handbook, *Voluntary Repatriation: International Protection*, UNHCR, Geneva, 1996.

2 T. Allen (ed.), *In Search of Cool Ground: War, Flight and Homecoming in Northeast Africa*, United Nations Research Institute for Social Development, Africa World Press and James Currey, London, 1996, p. 15.

3 B. Stein, 'Reintegrating returning refugees in Central America', in K. Kumar (ed), *Rebuilding Societies After Civil War: Critical Roles for International Assistance*, Lynne Rienner, Boulder, 1997, p. 161.

4 M. Ortega and P. Acevedo, 'Nicaraguan repatriation from Honduras and Costa Rica', in M. Larkin, F. Cuny and B. Stein (eds), *Repatriation Under Conflict in Central America*, Center for Immigration Policy and Refugee Assistance, Washington DC, 1991.

5 P. Weiss-Fagen and J. Eldridge, 'Salvadoran repatriation from Honduras', in *ibid*, p. 177.

6 For further details, see C. Robinson, *Something Like Home Again: The Repatriation of Cambodian Refugees*, US Committee for Refugees, Washington DC, 1994.

7 A. Mayne *et al*, 'Mid-term review of UNHCR programme for reintegration assistance in Afghanistan', UNHCR, Geneva, June 1996, p.1.

8 For some case studies of spontaneous repatriation see F. Cuny, B. Stein and P. Reed (eds), *Repatriation During Conflict in Africa and Asia*, Center for the Study of Societies in Crisis, Dallas, 1992.

9 J. Crisp, *Rebuilding a War-Torn Society: A Review of the UNHCR Reintegration Programme for Mozambican Returnees*, UNHCR, Geneva, 1996, p. 5.

10 See, for example, T. Allen, *op cit*; T. Allen and H. Morsink (eds), *When Refugees Go Home: African Experiences*, United Nations Research Institute for Social Development, Africa World Press and James Currey, Geneva, 1994; C. Watson, *The Flight, Exile and Return of Chadian Refugees*, United Nations Research Institute for Social Development, Geneva, 1996.

11 For a discussion of these issues, see T. Allen and D. Turton, 'Introduction', in T. Allen, *op cit*.

12 C. Sorensen, 'Alebu: Eritrean returnees restore their livelihoods', paper presented at the conference 'Reconstructing livelihoods: towards new approaches to resettlement', Oxford University, September 1996, p. 2.

13 C. Watson, *op cit*, p. 105.

14 'Bosnia: property disputes cloud repatriation prospects', *Forced Migration Monitor*, January 1997.

15 C. Watson, *op cit*, p. 119.

16 L. Studdert, 'An assessment of food security and livelihood of repatriated households in Cambodia', World Food Programme, Rome, 1995.

17 See, for example, the speakers and participants at a UNHCR/International Peace Academy conference at Princeton University, July 1996, reported in *Healing the Wounds: Refugees, Reconstruction and Reconciliation*, International Peace Academy, New York, 1996.

18 UNHCR, *The State of the World's Refugees: In Search of Solutions*, Oxford University Press, Oxford, 1995, p. 51.

19 S. Holtzman, 'Post-conflict reconstruction', Environment Department Work in Progress, World Bank, Washington DC, 1995, p.15.

20 *The State of the World's Refugees, op cit*, p. 106.

21 S. Holtzman, *op cit*, p. 7.

22 R. Hogg, 'Changing mandates in the Ethiopian Ogaden', in T. Allen, *op cit*, p. 162.

23 C. Sorensen, *op cit*, p. 2.

24 'Preparatory WSP mission to North-East Somalia: mission report', War-Torn Societies Project, United Nations Research Institute for Social Development, December 1996, pp. 6-7.

25 S. Holtzman, *op cit*, p. 15.

26 'Voluntary repatriation and other return movements: the role of UNHCR in the country of origin', internal paper, UNHCR, Geneva, August 1990, p. 4.

27 *The State of the World's Refugees, op cit*, p. 108.

28 'Voluntary repatriation', UNHCR Executive Committee Conclusion No. 40 of 1985, on *Refworld* CD-Rom, UNHCR, Geneva, 1997.

29 Human Rights Watch, 'Uncertain refuge: international failures to protect refugees', report 9/1, New York, April 1997, p. 9.

30 'Report of the 46th session of the Executive Committee of the High Commissioner's programme', UNHCR Executive Committee document A/AC.96/860, October 1995, on *Refworld, op cit*.

31 'UNHCR's role in national legal and judicial capacity building', UNHCR Executive Committee conference room paper EC/46/SC/CRP.31, May 1996, on *ibid*.

32 See, for example, Amnesty International, 'Rwanda: Amnesty delegates back from Rwanda report new wave of human rights abuses', press release AFR47/10/97, February 1997.

33 Human Rights Watch, 'Tajik refugees in northern Afghanistan: obstacles to repatriation', report 8/6, New York, May 1996, p. 28.

34 Human Rights Watch, 'Uncertain refuge', *op cit*.

35 This critique is developed in *Rebuilding a War-Torn Society*, *op cit*, and in *The State of the World's Refugees*, *op cit*, pp. 176-181.

36 S. Ogata, 'Towards healing the wounds: conflict-torn states and the return of refugees', statement presented at the conference 'The United Nations: the next fifty years', Korea University, April 1996.

37 K. Kumar, *op cit*.

38 For a useful review of the literature, see P. Weiss-Fagen, *The Challenge of Rebuilding War-Torn Societies: A Bibliographic Essay*, War-torn Societies Project, United Nations Research Institute for Social Development, Geneva, 1995.

39 See, for example, K. Bush, 'Towards a balanced approach to rebuilding war-torn societies', *Canadian Foreign Policy*, vol. 3, no. 3, 1995.

40 P. Weiss-Fagen, 'The meaning and modes of reintegration', paper presented at the conference 'People of concern', UNHCR, Geneva, November 1996, p. 1.

41 S. Ogata, 'From humanitarian relief to rehabilitation: a comprehensive response', statement presented at the advanced development management programme, Sophia University, Tokyo, October 1995, on *Refworld* CD-Rom, *op cit*.

42 See, for example, K. Kumar. *op cit*, pp. 32-33.

43 For further details of this initiative, see *The State of the World's Refugees*, *op cit*, pp. 50-51.

Chapter 5
The asylum dilemma

1 J. Kumin, 'Harmonization of refugee law: can the protection gap be closed?', address to the International Bar Association, Berlin, October 1996.

2 The statistics in this section are taken primarily from bulletins produced by Eurostat and the Secretariat of the Intergovernmental Consultations on Asylum, Refugee and Migration Policies in Europe, North America and Australia. See also *Populations of Concern to UNHCR: A Statistical Overview*, published annually by UNHCR, and the *World Refugee Survey*, published annually by the US Committee for Refugees.

3 L. Williams, 'Thousands seek asylum in South Africa', Panafrican News Agency despatch, 15 May 1997; 'South Africa: refugees and workers', *Migration News*, vol. 4, no. 5, 1997.

4 UNHCR, *The State of the World's Refugees: In Search of Solutions*, Oxford University Press, Oxford, 1995, p. 199.

5 E. Kjaergaard, 'The concept of 'safe third country' in contemporary European refugee law', *International Journal of Refugee Law*, vol. 6, no. 4, 1994.

6 *Overview of Readmission Agreements in Central Europe*, UNHCR, Geneva, 1993.

7 'Note on International Protection', UNHCR Executive Committee document no. A/AC.96/830, September 1994, on *Refworld* CD-Rom, UNHCR, Geneva, 1997.

8 *The State of the World's Refugees*, *op cit*, p. 201.

9 European Council on Refugees and Exiles, *Safe Third Countries: Myths and Realities*, London, 1995, pp. 7-9.

10 European Council on Refugees and Exiles, 'Position of ECRE on sharing the responsibility: protecting refugees and displaced persons in the context of large-scale arrivals', ECRE, London, 1996, para. 14.

11 *Forced Migration Alert*, no. 30, 27 May 1997.

12 C. Berthiaume, 'Asylum under threat', *Refugees*, no. 101, 1995.

13 *The Financial Times*, 12 January 1997.

14 For information on the subject of trafficking, see the newsletter *Trafficking in Migrants*, published by the International Organization for Migration. See also F. del Mundo, 'Trafficking in human lives', *Refugees*, no. 101, 1995.

15 *ibid*.

16 V. Crowe, 'Short report on Wilton Park Conference 497: Migration: prevention, control and management', April 1997.

17 S. Ogata, statement on the occasion of the publication of *The State of the World's Refugees* in German, Bonn, June 1994, on *Refworld* CD-Rom, *op cit*.

18 A. Shacknove, 'Asylum seekers in affluent states', paper presented to the UNHCR conference, 'People of concern', Geneva, November, 1996. This section also draws substantially on R. Byrne and A. Shacknove, 'The safe country notion in European asylum law', *Harvard Human Rights Journal*, vol. 9, Spring 1996.

19 R. Byrne and A. Shacknove, *ibid*.

20 *Refworld*, *op cit*. See also <http://www.unhcr.ch>.

21 This example is drawn from A. Shacknove, *op cit*, and from R. Byrne and A. Shacknove, *op cit*, pp. 225-6.

22 M. Kjaerum, 'Temporary protection in Europe in the 1990s', *International Journal of Refugee Law*, vol. 6, no. 3, 1994.

23 S. Ogata, statement at the Intergovernmental Consultations on Asylum, Refugee and Migration Policies in Europe, North America and Australia, Washington DC, May 1997.

24 'Progress report on informal consultations on the provision of international protection to all those who need it', UNHCR document no. EC/47/SC/CRP.27, Geneva, May 1997.

25 See, for example, S. Ogata, 'Preventing future genocide and protecting refugees', address at the Holocaust Memorial Museum, Washington DC, April 1997: "We should work to prevent the deportation of Bosnian refugees who cannot yet return to their own homes. It is wishful thinking to assume that my Office can make repatriation possible if political leaders in Bosnia are allowed to pursue their heinous policies of ethnic cleansing and if shelter is not reconstructed more quickly."

26 *ibid*.

27 J. Crush, 'A bad neighbour policy? Migrant labour and the new South Africa', *Southern Africa Report*, vol. 12, no.1, 1996.

28 D. Joly, 'An agenda for reception and integration: the Western European experience and Central Europe', paper prepared for the Third International Symposium on the Protection of Refugees in Central Europe, Budapest, April 1997.

29 A. Suhrke, 'Towards a better international refugee regime', unpublished paper, 1997, p. 15.

30 'Asylum in Europe and the return of rejected asylum seekers', internal UNHCR memorandum, 1 December 1995.

31 For a concise analysis of the CPA and its achievements, see *The State of the World's Refugees, op cit*, pp. 208-209.

32 C. Berthiaume, *op cit.*

33 This point has been made for many years. See, for example, Independent Commission on International Humanitarian Issues, *Refugees: The Dynamics of Displacement*, Zed Books, London, 1986, p. 41.

34 'Asylum in Europe and the return of rejected asylum seekers', *op cit.*

35 See W. Bohning and M. Schloeter-Paredes (eds), *Aid in Place of Migration?*, International Labour Office, Geneva, 1994.

36 P. Martin and J. Taylor, 'Managing migration: the role of economic policy', International Center for Migration, Ethnicity and Citizenship, New York, 1996, p. 31.

37 'Swedish refugee policy in global perspective: summary of a report to the Swedish government by the parliamentary Refugee Policy Commission', Stockholm, June 1995.

Chapter 6
Statelessness and citizenship

1   The terms citizenship and nationality are used as synonyms in this chapter.

2   Article 1, 1954 Convention relating to the Status of Stateless Persons.

3   For a fuller discussion of the legal dimensions of statelessness, see C. Batchelor, 'Stateless persons: some gaps in international protection', *International Journal of Refugee Law*, vol. 7, no. 2, 1995.

4   Independent Commission on International Humanitarian Issues, *Winning the Human Race*, Zed Books, London, 1988, p. 112.

5   K. Landgren, 'Foreword', *Refugee Survey Quarterly*, vol. 14, no. 3, 1995, p. viii.

6   D. Lloyd George, *The Truth about the Peace Treaties, Vol. II*, Victor Gollancz, London, 1938, p. 757.

7   H. Arendt, *The Origins of Totalitarianism*, Harcourt, Brace, Jovanovich, New York, 1973, p. 290.

8   See 'Repatriation of Biharis from Bangladesh', response to information request BDG6 of 3.3.94 on *Refworld* CD-Rom, UNHCR, Geneva, 1997.

9   The very complicated history of this group is examined in T. Lee, 'Stateless persons and the 1989 Comprehensive Plan of Action: Chinese nationality and the Republic of China (Taiwan)', *International Journal of Refugee Law*, vol. 7, no. 2, 1995.

10 This list has been drawn up from the databases which appear on the *Refworld* CD-Rom, UNHCR, Geneva, 1997.

11 S. Ogata, 'Statement to the 51st Session of the UN Commission on Human Rights', Geneva, February 1995, on *Refworld* CD-Rom, *op cit.*

12 W. R. Brubaker, 'Aftermaths of empire and the unmixing of peoples: historical and comparative perspectives', Ford Foundation paper no. DRU-563-FF, 1993. See also A. Zolberg, 'The unmixing of peoples in the post-Communist world', occasional paper, International Center for Migration, Ethnicity and Citizenship, New School for Social Research, New York, 1997.

13 W. R. Brubaker, 'Citizenship struggles in the Soviet successor states', *International Migration Review*, vol. 27, no. 2, 1992. For a more recent examination of these issues, see P. Kolstoe, *Russians in the Former Soviet Republics*, Hurst and Co., London, 1995.

14 V. Tishkov, *Ethnicity, Nationalism and Conflict in and after the Soviet Union: The Mind Aflame*, United Nations Research Institute for Social Development, International Peace Research Institute and Sage Publications, London, 1997, p. 241.

15 B. Nahaylo, 'Population displacement in the CIS: the background, problems and challenges', *The CIS Conference on Refugees and Migrants*, European Series, UNHCR Regional Bureau for Europe, vol. 2, no. 2, 1996.

16 The full name of the republic is the Former Yugoslav Republic of Macedonia.

17 J. Pejic, 'Citizenship and statelessness in the former Yugoslavia: the legal framework', *Refugee Survey Quarterly*, vol. 14, no. 3, 1995, p. 8.

18 *Forced Migration Monitor*, September 1996.

19 *Citizenship in the Context of the Dissolution of Czechoslovakia*, European Series, UNHCR Regional Bureau for Europe, vol. 2, no. 4, 1996, p. 6.

20 Earl Warren, quoted in Independent Commission on International Humanitarian Issues, *op cit*, p. 107.

21 UN Department of Social Affairs, *A Study on Statelessness*, United Nations, New York, 1949.

22 H. Arendt, *op cit*, p. 286.

23 C. Batchelor, 'Training package: statelessness and related nationality issues', UNHCR, Geneva, 1996, p. 35.

24 Independent Commission on International Humanitarian Issues, *op cit*, p. 109.

25 US Department of State, 'Country reports on human rights practices for 1993: Mauritania', on *Refworld*, *op cit.*

26 US Department of State, 'Country reports on human rights practices for 1995: Kuwait', on *Refworld* CD-Rom, *op cit.*

27 UN Commission on Human Rights, 'Rights of persons belonging to national or ethnic, religious and linguistic minorities: report of the Secretary-General', January 1996, para. 45, on *Refworld* CD-Rom, *op cit.*

28 T. Piper, 'The exodus of ethnic Nepalis from southern Bhutan', *Refugee Survey Quarterly*, vol. 14, no. 3, 1995, pp. 69-74.

29 UNHCR, *Different Time Different Place: UNHCR in Cambodia*, Phnom Penh, 1995, p. 21.

30 T. Piper, *op cit*, p. 77.

31 *Forced Migration Monitor*, May 1997.

32 C. Messina, 'Refugees, forced migrants or involuntarily relocating persons? Refugee definitions in the countries of the CIS', paper presented at a conference on refugee rights and realities, Nottingham, November 1996.

33 I. Brownlie, *Principles of Public International Law*, Clarendon Press, Oxford, 1990, p. 664.

34 Independent Commission on International Humanitarian Issues, *op cit*, p. 112.

35 C. Batchelor, 'Training package', *op cit*, p. 14.

36 M. Hudson, *Report on Nationality, Including Statelessness*, International Law Commission, 1952.

37 General Assembly Resolution 50/152, February 1996.

38 See Box 1.3 for additional details of this conference.

39 For bibliographies on statelessness, see *Refugee Survey Quarterly*, vol. 14, no. 3, 1995, pp. 157-165; and *Austrian Journal of Public and International Law*, vol. 49, no. 1, 1995, pp. 105-108.

40 P. van Krieken, 'Disintegration and statelessness', *Netherlands Quarterly of Human Rights*, vol. 12, no. 1, 1994, p. 32.

41 C. Batchelor, 'UNHCR and issues related to nationality', *Refugee Survey Quarterly*, vol. 14, no. 3, 1995, p. 112.

Conclusion
An agenda for action

1 C. Sommaruga, introductory address to the humanitarian forum, Wolfsberg, June 1997.

2 The following account of this meeting is drawn from A. Penketh, 'Security Council cool to appeals for humanitarian enforcement', AFP despatch, 21 May 1997.

3 These doubts are expressed in M. Goulding, 'United Nations reform: new approaches to peace and security?', Olof Palme Memorial Lecture, Stockholm, June 1997.

4 See, for example, T. Weiss and C. Collins, *Humanitarian Challenges and Intervention: World Politics and the Dilemmas of Help*, Westview Press, Boulder, 1996, pp. 13-18.

5 *Working in a War Zone: A Review of UNHCR's Operations in Former Yugoslavia*, Central Evaluation Section, UNHCR, Geneva, April 1994, p. 8.

6 M. Anderson, 'International assistance and conflict: an exploration of negative impacts', Cambridge, Mass., 1995, p. 4.

7 B. Barber, 'Feeding refugees, or war?', *Foreign Affairs*, vol. 76, no. 4, 1997.

8 C. Sommaruga, *op cit*.

9 S. Ogata, 'Peace, security and humanitarian action,' Alastair Buchan Memorial Lecture, International Institute for Strategic Studies, London, April 1997.

10 African Rights, 'Humanitarianism unbound? Current dilemmas facing multi-mandate relief operations in political emergencies', discussion paper no. 5, November 1994.

11 See, for example, Amnesty International, 'Rwanda: human rights overlooked in mass repatriation', report no.

AFR47/02/97, January 1997, and 'Great Lakes region: still in need of protection: repatriation, refoulement and the safety of refugees and the internally displaced', report no. AFR02/07/97, January 1997.

12 This theme is explored in detail in M. Cranna (ed), *The True Cost of Conflict*, Saferworld and Earthscan Publications, London, 1994.

13 S. Ogata, 'Assuring the security of people: the humanitarian challenge of the 21st century', Olof Palme Memorial Lecture, Stockholm, June 1995, on *Refworld* CD-Rom, UNHCR, Geneva, 1997.

14 S. Ogata, statement to the Third Committee of the UN General Assembly, November 1994, on *Refworld* CD-Rom, UNHCR, Geneva, 1997.

15 See, for example, the ConflictNet website, <http://www.igc.apc.org/conflictnet/>.

16 United Nations Development Programme, *Human Development Report 1997*, Oxford University Press, New York, 1997.

17 See 'Rebuilding war-torn societies', Chapter Seven of *States of Disarray: The Social Effects of Globalization*, United Nations Research Institute for Social Development, Geneva, 1995.

18 J. Whitman, 'Those that have power to hurt but would do none: the military and humanitarianism', address given at the Royal Military Academy, Sandhurst, January 1997, *Journal of Humanitarian Assistance*, website <www-jha.sps.cam.ac.uk>.

19 L. Diamond, *Promoting Democracy in the 1990s: Actors and Instruments, Issues and Imperatives*, Carnegie Commission on Preventing Deadly Conflict, New York, 1995.

20 See M. Weiner and R. Munz, 'Migrants, refugees and foreign policy: prevention and intervention strategies', *Third World Quarterly*, vol. 18, no. 3, 1997, pp. 43-47.

21 Commission on Global Governance, *Our Global Neighbourhood*, Oxford University Press, New York, 1995.

22 L. Diamond, *op cit*, pp. 51-59.

23 'Comprehensive and regional approaches within a protection framework', UNHCR Executive Committee conclusion no. 80 of 1996, on *Refworld* CD-Rom, *op cit*.

24 W. Shawcross, statement to the Wolfsberg humanitarian forum, Wolfsberg, June 1997.

25 B. Frelick, 'Unsafe havens: reassessing security in refugee crises', *Harvard International Review*, Spring 1997.

Statistics

There is a constant demand for accurate and topical refugee statistics from academic researchers, aid agencies, the media and others with an interest in humanitarian affairs. In order to meet this demand and to facilitate the planning and implementation of its own activities, UNHCR has steadily enhanced the quality and quantity of the statistical data which it collects and disseminates. The most recent compilation of data, a 60-page report entitled *Refugees and Others of Concern to UNHCR: 1996 Statistical Overview,* is available free of charge from the Programme Coordination Section, Division of Operational Support, UNHCR, CP 2500, CH-1211 Geneva, Switzerland. Refugee statistics can also be found on *Refworld,* the UNHCR CD-Rom, and on the UNHCR website (see 'Further reading' for details).

Table 1:   People of concern to UNHCR

Country of asylum/ present residence	Major countries of origin	Number	People of concern	Country of asylum/ present residence	Major countries of origin	Number	People of concern
REFUGEES IN AFRICA							
Algeria			190,267	Ethiopia			390,528
	Mali	15,056			Djibouti	18,000	
	Niger	10,181			Kenya	8,678	
	Saharawis	165,000			Somalia	287,761	
Angola			9,381		Sudan	75,743	
	D.R. Congo (ex-Zaire)	9,341		Gambia			6,924
Benin			5,960	Ghana			35,617
Burkina Faso			28,381		Liberia	15,178	
Côte d'Ivoire			327,696		Togo	20,258	
	Liberia	327,288		Guinea			663,854
Cameroon			46,407		Liberia	415,003	
	Chad	44,566			Sierra Leone	248,827	
Central African Republic			36,564	Guinea-Bissau			15,401
	Chad	5,491			Senegal	15,000	
	Sudan	30,671		Kenya			223,640
Congo			20,451		Ethiopia	7,109	
	Angola	20,201			Rwanda	5,487	
D.R. Congo (ex-Zaire)			675,973		Somalia	171,347	
	Angola	108,284			Sudan	33,477	
	Burundi	30,226			Uganda	5,425	
	Rwanda	423,561		Liberia			120,061
	Sudan	96,529			Sierra Leone	120,001	
	Uganda	17,289		Libya			7,747
Djibouti			25,076	Mali			18,234
	Somalia	23,010			Mauritania	16,764	
Egypt			6,035	Mauritania			15,880
					Mali	15,872	

Country of asylum/ present residence	Major countries of origin	Number	People of concern
Niger			25,845
	Mali	24,000	
Nigeria			8,486
	Liberia	5,278	
Rwanda			25,257
	Burundi	9,611	
	D.R. Congo (ex-Zaire)	15,397	
Senegal			65,044
	Mauritania	64,030	
Sierra Leone			13,532
	Liberia	13,521	
South Africa			22,645
Sudan			393,874
	Eritrea	328,307	
	Ethiopia	51,467	
Tanzania			498,732
	Burundi	385,452	
	Mozambique	33,202	
	Rwanda	20,020	
	D.R. Congo (ex-Zaire)	55,214	
Togo			12,589
	Ghana	12,285	
Uganda			264,294
	Rwanda	11,236	
	Sudan	223,720	
	D.R. Congo (ex-Zaire)	28,611	
Zambia			131,139
	Angola	109,623	
	D.R. Congo (ex-Zaire)	14,180	
Africa: other countries			9,966
TOTAL REFUGEES IN AFRICA			**4,341,480**

REFUGEES IN ASIA

Country of asylum/ present residence	Major countries of origin	Number	People of concern
Afghanistan			18,775
	Tajikistan	18,769	
Armenia			218,950
	Azerbaijan	200,000	
Azerbaijan			233,000
	Armenia	185,000	
	Uzbekistan	48,000	
Bangladesh			30,692
	Myanmar	30,578	

Country of asylum/ present residence	Major countries of origin	Number	People of concern
China			290,100
	Viet Nam	288,805	
Hong Kong			6,875
	Viet Nam	6,872	
India			233,370
	Afghanistan	18,607	
	Bangladesh	53,500	
	China	98,000	
	Sri Lanka	62,226	
Iran			2,030,359
	Afghanistan	1,414,659	
	Iraq	579,200	
Iraq			112,957
	Iran	34,194	
	Palestinians	62,635	
	Turkey	14,986	
Kazakstan			15,577
	Russian Federation	6,000	
	Tajikistan	6,000	
Kyrgyzstan			16,707
	Tajikistan	16,436	
Nepal			126,815
	Bhutan	106,801	
	China	20,005	
Pakistan			1,202,703
	Afghanistan	1,200,000	
Saudi Arabia			9,852
	Iraq	9,701	
Syria			27,759
	Iraq	26,817	
Thailand			107,962
	Myanmar	104,033	
Turkey			8,166
Turkmenistan			15,580
	Tajikistan	12,170	
Viet Nam			34,400
	Cambodia	34,400	
Yemen			53,546
	Palestinians	6,000	
	Somalia	43,871	
Asia: other countries			14,479
TOTAL REFUGEES IN ASIA			**4,808,624**

REFUGEES IN EUROPE

Country of asylum/ present residence	Major countries of origin	Number	People of concern
Austria			29,745

Country of asylum/ present residence	Major countries of origin	Number	People of concern
Belarus			30,525
Belgium			36,060
Croatia			165,395
Denmark			53,302
Finland			10,248
Macedonia (F.Y.R.)			5,089
France			151,329
Germany			1,266,000
Greece			5,780
Hungary			7,537
Italy			71,630
Netherlands			103,425
Norway			57,000
Russian Federation			205,458
Slovenia			10,014
Spain			5,685
Sweden			191,200
Switzerland			84,413
United Kingdom			96,905
Yugoslavia (F.R.)			563,215
Europe: other countries			16,084
TOTAL REFUGEES IN EUROPE			**3,166,039**

REFUGEES IN LATIN AMERICA

Country of asylum/ present residence	Major countries of origin	Number	People of concern
Argentina			10,430
Belize			8,534
	El Salvador	5,770	
Costa Rica			23,176
	Nicaragua	17,990	
Mexico			34,569
	Guatemala	32,593	
Latin America: other countries			11,721
TOTAL REFUGEES IN LATIN AMERICA			**88,430**

REFUGEES IN NORTH AMERICA

Country of asylum/ present residence	Major countries of origin	Number	People of concern
Canada			123,219
United States of America			596,900
TOTAL REFUGEES IN NORTH AMERICA			**720,119**

REFUGEES IN OCEANIA

Country of asylum/ present residence	Major countries of origin	Number	People of concern
Australia			59,029
Papua New Guinea			10,176
	Indonesia	10,175	
Oceania: other countries			5,749
TOTAL REFUGEES IN OCEANIA			**74,954**

GRAND TOTAL REFUGEES			**13,199,646**

IDPS IN AFRICA

Country of asylum/ present residence	Major countries of origin	Number	People of concern
Burundi			882,900
Liberia			320,000
Sierra Leone			654,600
Somalia			200,000
TOTAL IDPs IN AFRICA			**2,057,500**

IDPS IN ASIA

Country of asylum/ present residence	Major countries of origin	Number	People of concern
Afghanistan			273,840
Armenia			72,000
Azerbaijan			549,030
Cambodia			29,406
Cyprus			265,000
Georgia			272,359
Iraq			32,000
Sri Lanka			200,000
Tajikistan			25,285
TOTAL IDPs IN ASIA			**1,718,920**

IDPS IN EUROPE

Country of asylum/ present residence	Major countries of origin	Number	People of concern
Bosnia and Herzegovina			760,146
Croatia			144,147
Russian Federation			161,312
Europe: other countries			487
TOTAL IDPs IN EUROPE			**1,066,092**

IDPS IN LATIN AMERICA

Country of asylum/ present residence	Major countries of origin	Number	People of concern
Guatemala			11,200
TOTAL IDPs IN LATIN AMERICA			**11,200**

GRAND TOTAL IDPs			**4,853,712**

Country of asylum/ present residence	Major countries of origin	Number	People of concern
RETURNEES IN AFRICA			
Angola			59,467
Burundi			71,031
Eritrea			24,727
Ethiopia			27,907
Liberia			11,084
Mali			73,284
Mauritania			35,000
Rwanda			1,300,582
Somalia			14,435
Togo			73,283
Africa: other countries			1,704
TOTAL RETURNEES IN AFRICA			**1,692,504**
RETURNEES IN ASIA			
Afghanistan			613,390
Azerbaijan			60,402
Cambodia			34,734
Iraq			115,330
Laos			27,307
Myanmar			219,282
Sri Lanka			54,000
Turkmenistan			6,750
Viet Nam			105,614
Asia: other countries			4,735
TOTAL RETURNEES IN ASIA			**1,241,544**
RETURNEES IN EUROPE			
Bosnia and Herzegovina			252,256
Croatia			55,252
Europe: other countries			441
TOTAL RETURNEES IN EUROPE			**307,949**
RETURNEES IN LATIN AMERICA			
El Salvador			30,887
Guatemala			37,791
Latin America: other countries			548
TOTAL RETURNEES IN LATIN AMERICA			**69,226**
GRAND TOTAL RETURNEES			**3,311,233**

Country of asylum/ present residence	Major countries of origin	Number	People of concern
ASIA: OTHERS OF CONCERN			
Kuwait	Stateless		120,000
Yemen			36,000
TOTAL ASIA: OTHERS OF CONCERN			**156,000**
EUROPE: OTHERS OF CONCERN			
Belarus			160,000
Bosnia and Herzegovina			200,000
	Bosnia and Herzegovina		200,000
Russian Federation			847,138
	Russian Federation		847,138
Europe: other countries			1,514
TOTAL EUROPE: OTHERS OF CONCERN			**1,208,652**
GRAND TOTAL OTHERS OF CONCERN			**1,364,652**
PEOPLE OF CONCERN TO UNHCR: GRAND TOTAL			**22,729,233**

Statistics at 1 January 1997. The table shows only countries with over 5,000 people of concern to UNHCR and shows countries of origin only for refugee populations of over 5,000 which are located outside of Europe, North America and Australasia. 'IDPs' refers to internally displaced people. 'Returnees' include former refugees and former IDPs of concern to UNHCR. 'Others of concern' includes war-affected populations in former Yugoslavia, relocating populations in the Russian Federation (from other CIS countries and the Baltic states) and stateless people.

Table 2: Asylum applications and admissions to the industrialized states, 1987-96

Country	1987	1988	1989	1990	1991	1992	1993	1994	1995	1996
Australia										
Asylum applications	..	..	1,262	12,128	16,743	6,054	7,198	6,264	7,632	9,611
1951 Convention status	..	..	80	91	189	614	992	1,031	681	1,380
Humanitarian status	5,111	5,772	7,264	10,411	6,478	4,772	8,251	7,505	9,626	8,135
Rejections	..	..	331	195	1,469	9,949	9,066	6,716	6,793	6,218
Resettlement arrivals	5,990	5,304	3,623	1,537	1,267	2,385	2,688	3,845	4,006	3,118
Austria										
Asylum applications	11,406	15,790	21,882	22,789	27,306	16,238	4,745	5,082	5,919	6,991
1951 Convention status	1,120	1,790	2,900	860	2,470	2,290	1,200	680	990	716
Rejections	..	4,933	12,134	11,784	17,217	21,196	14,197	8,335	6,634	8,032
Belgium										
Asylum applications	6,000	5,078	8,112	12,963	15,172	17,647	26,880	14,353	11,420	12,433
1951 Convention status	2,680	910	800	680	600	760	1,040	1,510	1,300	1,581
Rejections	..	1,477	830	1,153	1,683	2,006	2,524	3,274	2,750	4,065
Canada										
Asylum applications	38,000	48,000	19,934	36,735	32,347	37,748	20,292	22,006	26,072	26,120
1951 Convention status	1,080	1,295	4,744	10,710	19,425	17,437	14,101	15,224	9,614	9,541
Humanitarian status	2,900	2,090	2,490	3,330	2,410	880	3,870	2,290	1,550	..
Rejections	5,562	1,774	1,132	3,842	8,868	11,070	11,448	6,442	4,096	7,037
Resettlement arrivals	20,078	26,065	35,438	31,917	24,887	14,726	11,560	10,100	10,919	10,935
Czech Republic										
Asylum applications	0	0	0	1,792	1,977	817	2,193	1,188	1,413	2,156
1951 Convention status	0	0	0	26	720	228	242	112	56	95
Rejections	0	0	0	0	1	9	11	169	20	24
Denmark										
Asylum applications	2,750	4,668	4,488	5,292	4,609	13,884	14,347	6,651	5,104	5,893
1951 Convention status	..	1,018	1,211	710	990	760	650	680	4,970	1,214
Humanitarian status	268	1,870	2,220	1,430	1,910	1,970	1,960	1,420	14,510	3,622
Rejections	..	638	..	..	..	..	..	..	3,496	2,212
Resettlement arrivals	..	440	1,000	910	860	550	500	430	530	470
Finland										
Asylum applications	50	64	200	2,730	2,137	3,634	2,023	840	854	711
1951 Convention status	..	5	10	15	16	12	9	15	4	11
Humanitarian status	..	10	40	140	1,700	570	2,073	301	219	334
Rejections	..	21	..	332	628	1,344	1,435	492	269	248
Resettlement arrivals	..	294	540	410	500	670	520	350	640	840

Country	1987	1988	1989	1990	1991	1992	1993	1994	1995	1996
France										
Asylum applications	27,672	34,352	61,422	54,813	47,380	28,872	27,564	25,964	20,170	17,405
1951 Convention status	8,700	8,790	8,770	13,490	15,470	10,270	9,910	7,030	4,530	4,344
Rejections	17,924	16,631	22,400	73,866	62,975	26,380	25,575	22,685	24,434	17,859
Germany										
Asylum applications	57,379	103,076	121,318	193,063	256,112	438,191	322,614	127,210	166,951	149,193
1951 Convention status	8,231	7,621	5,991	6,500	11,597	9,189	16,400	25,600	23,470	24,000
Humanitarian status	-	-	-	-	-	-	-	-	3,630	2,082
Rejections	62,000	62,983	89,866	116,268	128,820	163,637	347,991	238,386	114,376	124,575
Greece										
Asylum applications	6,950	8,400	3,000	6,166	2,672	1,850	813	1,303	1,312	1,560
1951 Convention status	..	230	290	170	120	60	40	90	200	160
Rejections	..	542	804	2,331	5,207	1,737	711	666	1,045	648
Ireland										
Asylum applications	..	..	..	..	..	39	91	362	424	1,179
1951 Convention status	..	..	..	..	..	7	9	18	14	2
Humanitarian status	..	..	..	..	..	7	5	5	2	0
Rejections	..	..	..	..	..	22	23	32	8	2
Italy										
Asylum applications	11,050	1,300	2,250	4,827	26,472	6,042	1,647	1,786	1,732	675
1951 Convention status	370	210	130	824	803	336	126	298	285	172
Rejections	4,662	5,795	101	562	15,662	6,624	1,300	1,386	1,433	522
Japan										
Asylum applications	48	47	50	32	42	68	50	73	52	147
1951 Convention status	6	12	2	2	1	3	6	1	1	1
Rejections	35	62	23	31	13	41	33	41	32	43
Netherlands										
Asylum applications	13,460	7,486	13,898	21,208	21,615	17,462	35,399	52,573	29,258	22,170
1951 Convention status	237	589	1,032	694	775	4,923	10,338	6,654	7,980	8,810
Humanitarian status	896	930	1,076	857	1,920	6,891	4,674	9,235	6,203	7,384
Rejections	7,425	7,337	9,674	8,998	14,544	20,304	15,759	32,146	32,297	15,297
Resettlement arrivals	560	780	590	700	589	643	659	554	605	475
New Zealand										
Asylum applications	..	..	..	..	..	324	375	445	712	1,321
1951 Convention status	..	..	..	..	..	114	60	51	80	89
Rejections	..	..	..	..	..	615	898	272	224	578

Country	1987	1988	1989	1990	1991	1992	1993	1994	1995	1996
Norway										
Asylum applications	..	..	..	3,962	4,569	5,236	12,876	3,379	1,460	1778
1951 Convention status	271	147	338	108	101	63	54	22	29	6
Humanitarian status	2,379	4,110	3,667	1,219	1,654	1,574	7,681	2,007	1,625	1,198
Rejections	846	2,115	2,927	2,059	2,265	2,884	4,685	2,963	1,414	1,410
Resettlement arrivals	803	774	1,075	974	1,142	2,037	1,474	694	1,591	788
Portugal										
Asylum applications	450	350	150	75	255	686	2,090	767	450	269
1951 Convention status	..	12	25	9	25	17	75	31	49	5
Rejections	..	19	29	41	180	442	567	426	514	167
Spain										
Asylum applications	2,500	4,516	4,077	8,647	8,138	11,708	12,615	11,999	5,678	4,730
1951 Convention status	513	555	264	490	555	264	1,287	627	464	243
Humanitarian status	..	..	..	..	..	..	..	..	230	193
Rejections	..	..	..	..	5,475	10,590	16,250	12,209	6075	4,539
Sweden										
Asylum applications	18,114	19,595	30,335	29,347	27,351	84,018	37,583	18,640	9,047	5,753
1951 Convention status	2,330	3,700	3,080	2,170	1,400	620	1,030	790	150	130
Humanitarian status	8,580	9,780	20,110	9,310	15,510	8,770	34,520	36,650	3,540	3,070
Rejections	..	4,061	..	..	20,376	..	41,417	10,301	5,568	3,104
Resettlement arrivals	1,457	1,476	1,559	1,455	1,732	3,402	937	7,431	1,956	1,629
Switzerland										
Asylum applications	10,913	16,726	24,425	35,836	41,629	17,960	24,739	16,134	17,021	18,001
1951 Convention status	830	680	654	571	880	1,410	3,830	2,940	2,650	2,267
Humanitarian status	..	2,036	1,950	4,879	..	..	..	9,590	8,600	5,249
Rejections	8,292	8,844	12,708	11,149	28,478	30,134	18,704	18,735	13,457	14,232
United Kingdom										
Asylum applications	5,863	5,739	16,775	38,195	73,400	32,300	28,000	42,200	55,000	34,800
1951 Convention status	460	980	3,340	1,590	800	1,900	2,860	1,400	2,200	2,765
Humanitarian status	2,230	2,290	5,840	3,600	2,950	21,700	15,480	5,450	6,780	7,790
Rejections	786	624	1,095	855	5,390	35,480	18,550	20,915	26,220	38,485
Resettlement arrivals	440	720	720	650	490	620	510	260	70	20
United States										
Asylum applications (est.)	37,855	88,067	147,435	106,774	81,650	150,748	209,041	212,379	223,973	195,617
1951 Convention status	5,093	7,340	9,229	5,672	2,908	3,959	7,464	11,764	17,493	16,600
Rejections (est.)	5,181	12,873	47,321	24,156	6,251	9,759	26,969	43,338	17,356	24,700
Resettlement arrivals	64,800	76,500	107,200	122,300	112,800	132,200	119,500	112,700	99,500	75,682

All decisions indicated are first instance decisions. The table does not generally include former Yugoslav citizens granted temporary protection. The symbol '..' is used when no figure is available. *Australia:* arrival data reported by fiscal year, July-June. *Norway* and *Sweden:* humanitarian status includes former Yugoslav citizens. *Portugal:* No breakdown available between Convention status and humanitarian status for positive decisions. *USA:* data reported by fiscal year, October-September. US asylum applications are estimated on the basis of number of applications x 1.45 (average family size). Rejections are estimated on the basis of number of rejections x 1.5 (average family size).

Further reading

Much of the data presented in this book is drawn from unpublished reports and documents prepared by UNHCR and its operational partners. The book has also made extensive use of the documentation available on *Refworld*, the UNHCR CD-Rom (for details see below). The following bibliography, which is organized on a chapter-by-chapter basis, identifies some of the most accessible and useful literature on the issues examined in the book, focusing on publications issued in 1996 and 1997. Additional sources are also cited in the endnotes to each chapter. The inclusion of any item in this bibliography does not imply its endorsement by UNHCR.

Safeguarding human security

ANDERSON, M, *Frontiers: Territory and State Formation in the Modern World*, Polity Press, Cambridge, 1996

BARBER, B, 'Feeding refugees, or war?', *Foreign Affairs*, vol. 76, no. 4, 1997

BOOTH, K, 'Human wrongs and international relations', *International Affairs*, vol. 71, no. 1, 1995

BROWN, M (ed), *The International Dimensions of Internal Conflict*, MIT Press, Cambridge MA, 1996

BUSH, K, 'Rocks and hard places: bad governance, human rights abuse and population displacement', *Canadian Foreign Policy*, vol. 4, no. 1, 1996

CLARKE, W and HERBST, W, 'Somalia and the future of humanitarian intervention', *Foreign Affairs*, vol. 75, no. 2, 1996

COHEN, R, 'Diasporas and the nation state: from victims to challengers', *International Affairs*, vol. 72, no. 3, 1996

DUFFIELD, M, 'Humanitarian intervention in Africa: the new aid paradigm and separate development', *New Political Economy*, Summer 1997

ELLIS, S, 'Africa after the cold war: new patterns of government and politics', *Development and Change*, vol. 27, no. 1, 1996

HELTON, A, 'The CIS migration conference: a chance to prevent and ameliorate forced movements of people in the former Soviet Union', *International Journal of Refugee Law*, vol. 8, no. 1/2, 1996

HOFFMANN, S, 'The politics and ethics of military intervention', *Survival*, vol. 37, no. 4, 1995-96

HUMAN RIGHTS WATCH, 'Refugees and internally displaced persons in Armenia, Azerbaijan, Georgia, the Russian Federation and Tajikistan', report no. D807, New York, 1996

IKENBERRY, J, 'The myth of post-cold war chaos', *Foreign Affairs*, vol. 75, no. 3, 1996

JEAN, F and RUFIN, J-C (eds), *Economie des Guerres Civiles*, Editions Pluriel/Hachette, Paris, 1996

JOLLY, R, 'Human development: the world after Copenhagen', *Global Governance*, vol. 3, no. 2, 1997

KALDER, M, 'A cosmopolitan response to new wars', *Peace Review*, vol. 8, no. 4, 1996

MACRAE, J and ZWI, A (eds), *War and Hunger: Rethinking International Responses to Complex Emergencies*, Zed Books, London, 1995

MEDECINS SANS FRONTIERES, *World in Crisis: The Politics of Survival at the End of the 20th Century*, Routledge, London, 1997

MOONEY, E, 'Conference report: CIS conference on refugees and migrants', *International Journal on Minority and Group Rights*, vol. 4, no. 1, 1996-97

PETTIFORD, L, 'Changing conceptions of security in the Third World', *Third World Quarterly*, vol. 17, no. 3, 1996

PRENDERGAST, J, *Frontline Diplomacy: Humanitarian Aid and Conflict in Africa*, Lynne Rienner, Boulder, 1996

PRUNIER, G, 'The Great Lakes crisis', *Current History*, vol. 96, no. 610, 1997

RICHARDS, P, *Fighting for the Rain Forest: War, Youth and Resources in Sierra Leone*, James Currey, London, 1996

ROBERTS, A, *Humanitarian Action in War*, Adelphi Paper no. 305, International Institute for Strategic Studies, London, 1996

ROTBERG, R and WEISS, T (eds), *From Massacres to Genocide: The Media, Public Policy and Humanitarian Crises*, Brookings Institution/World Peace Foundation, Cambridge MA, 1996

SORENSEN, G, 'Individual security and national security: the state remains the principal problem', *Security Dialogue*, vol. 27, no. 4, 1996

SWAIN, A, 'Environmental migration and conflict dynamics', *Third World Quarterly*, vol. 17, no. 5, 1996

THIRD WORLD QUARTERLY, vol. 18, no. 3, 1997, special issue: beyond UN subcontracting: task-sharing with regional security arrangements and service-providing NGOs

TISHKOV, V, *Ethnicity, Nationalism and Conflict in and after the Soviet Union: The Mind Aflame*, United Nations Institute for Social Development, International Peace Research Institute and Sage Publications, London, 1997

UNDP (United Nations Development Programme), *Human Development Report 1997*, Oxford University Press, New York, 1997

UNHCR (Office of the United Nations High Commissioner for Refugees), *The State of the World's Refugees: In Search of Solutions*, Oxford University Press, Oxford, 1995

UNHCR (Office of the United Nations High Commissioner for Refugees), *The CIS Conference on Refugees and Migrants*, European Series, vol. 2, no. 2, Geneva, 1996

WALKER, P, 'Whose disaster is it anyway? Rights, responsibilities and standards in crisis', *Journal of Humanitarian Assistance*, website <www-jha.sps.cam.ac.uk>

WEINER, M, 'Bad neighbors, bad neighborhoods: an enquiry into the causes of refugee flows', *International Security*, vol. 21, no. 1, 1996

WEISS, T and COLLINS, C, *Humanitarian Challenges and Intervention: World Politics and the Dilemmas of Help*, Westview Press, Boulder, 1996

Defending refugee rights

AMNESTY INTERNATIONAL, *Refugees: Human Rights Have No Borders*, London, 1997

BARUTCISKI, M, 'The reinforcement of non-admission policies and the subversion of UNHCR: displacement and internal assistance in Bosnia, Herzegovina (1992-94)', *Journal of Refugee Studies*, vol. 8, no. 1/2, 1996

BASCOM, J, *Losing Place: Refugee Populations and Rural Transformations in East Africa*, Berghahn Books, Providence, 1996

CRISP, J, 'Meeting the needs and realizing the rights of refugee children and adolescents: from policy to practice', *Refugee Survey Quarterly*, vol. 15, no. 3, 1996

DOWTY, A and LOESCHER, G, 'Refugee flows as grounds for international action', *International Security*, vol. 21, no. 1, 1996

FRELICK, B, 'Assistance without protection', in *World Refugee Survey 1997*, United States Committee for Refugees, Washington DC, 1997

GOODWIN-GILL, G, *The Refugee in International Law*, Oxford University Press, Oxford, 1996

GOWLLAND-DEBBAS, V, *The Problem of Refugees in the Light of Contemporary International Law*, Martinus Nijhoff, The Hague, 1996

HUMAN RIGHTS WATCH, 'Discussion paper: protection in the decade of voluntary repatriation', New York, 1996

HUMAN RIGHTS WATCH, "The Rohingya Muslims: ending a cycle of exodus?', report no. C809, New York, 1996

HUMAN RIGHTS WATCH, 'Uncertain refuge: international failures to protect refugees', report no. 9/1(G), New York, 1997

JACOBSON, K, 'Factors influencing the policy responses of host governments to mass refugee influxes', *International Migration Review*, vol. 30, no. 3, 1996

JACOBSON, K, 'Refugees' environmental impact: the effects of patterns of settlement', *Journal of Refugee Studies*, vol. 10, no. 1, 1997

JOURNAL OF REFUGEE STUDIES, vol. 9, no. 3, 1996, special issue on the Rwanda emergency: causes, responses and solutions

KEELY, C, 'How nation-states create and respond to refugee flows', *International Migration Review*, vol. 30, no. 4, 1996

KIBREAB, G, *People on the Edge in the Horn: Displacement, Land Use and the Environment in the Gedaref Region, Sudan*, James Currey, London, 1996

KIBREAB, G, 'Eritrean and Ethiopian urban refugees in Khartoum: what the eye refuses to see', *African Studies Review*, vol. 39, no. 3, 1996

KIBREAB, G, 'Environmental causes and impact of refugee movements: a critique of the current debate', *Disasters*, vol. 21, no. 1, 1997

KUHLMAN, T, *Asylum or Aid? The Economic Integration of Ethiopian and Eritrean Refugees in the Sudan*, Avebury, Aldershot, 1995

LAWYERS COMMITTEE FOR HUMAN RIGHTS, *African Exodus: Refugee Crisis, Human Rights and the 1969 OAU Convention*, New York, 1995

MALKKI, L, *Purity and Exile: Violence, Memory and National Cosmology among Hutu Refugees in Tanzania*, University of Chicago Press, Chicago, 1995

SAULNIER, F, 'Rwanda: the human shield strategy', *The World Today*, January 1996

Internal conflict and displacement

AFRICAN RIGHTS, *Sudan's Invisible Citizens: The Policy of Abuse against Displaced People in the North*, African Rights, London, 1995

CHIMNI, B, 'The incarceration of victims: deconstructing safety zones', in N. Al-Naumi and R. Meese (eds), *International Legal Issues Arising Under the United Nations Decade of International Law*, Martinus Nijhoff, The Hague, 1995

COHEN, R, 'Protecting the internally displaced', in *World Refugee Survey 1996*, United States Committee for Refugees, Washington DC, 1996

COHEN, R and CUENOD, J, *Improving Institutional Arrangements for the Internally Displaced*, Brookings Institution and Refugee Policy Group, Washington DC, 1995

CURTIS, P, 'Urban household coping strategies during war: Bosnia-Hercegovina', *Disasters*, vol. 19, no. 1, 1995

DENG, F, 'Dealing with the displaced: a challenge to the international community', *Global Governance*, vol. 1, no. 1, 1995

FLECK, D, *The Handbook of Humanitarian Law in Armed Conflicts*, Oxford University Press, Oxford, 1996

FORSYTHE, D, 'The International Committee of the Red Cross and humanitarian assistance: a policy analysis', *International Review of the Red Cross*, no. 314, 1996

FRANCO, L, 'An examination of safety zones for internally displaced persons as a contribution toward prevention and solution of refugee problems', in N. Al-Naumi and R. Meese (eds), *International Legal Issues Arising Under the*

United Nations Decade of International Law, Martinus Nijhoff, The Hague, 1995

HUMAN RIGHTS WATCH, 'Turkey's failed policy to aid the forcibly displaced in the southeast', report no. D809, New York, 1996

HUMAN RIGHTS WATCH, *Failing the Internally Displaced: The UNDP Displaced Persons Program in Kenya*, New York, 1997

HUMAN RIGHTS WATCH, 'Zaire: 'attacked by all sides'. Civilians and the war in eastern Zaire', report no. 9/1(A), New York, 1997

KLEINE-AHLBRANDT, S, *The Protection Gap: The International Protection of Internally Displaced People: The Case of Rwanda*, Institut Universitaire de Hautes Etudes Internationales, Geneva, 1996

KUMAR, R, 'The troubled history of partition', *Foreign Affairs*, vol. 76, no. 1, 1997

LAVOYER, P, 'Refugees and internally displaced persons: international humanitarian law and the role of the ICRC', *International Review of the Red Cross*, no. 305, 1995

LEE, L, 'Internally displaced persons and refugees: toward a legal synthesis?, *Journal of Refugee Studies*, vol. 9, no. 1, 1996

MOONEY, E, 'Internal displacement and the conflict in Abkhazia', *International Journal on Minority and Group Rights*, vol. 3, no. 3, 1996

McDOWELL, C (ed), *Understanding Impoverishment: The Consequences of Development-Induced Displacement*, Berghahn Books, Providence, 1996

POSEN, B, 'Military responses to refugee disasters', *International Security*, vol. 21, no. 1, 1996

RIEFF, D, 'Nagorno-Karabakh: case study in ethnic strife', *Foreign Affairs*, vol. 76, no. 2, 1997

REFUGEE SURVEY QUARTERLY, vol. 14, no. 1/2, 1995, special issue and select bibliography on internally displaced people

ROHDE, D, *A Safe Area: Srebrenica: Europe's Worst Massacre Since the Second World War*, Simon and Schuster, New York, 1997

UNHCR (Office of the United Nations High Commissioner for Refugees), *UNHCR's Operational Experience with Internally Displaced Persons*, Geneva, 1994

YETT, S, 'Masisi, down the road from Goma: ethnic cleansing and displacement in eastern Zaire', United States Committee for Refugees, Washington DC, 1996

Return and reintegration

ALLEN, T (ed), *In Search of Cool Ground: War, Flight and Homecoming in Northeast Africa*, United Nations Research Institute for Social Development, Africa World Press and James Currey, London, 1996

AMNESTY INTERNATIONAL, 'Rwanda: human rights overlooked in mass repatriation', report no. AFR47/02/97, London, 1997

AMNESTY INTERNATIONAL, 'Great Lakes region: still in need of protection: repatriation, refoulement and the safety of refugees and the internally displaced', report no. AFR02/07/97, London, 1997

AMNESTY INTERNATIONAL, 'Who's living in my house? Obstacles to the safe return of refugees and internally displaced people', report no. EUR/ID, London, 1997

BALL, N, *Making Peace Work: The Role of the International Development Community*, Overseas Development Council, Washington DC, 1996

BERDAL, M, *Disarmament and Demobilisation After Civil Wars*, Adelphi paper no. 303, International Institute for Strategic Studies, London, 1996

BARANYI, S, 'The challenge in Guatemala: verifying human rights, strengthening national protection and enhancing an integrated approach to peace', *Journal of Humanitarian Assistance*, website <www-jha.sps.cam.ac.uk>

BOUTWELL, J et al (eds), *Lethal Commerce: The Global Trade in Small Arms and Light Weapons*, American Academy of Arts and Sciences, Cambridge MA, 1995

BUSH, K, 'Towards a balanced approach to rebuilding war-torn societies', *Canadian Foreign Policy*, vol. 3, no. 2, 1995

COLETTA, N et al, *The Transition from War to Peace in Sub-Saharan Africa*, World Bank, Washington DC, 1996

CRISP, J, *Rebuilding a War-Torn Society: A Review of UNHCR's Reintegration Programme for Mozambican Returnees*, UNHCR, Geneva, 1996

DOYLE, M, *UN Peacekeeping in Cambodia: UNTAC's Civil Mandate*, Lynne Rienner, Boulder, 1995

FERRIS, E, 'After the wars are over: reconstruction and repatriation', Working Paper no. 10, Migration Policy in Global Perspective Series, International Center for Migration, Ethnicity and Citizenship, New School for Social Research, New York, 1997

HUMAN RIGHTS WATCH, 'Bosnia-Herzegovina: a failure in the making. Human rights and the Dayton agreement', report no. D808, New York, 1996

HUMAN RIGHTS WATCH, 'Guatemala: return to violence: refugees, civil patrollers and impunity', report no. B801, 1996

HUMAN RIGHTS WATCH, 'Tajikistan: Tajik refugees in northern Afghanistan: obstacles to repatriation', report no. 8.6 (D), New York, 1996

KIBREAB, G, *Ready and Willing but Still Waiting: Eritrean Refugees in Sudan and the Dilemmas of Return*, Life and Peace Institute, Uppsala, 1996

KOSER, K, 'Information and repatriation: the case of Mozambican refugees in Malawi', *Journal of Refugee Studies*, vol. 10, no. 1, 1997

KUMAR, K (ed), *Rebuilding Societies After Civil War: Critical Roles for International Assistance*, Lynne Rienner, Boulder, 1997

MERON, T, 'Answering for war crimes: lessons from the Balkans', *Foreign Affairs*, vol. 76, no. 1, 1997

MOORE, J, *The UN and Complex Emergencies: Rehabilitation in Third World Transitions*, War-Torn Societies Project, United Nations Research Institute for Social Development, Geneva, 1996

PAINTER, R, 'Property rights of returning displaced persons: the Guatemalan experience', *Harvard Human Rights Journal*, vol. 9, Spring 1996

POTTIER, J, 'Relief and repatriation: views by Rwandan refugees, lessons for humanitarian aid workers', *African Affairs*, vol. 95, no. 380, 1996

ROBERTS, S and WILLIAMS, J, *After the Guns Fall Silent: The Enduring Legacy of Landmines*, Vietnam Veterans of America Foundation, Washington DC, 1995

SCHEAR, J, 'Bosnia's post-Dayton traumas', *Foreign Policy*, no. 104, 1996

WATERS, T, 'The coming Rwandan demographic crisis: or why current repatriation policies will not solve Tanzania's (or Zaire's) refugee problems', *Journal of Humanitarian Assistance*, website <www-jha.sps.cam.ac.uk>

WATSON, C, *The Flight, Exile and Return of Chadian Refugees*, United Nations Research Institute for Social Development, Geneva, 1996

UNHCR and IPA (International Peace Academy), *Healing the Wounds: Refugees, Reconstruction and Reconciliation*, Geneva and New York, 1996

ZIECK, M, *UNHCR and Voluntary Repatriation: A Legal Analysis*, University of Amsterdam (doctoral thesis), Amsterdam, 1997

The asylum dilemma

AMNESTY INTERNATIONAL, *Cell Culture: The Detention and Imprisonment of Asylum Seekers in the United Kingdom*, London, 1997

ANDERSON, E, 'The role of asylum states in promoting safe and peaceful repatriation under the Dayton agreements', *European Journal of International Law*, vol. 7, no. 2, 1996

BYRNE, R and SHACKNOVE, A, 'The safe country notion in European asylum law', *Harvard Human Rights Journal*, vol. 9, Spring 1996

CARLIER, J-Y and VANHEULE, D (eds), *Europe and Refugees: A Challenge?*, Kluwer, The Hague, 1997

CARLIER, J-Y et al (eds), *Who is a Refugee? A Comparative Case Law Study*, Kluwer, The Hague, 1997

COHEN, R, *The Cambridge Survey of World Migration*, Cambridge University Press, Cambridge, 1995

DAOUST, I and FOLKELIUS, K, 'UNHCR symposium on gender-based persecution', *International Journal of Refugee Law*, vol. 8, no. 1/2, 1996

DIAZ-BRIQUETS, S and PEREZ-LOPEZ, J, 'Refugee remittances: conceptual issues and the Cuban and Nicaraguan experiences', *International Migration Review*, vol. 31, no. 2, 1997

ECRE (European Council on Refugees and Exiles), *Safe Third Countries: Myths and Realities*, London, 1996

HUMAN RIGHTS WATCH, 'Crime or simply punishment? Racist attacks by Moscow law enforcement authorities', report no. D712, New York, 1995

INTERNATIONAL MIGRATION REVIEW, vol. 30, no. 1, 1996, special issue on ethics, migration and global stewardship

IOM (International Organization for Migration), *The Baltic Route: The Trafficking of Migrants Through Lithuania*, Geneva, 1997

JOLY, D, *Haven or Hell? Asylum Policies and Refugees in Europe*, Macmillan, London, 1996

MARSHALL, B, *British and German Refugee Policies in the European Context*, Royal Institute of International Affairs, London, 1996

McDOWELL, C, *A Tamil Diaspora: Sri Lankan Migration, Settlement and Politics in Switzerland*, Berghahn Books, Providence, 1997

NEWLAND, K, *US Refugee Policy: Dilemmas and Directions*, Carnegie Endowment for International Peace, Washington DC, 1995

PAPADEMETRIOU, D and HAMILTON, K, *Converging Paths: French, Italian and British Responses to Immigration*, Carnegie Endowment for International Peace, Washington DC, 1996

PLAUT, W, *Asylum: A Moral Dilemma*, Praeger, Westport, 1995

PREEG, E, *The Haitian Dilemma: A Case Study in Demographics, Development and US Foreign Policy*, Westview Press, Boulder, 1996

RAOUL WALLENBERG INSTITUTE, *Temporary Protection: Problems and Prospects*, report no. 22, Lund, 1996

SIMMONS, A (ed), *International Migration, Refugee Flows and Human Rights in North America: The Impact of Free Trade and Restructuring*, Center for Migration Studies, New York, 1995

TEITELBAUM, M and WEINER, M (eds), *Threatened Peoples, Threatened Borders: World Migration and US Policy*, W.W. Norton, New York, 1995

WEINER, M and MUNZ, R, 'Migrants, refugees and foreign policy: prevention and intervention strategies', *Third World Quarterly*, vol. 18, no. 1, 1997

ZUCKER, N and ZUCKER, N, *Desperate Crossings: Seeking Refuge in America*, M.E. Sharpe, Armonk NY, 1996

Statelessness and citizenship

ARZT, D, *Refugees Into Citizens: Palestinians and the end of the Arab/Israeli Conflict*, Council on Foreign Relations, New York, 1997

AUSTRIAN JOURNAL OF PUBLIC AND INTERNATIONAL LAW, special issue and bibliography on state succession and nationality, vol. 49, no. 1, 1995

BATCHELOR, C, 'Stateless persons: some gaps in international protection', *International Journal of Refugee Law*, vol. 7, no. 2, 1995

BATCHELOR, C, 'UNHCR and issues related to nationality', *Refugee Survey Quarterly*, vol. 14, no. 3, 1995

BATT, J, *The New Slovakia: National Identity, Political Integration and the Return to Europe*, Royal Institute of International Affairs, London, 1996

BREMER, I and TARAS, R, *New States, New Politics: Building the Post-Soviet Nations*, Cambridge University Press, Cambridge, 1997

BRUNNER, G, *Nationality Problems and Minority Conflicts in Eastern Europe*, Bertelsman Foundation Publishers, Guetersloh, 1996

CHINN, J and KAISER, R, *Russians as the New Minority: Ethnicity and Nationalism in the Soviet Successor States*, Westview Press, Boulder, 1996

COUNCIL OF EUROPE (Parliamentary Assembly), *The Child as Citizen*, Strasbourg, 1996

DARWEISH, M and RIGBY, A, 'Palestinians in Israel: nationality and citizenship', Department of Peace Studies, University of Bradford, Peace Report Series no. 35, 1996

FONCESCA, I, *Bury me Standing: The Gypsies and their Journey*, Vintage, London, 1996

HUMAN RIGHTS WATCH, 'The Bedoons of Kuwait: citizens without citizenship', report no. 1568, New York, 1995

HUMAN RIGHTS WATCH, 'Cambodia: deterioration of human rights in Cambodia', report no. 8/11(C), New York, 1996

HUMAN RIGHTS WATCH, 'Syria: the silenced Kurds', report no. 8/4(E), New York, 1996

HUMAN RIGHTS WATCH, 'Burma: children's rights and the rule of law', report no. 9/1(C), New York, 1997

HUTT, M, 'Ethnic nationalism, refugees and Bhutan', *Journal of Refugee Studies*, vol. 8, no. 4, 1996

KHAN, I, 'UNHCR's mandate relating to statelessness and UNHCR's preventive strategy', *Austrian Journal of Public and International Law*, vol. 49, no. 1, 1995

OPEN SOCIETY INSTITUTE (Forced Migration Projects), *Crimean Tatars: Repatriation and Conflict Prevention*, New York, 1996

OPEN SOCIETY INSTITUTE (Forced Migration Projects), *Roma and Forced Migration: An Annotated Bibliography*, New York, 1997

PEJIC, J, 'Citizenship and statelessness in the former Yugoslavia: the legal framework', *Refugee Survey Quarterly*, vol. 14, no. 3, 1995

PIPER, T, 'The exodus of ethnic Nepalis from southern Bhutan', *Refugee Survey Quarterly*, vol. 14, no. 3, 1995

REFUGEE SURVEY QUARTERLY, vol. 14, no. 3, 1995, special issue and bibliography on statelessness

SHIBLAK, A, 'Residency status and civil rights of Palestinian refugees in Arab countries', *Journal of Palestine Studies*, vol. 25, no. 3, 1996

UNHCR (Office of the United Nations High Commissioner for Refugees), *Citizenship in the Context of the Dissolution of Czechoslovakia*, European Series, vol. 2, no. 4, Geneva, 1996

YEE, S, 'The new constitution of Bosnia and Herzegovina', *European Journal of International Law*, vol. 7, no. 2, 1996

ZOLBERG, A, 'The unmixing of peoples in the post-communist world', occasional paper, International Center for Migration, Ethnicity and Citizenship, New School for Social Research, New York, 1997

Periodicals

In Defense of the Alien, published annually by the Center for Migration Studies, New York

International Journal of Refugee Law, published quarterly by Oxford University Press

International Migration Review, published quarterly by the Center for Migration Studies, New York

International Review of the Red Cross, published six times a year by the International Committee of the Red Cross

Journal of Refugee Studies, published quarterly by Oxford University Press

Refugee Survey Quarterly, published quarterly by Oxford University Press

World Disaster Report, published annually by the International Federation of Red Cross and Red Crescent Societies

World Refugee Survey, published annually by the US Committee for Refugees, Washington DC

Selected websites

United Nations sites:
UNHCR:
   http://www.unhcr.ch
UNHCR Refworld:
   http://www.unhcr.ch/refworld/refworld.htm
United Nations:
   http://www.un.org
UN Centre for Human Rights:
   http://www.unhchr.ch
UN ReliefWeb:
   http://www.reliefweb.int/

Other sites:
Amnesty International:
   http://www.amnesty.org/
European Council on Refugees and Exiles:
   http://www.poptel.org.uk/ein/ecre/
Human Rights Watch:
   http://www.hrw.org
Institute for Global Communications:
   http://www.igc.org/igc/
InterAction:
   http://www.interaction.org/
International Committee of the Red Cross:
   http://www.icrc.org/
International Crisis Group:
   http://www.intl-crisis-group.org/
International Federation of Red Cross and Red Crescent Societies:
   http://www.ifrc.org/
Journal of Humanitarian Assistance:
   http://www-jha.sps.cam.ac.uk
Lawyers Committee for Human Rights:
   http://www.lchr.org/
Migration and ethnic relations:
   http://www.ercomer.org/wwwvl/

Open Society Institute, Forced Migration Projects:
  http://www.soros.org/fmp2/html
Oxford Refugee Studies Programme:
  http://www.users.ox.ac.uk/~rspnet/
Palestinian refugees:
  http://www.Palestine-net.com/palestine.html

Refworld: UNHCR's CD-Rom

Refworld is a reference tool designed to meet the information needs of everyone who has an interest in the problem of forced displacement: governments, international organizations, voluntary agencies, academic institutions and lawyers. This CD-Rom is a collection of full-text databases which is updated twice a year, providing easy access to the most comprehensive and reliable refugee information available, drawn from the most current and reliable sources. The information available on *Refworld* includes: data on conditions in refugees' countries of origin; national legislation and case law; international treaties and documents on human rights and refugee law; UN General Assembly and Security Council documents; official UNHCR documents; refugee statistics; and the catalogue of UNHCR's Centre for Documentation and Research.

Refworld is updated on a six-monthly basis and is available on an annual subscription basis for $250. Additional subscriptions can be ordered at a reduced rate of $125 per year. For more information and a demonstration disc allowing five hours of free access, contact *Refworld*, UNHCR Centre for Documentation and Research, CP2500, CH-1211 Geneva 2, Switzerland. Fax: (41-22) 739-8488; e-mail: <cdr@unchr.ch>.